# My Cape May

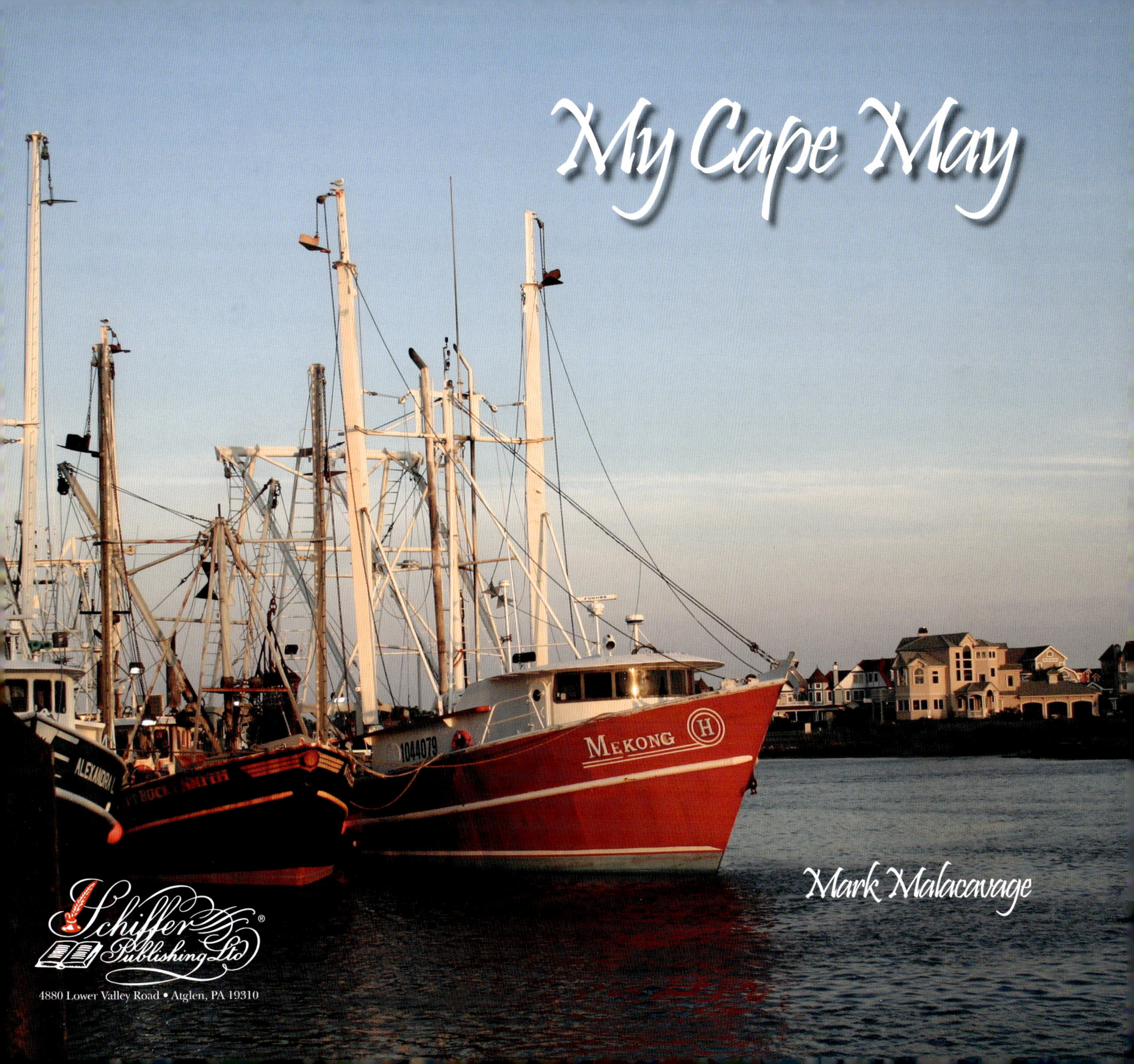


Mark Malacavage

Schiffer Publishing Ltd
4880 Lower Valley Road • Atglen, PA 19310

# Acknowledgments

I would like to thank my parents for first introducing me to Cape May as a young child.

A special thanks to "Oma" and "Pooey" for the continued blessing of the "beach house" that is now helping another generation to grow up knowing the wonder of Cape May.

My undying love and appreciation goes out to my best friend and wife, Leeann, for her love and support...and for putting up with my tramping off to who-knows-where-now with my camera bag over my shoulder.

Last, but certainly not least, I would be remiss if I didn't acknowledge my Lord and Savior, Jesus Christ. With God, all things are possible and His creation is beautiful to behold.



Library of Congress Control Number: 2013943325



Cover and book designed by: Bruce Waters
Type set in Zurich BT

ISBN: 978-0-7643-4470-1
Printed in China

Published by Schiffer Publishing, Ltd.
4880 Lower Valley Road
Atglen, PA 19310
Phone: (610) 593-1777; Fax: (610) 593-2002
E-mail: Info@schifferbooks.com

For our complete selection of fine books on this and related subjects, please visit our website at www.schifferbooks.com. You may also write for a free catalog.

This book may be purchased from the publisher. Please try your bookstore first.

We are always looking for people to write books on new and related subjects. If you have an idea for a book, please contact us at proposals@schifferbooks.com.

Schiffer Publishing's titles are available at special discounts for bulk purchases for sales promotions or premiums. Special editions, including personalized covers, corporate imprints, and excerpts can be created in large quantities for special needs. For more information, contact the publisher.

# Contents



*"You can shake the sand from your shoes,*
*but it will never leave your soul."*
~ Unknown

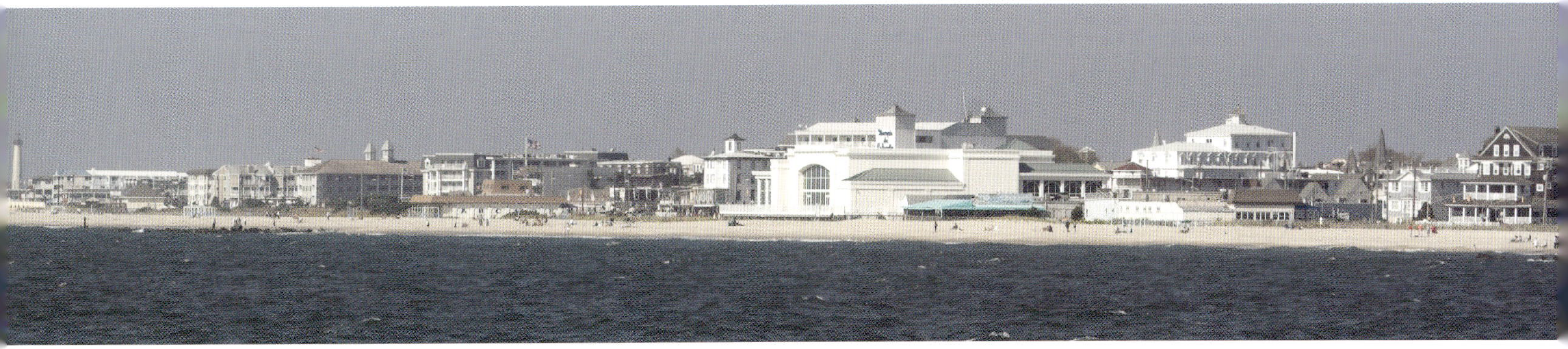

# Dedication

To my daughter Joy...
I have been granted the priceless gift of getting to discover Cape May all over again through her eyes.

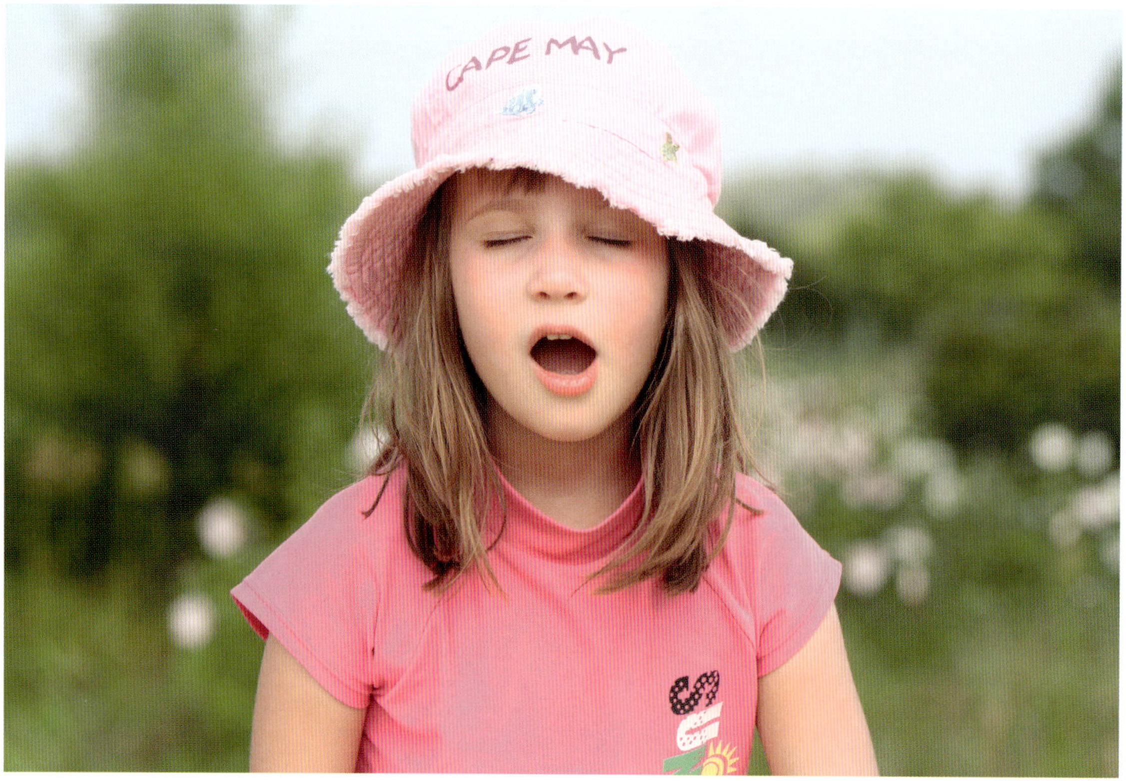

Chapter One

# Welcome to... *My Cape May*

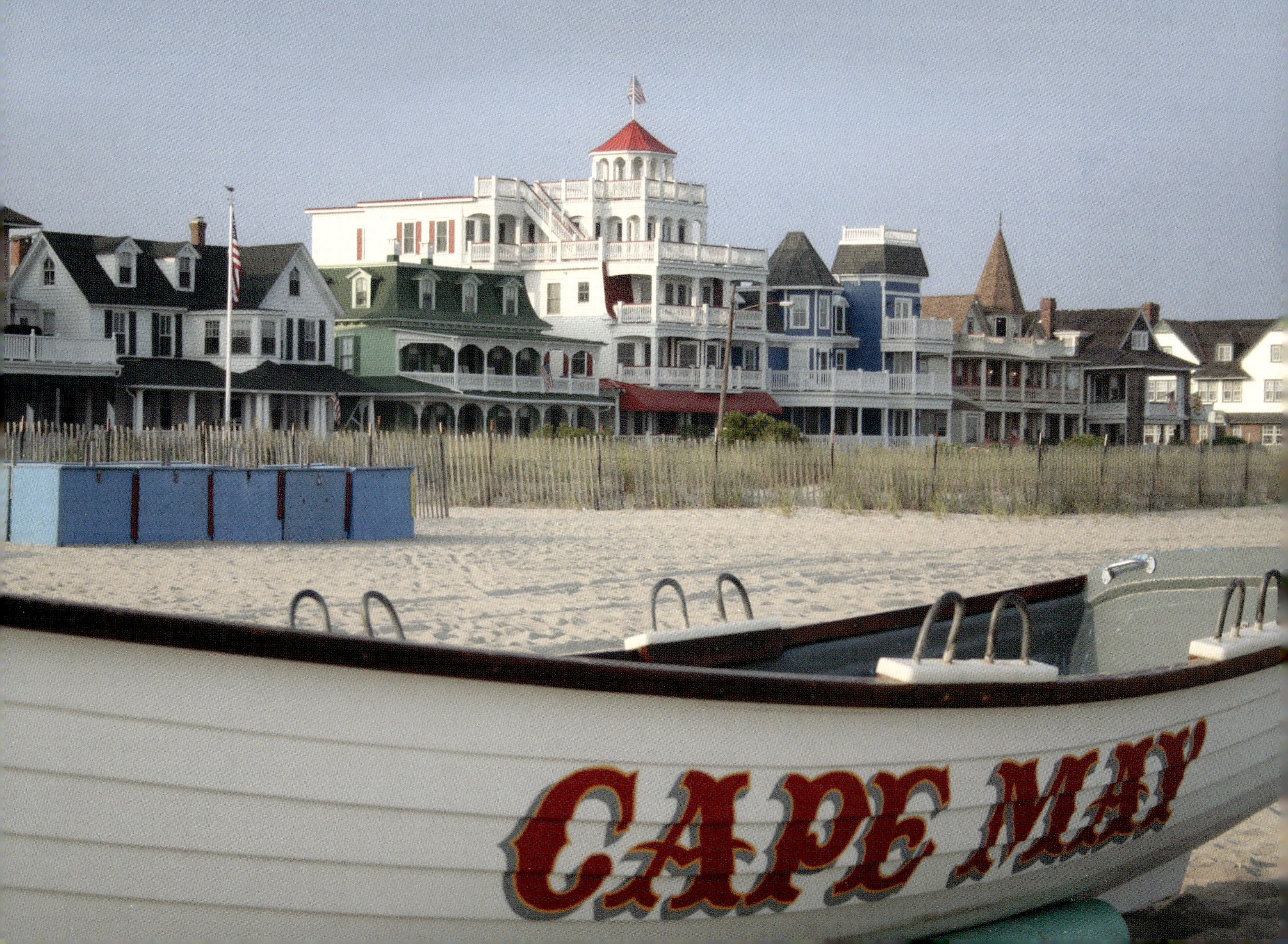

There are countless places where one could chose to live or to visit. Each has its own unique character and draw, but there are some places that are so much more than just a geographic location or even a community of people. There are those rare places that have that intangible something, a something that speaks to the very depths of your soul. Once you have been there, that place never leaves you. *You* may leave there; in fact, you may have only visited briefly, but a part of that place stays with you and calls you back no matter the distance.

Cape May, New Jersey, is one of those magical places that people fall in love with. If you have experienced that personal connection to Cape May for yourself, then you know what I am talking about and it is probably of little wonder to you why almost fifty thousand people flock to this little seaside resort every year and why a lucky few choose to call it their year-round home. If you have not yet had the opportunity to experience that magical connection, I hope you get a chance to visit soon.

Located at the southernmost tip of New Jersey, just below the Mason-Dixon line, on a peninsula flanked by the Delaware Bay and the Atlantic Ocean, the region of Cape Island, as it was once known, has a history as old as our nation's...in fact, older. Many a fine history book has been written about Cape May and the surrounding region. These books will tell of the Lenni-Lenape Indians who lived off the land when it was first sighted by Sir Henry Hudson in 1609, and then later explored by Cornelius Jacobsen Mey in 1621. It was for him the Cape was named, with a change in spelling occurring over time to May. They also give accounts about the earliest attempts to establish whaling settlements and then later the growth of agriculture communities in Southern New Jersey, as well as weave the true and fascinating tale of how Cape May rose to be what is generally recognized as the first seaside resort town in the nation. It first served Philadelphians escaping the summer heat of the city and then, later, visitors from all points. Of course, these books will include discussions of topics such as land speculation and development, a later collapse into malaise in the late nineteenth century, the role of the Cape in the First and Second World Wars, and the city's rise back to prominence as a resort destination once again in the latter half of the twentieth century. This is not one of those books.

No discussion of Cape May, its history, or its present would be complete without mention of the city's abundance of vintage Victorian architecture. Books have been written on the topic of Cape May's "Painted Ladies," explaining how this small city has managed to come into the twenty-first century with such an extensive collection of carefully restored and well-maintained examples of Victorian architecture. The devastating fire of 1878 that destroyed thirty-five acres of the city, the subsequent reconstruction of that large portion of the city in the popular architectural styles of the day, the later successful attempts by preservationists to have the city of Cape May placed on the National Register of Historic Places, and the resultant renewed pride in ownership and the blossoming of the Bed and Breakfast industry are all topics of such informative books. This is not one of those books.

There is so much to see and do and eat in Cape May. If you find yourself bored in Cape May, you have no one to blame but yourself...unless of course you have chosen to be bored. As anyone who has ever sat in a chair at the water's edge and done absolutely nothing except let the cares of the world seep down through their feet and out into the sand will tell you, there are times that boredom can be a virtuous pursuit. In addition to beach activities, there is boating, fishing, and other water sports; birding; hiking; shopping and sight-seeing tours; historical reenactments, trolley and horse-drawn carriage rides; movie nights on the beach; fireworks; concerts; a free zoo nearby; the jazz festival; and the nightlife with an active music scene. The list goes on. Cape May offers an extensive range of dining experiences — a hotdog stand with a cult-like following, a '50s-style soda fountain in the five and dime, crab shacks and seafood houses, family dining, and many world-renowned and award-winning fine dining establishments can all be found in and around the Cape. There are many great visitors' guide books that can tell a first-time vacationer where to stay, what to see and do, and where to eat. This is not one of those books.

What then is this that you hold in your hands? It is *my* Cape May...as seen through *my* eyes, through *my* camera lens. It is my modest attempt to represent the beauty and character of Cape May that I see as I walk its streets, hike its beaches, and explore its natural wonders. Certainly, it is very much my own personal view of Cape May, the town that I have been fortunate enough to know since I was a small child. I did not start out with the intent of capturing Cape May for the purpose of sharing it with others. It was merely the inevitable collision of two of my passions: photography and Cape Island. Likely, it has also, unknowingly, been an attempt to capture that intangible something that calls to me when I cannot be there.

As I began the process of putting this body of work together, I gave much thought to how I would approach it. I began selecting photos and thinking about captions and explanations when I realized that I had so much to say about Cape May that the words would soon overwhelm the images. It was never meant to be about the words. While I can manage to stumble my way around my native tongue, the English language, I wasn't invited to put this work together because of my words — it was because of the images.

As a result, I have chosen a minimalist approach. To make some order out of the chaos, I have arranged the images in three sections and, aside from a brief introduction to each section, there are few words. The words you will find are not my own, but a few quotes that I think complement the images. Aside from that, I want the images to speak and to tell the story of my Cape May. No captions. No explanations. Just images.

Now, if after you have had an opportunity to let the images tell you their story and you close this book and still find yourself dissatisfied and asking of a particular image "Where is that? What is that? Tell me more.", I have good news for you. We live in an age of technological wonder and (for better or for worse) social media, so I invite you to reach out to me on *www.facebook.com/CapeMayPics*. There I would be happy to attempt to answer any questions you may have about any of these photographs. I would also like to hear from you if one of my images stirred up a Cape May memory for you or if you have a Cape May story of your own to share. You can view additional images there that are not found in this book and individual prints of these images and more can be purchased at *www.CapeMayPics.com*.

I have said that this collection is from my personal perspective, but I hope that my Cape May will resonate with you and, in it, you will see some of the things that you love about Cape May, if you are already familiar with her. My wish is that you may find that *my* Cape May is also *your* Cape May.

## Chapter Two
# Around Town

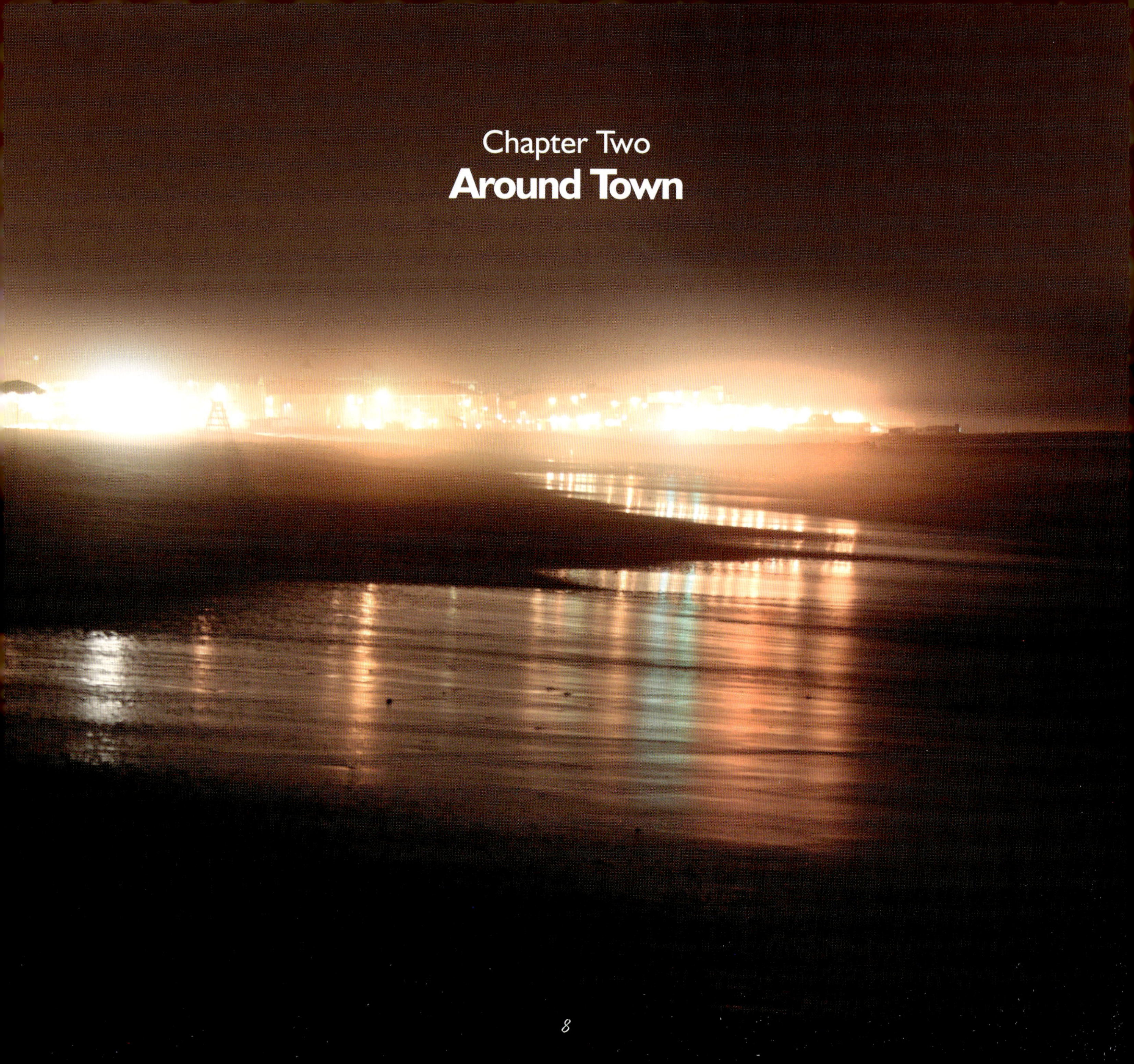

Take a journey around the streets of Cape May and beyond the city limits. Experience the tree-lined streets, the beautiful gardens, and, of course, that famous Cape May architecture. Perhaps take a tour by horse-drawn carriage or stroll the Washington Street pedestrian mall on a hot summer's night with a cool breeze blowing in from the ocean just a couple of blocks away. Discover the quirky side of Cape May or sample the local cuisine. Don't forget the rich history of the area. There are many with ties to the legendary ship, the *Mayflower*, who now rest in the soil around Cape May. Agricultural and maritime pursuits were a part of the earliest days of Cape May and you only need to look to see that they are a part of her present as well. Along the way, on the journey you will take through the following pages, you may spot the ghosts of a building or two that are no longer standing today.

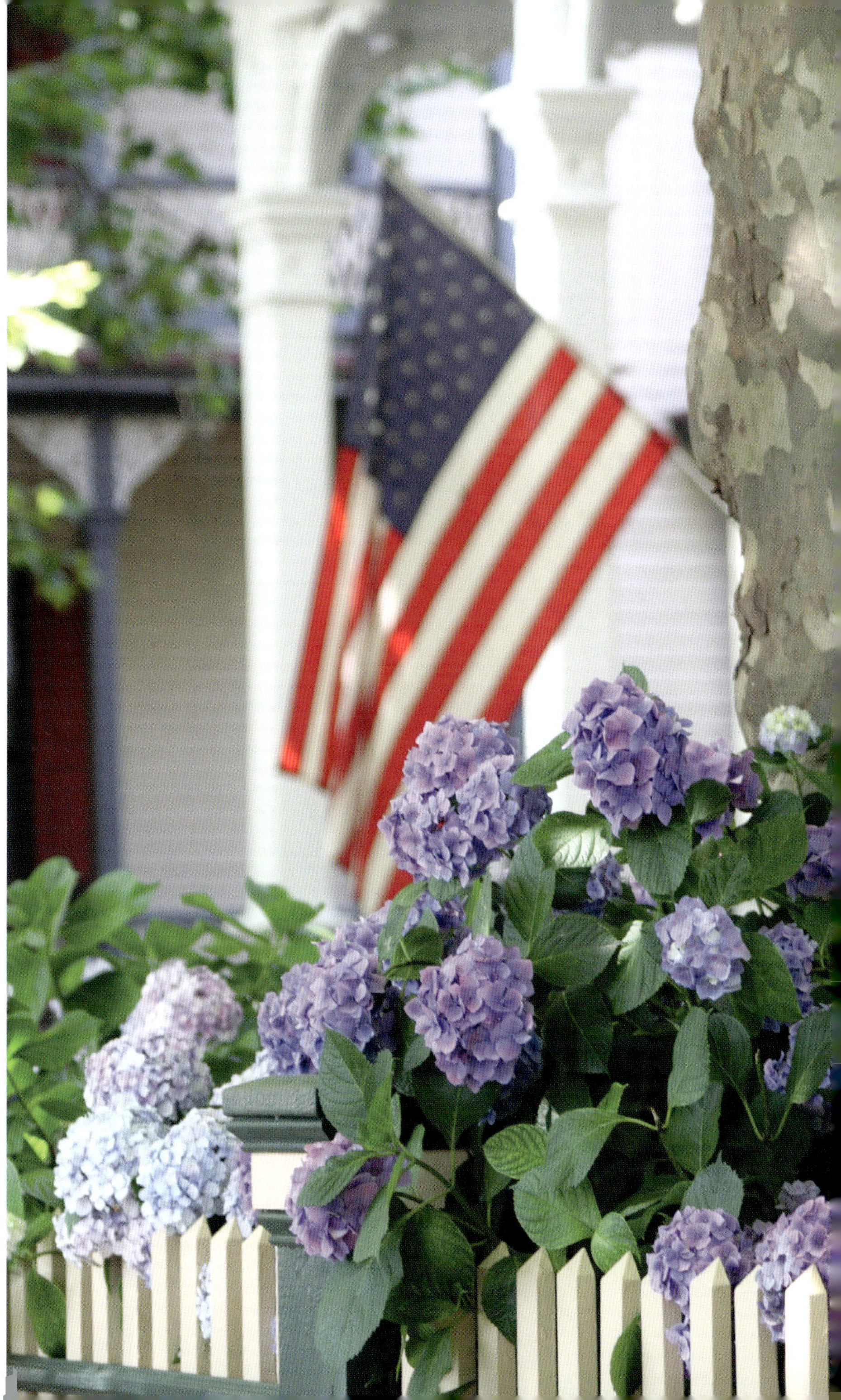

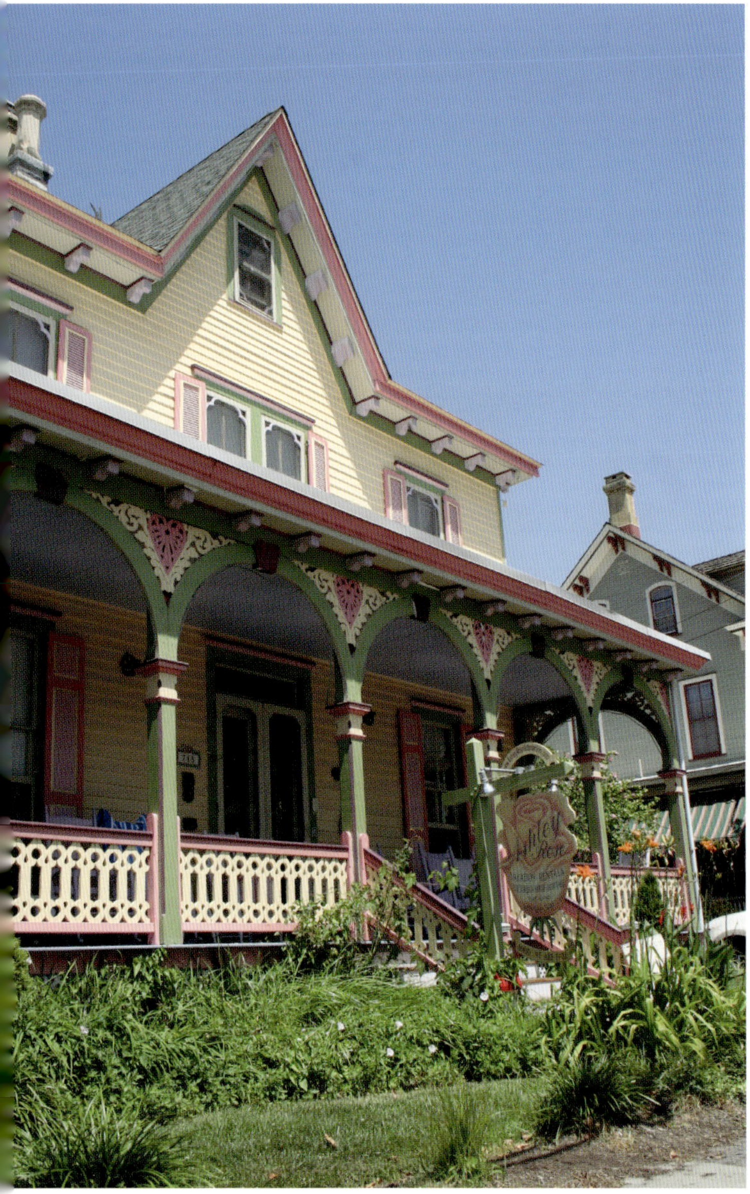

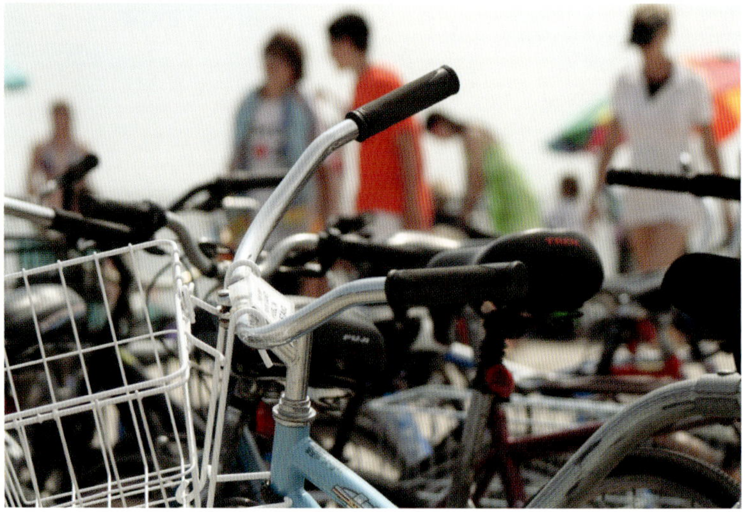

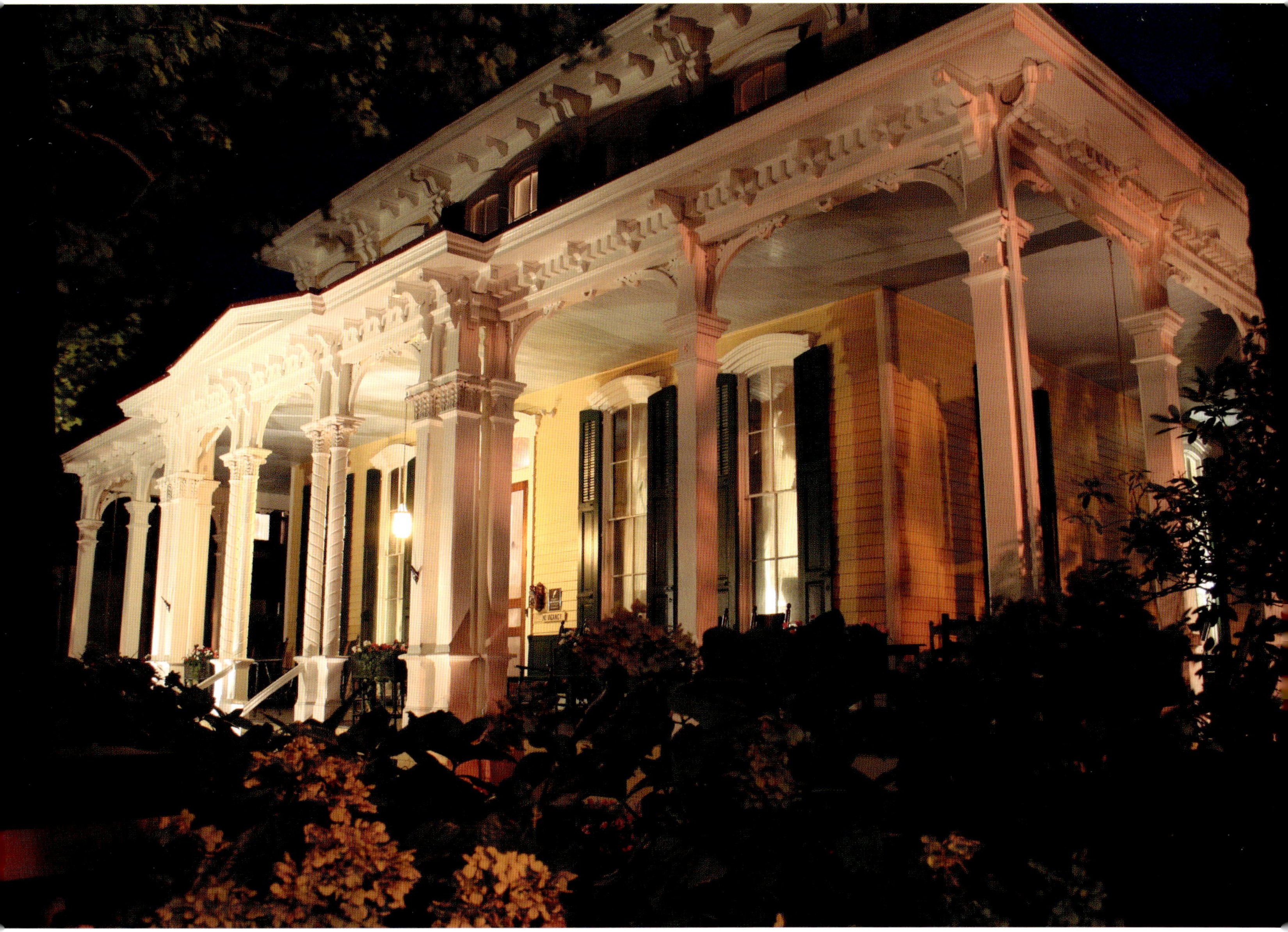

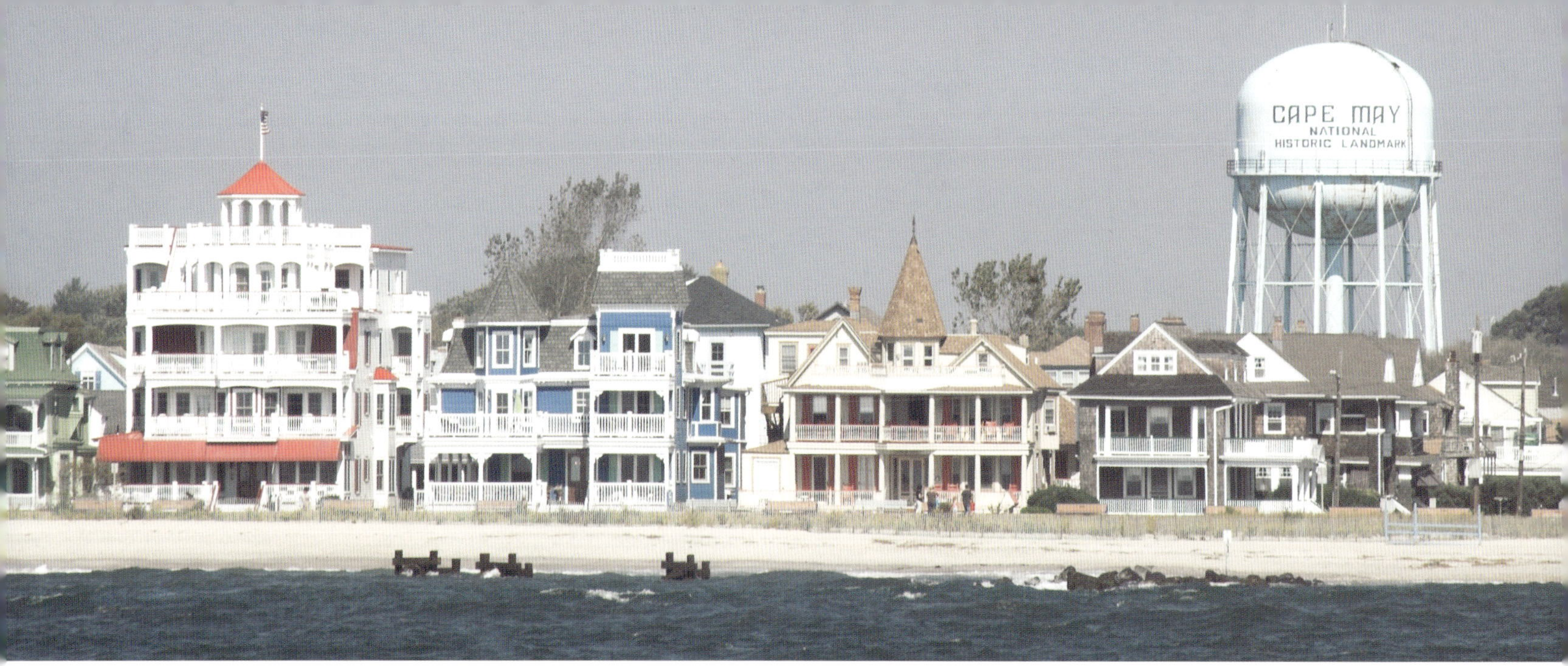
CAPE MAY
NATIONAL
HISTORIC LANDMARK

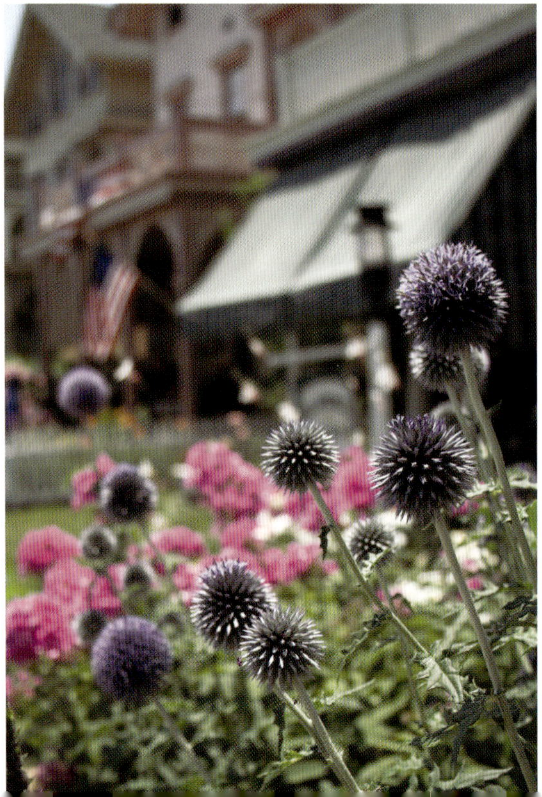

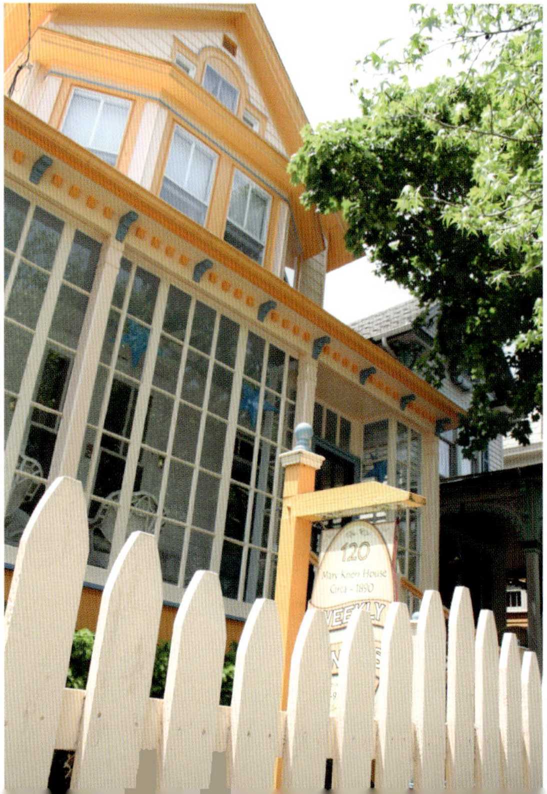
120
Circa - 1890

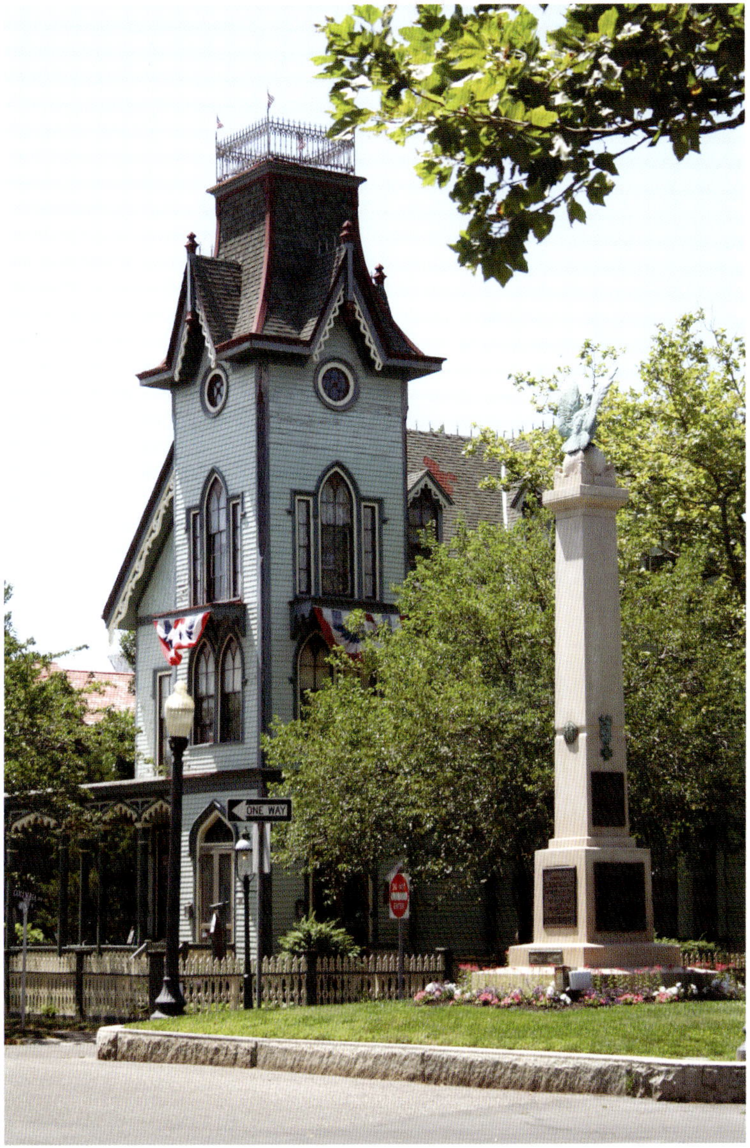
ONE WAY

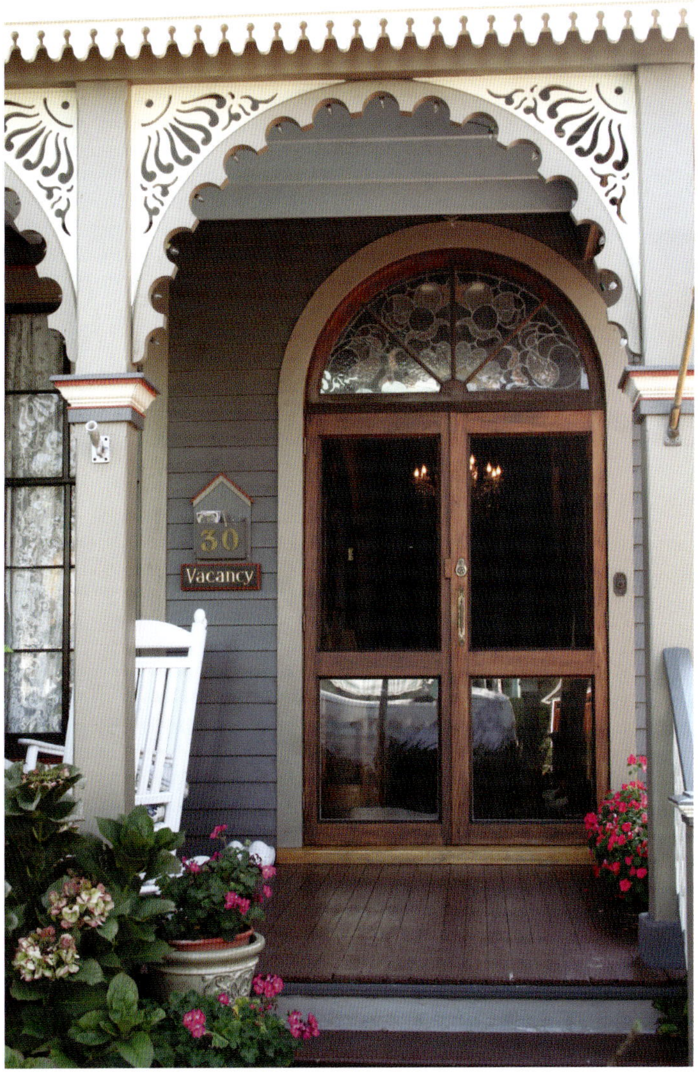
30
Vacancy

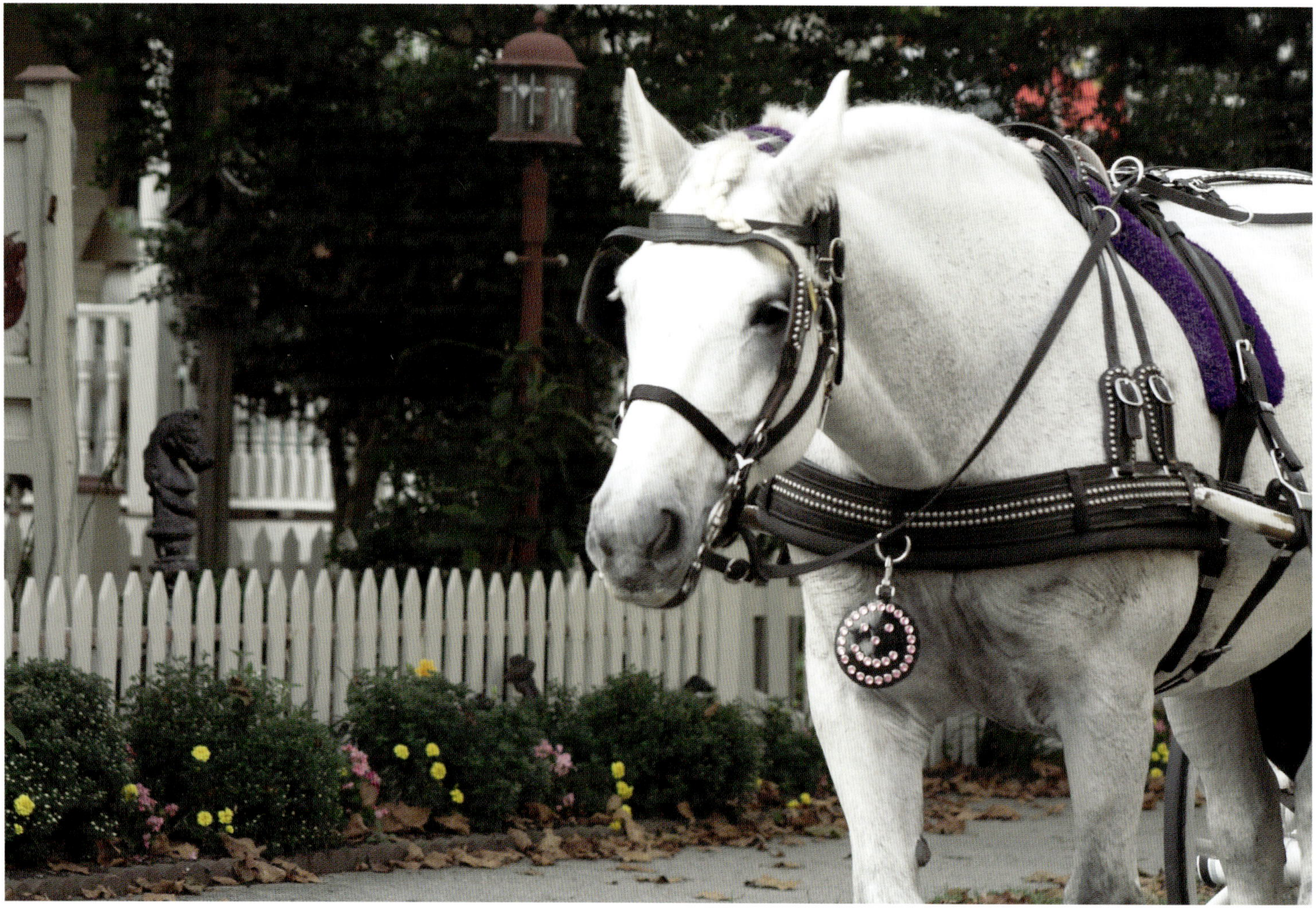

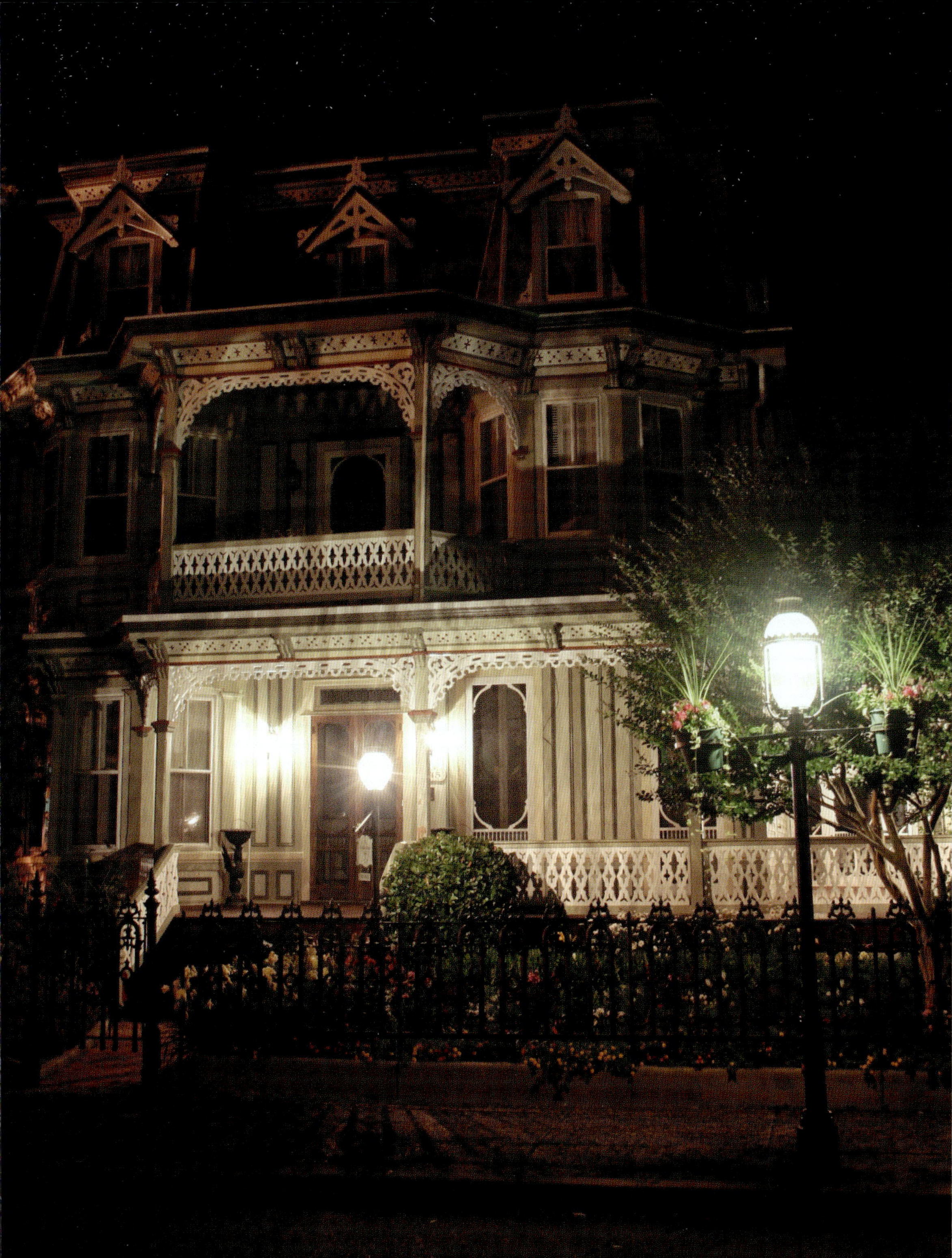

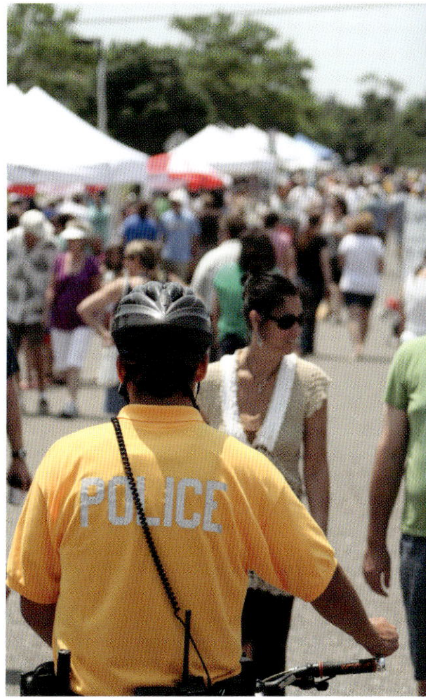
POLICE

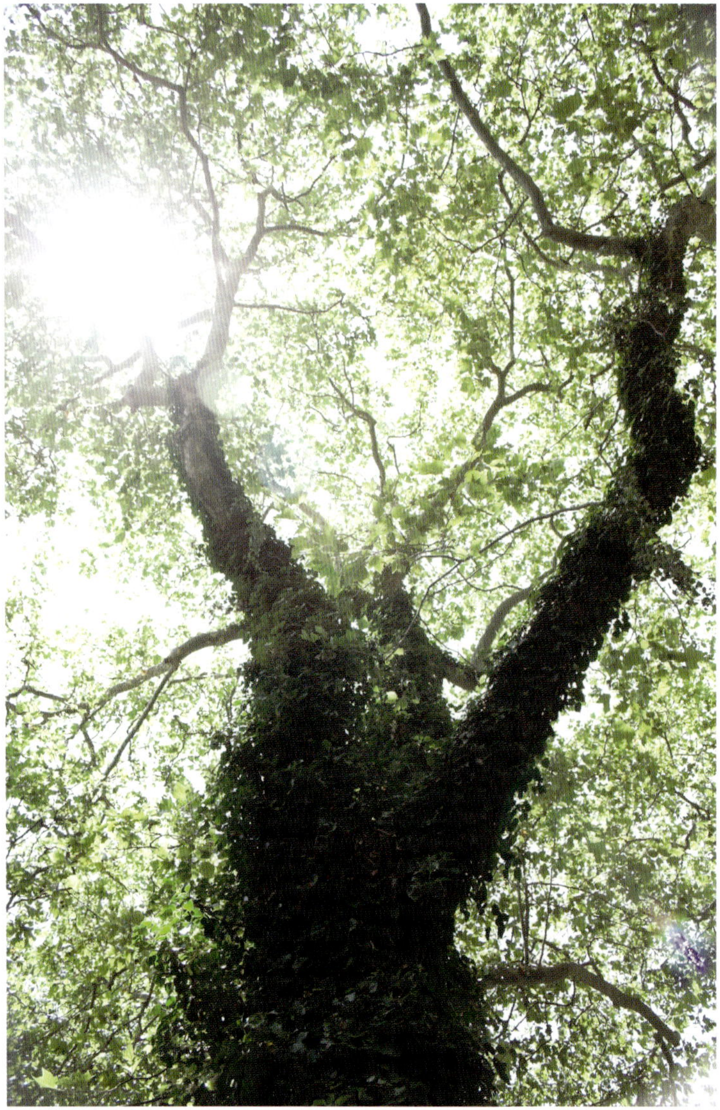

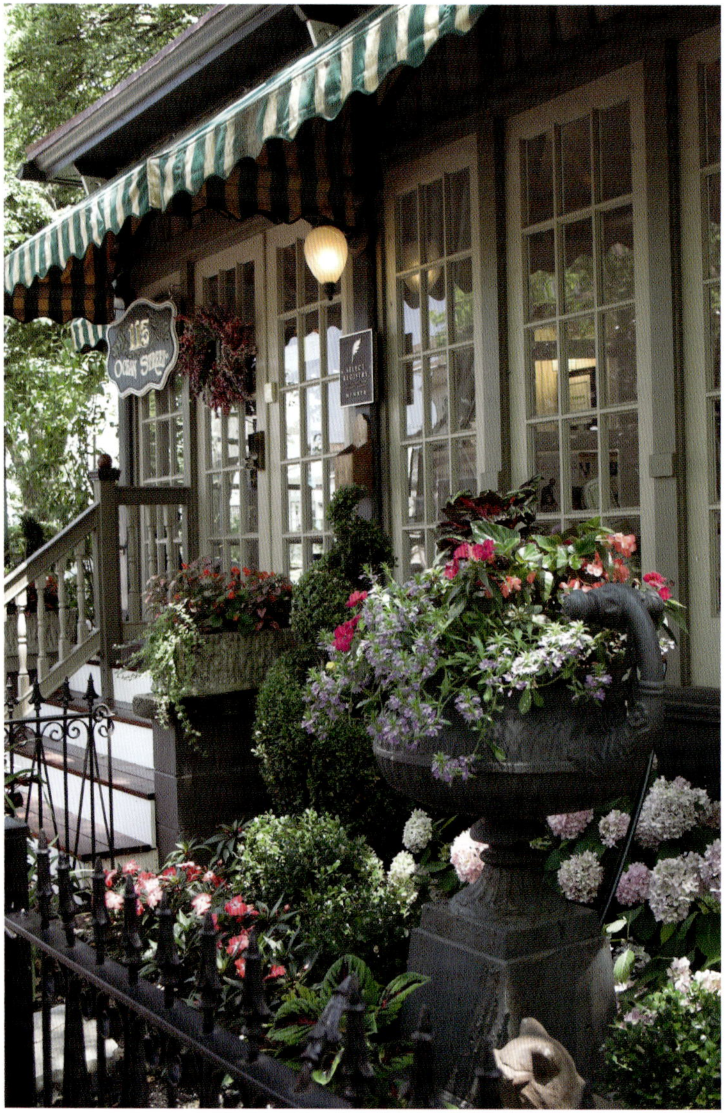
115

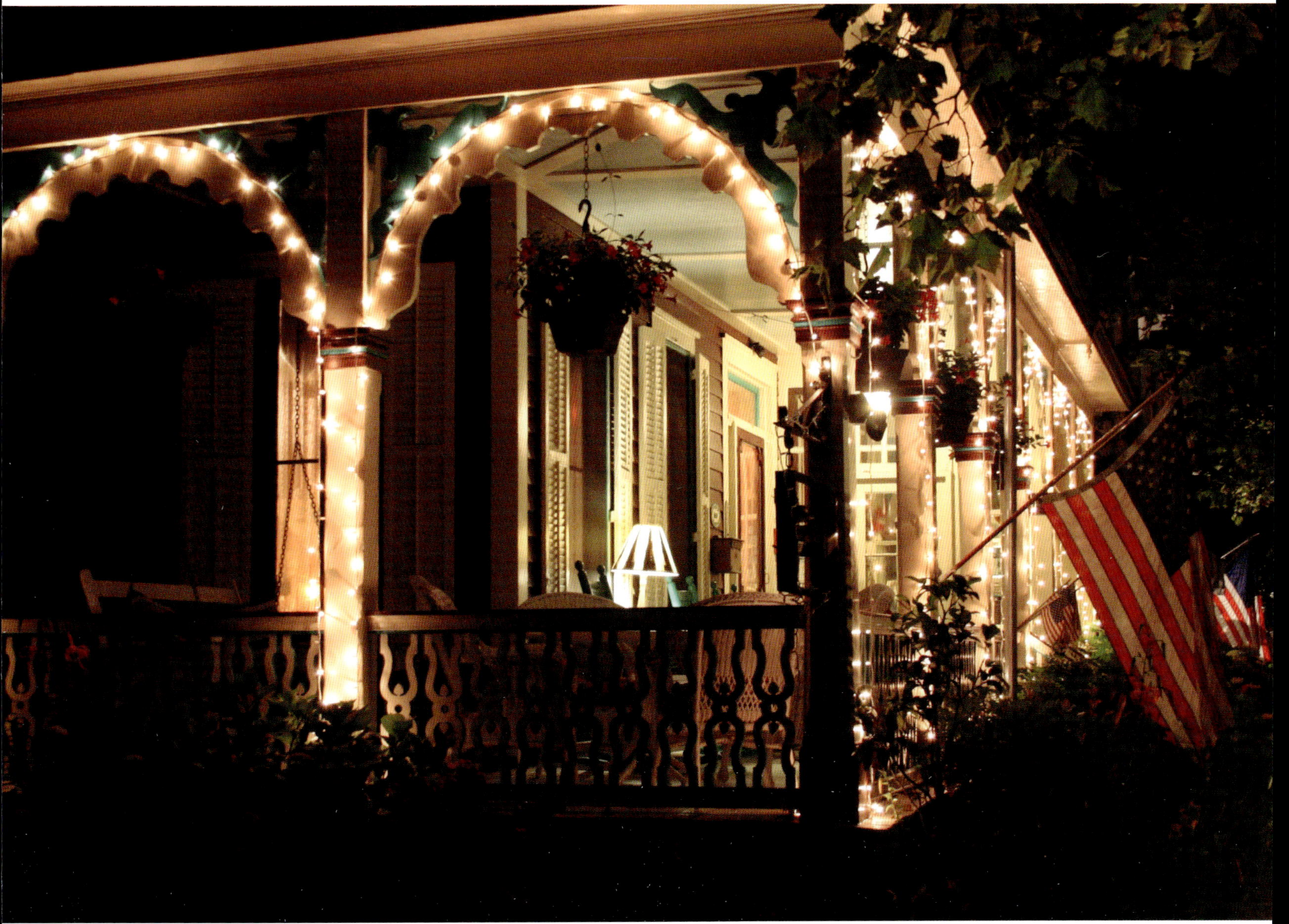

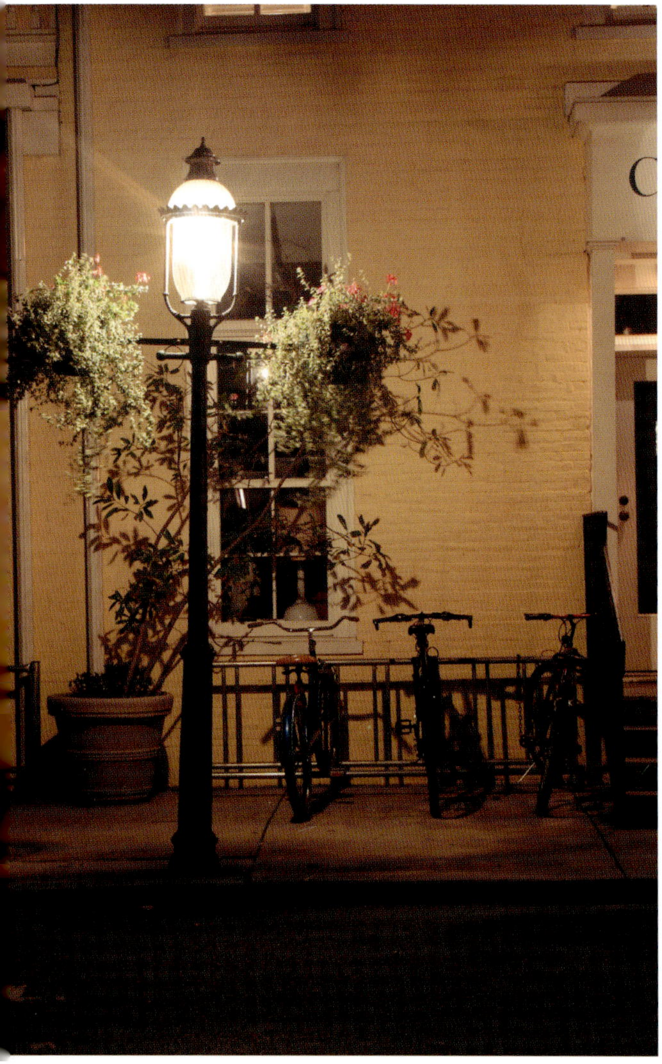

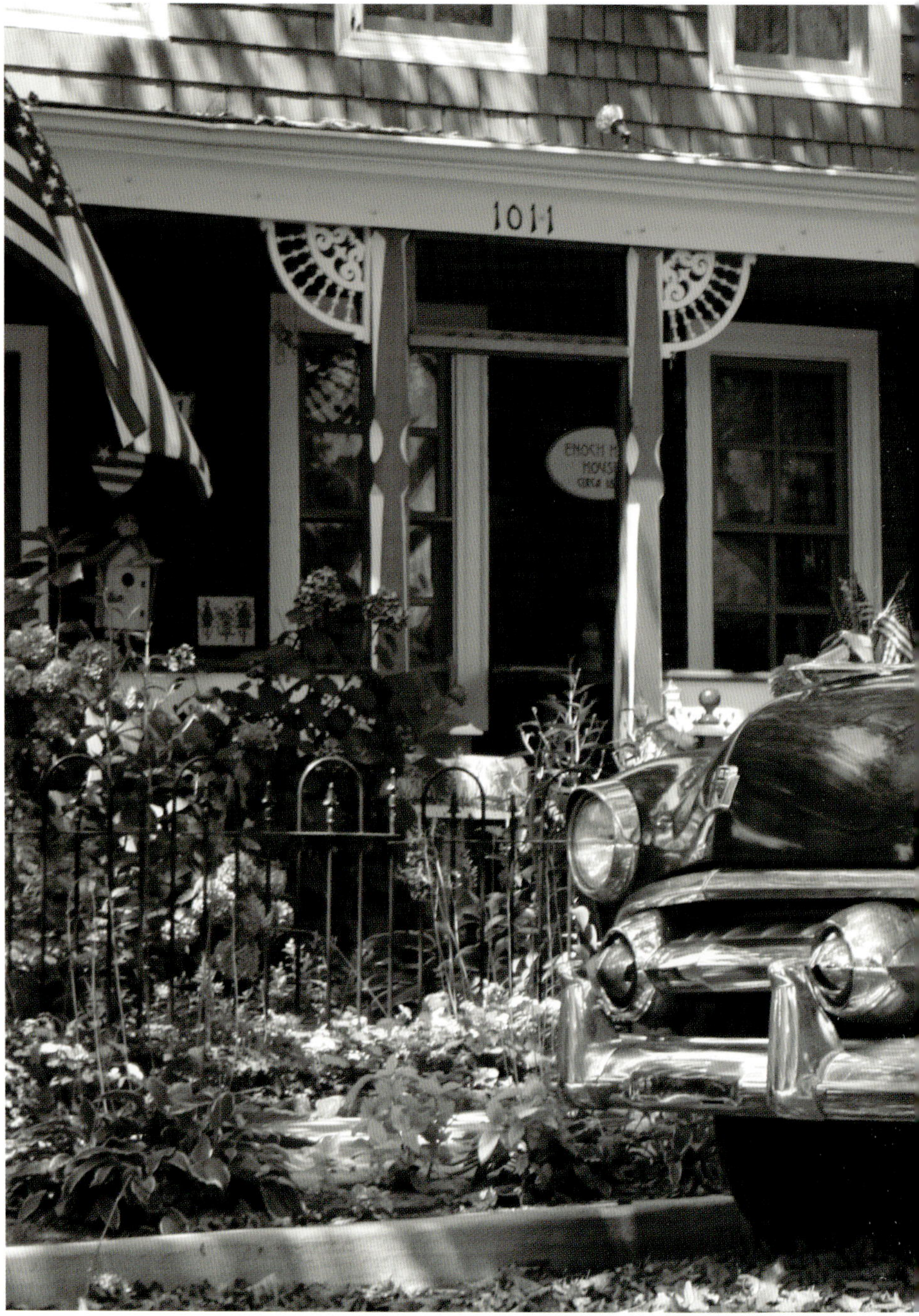
1011

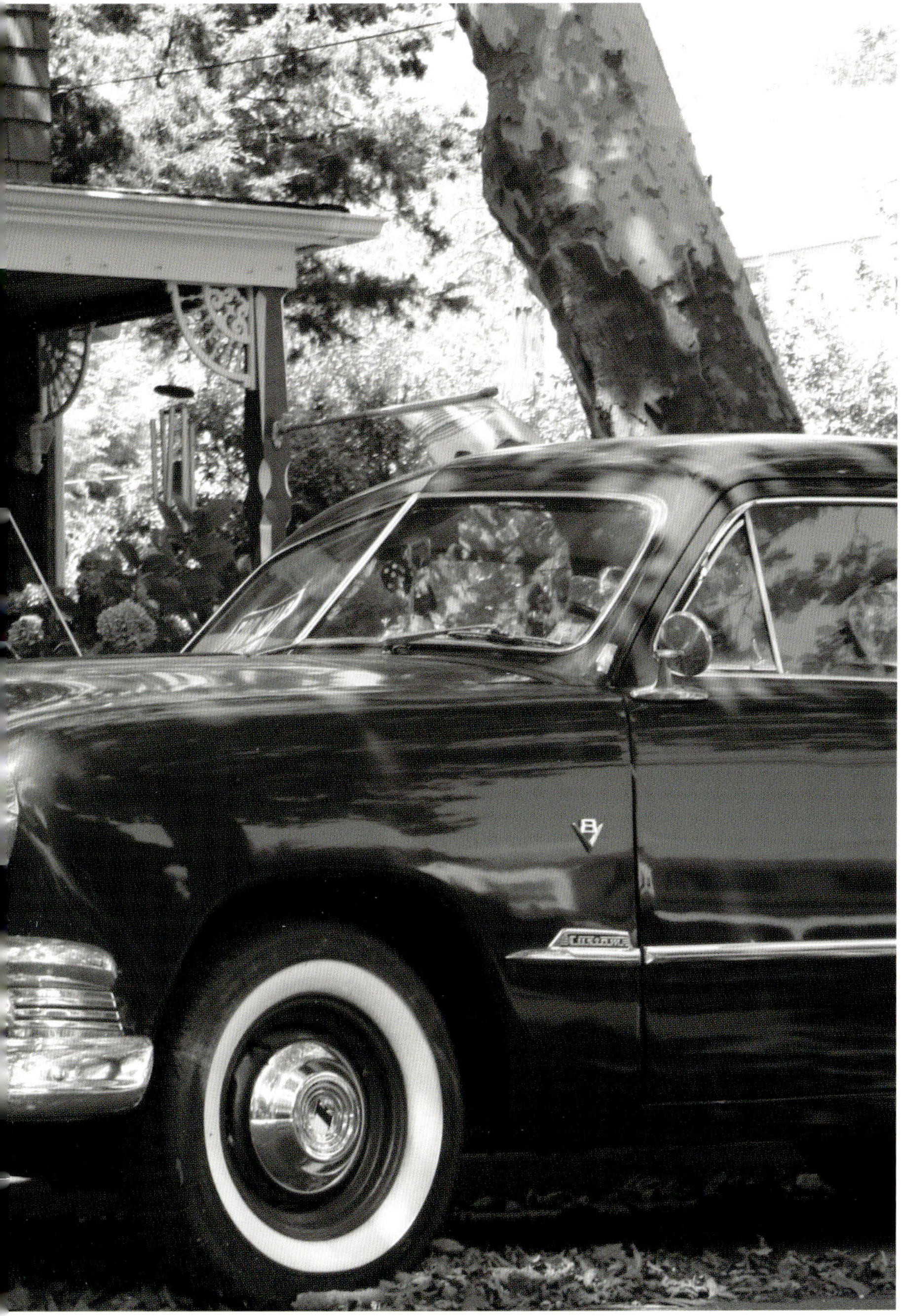

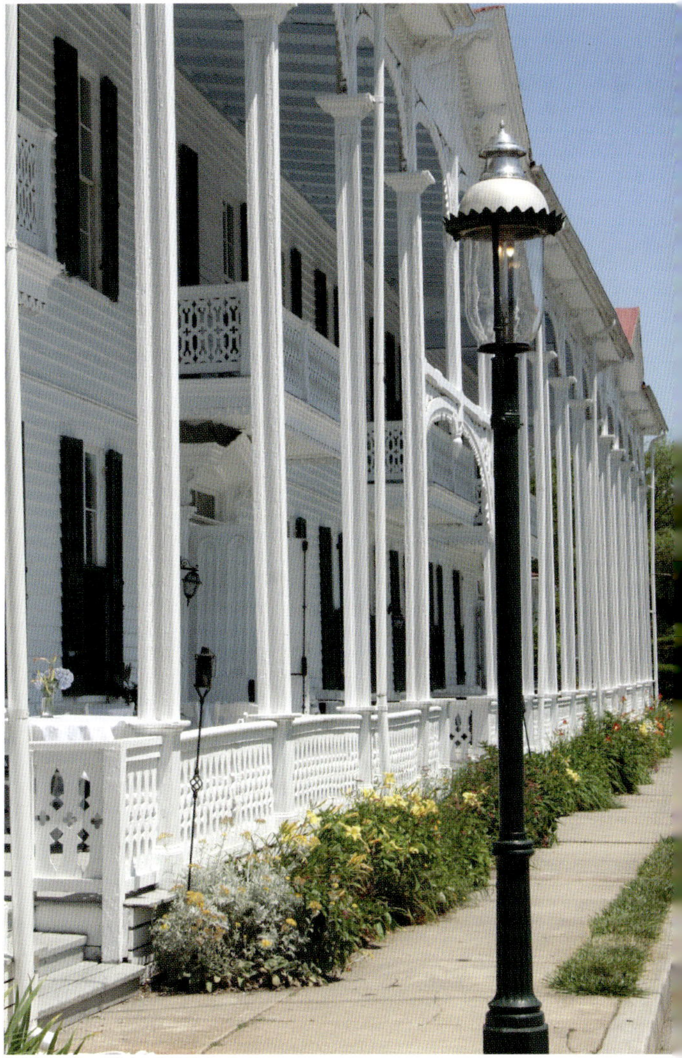

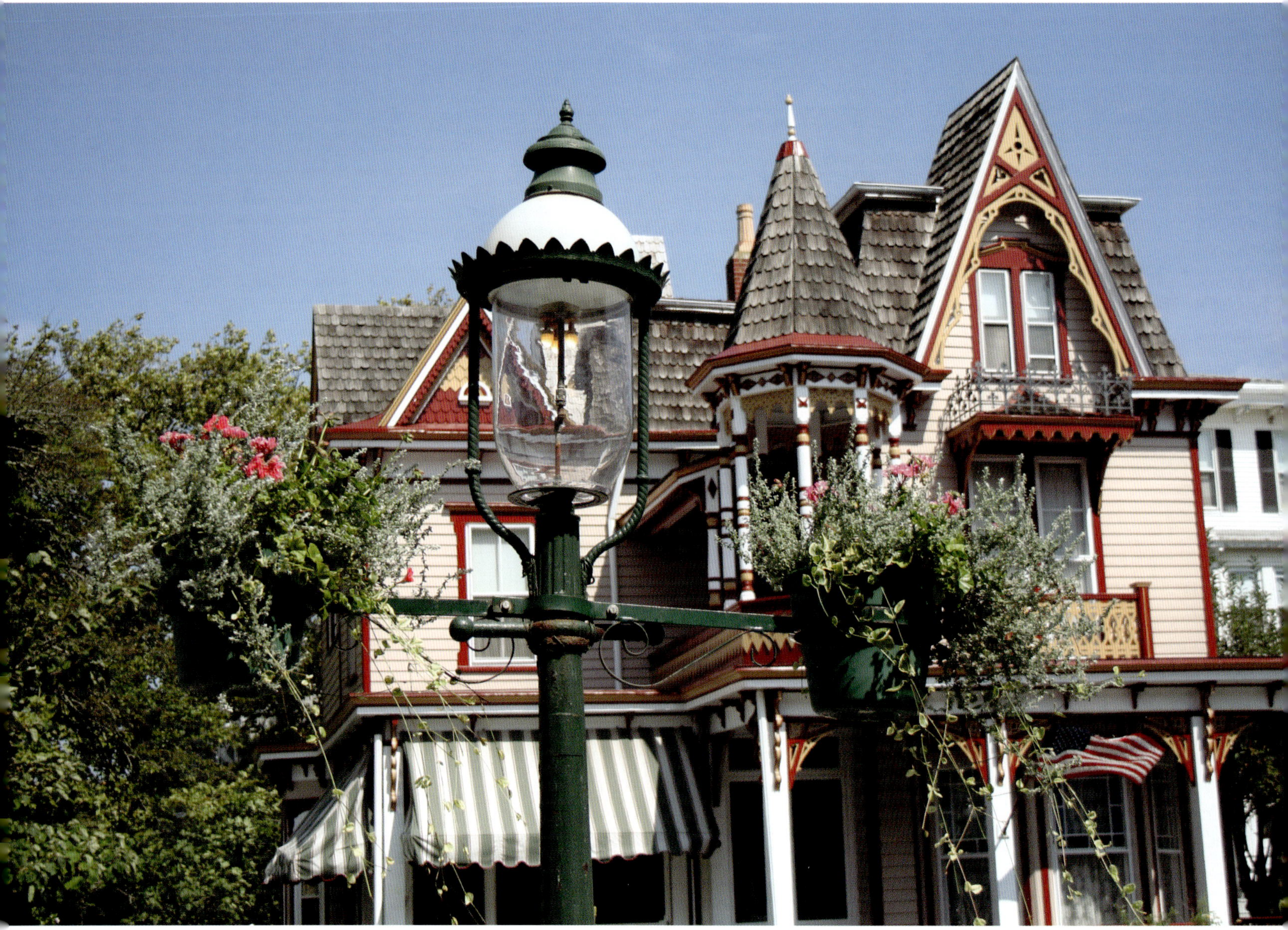

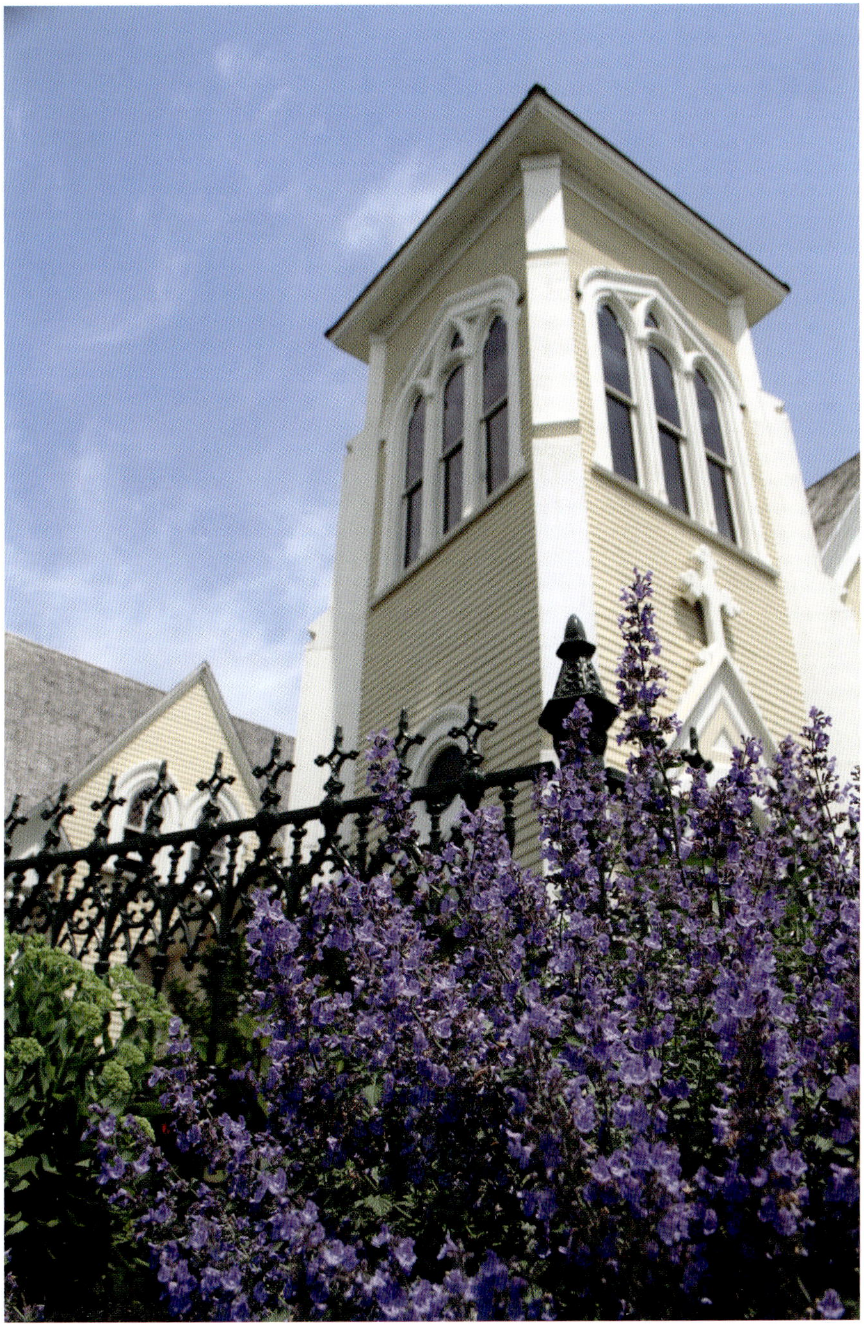

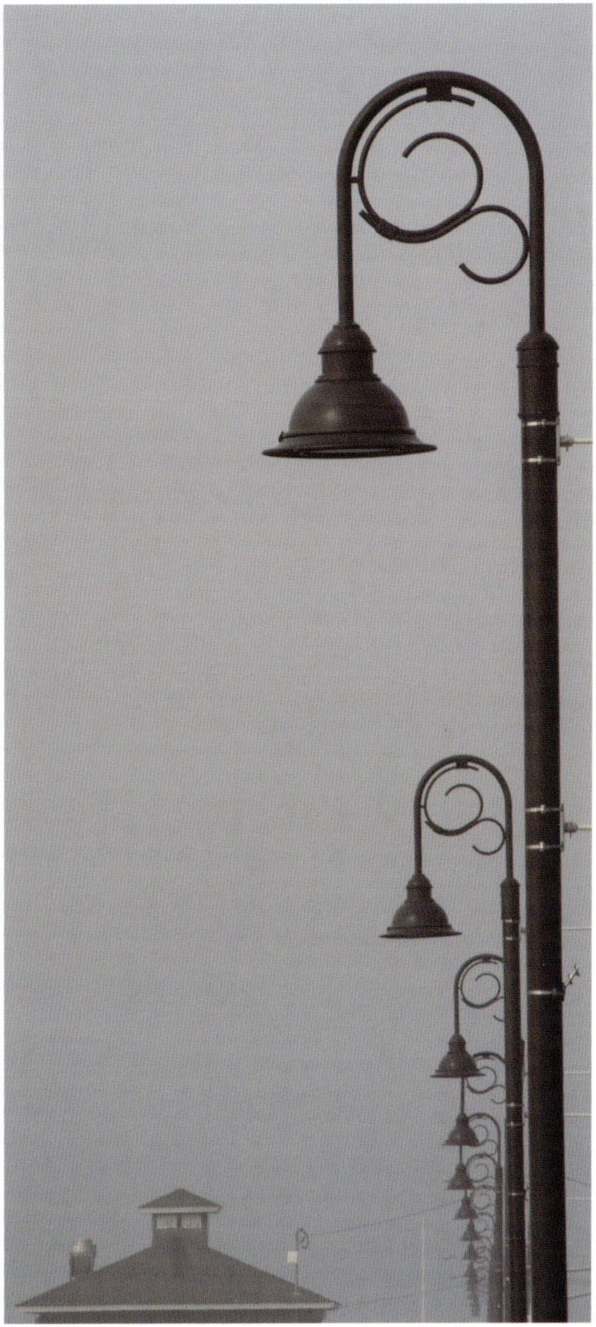

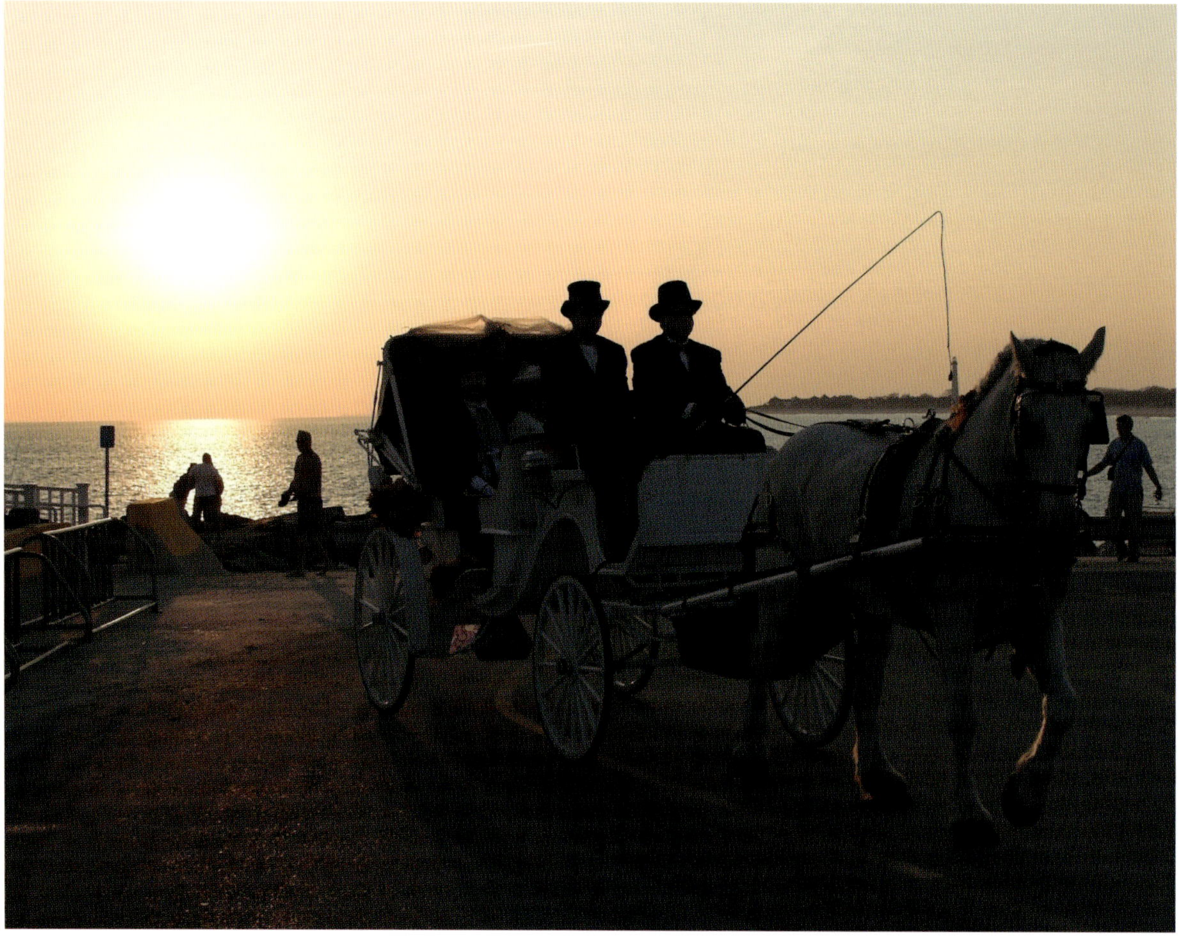

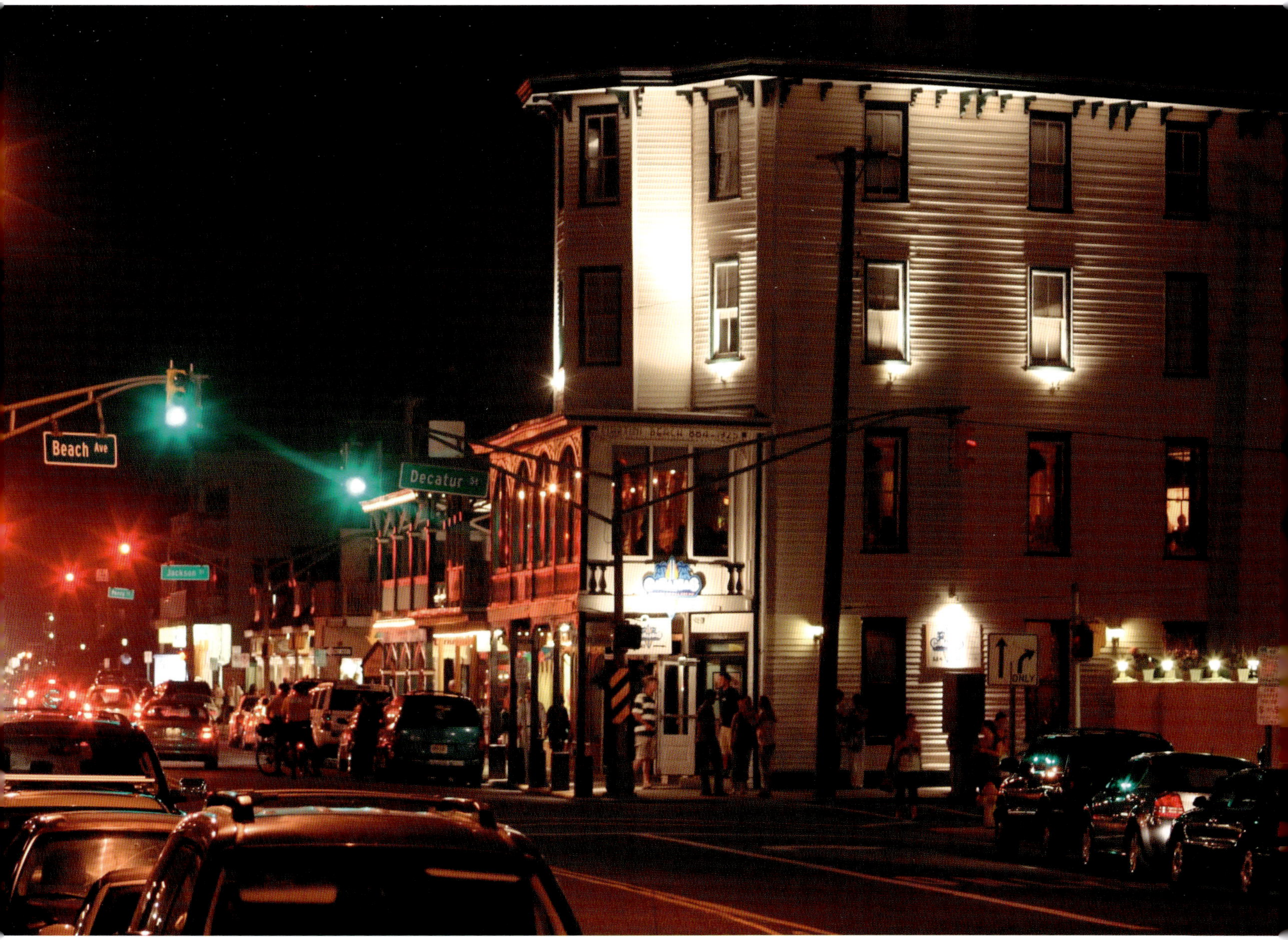
Beach Ave
Decatur St
Jackson St
ONLY

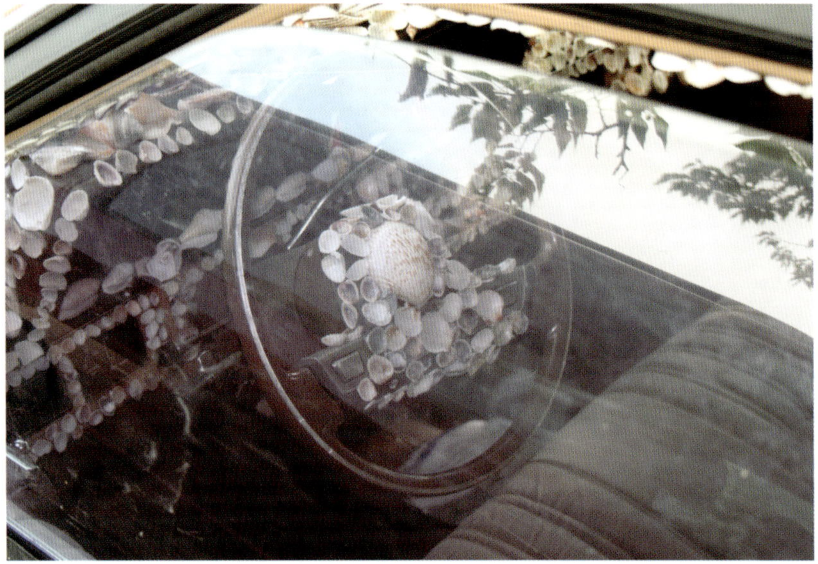

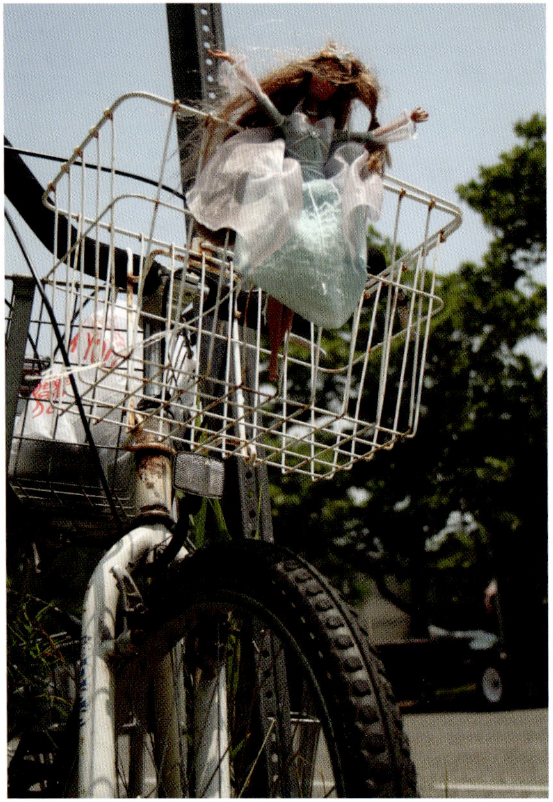

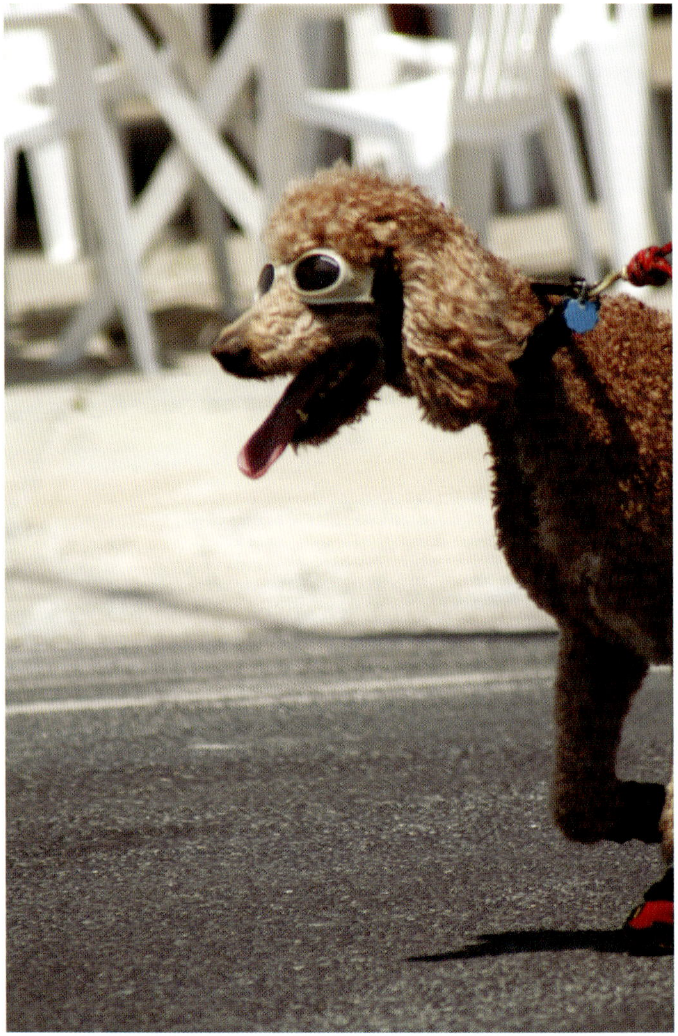

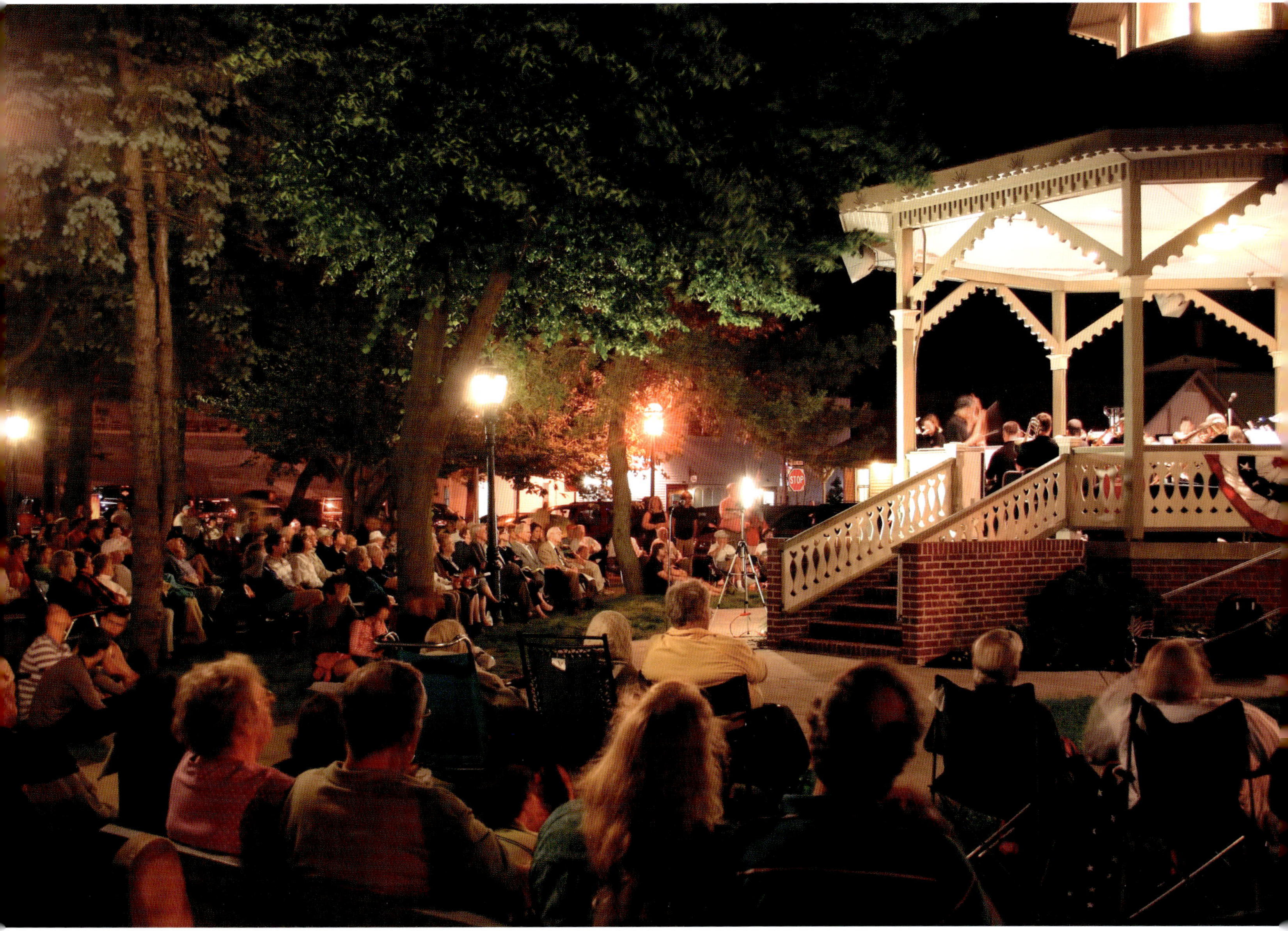
STOP

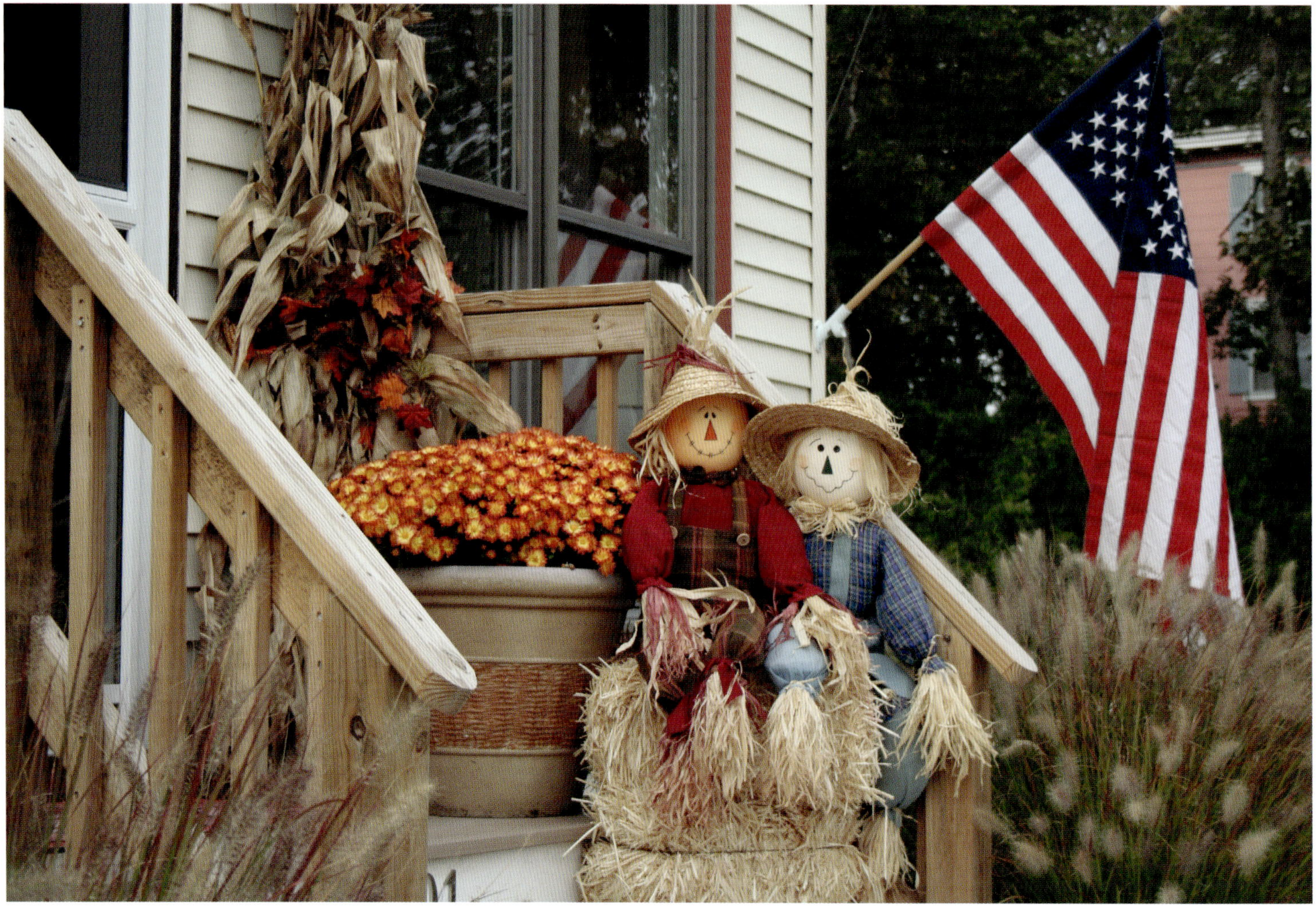

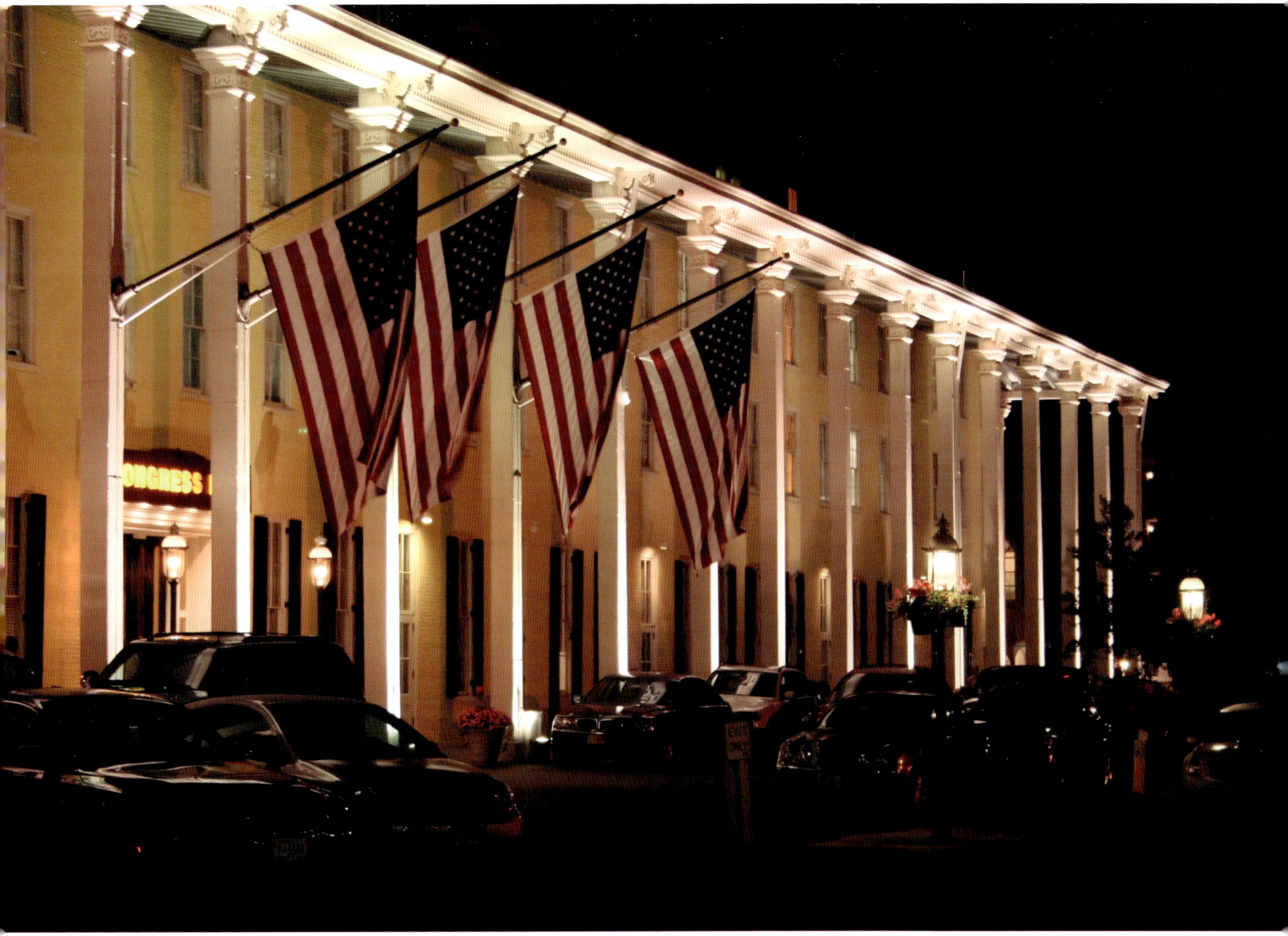
ONGRESS

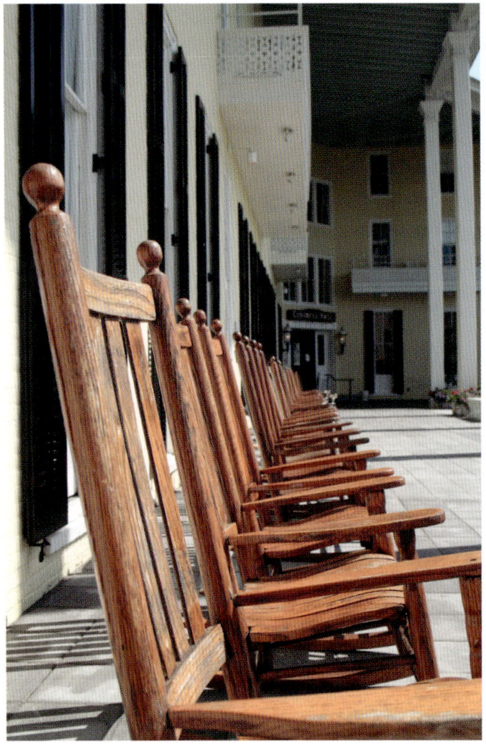

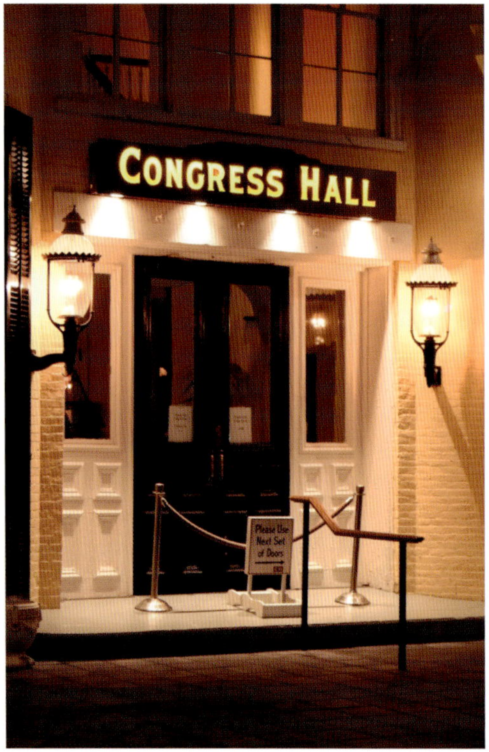
CONGRESS HALL
Please Use
Next Set
of Doors

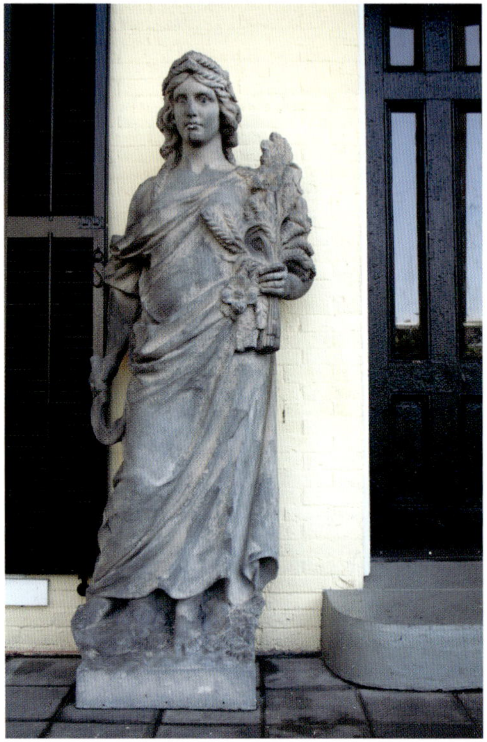

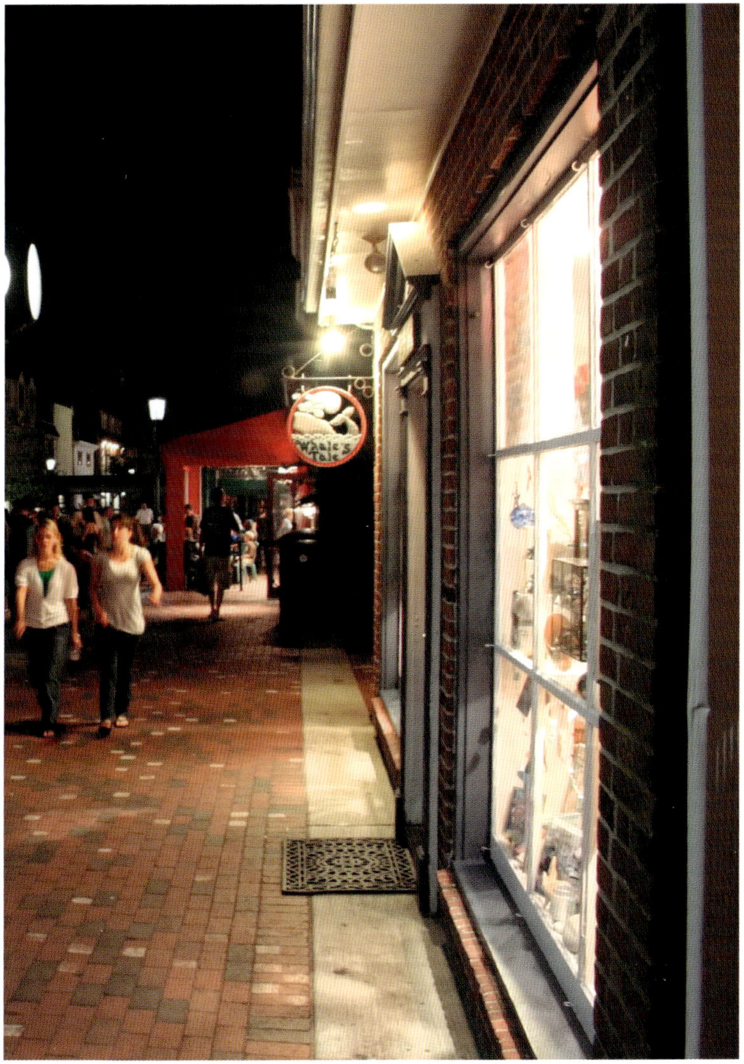
Whale's Tale

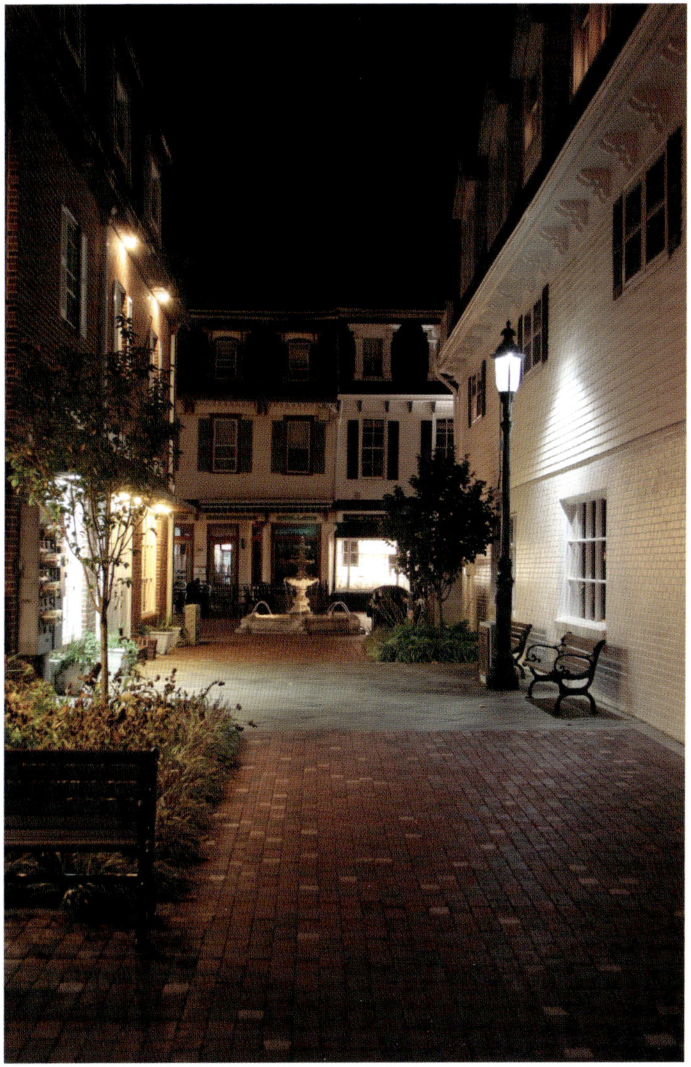

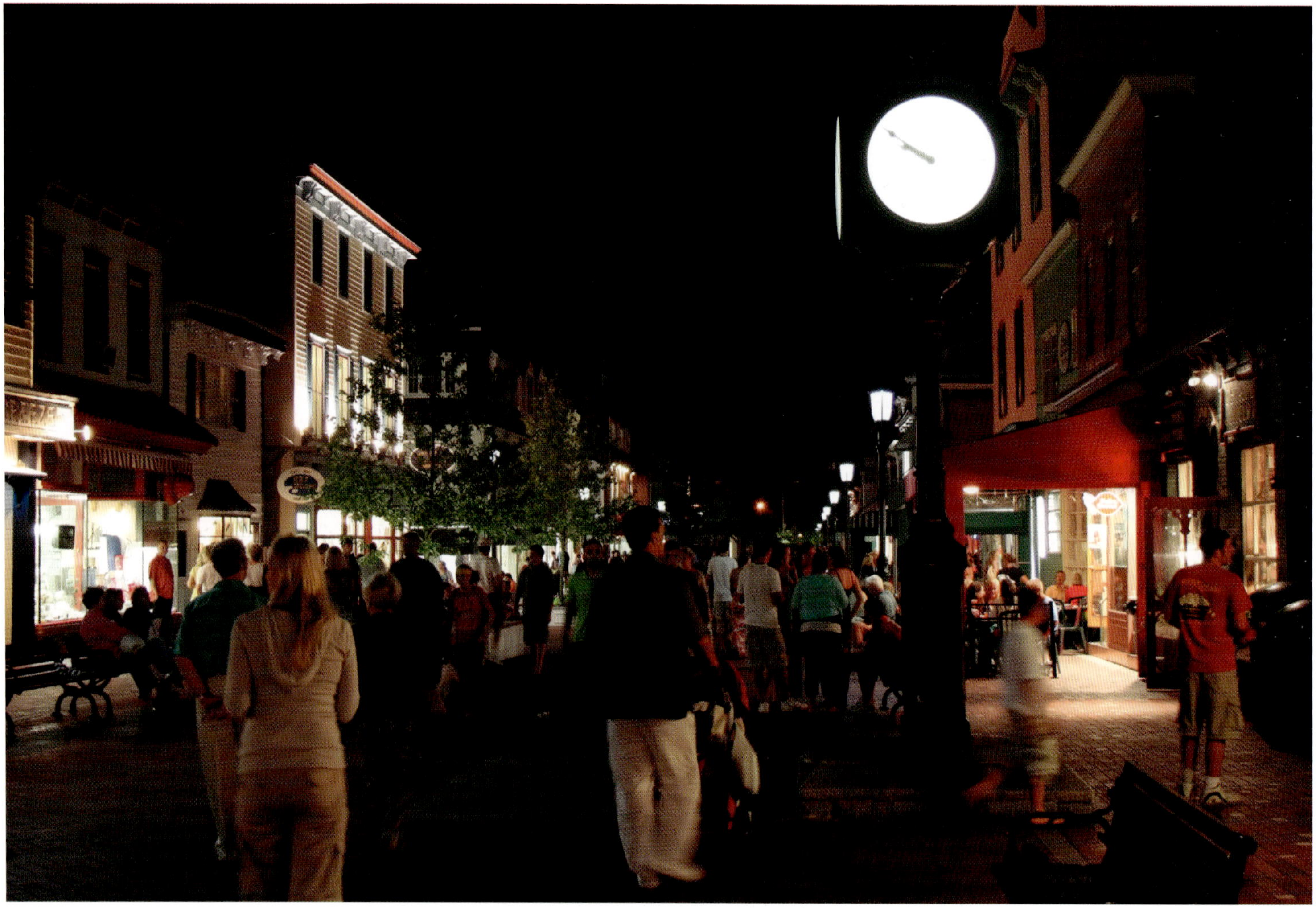

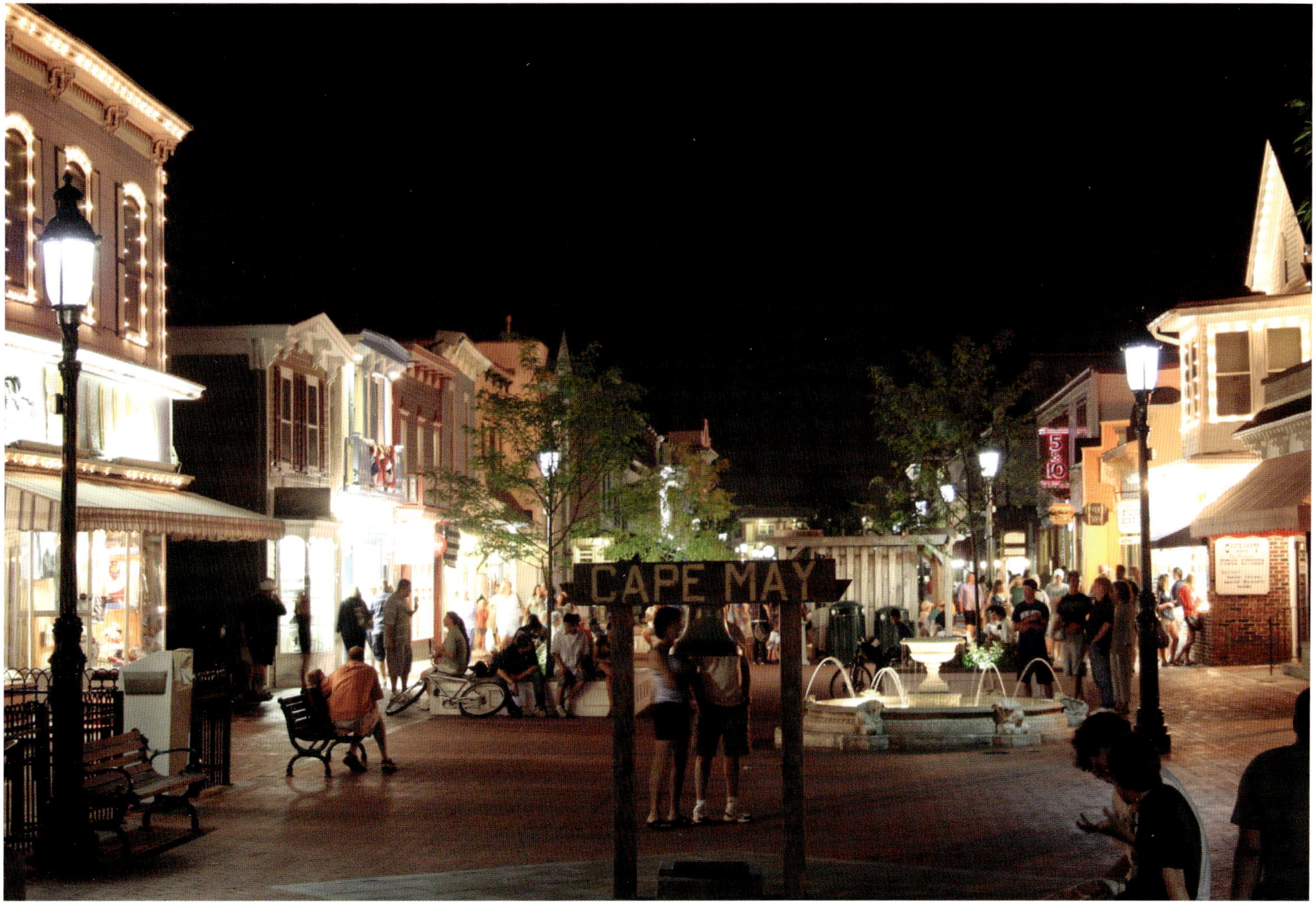
CAPE MAY

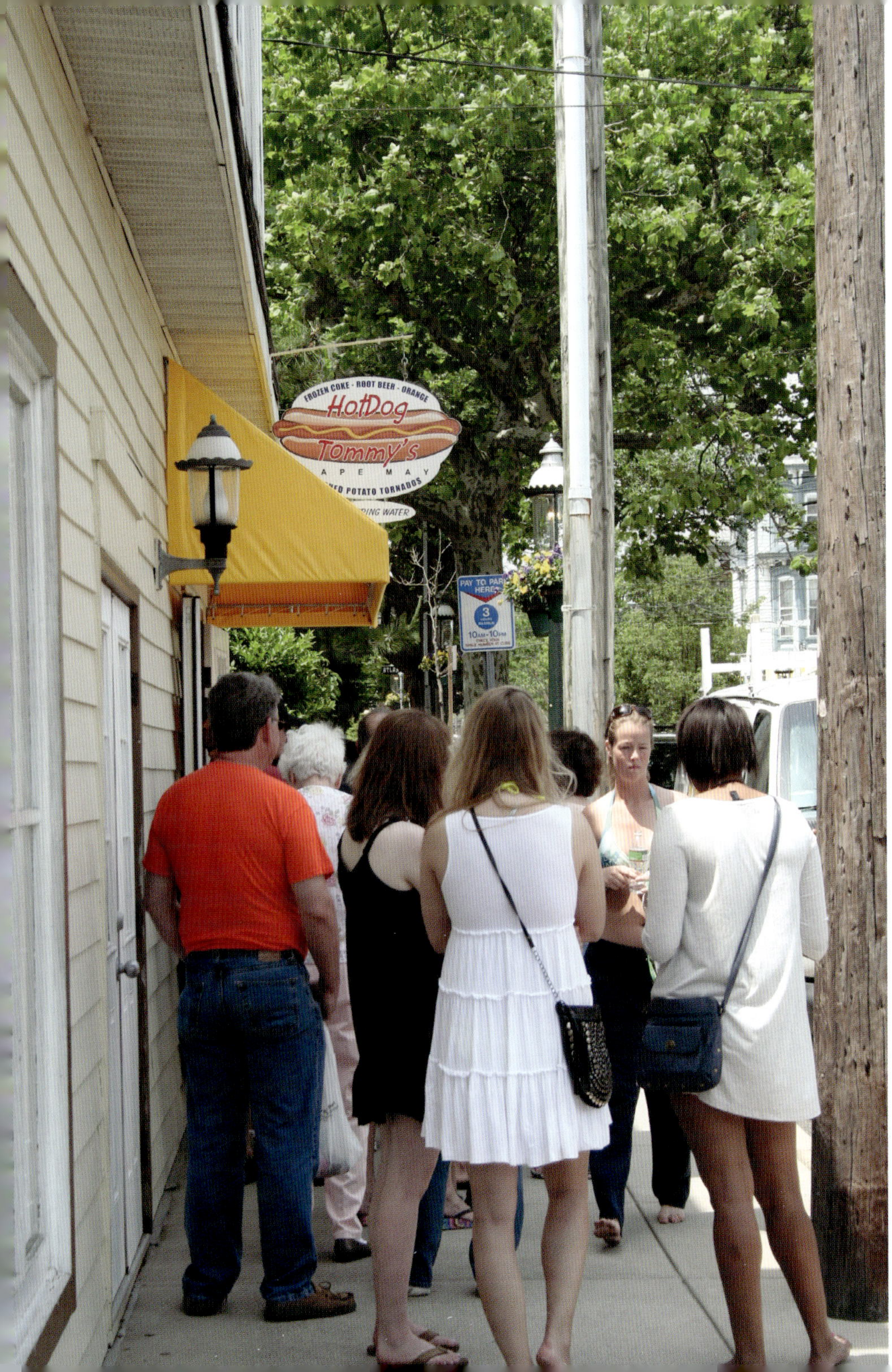
FROZEN COKE · ROOT BEER · ORANGE
HotDog
Tommy's

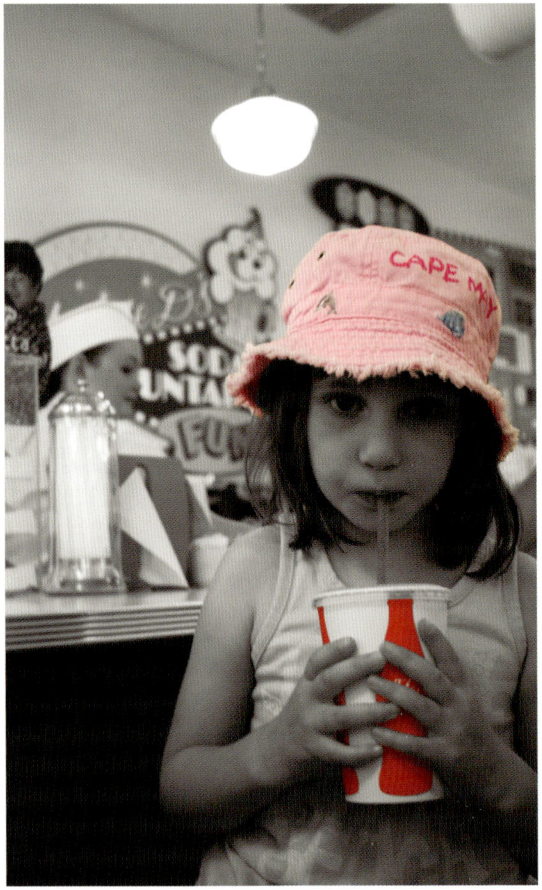
CAPE MAY

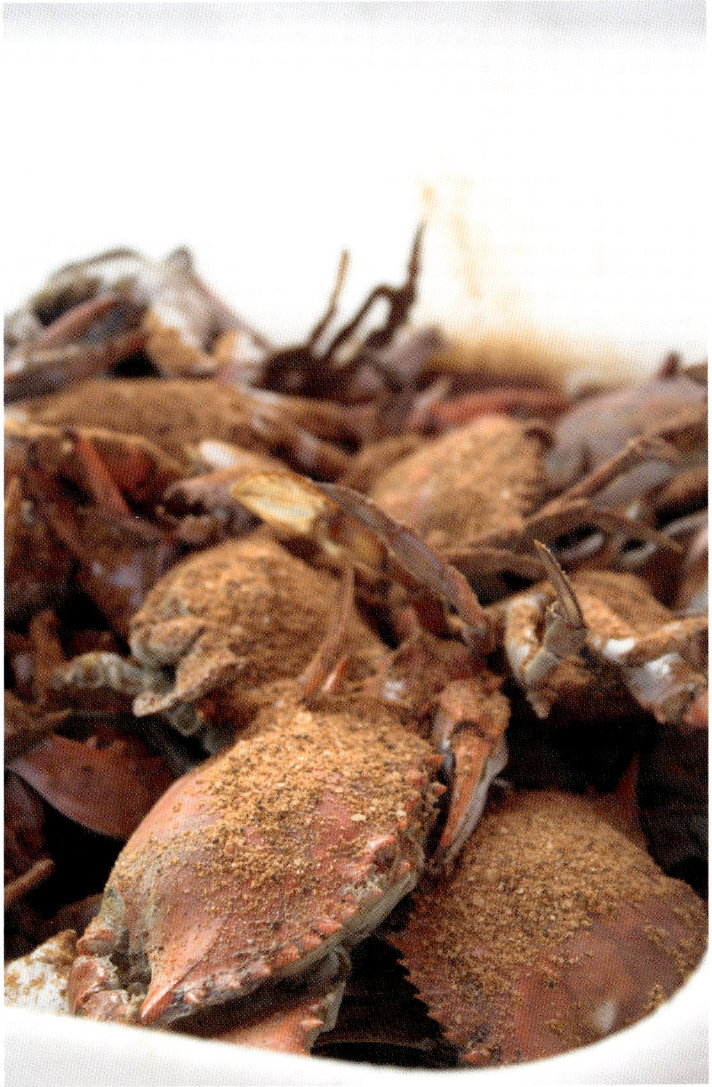

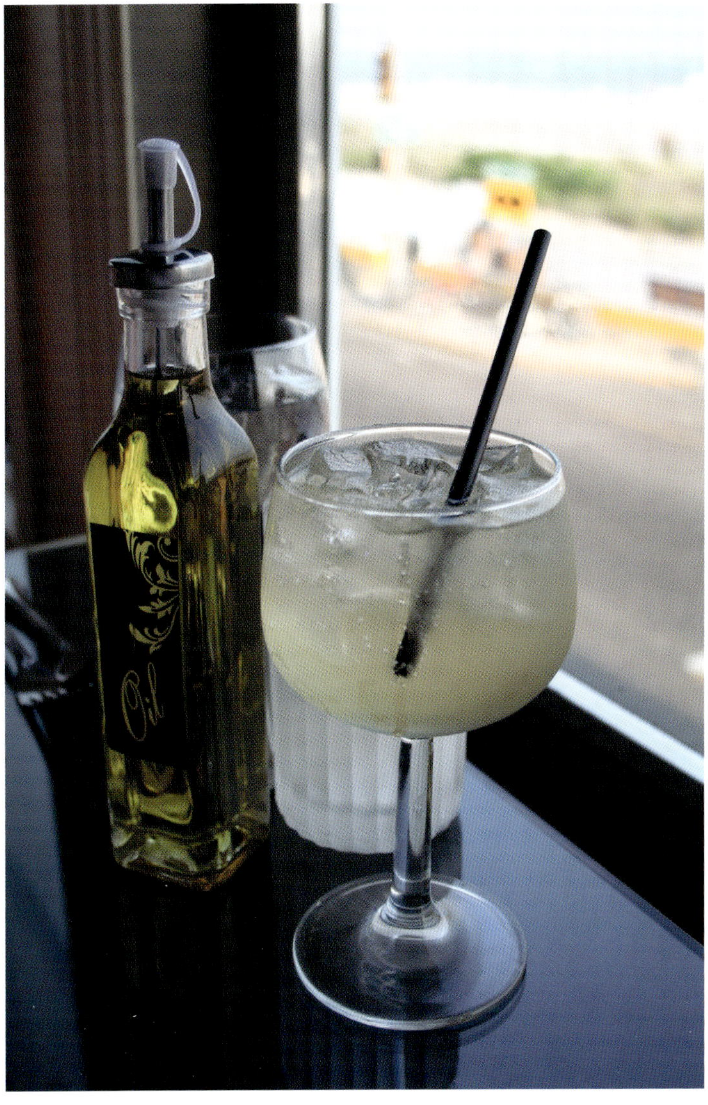
Oil

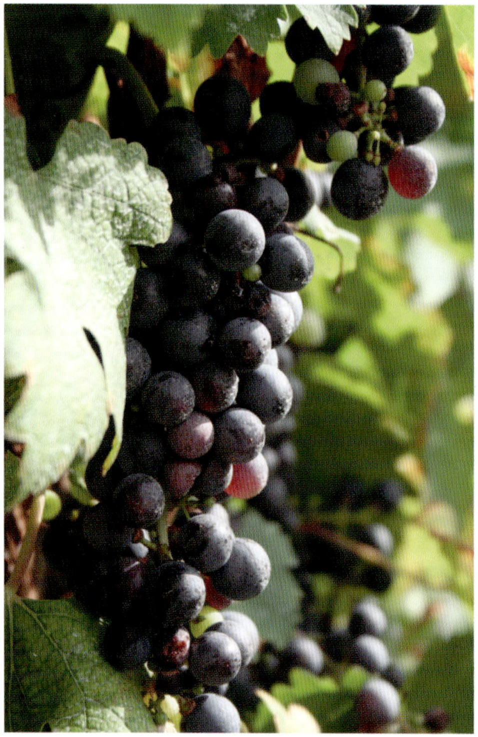

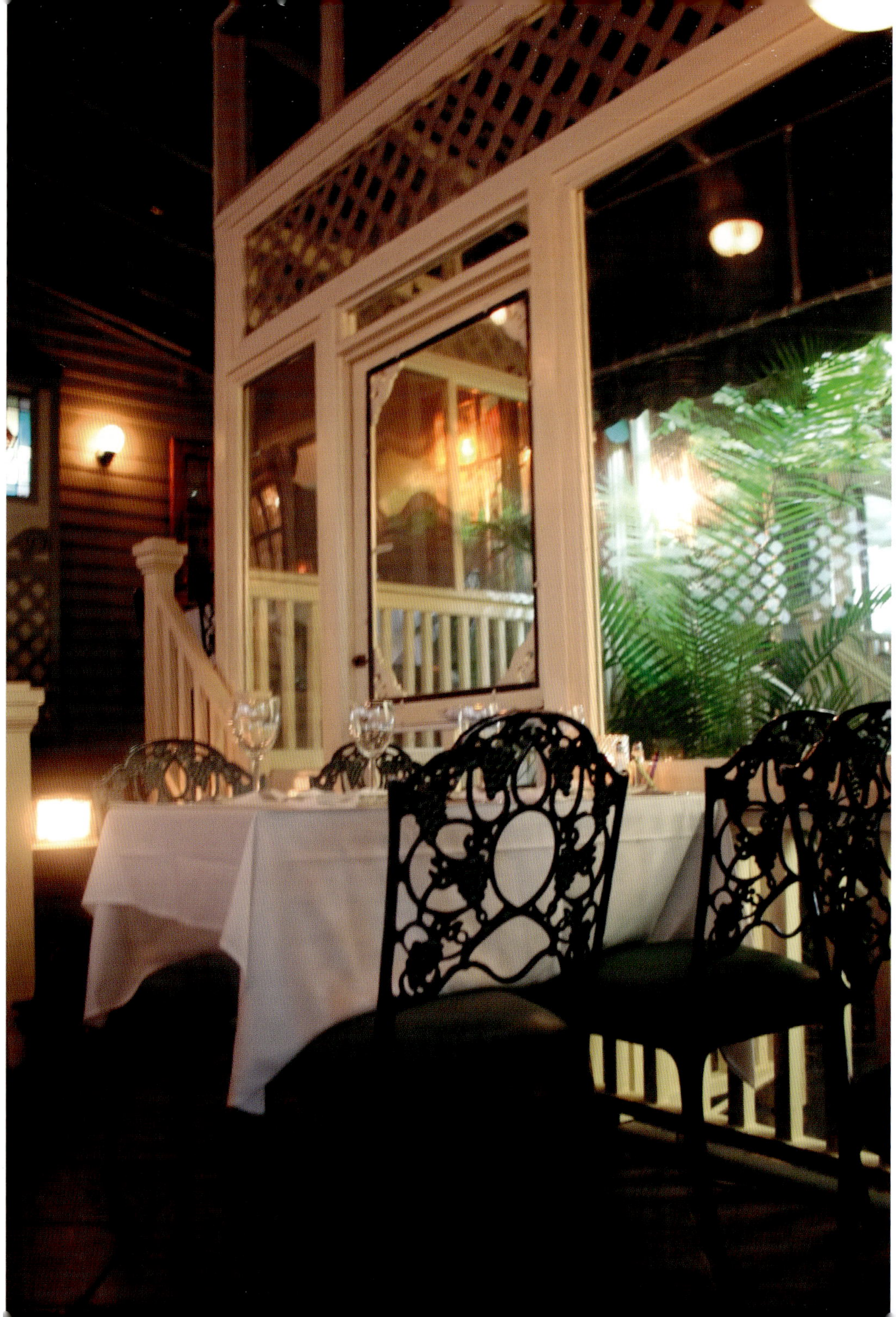

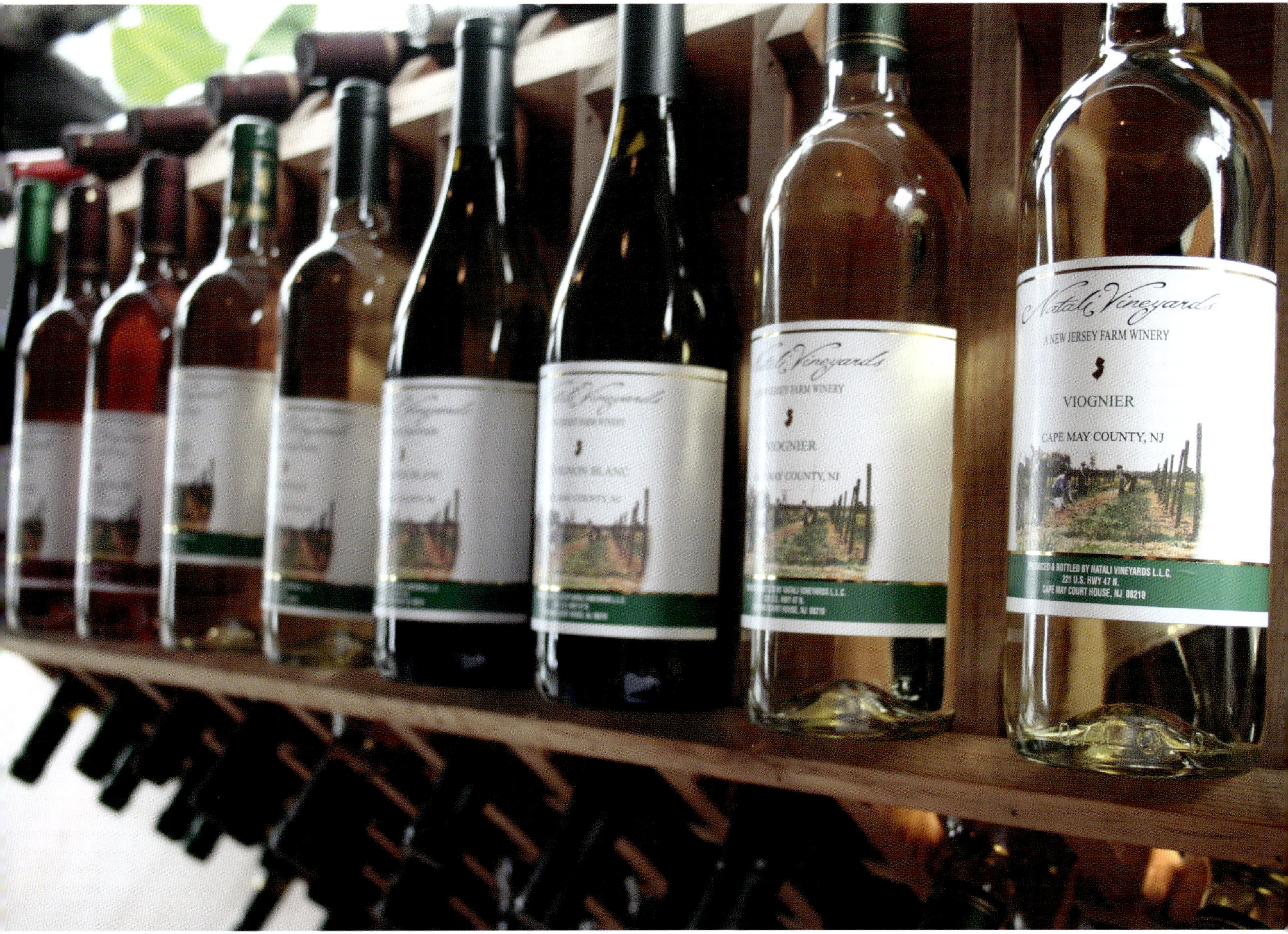
Natali Vineyards
A NEW JERSEY FARM WINERY
VIOGNIER
CAPE MAY COUNTY, NJ
PRODUCED & BOTTLED BY NATALI VINEYARDS L.L.C.
221 U.S. HWY 47 N.
CAPE MAY COURT HOUSE, NJ 08210

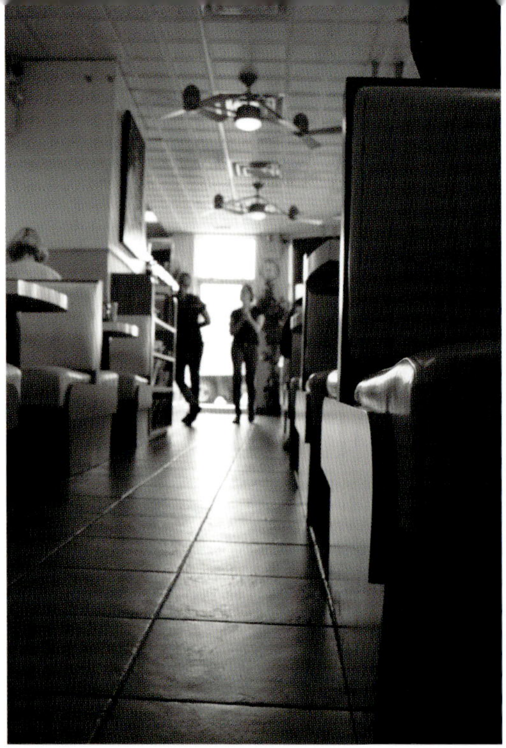

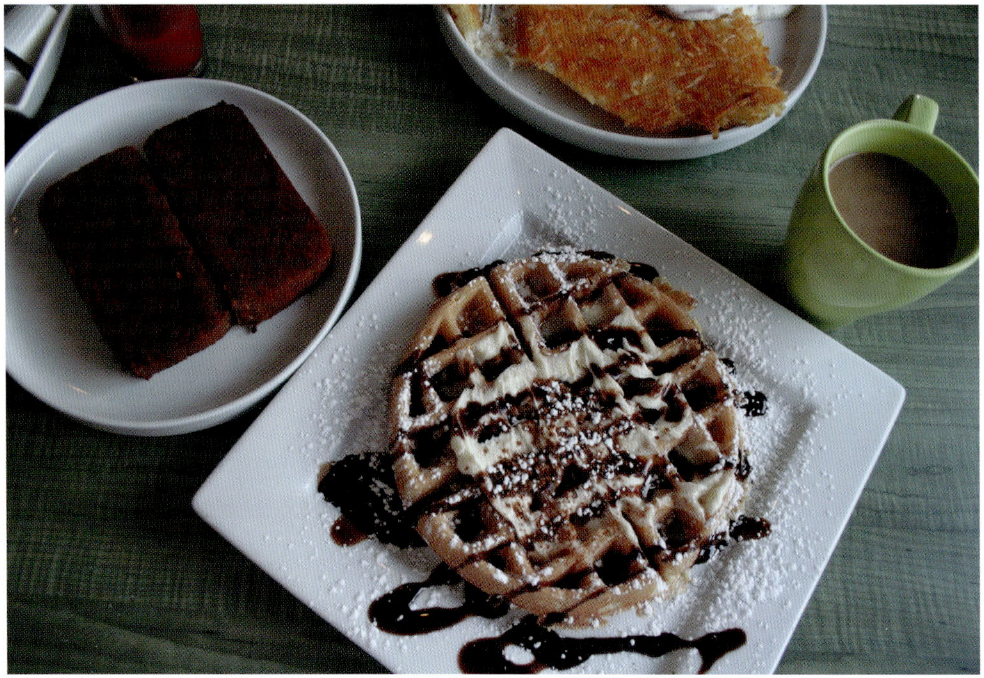

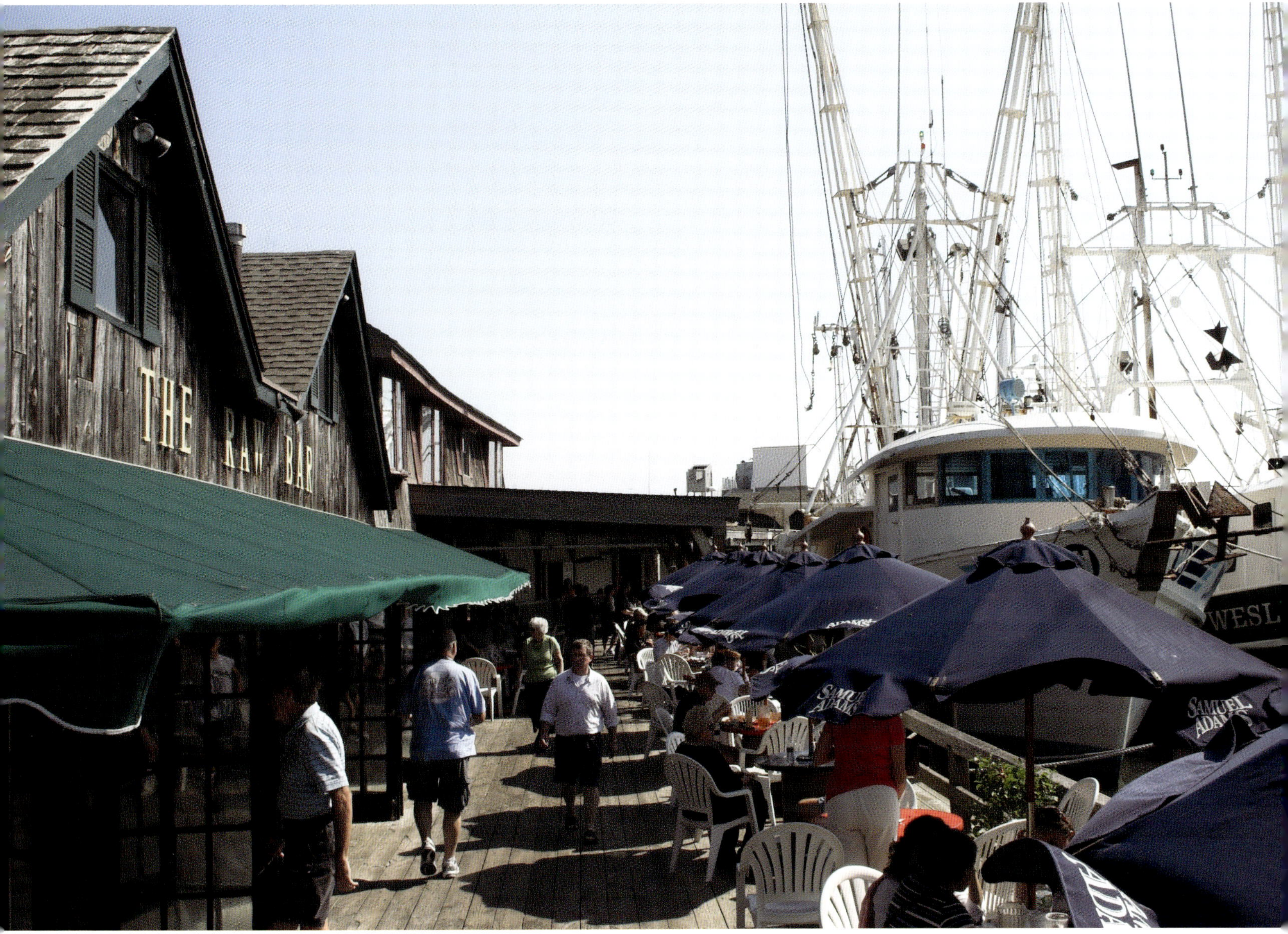
THE RAW BAR
SAMUEL ADAMS

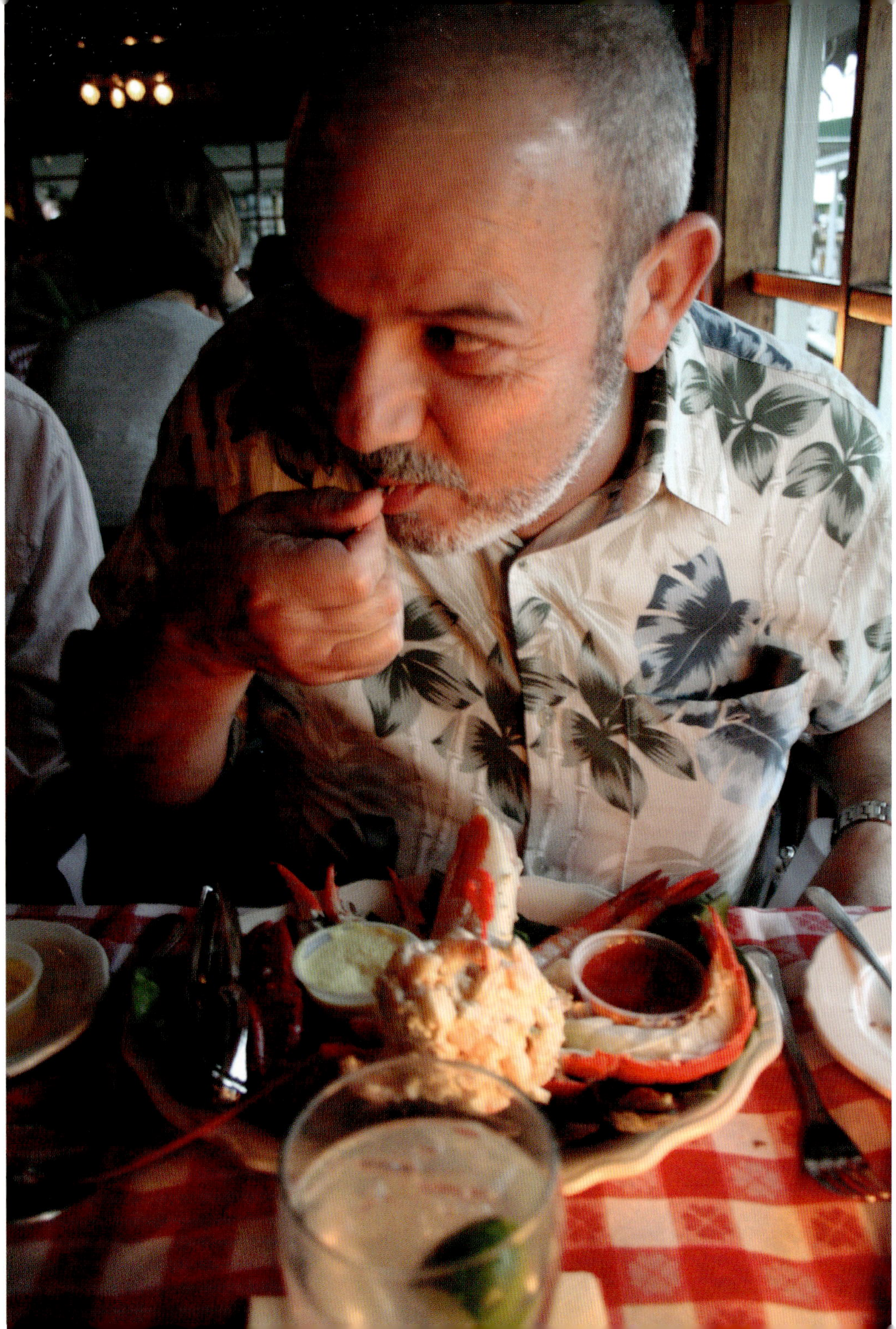

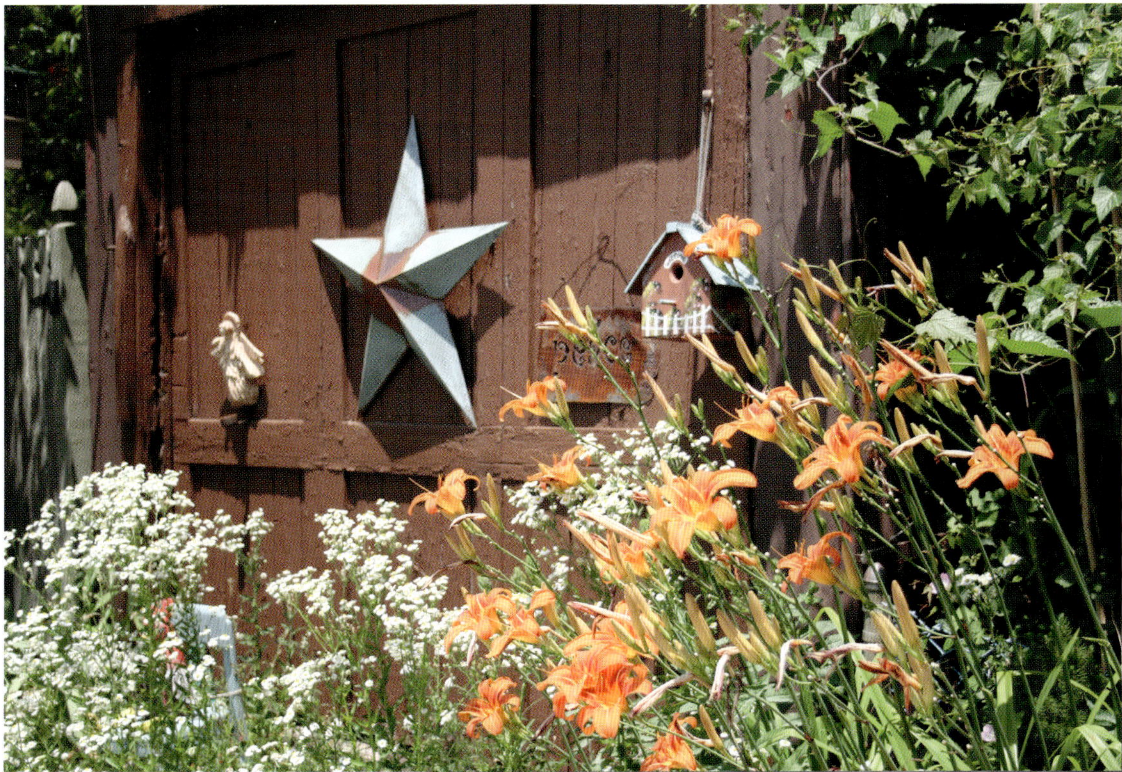

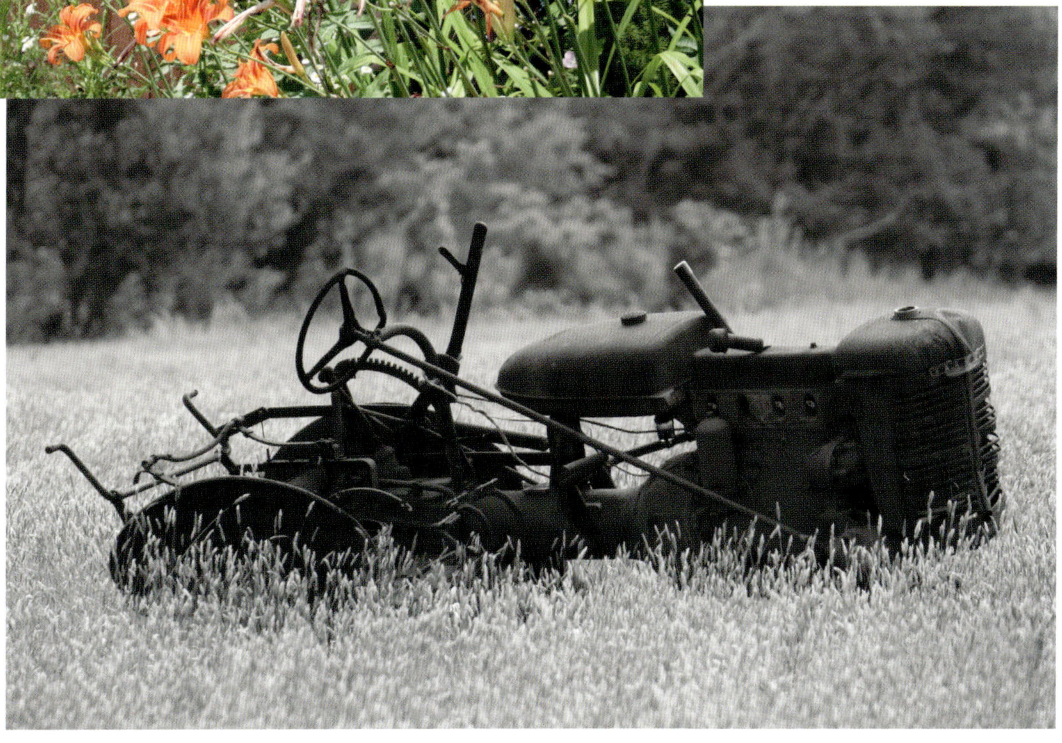

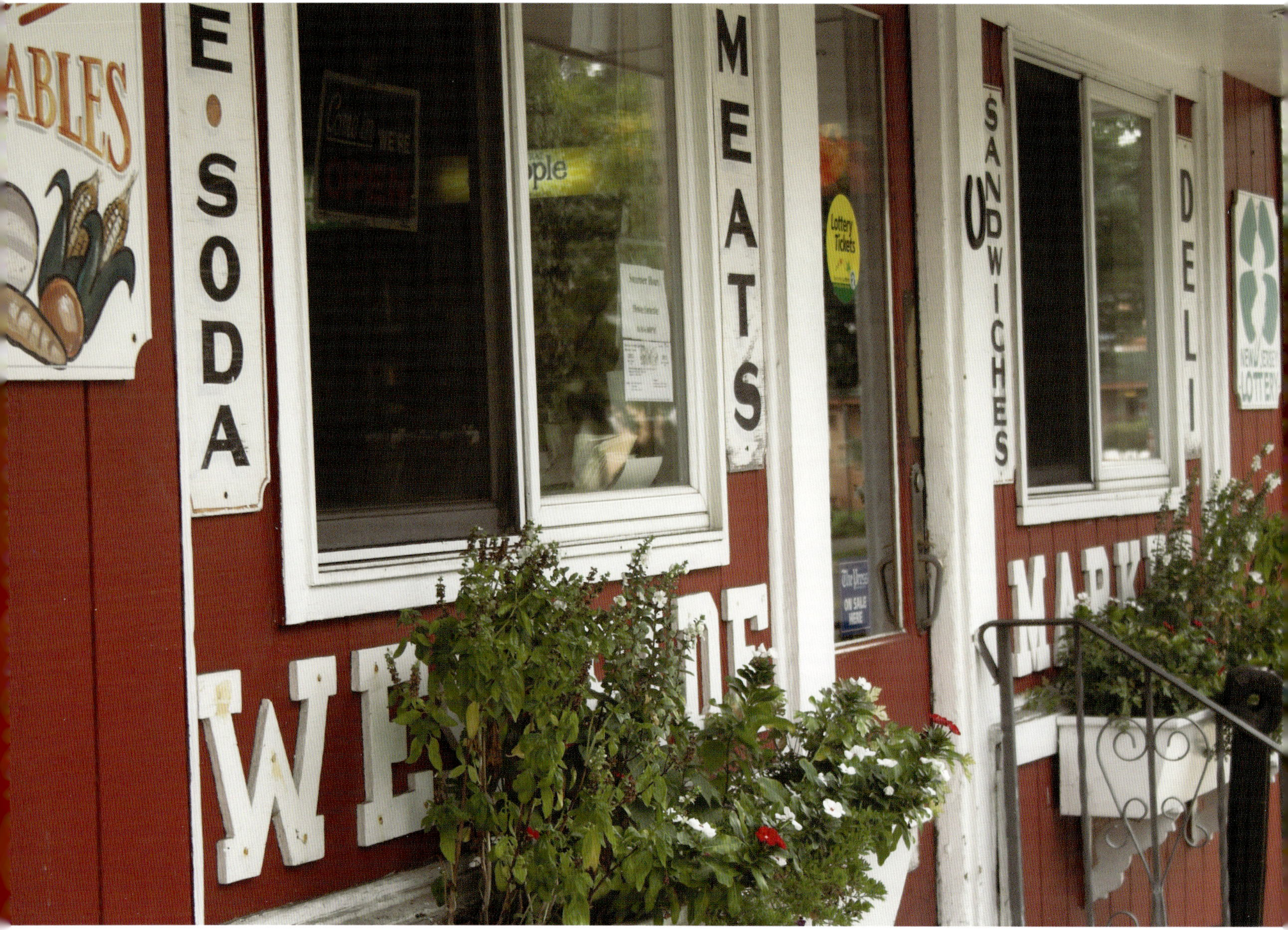
SODA
MEATS
SANDWICHES
DELI
Lottery Tickets
NEW JERSEY LOTTERY

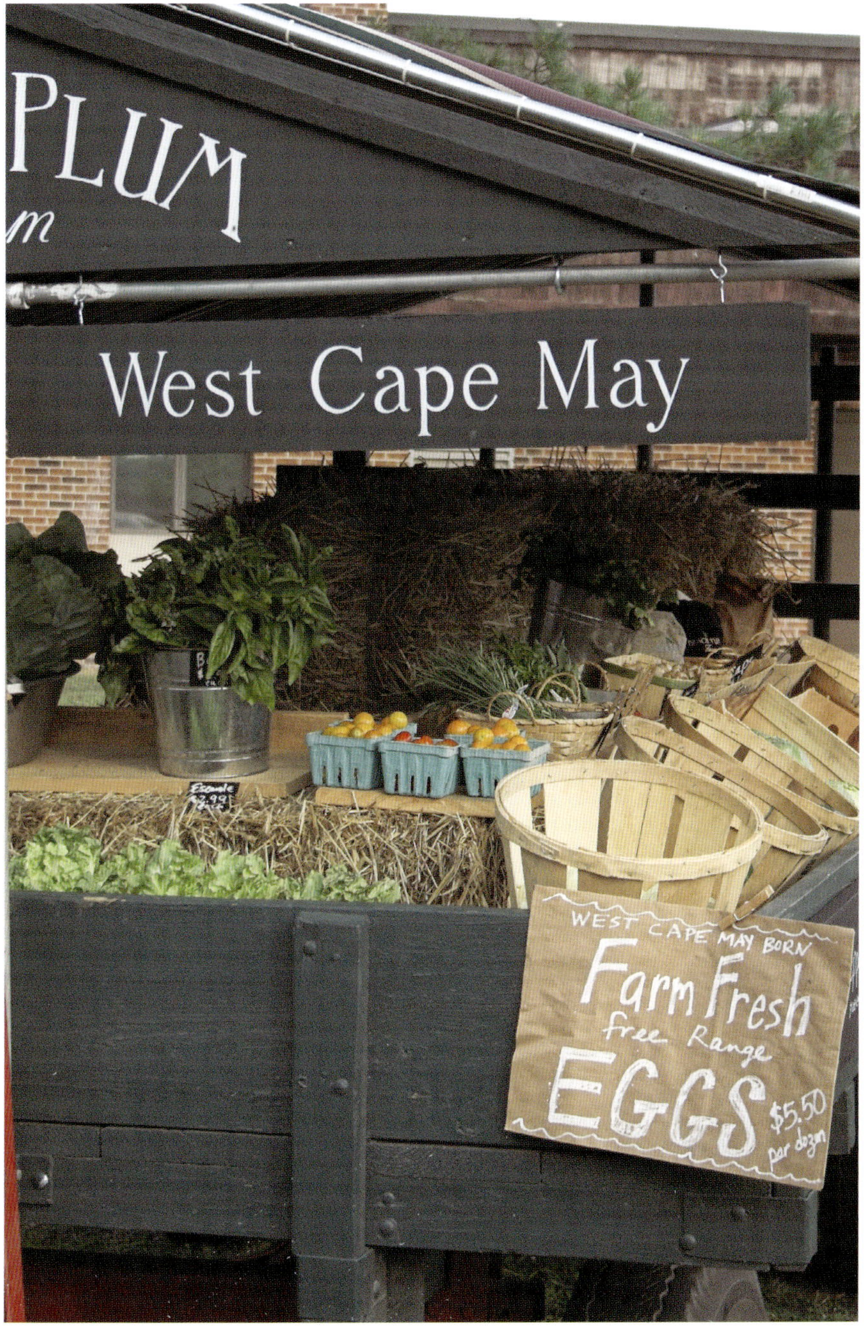
PLUM
West Cape May
WEST CAPE MAY BORN
Farm Fresh
free Range
EGGS
$5.50
per dozen

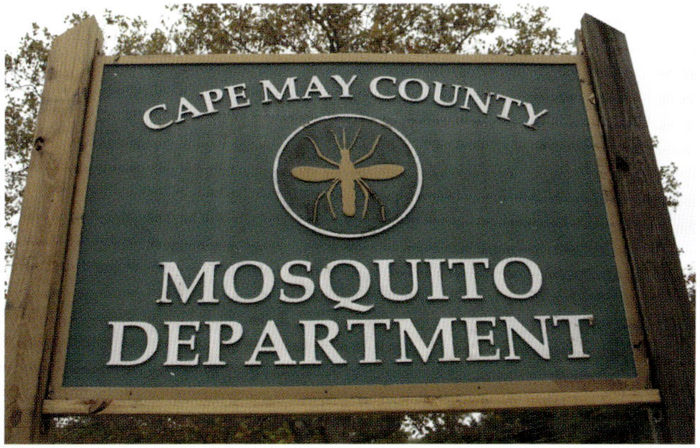
CAPE MAY COUNTY
MOSQUITO
DEPARTMENT

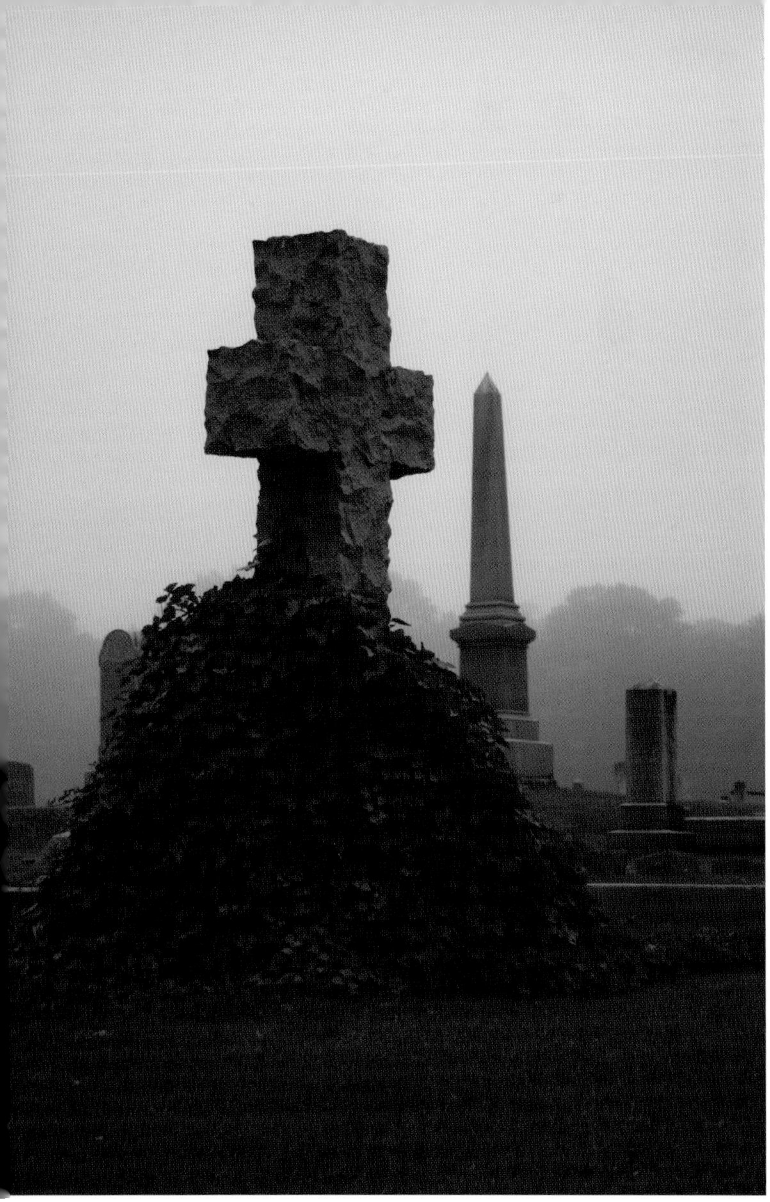

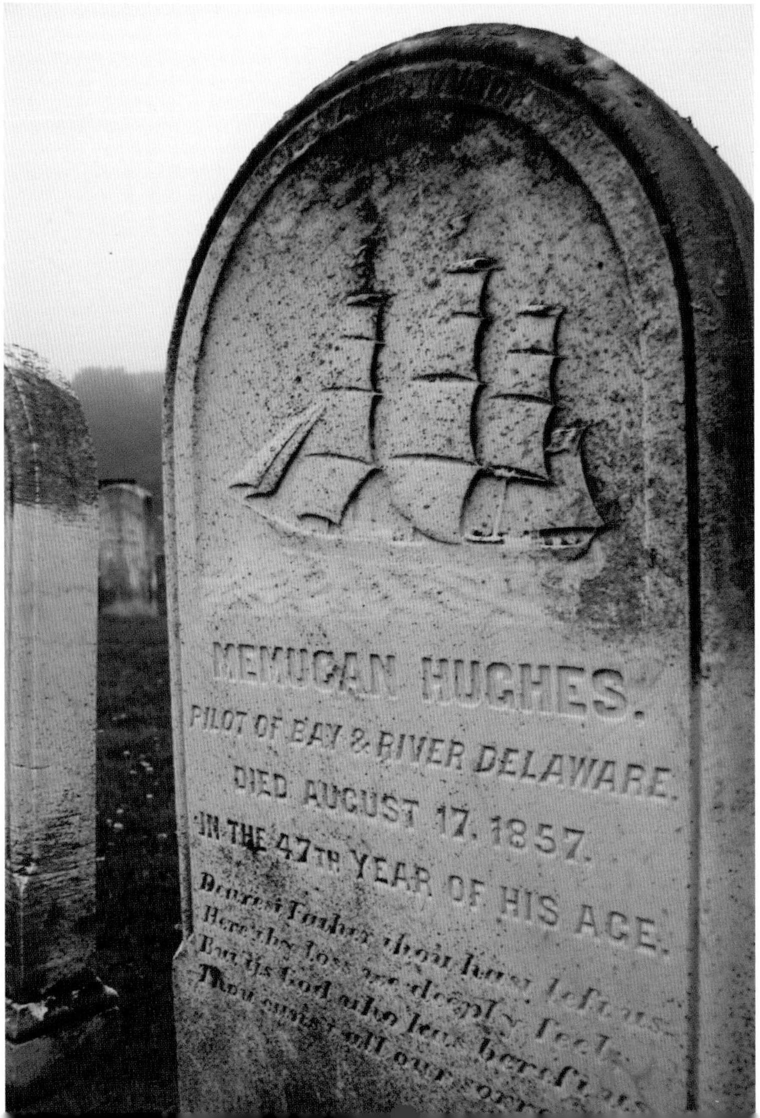
MEMUCAN HUGHES.
PILOT OF BAY & RIVER DELAWARE.
DIED AUGUST 17, 1857.
IN THE 47TH YEAR OF HIS AGE.

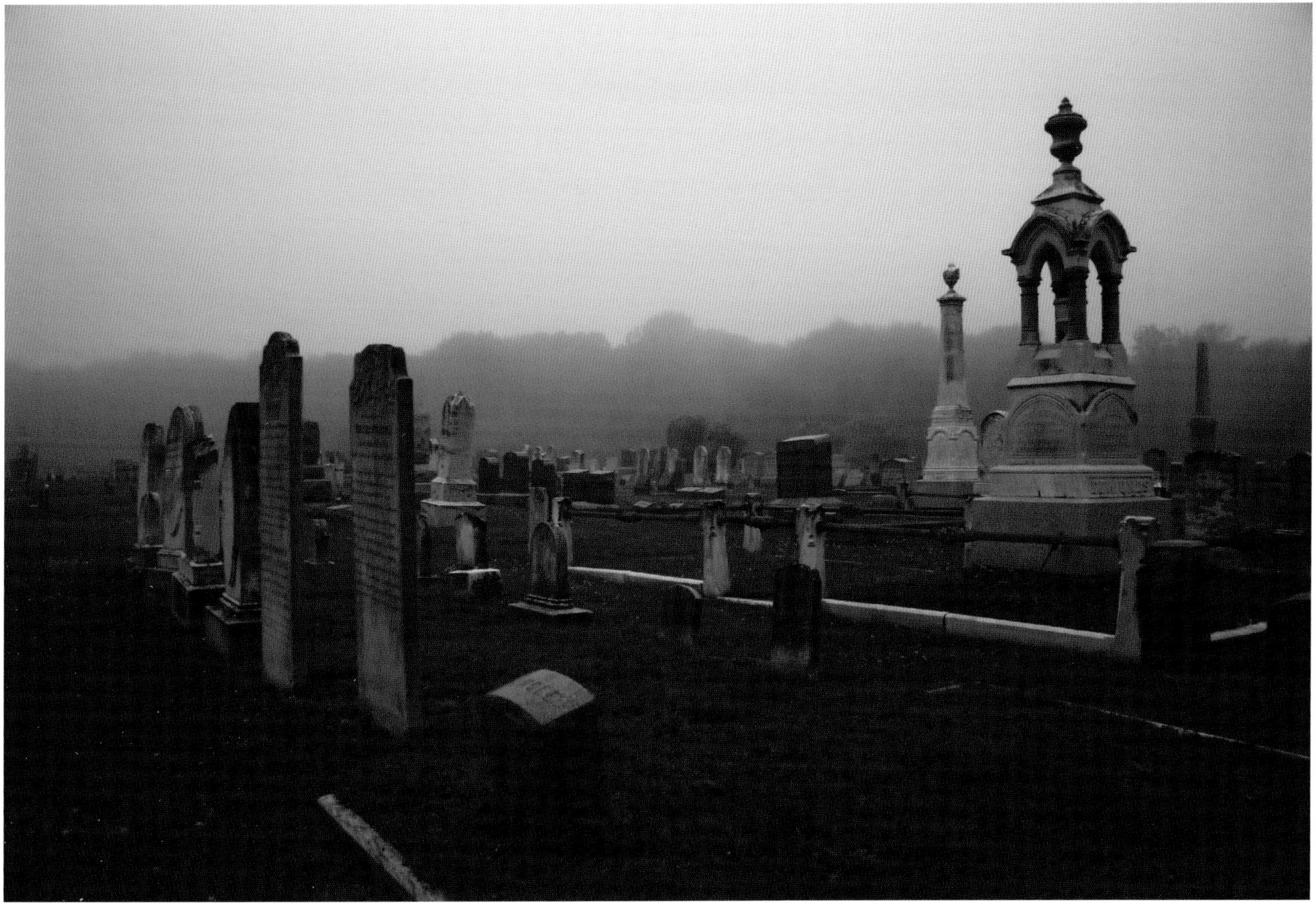

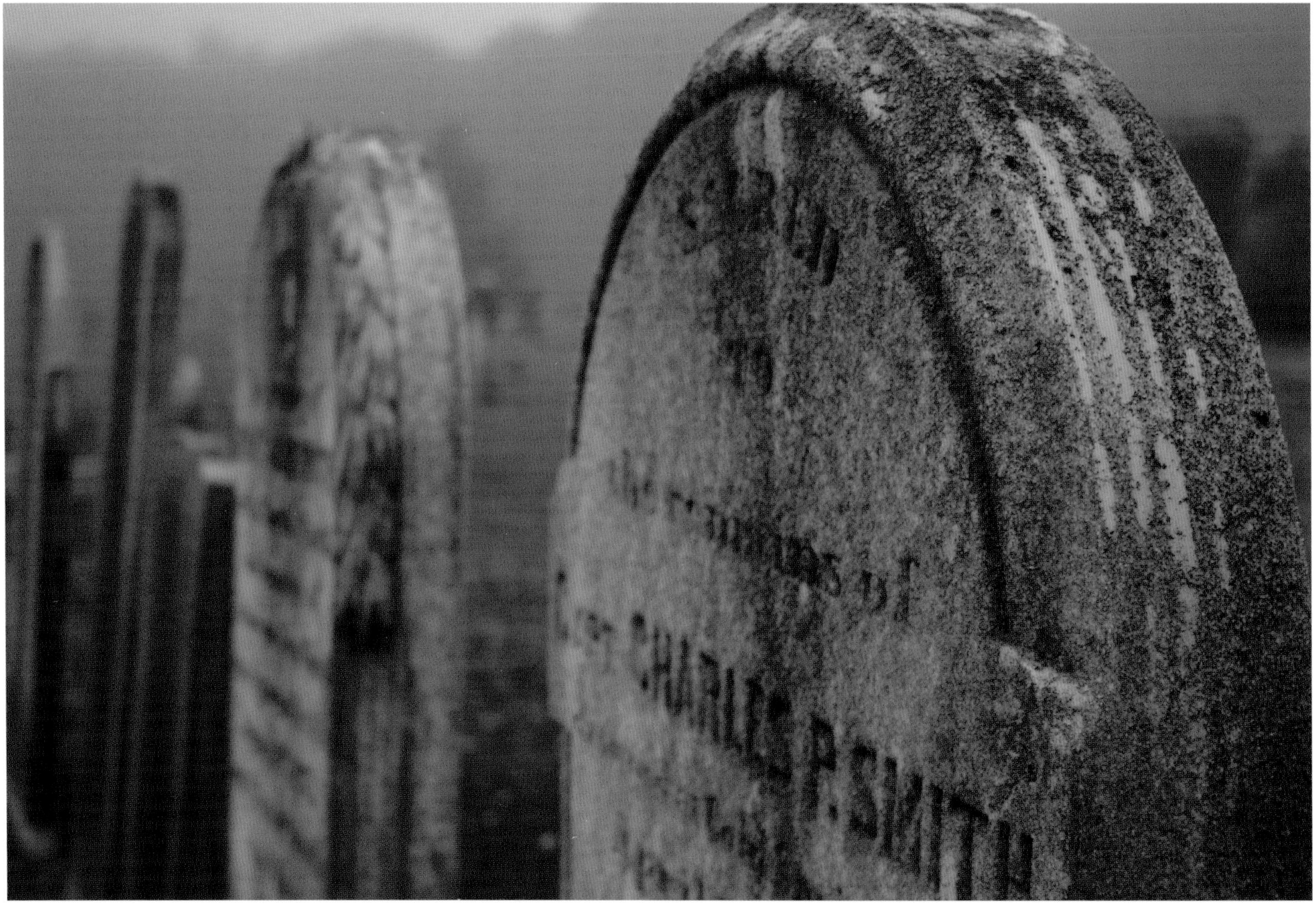

*"He who can no longer pause to wonder and stand rapt in awe, is as good as dead; his eyes are closed."*

~ Albert Einstein

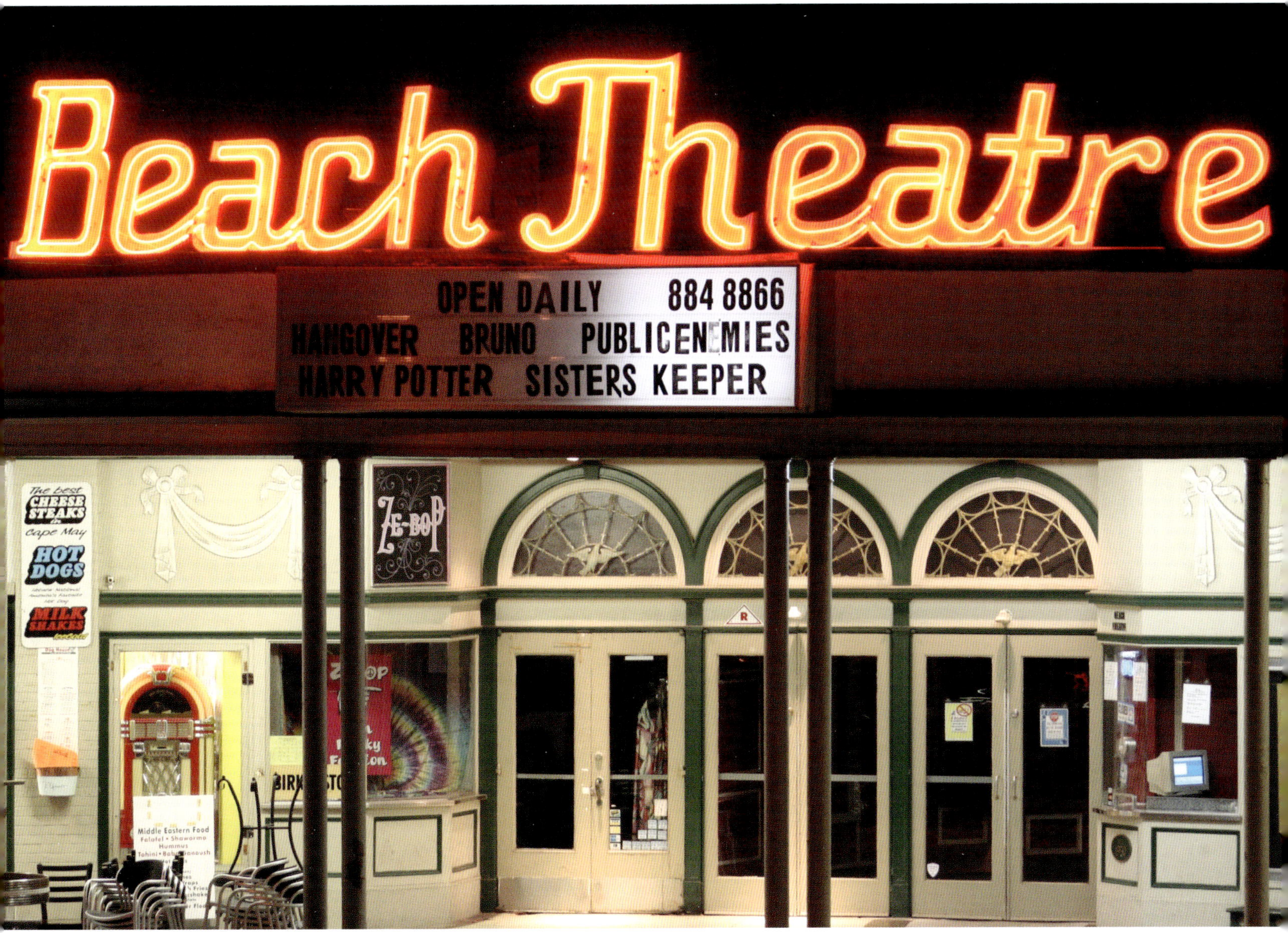
Beach Theatre
OPEN DAILY 884 8866
HANGOVER BRUNO PUBLICENEMIES
HARRY POTTER SISTERS KEEPER
The best CHEESE STEAKS in Cape May
HOT DOGS
MILK SHAKES
ZE-BOP
Middle Eastern Food

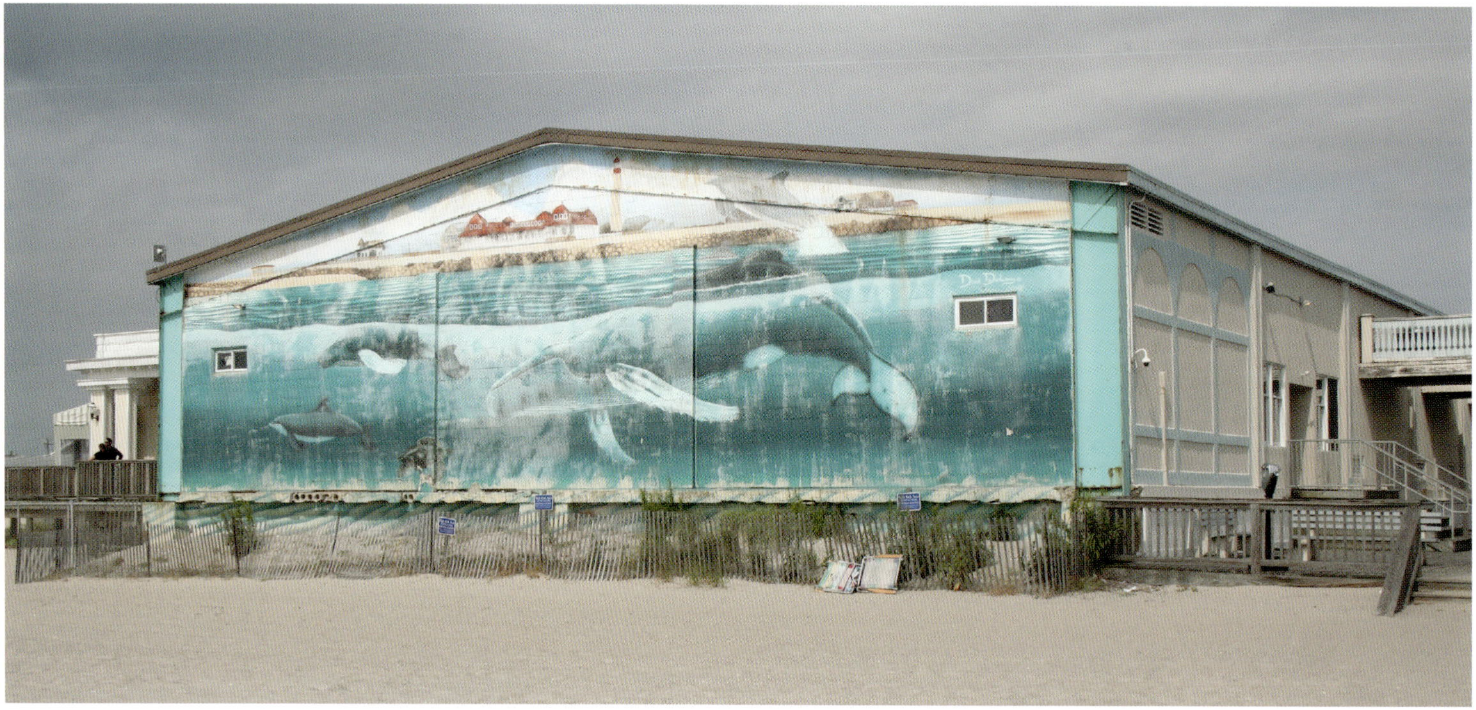

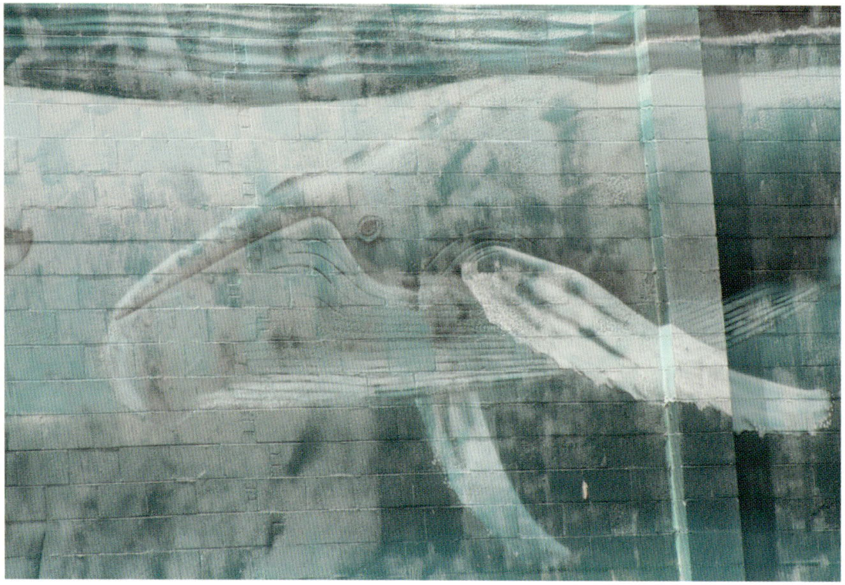

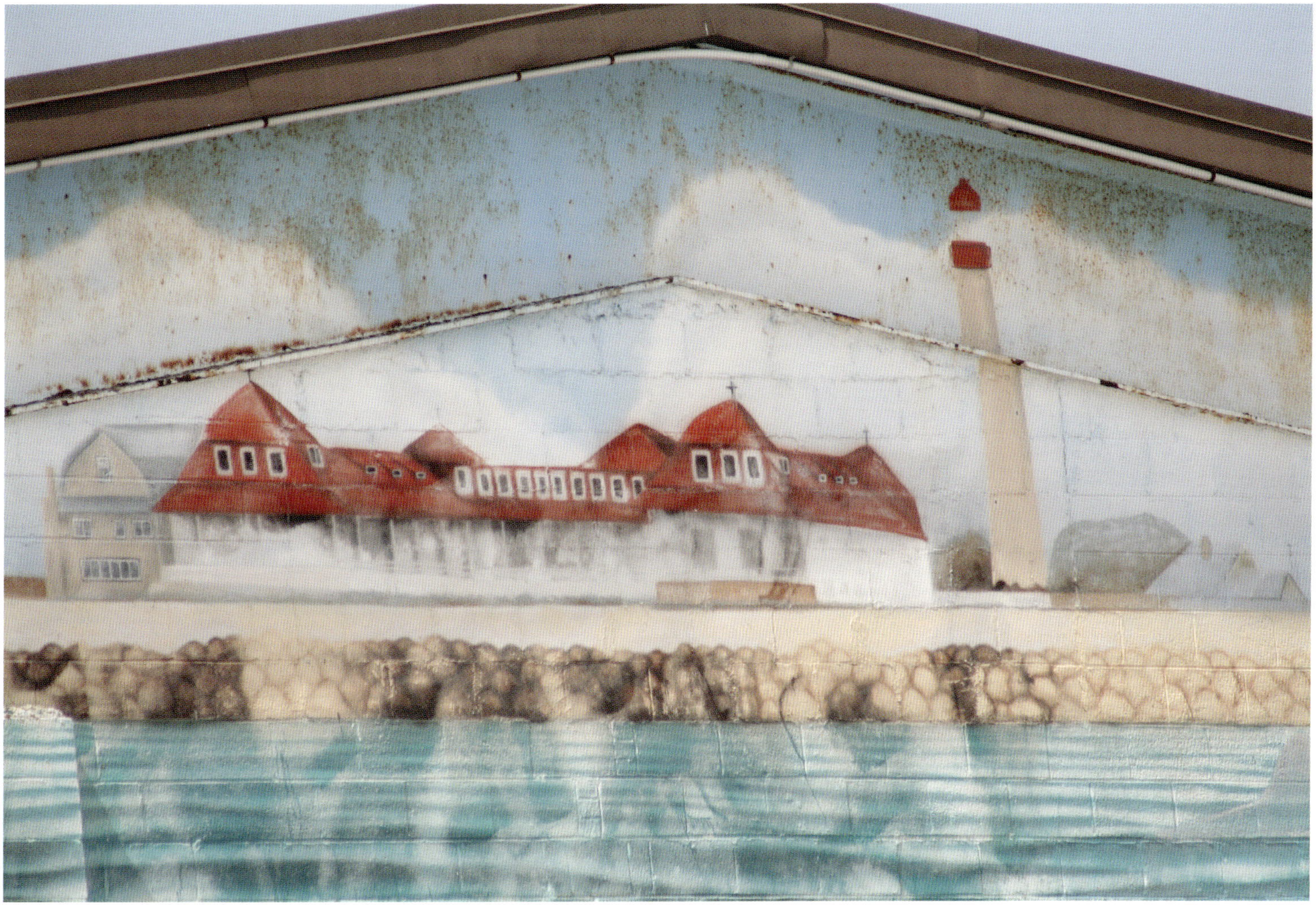

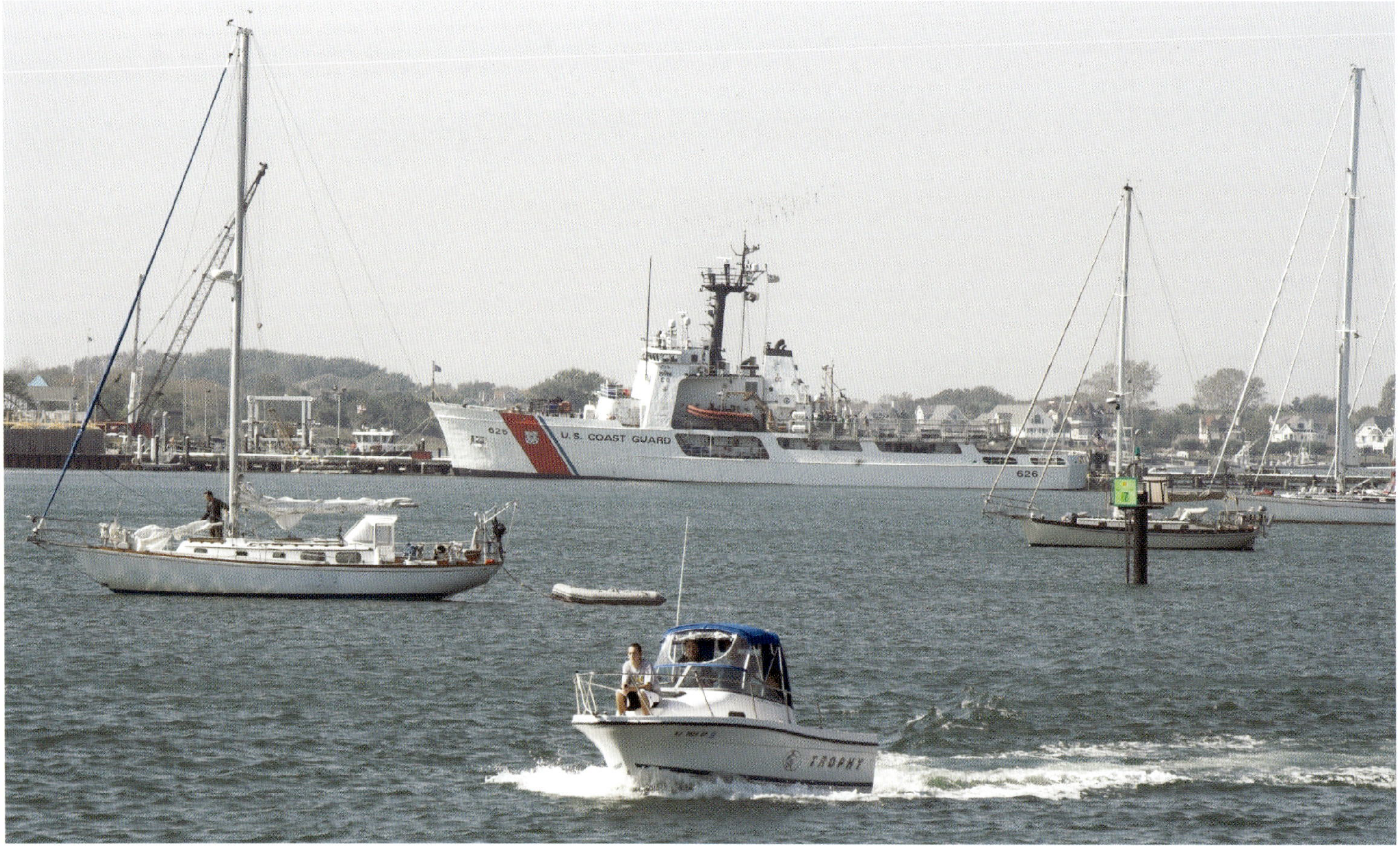


*"Believe me, my young friend, there is nothing —*
*absolutely nothing — half so much worth doing*
*as simply messing about in boats."*

~ Kenneth Grahame, *Wind in The Willows*

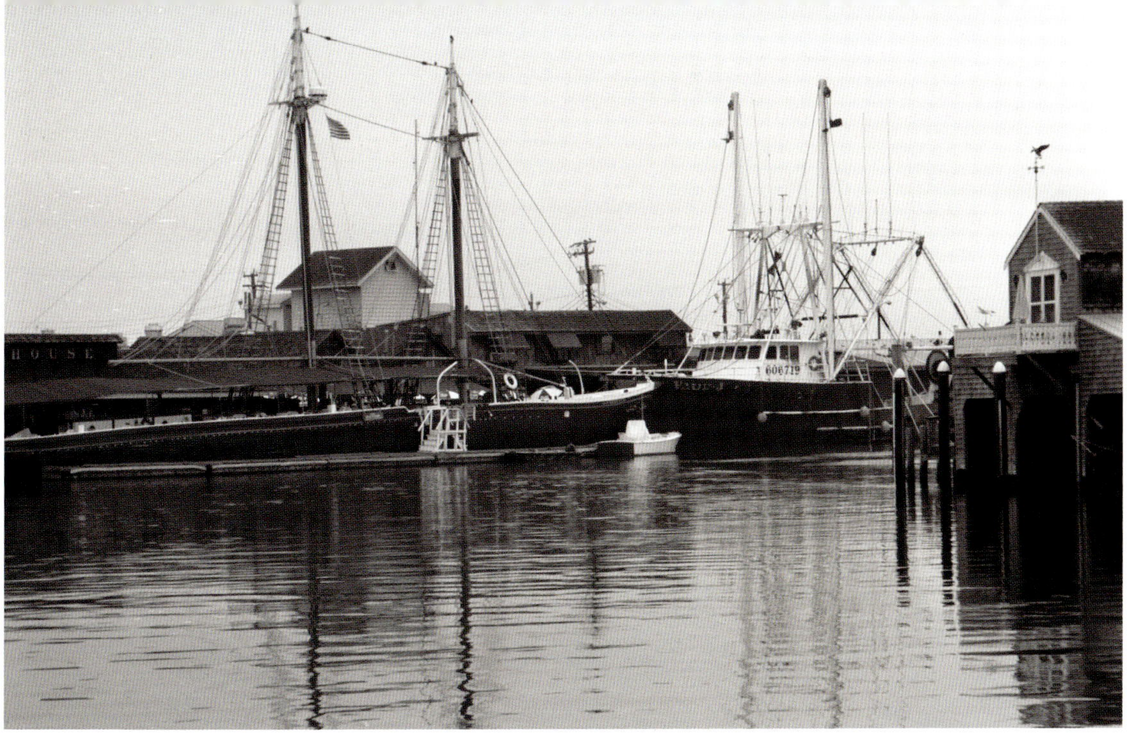
HOUSE
606719

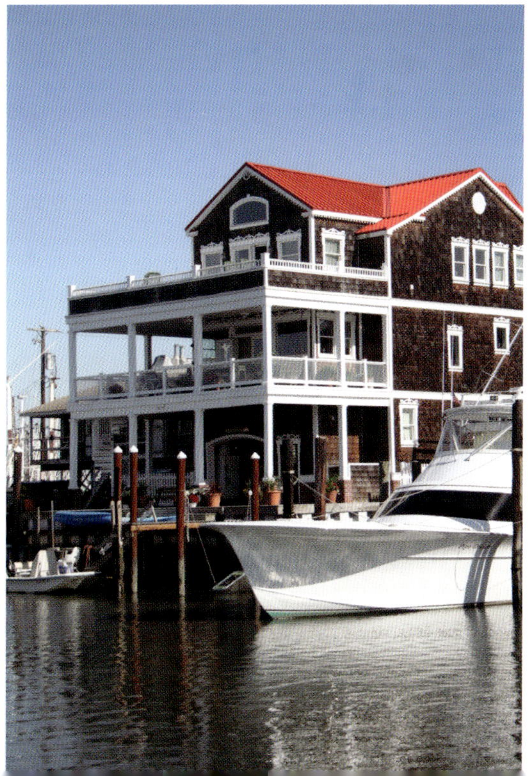

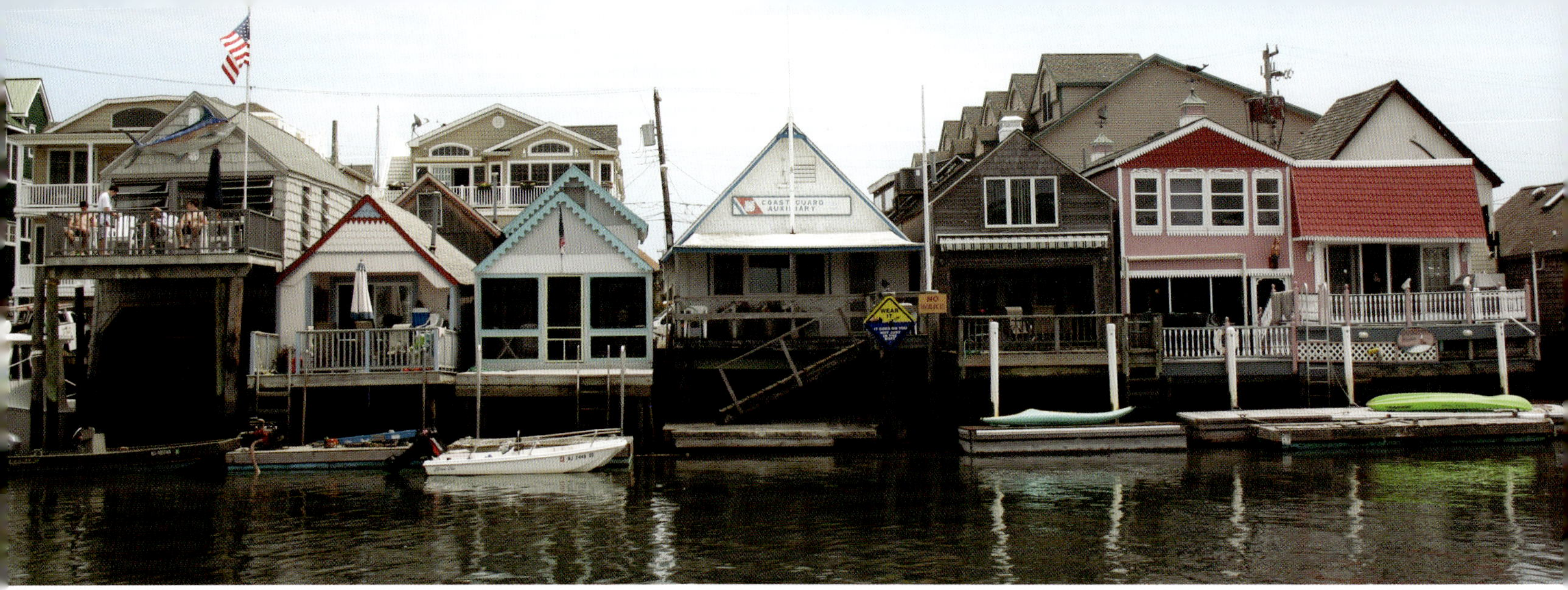
COAST GUARD AUXILIARY

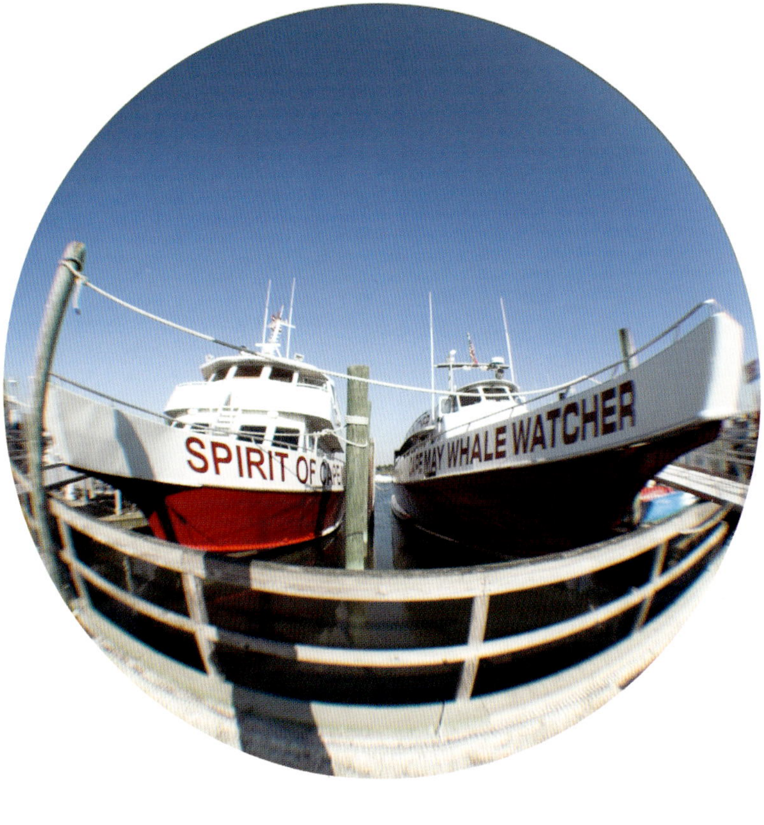
SPIRIT OF
WHALE WATCHER

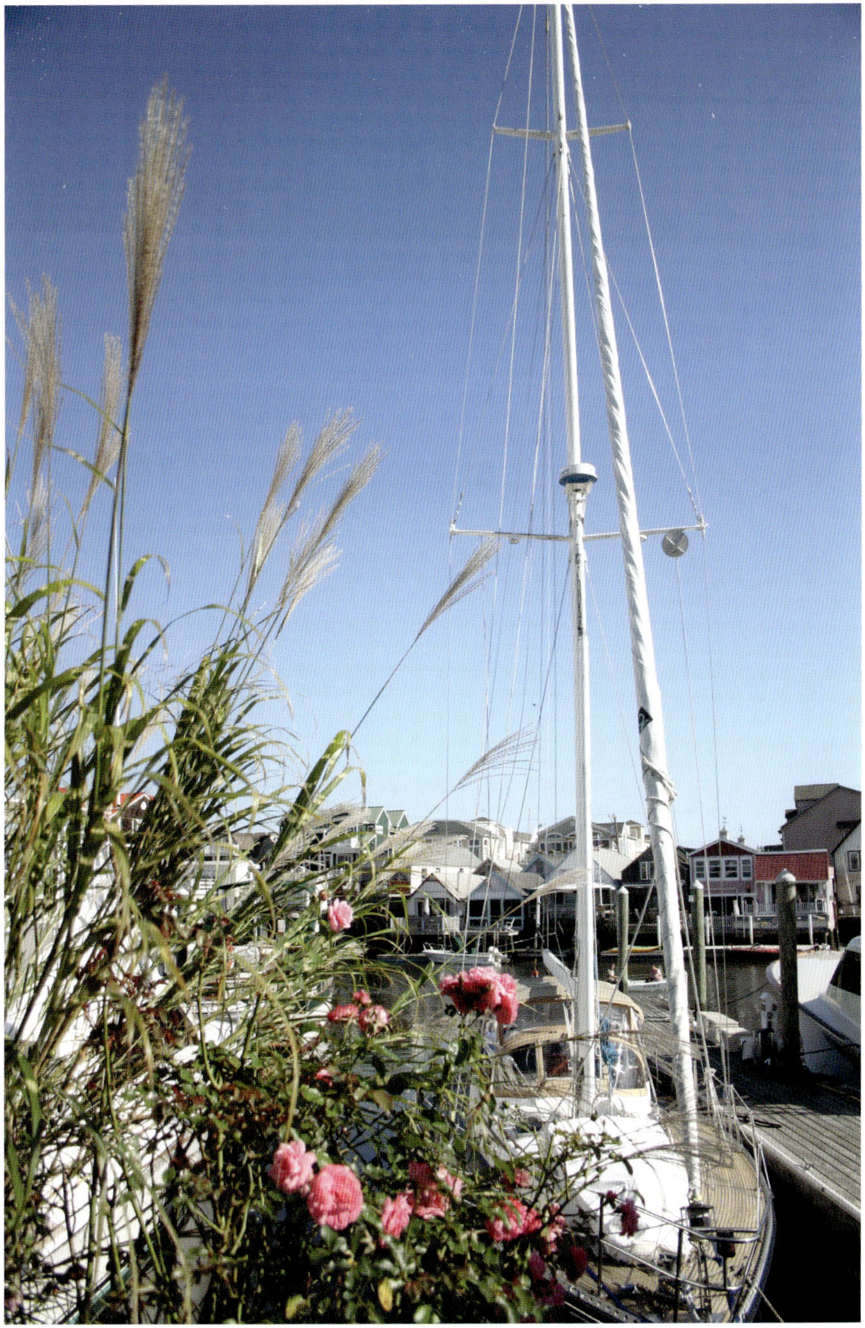

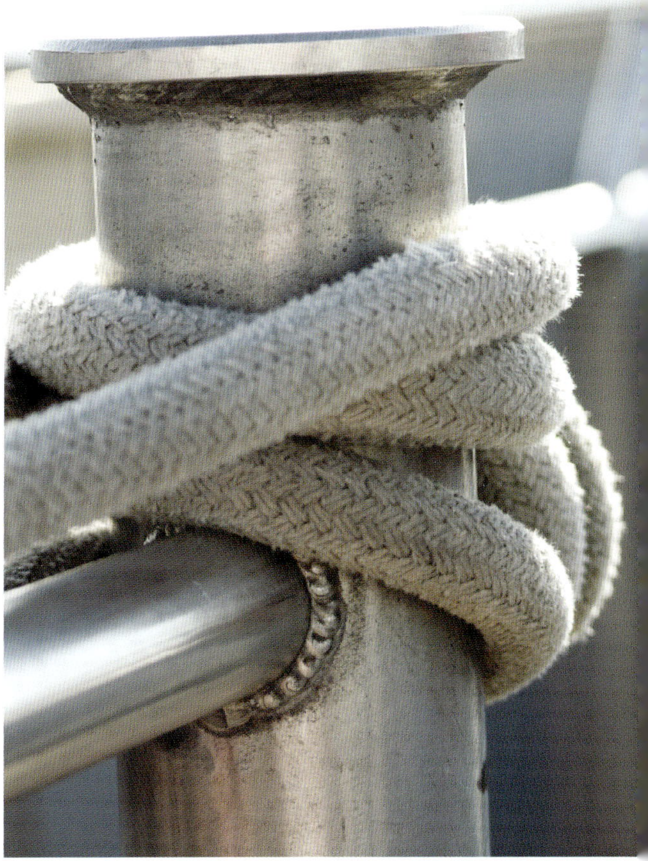

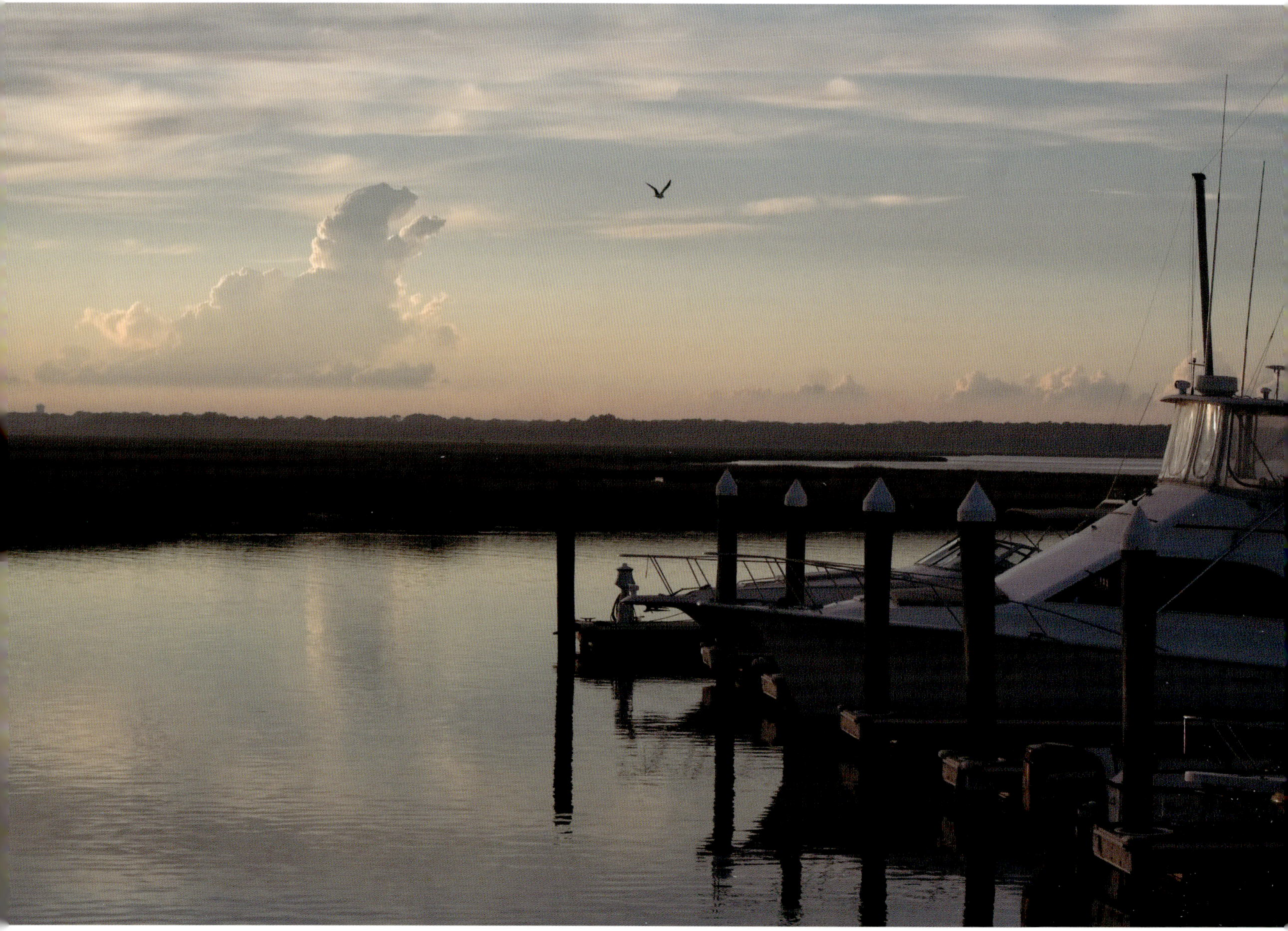

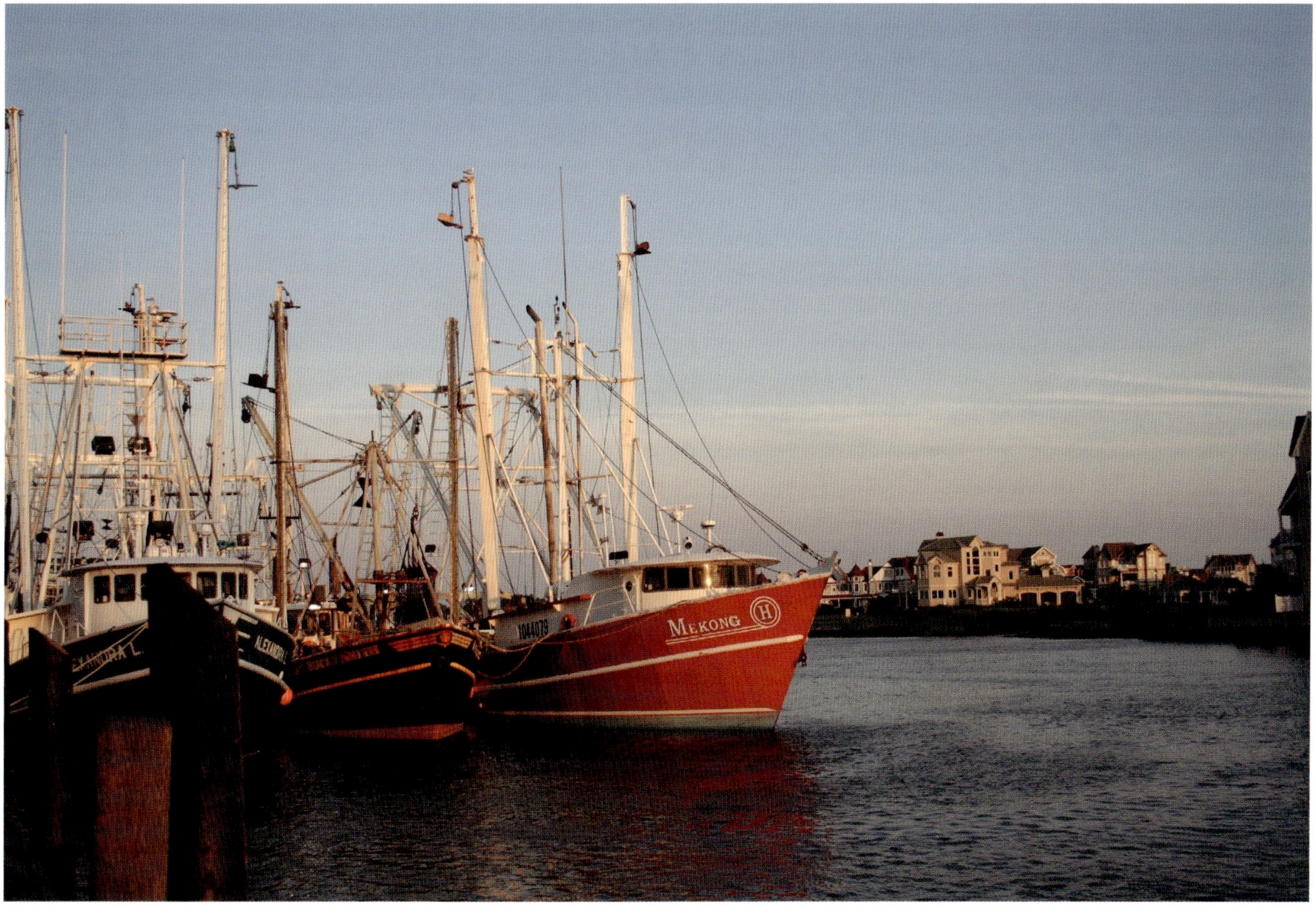
MEKONG
1044079

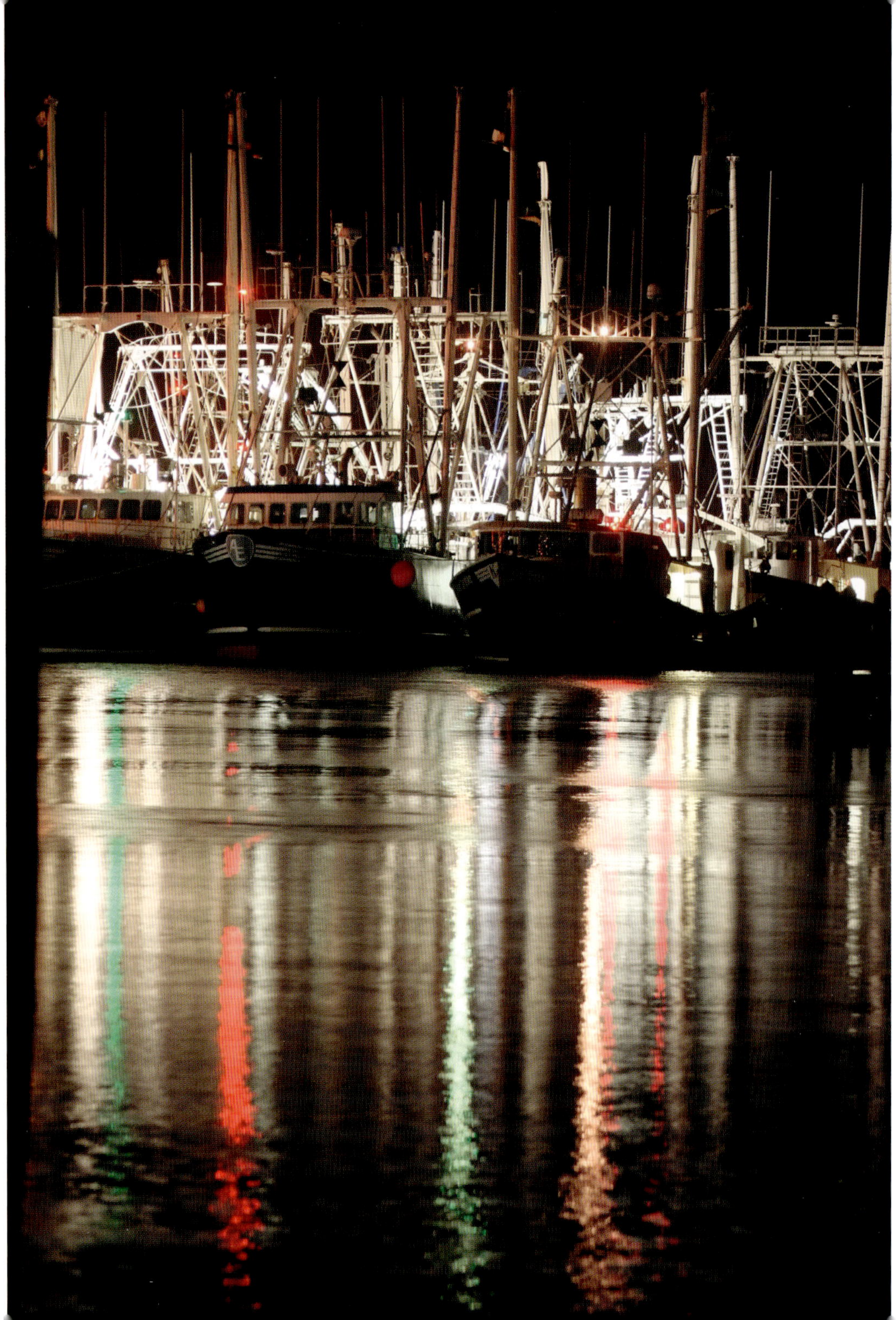

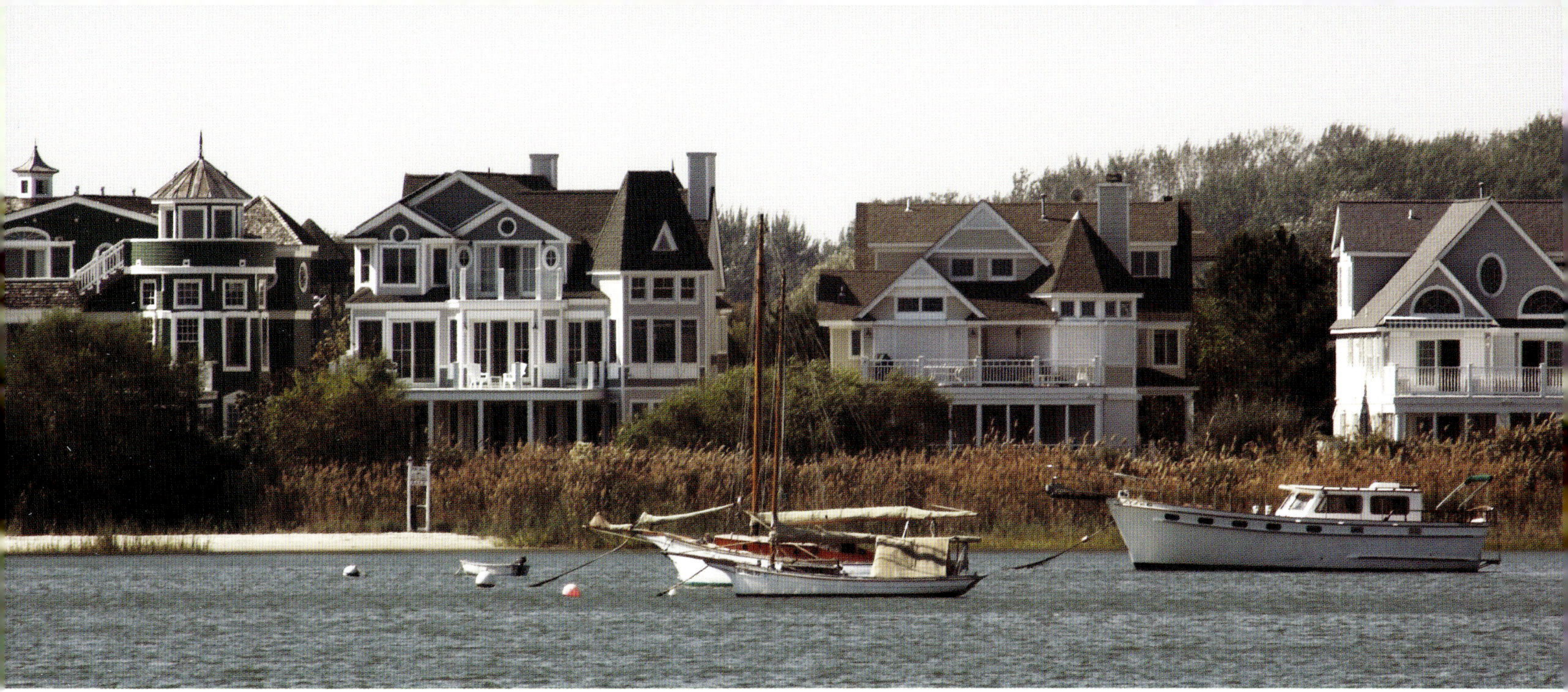

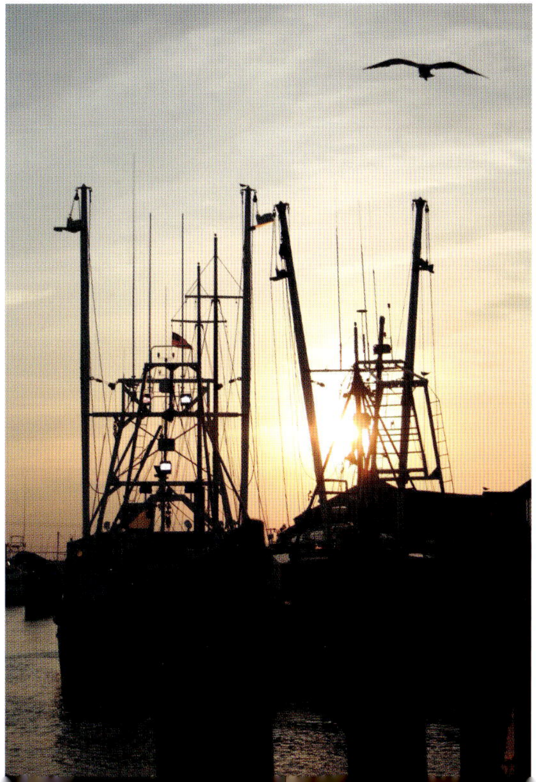

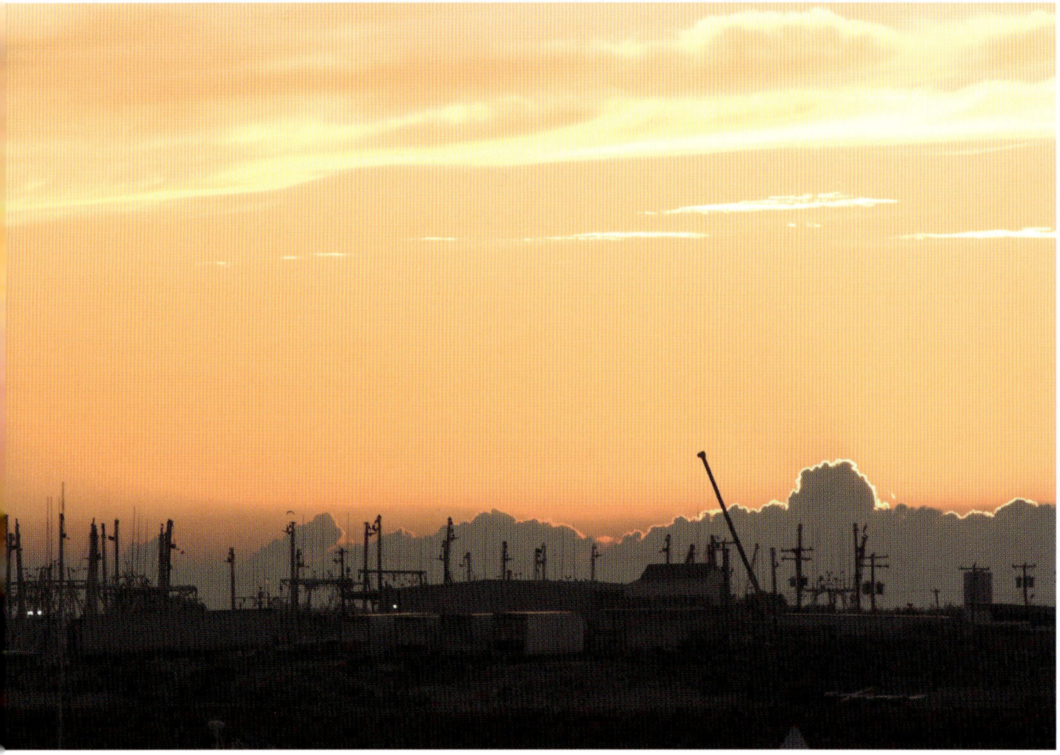

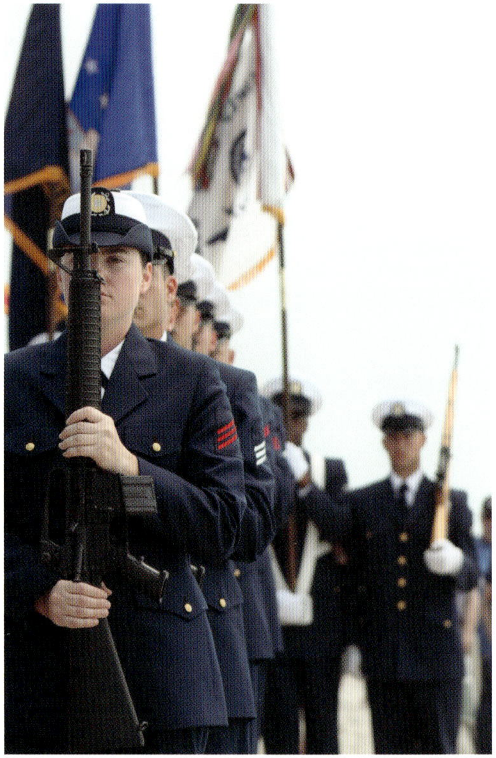

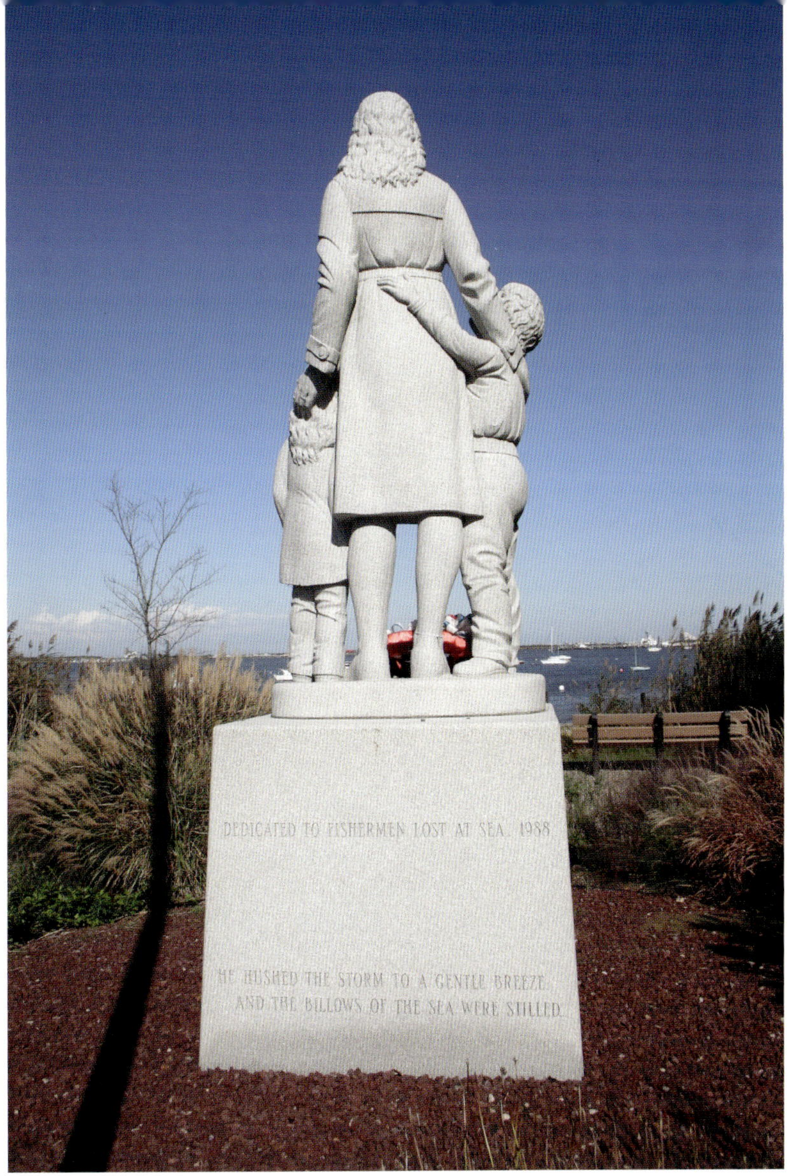


*"The fishermen know that the sea is dangerous and the storm terrible, but they have never found these dangers sufficient reason for remaining ashore."*

~ Vincent Van Gogh

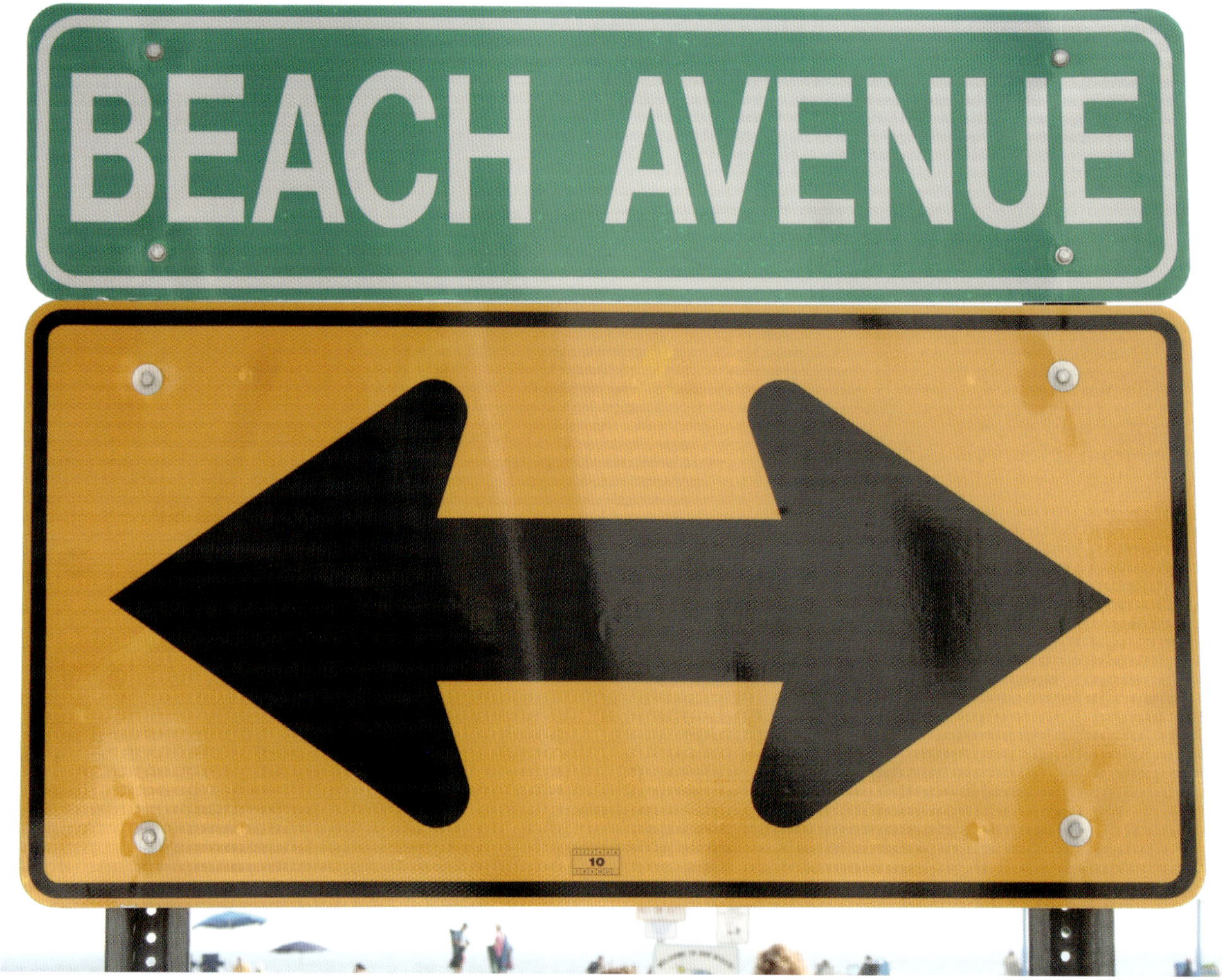
BEACH AVENUE
10

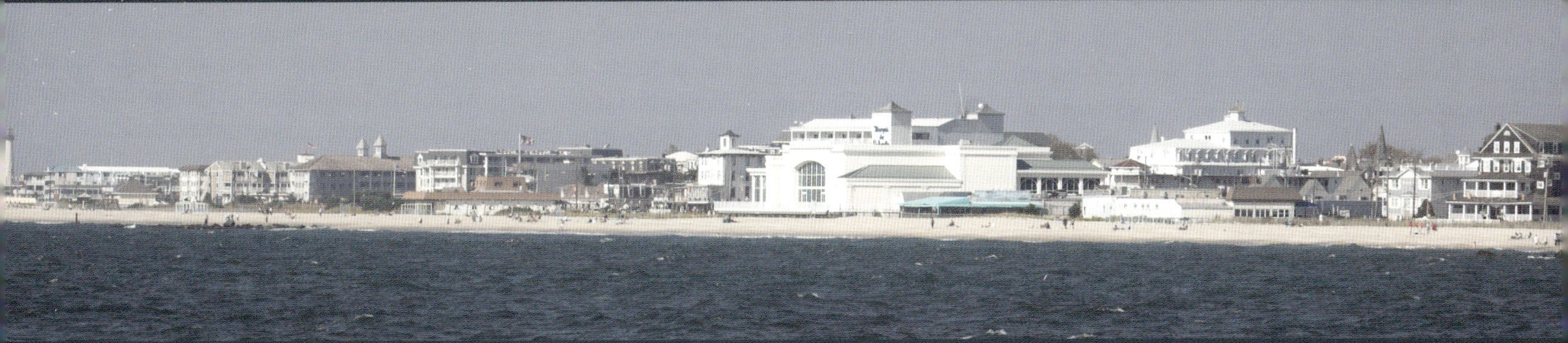

Chapter Three
# At the Beach

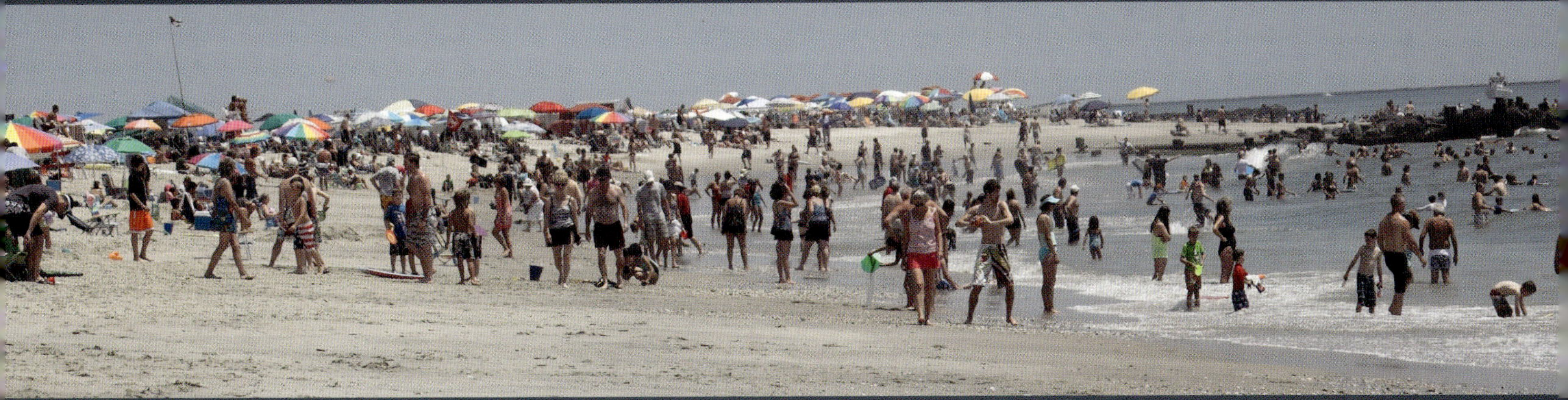

# The City Beaches

Collectively, Cape May's city beaches were ranked the second best beach in the United States and the ninth best beach in the world by the online travel site TripAdvisor® 2011 Travelers' Choice Best Beach Awards. With names like Poverty, Decatur, Steger's, Congress, Grant, and Broadway, the beaches of Cape May are *the* place for summer fun. Grab your beach tags and don't forget some quarters for the parking meters.

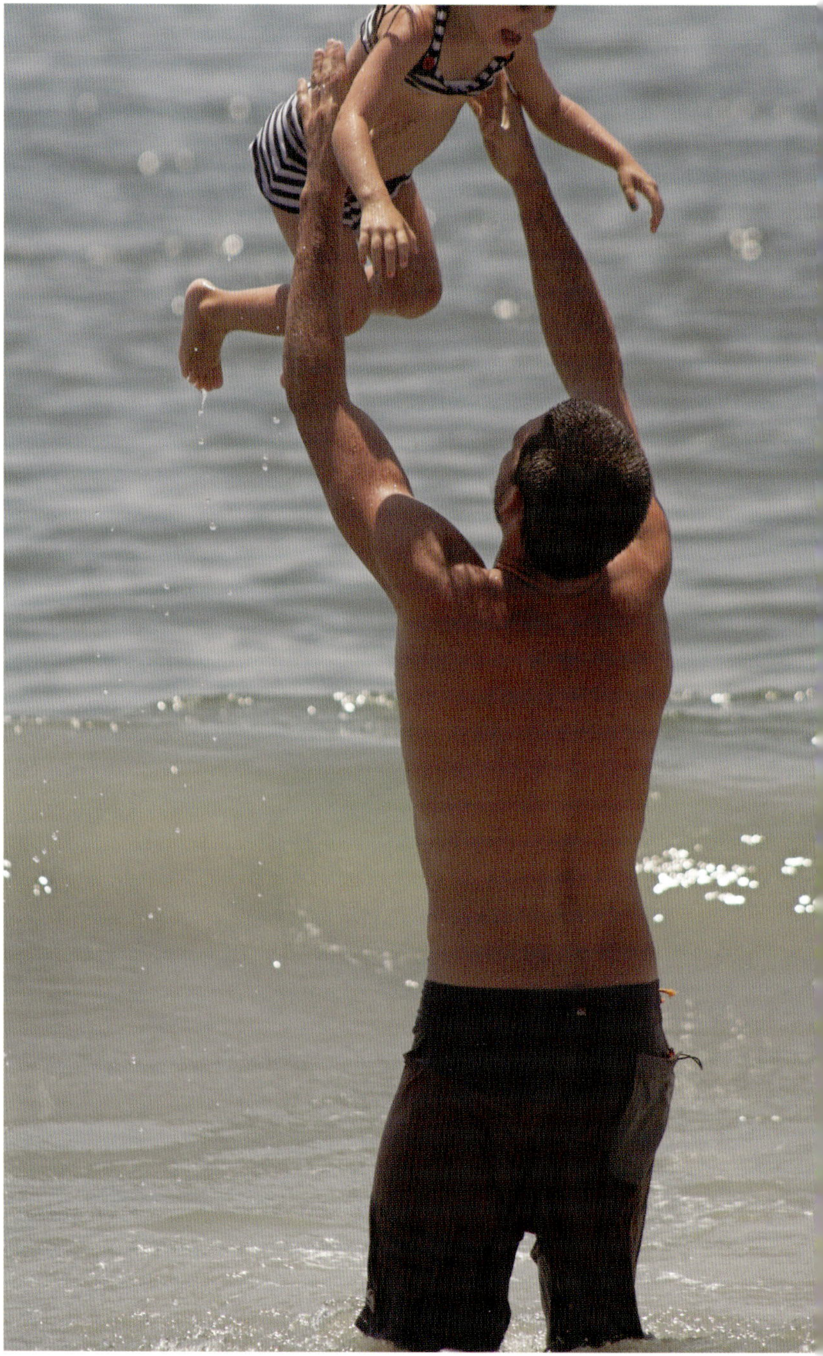

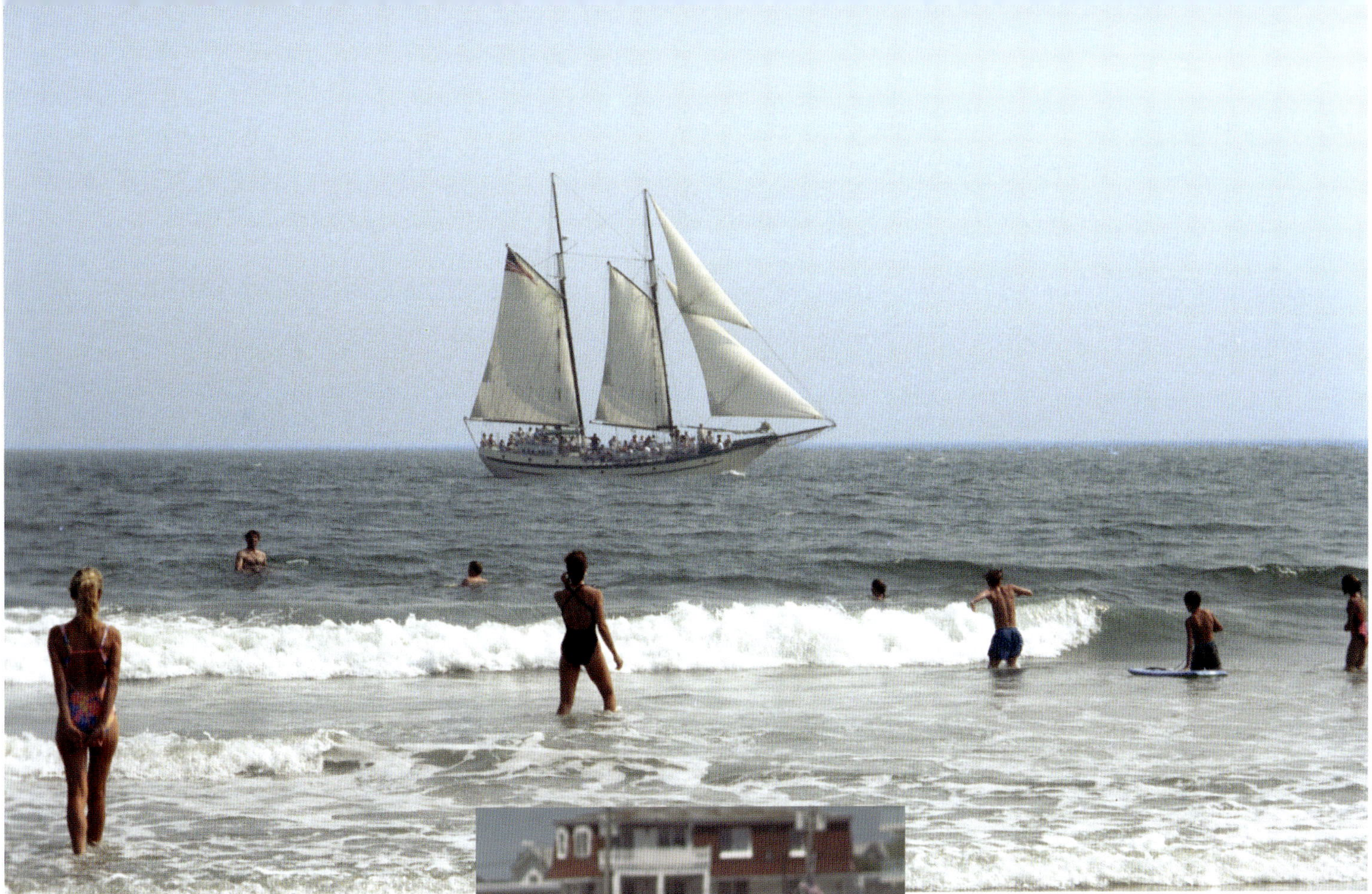
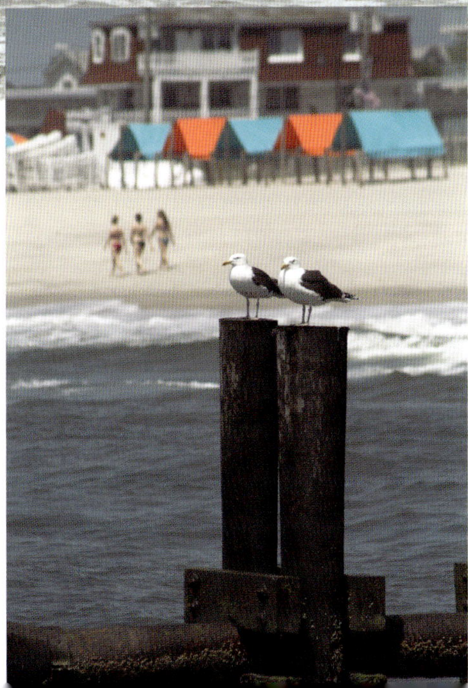

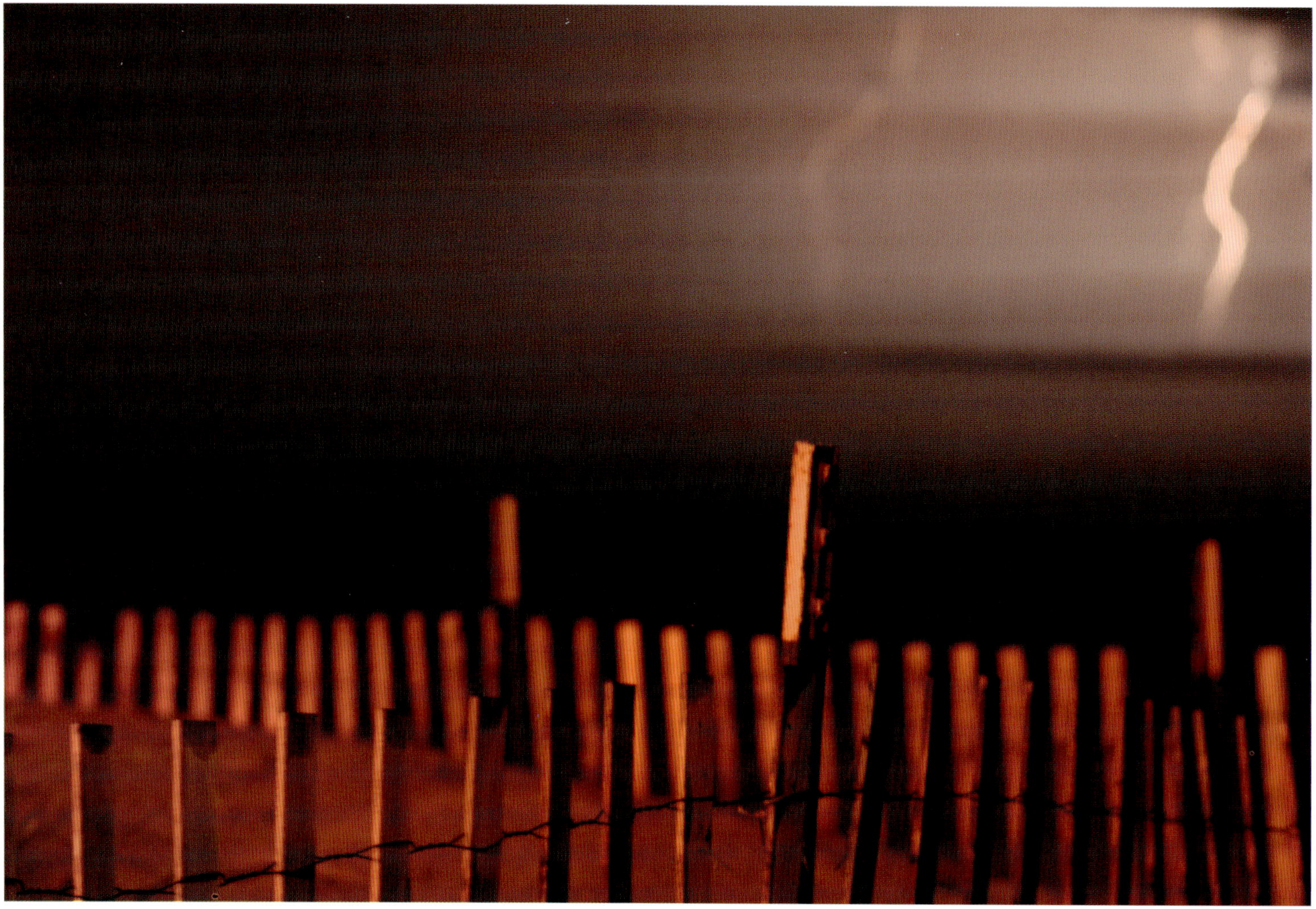

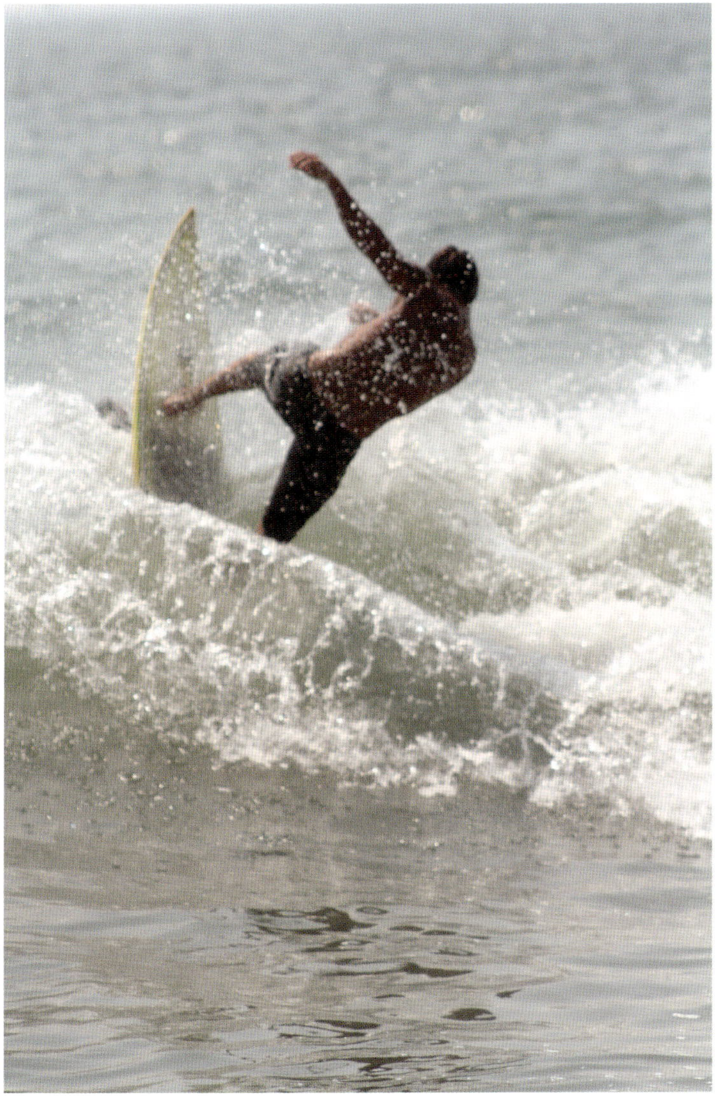

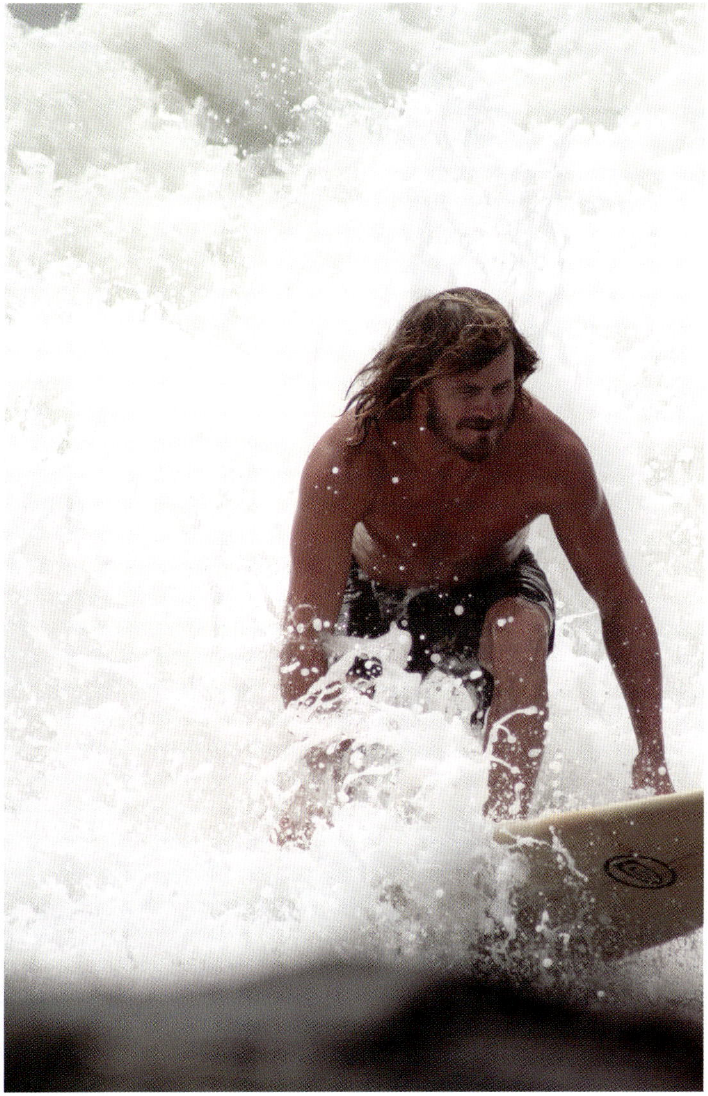

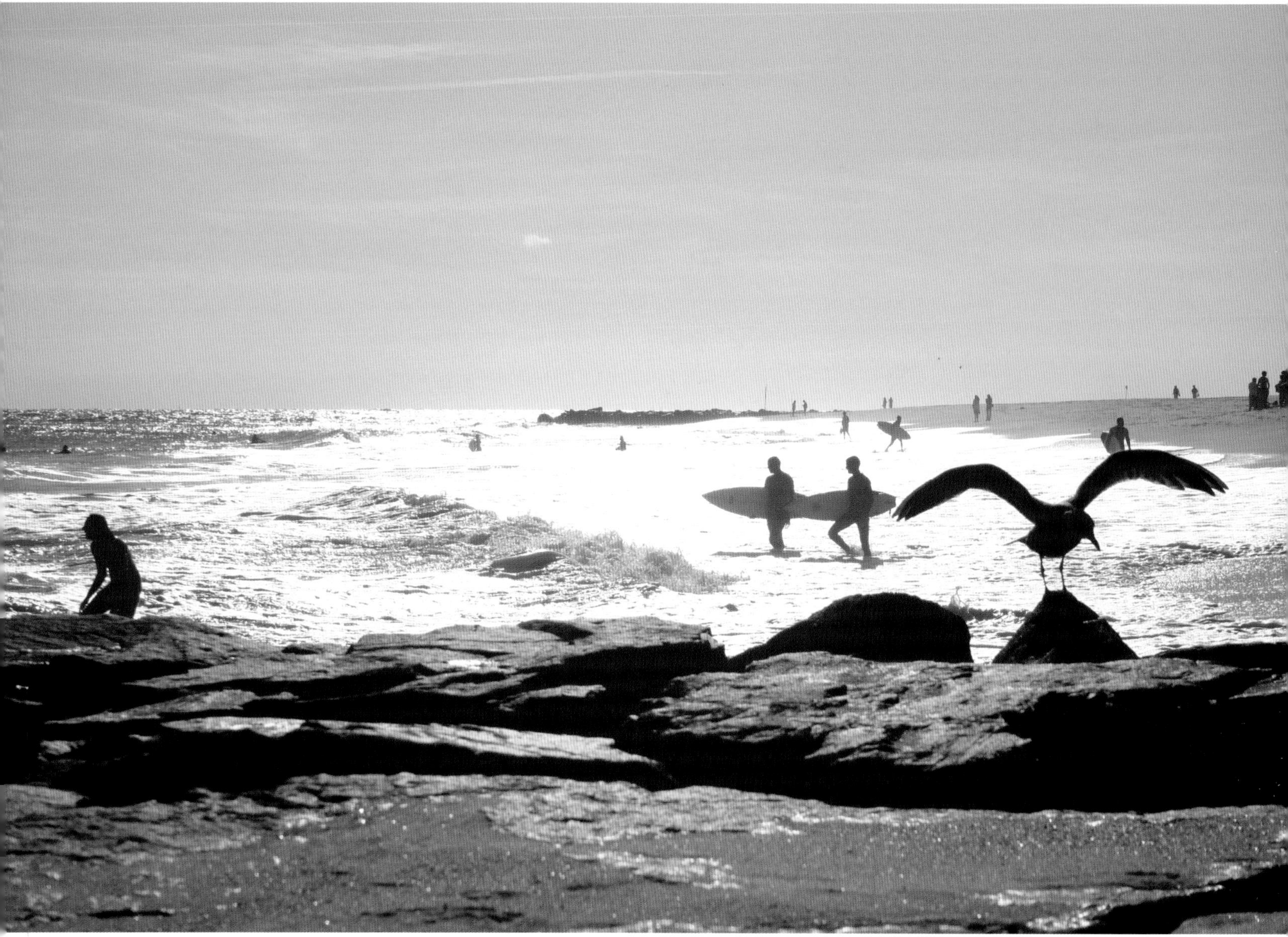

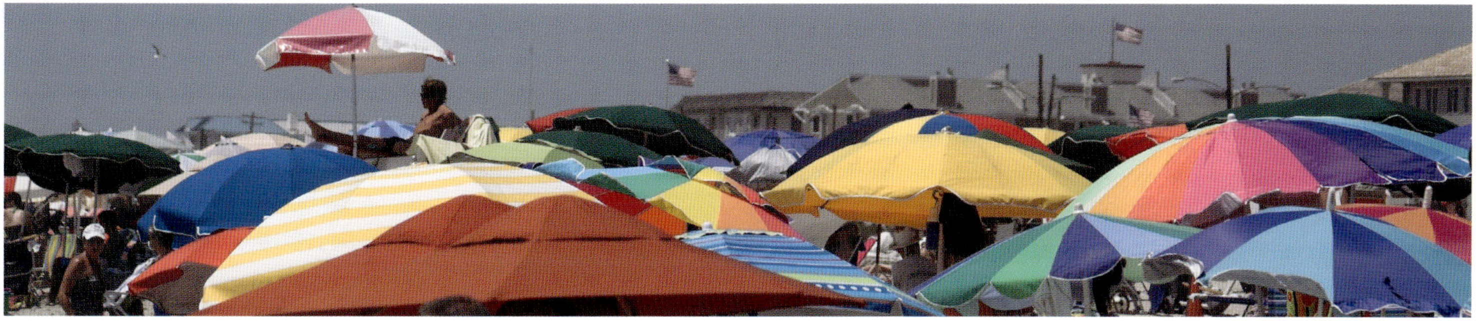

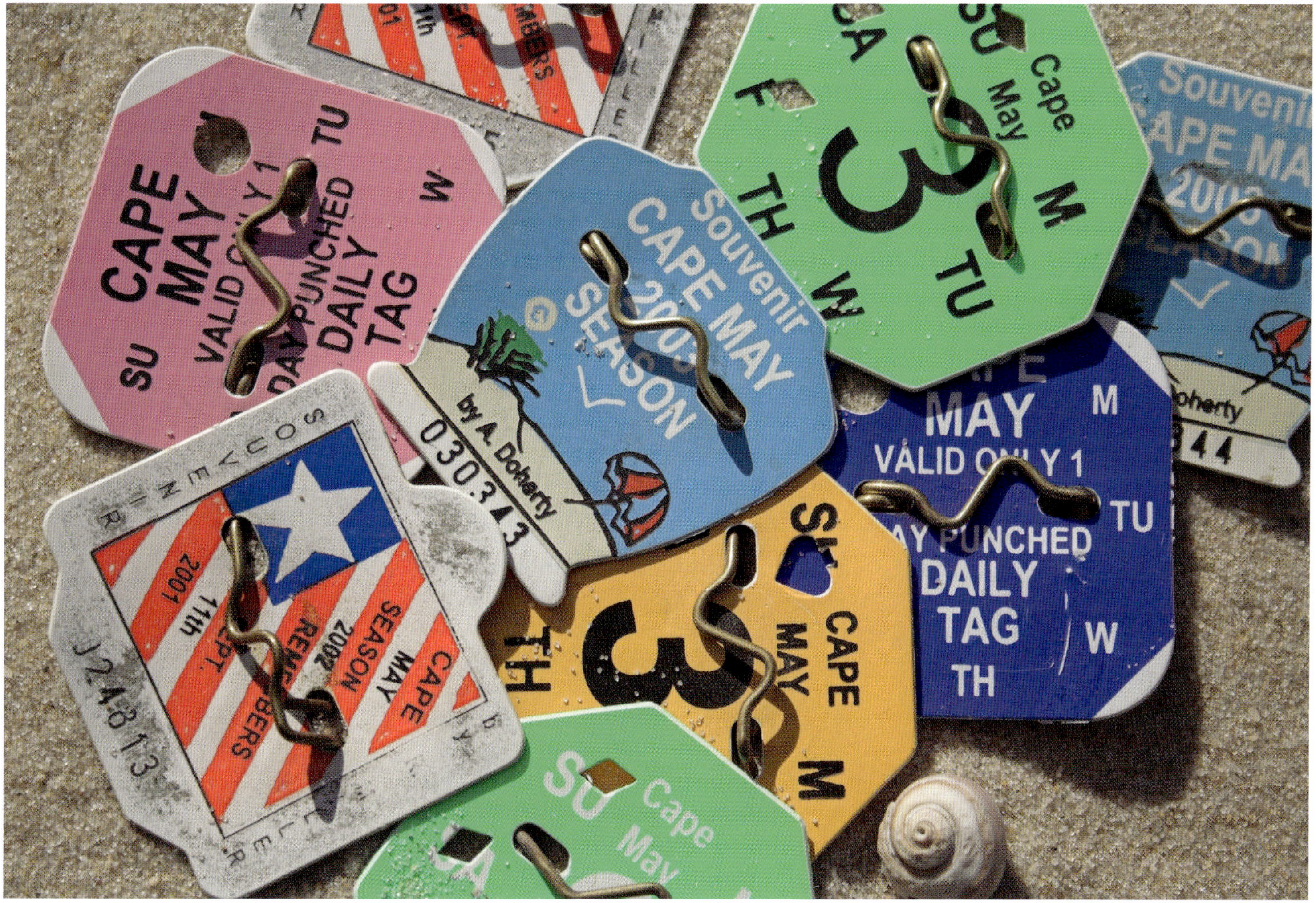
CAPE MAY
VALID ONLY 1
DAY PUNCHED
DAILY
TAG
Souvenir
CAPE MAY
SEASON
by A. Doherty
MAY
VALID ONLY 1
DAILY
TAG
Cape
May
CAPE
MAY
2002
SEASON
2001
11th
SEPT.
REMEMBERS

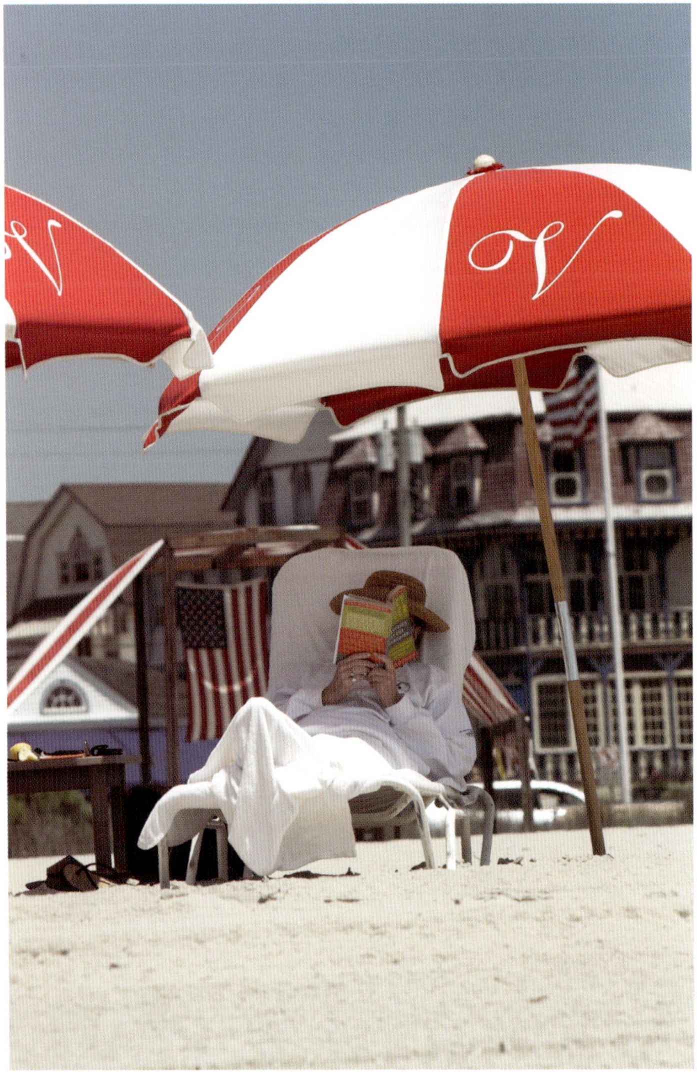

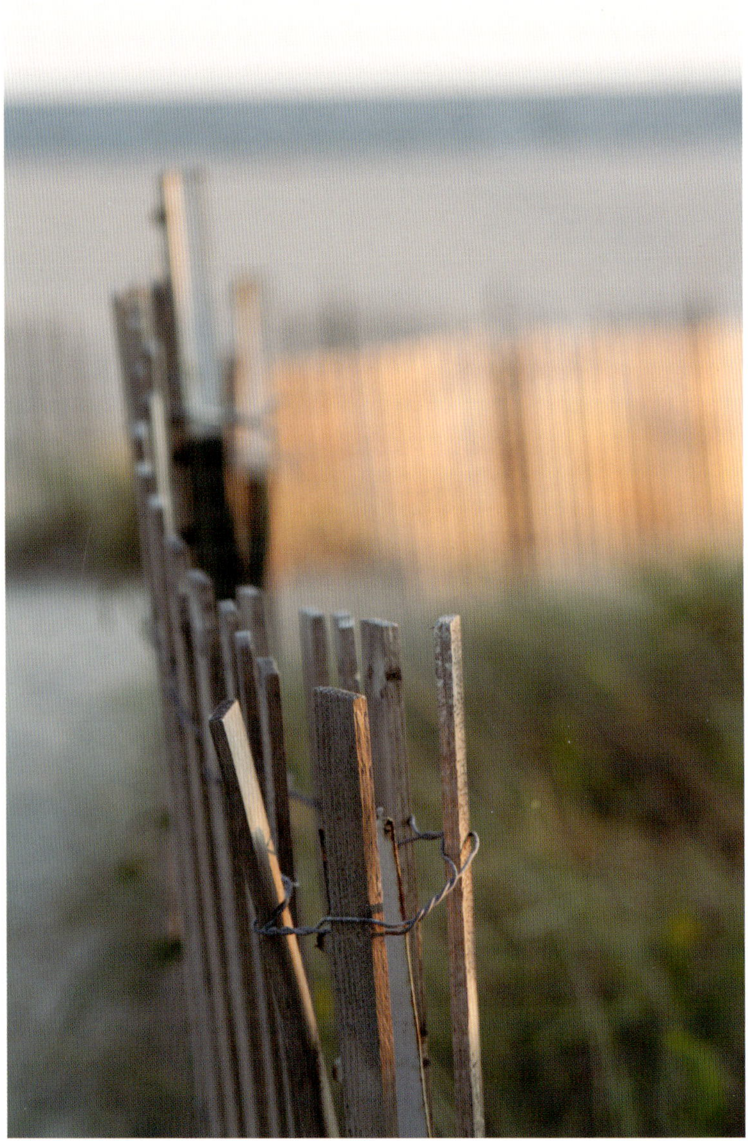

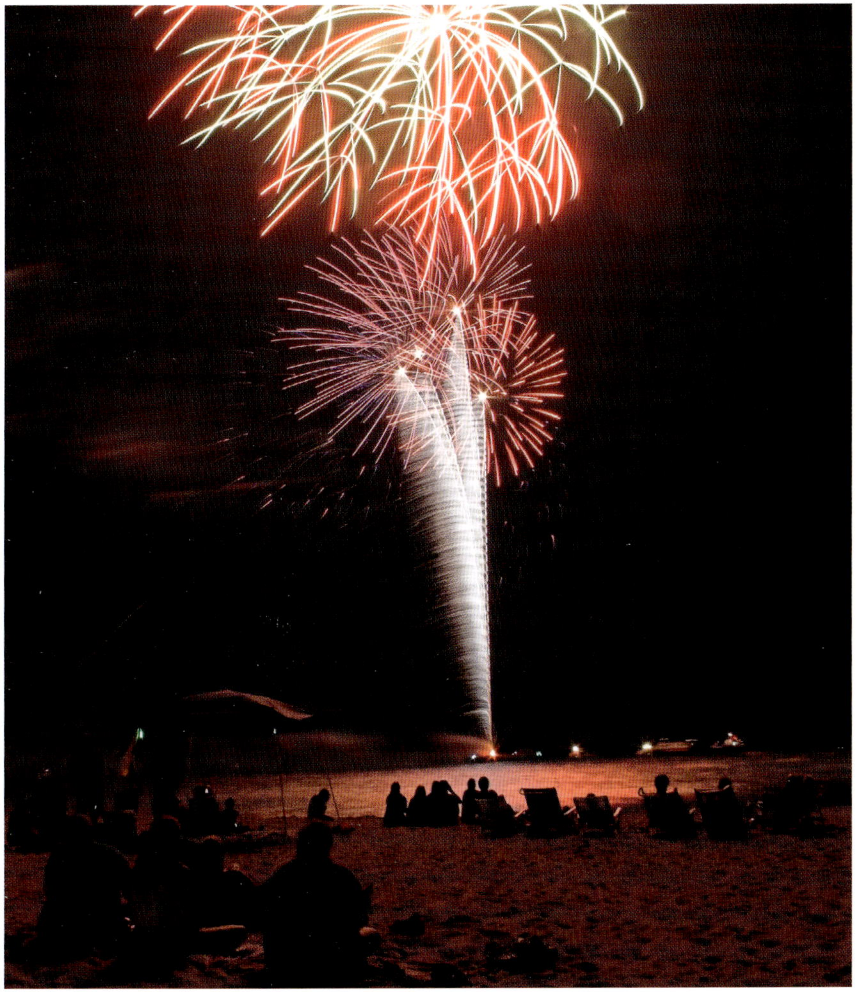

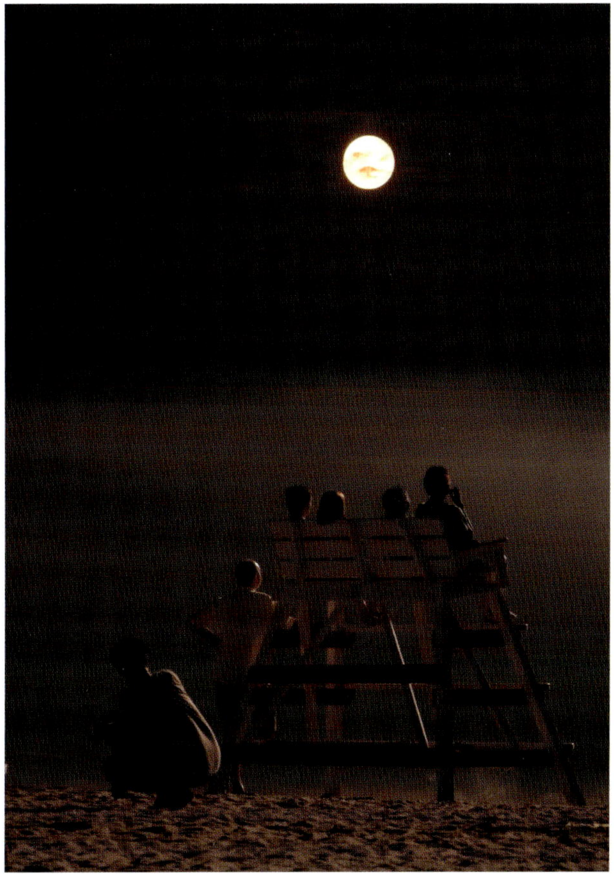

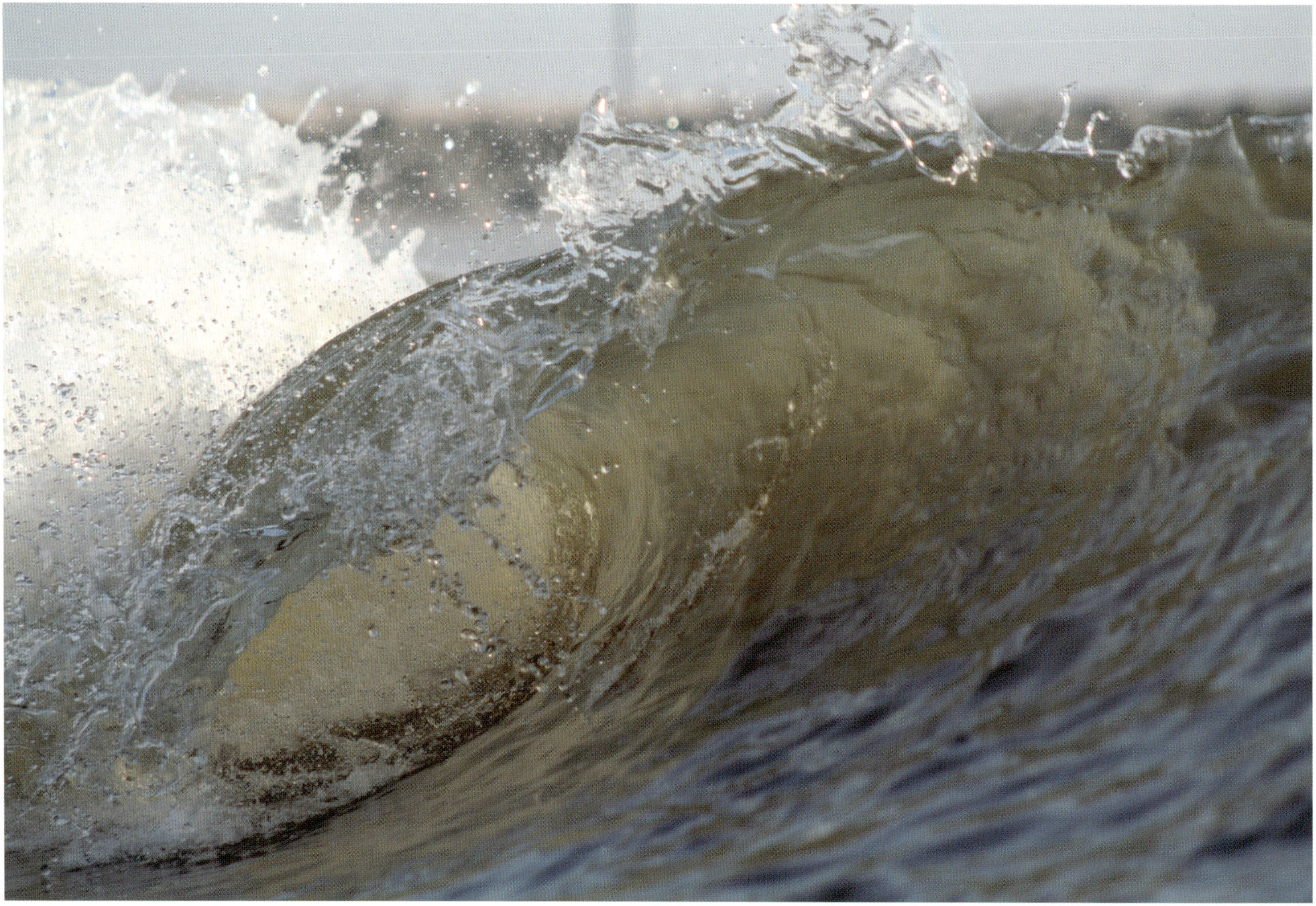

*"The cure for anything is salt water*
*– sweat, tears, or the sea."*
~ Isak Dinesen

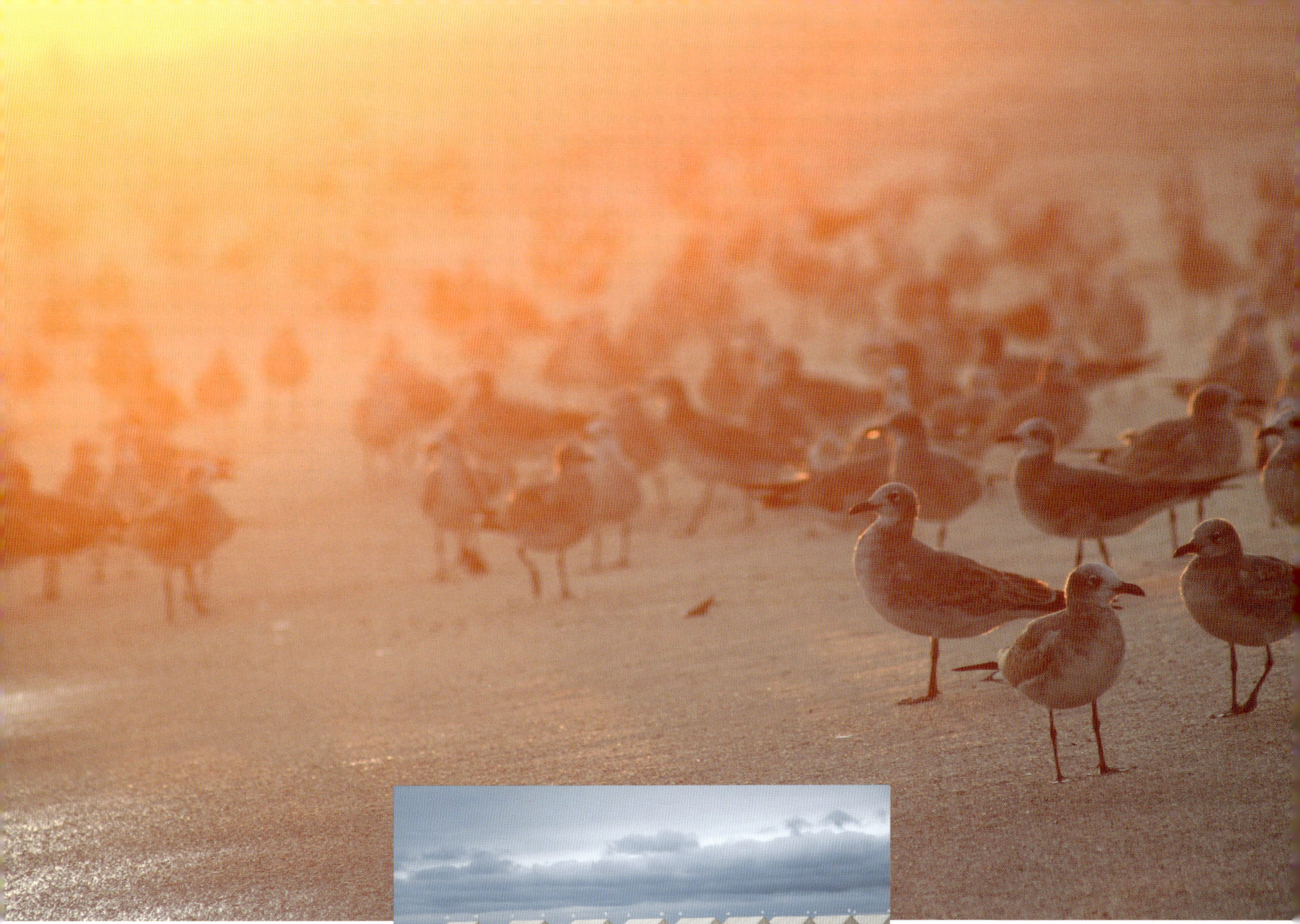

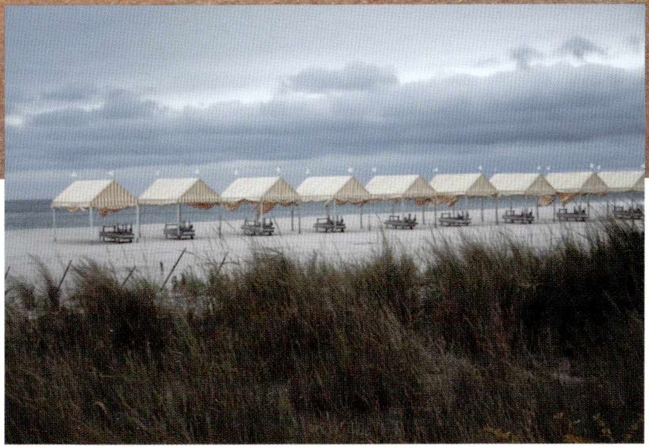

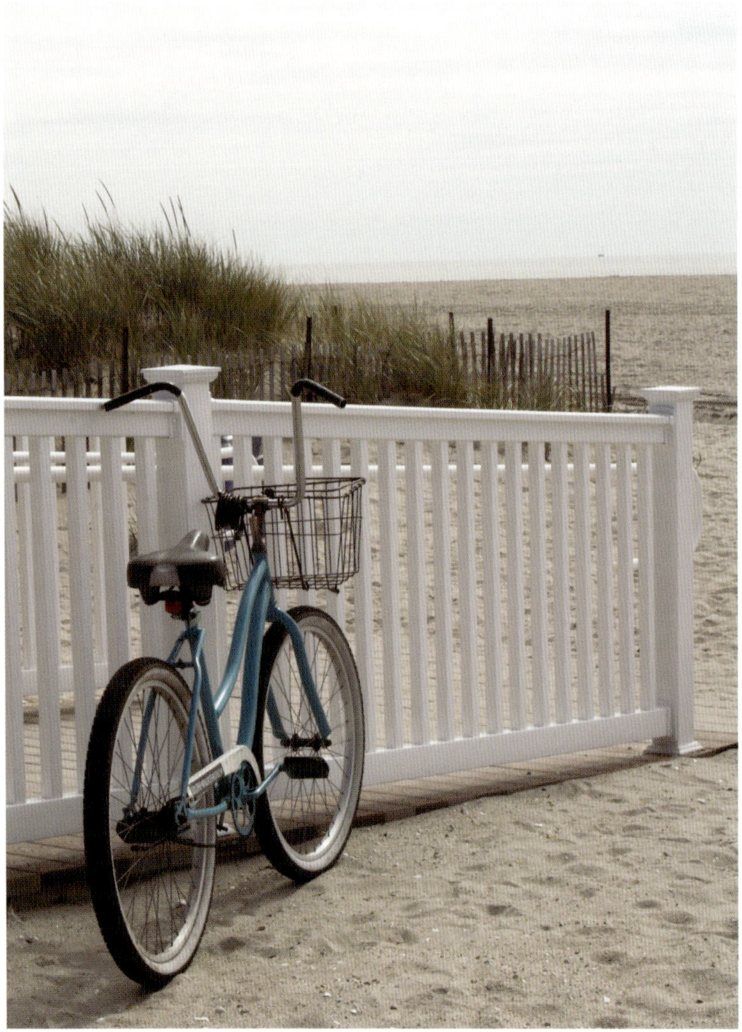

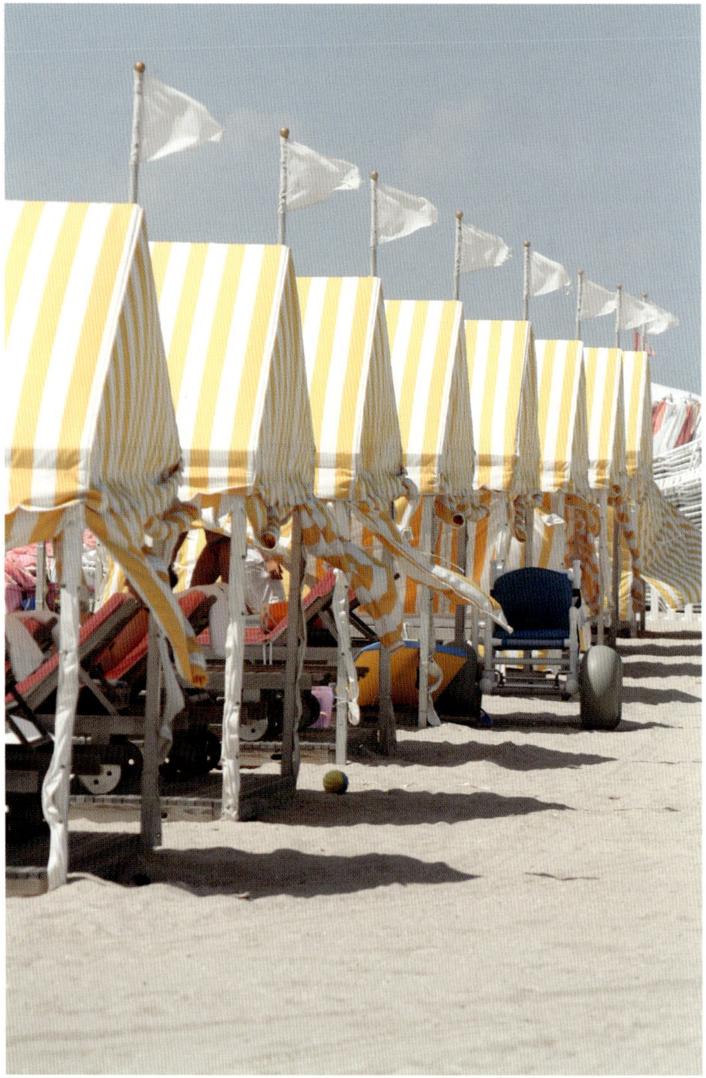

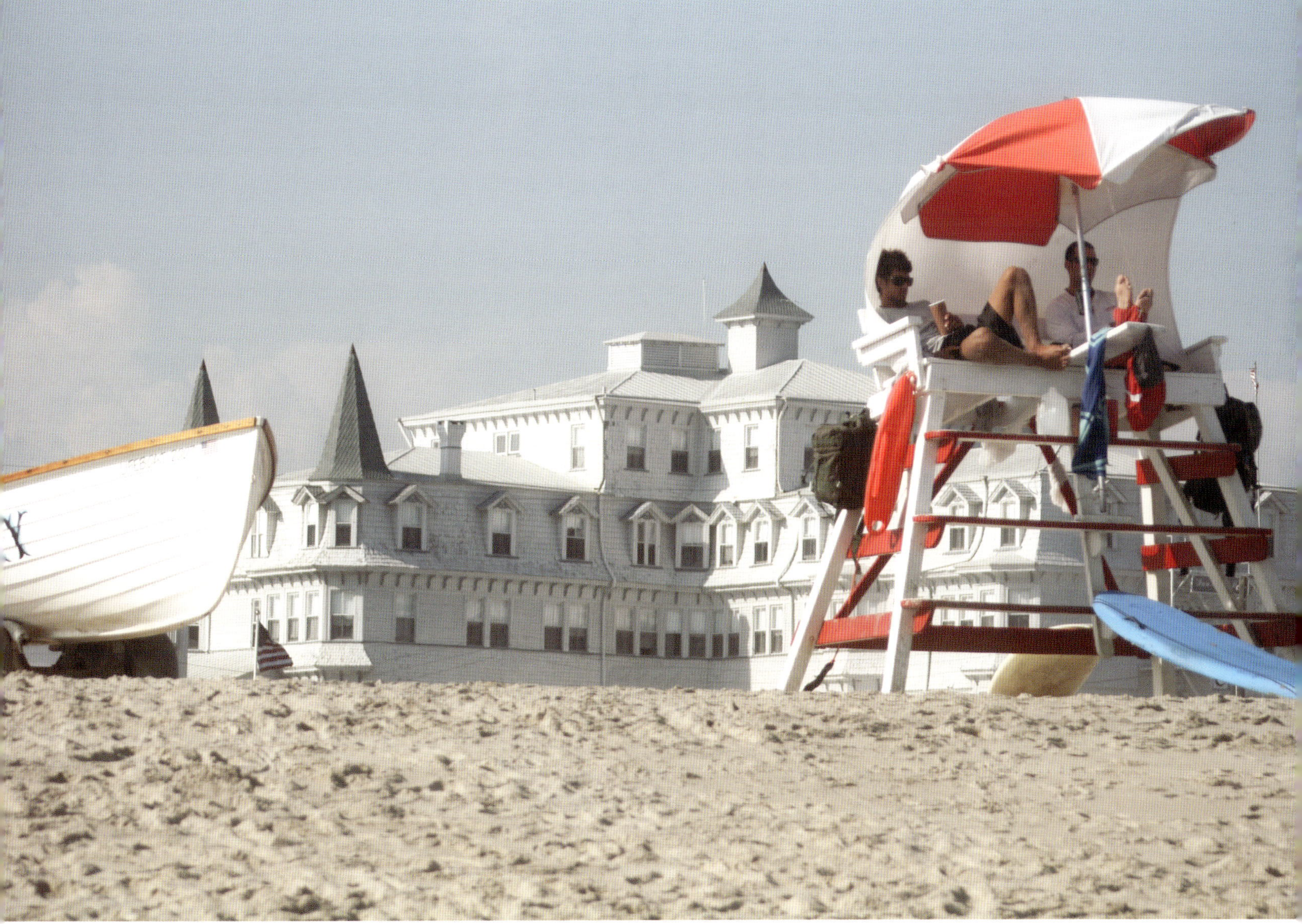

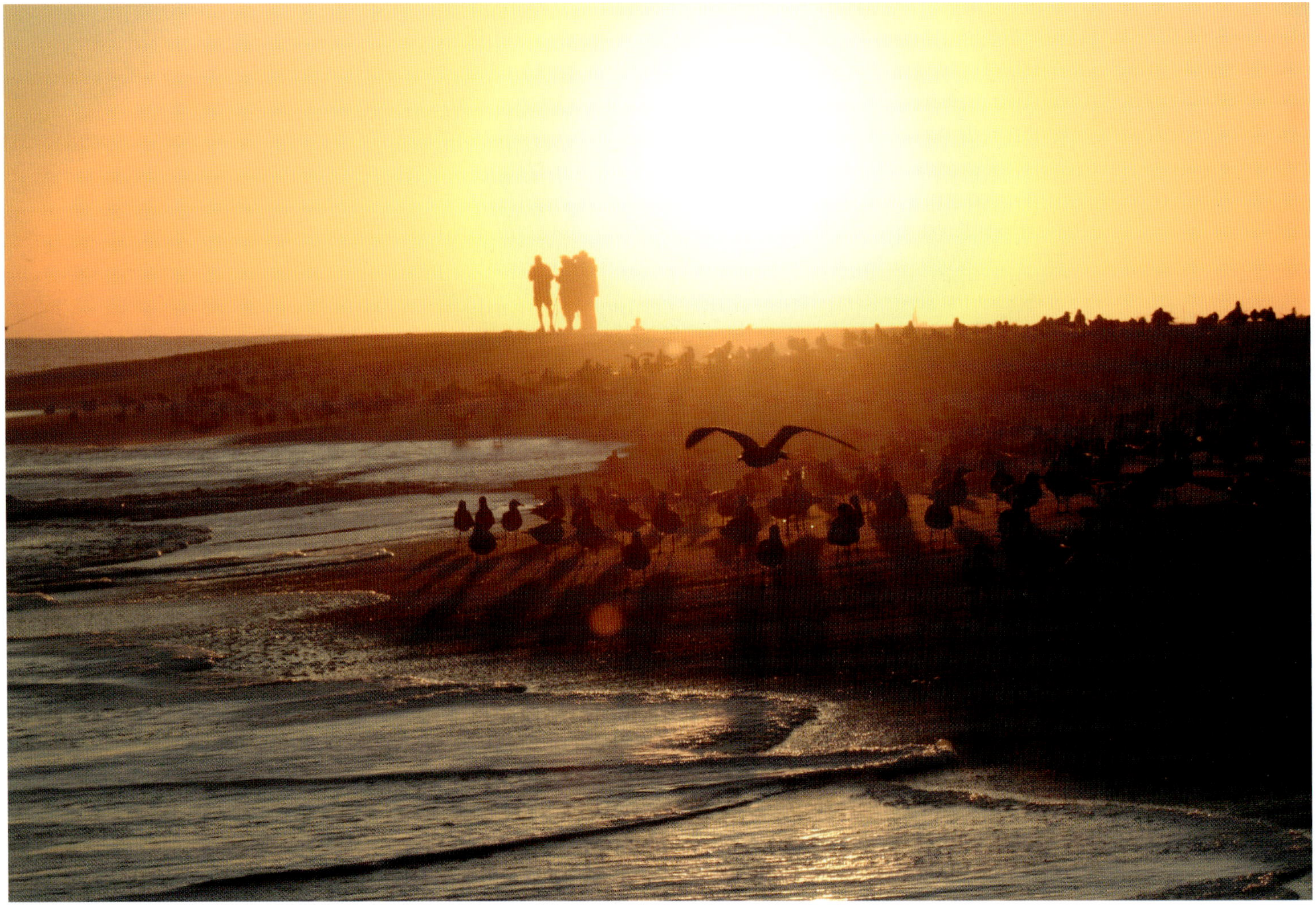

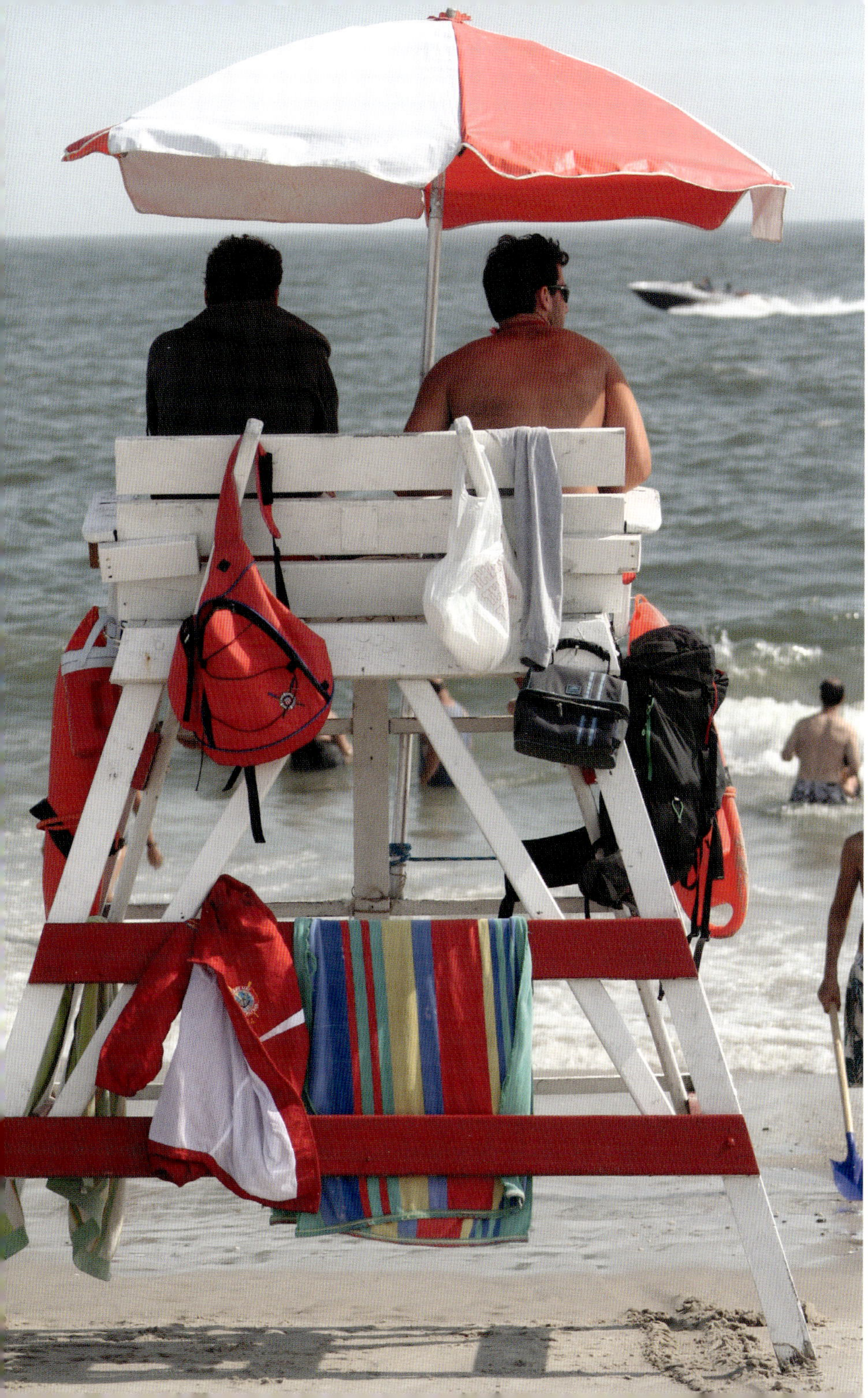
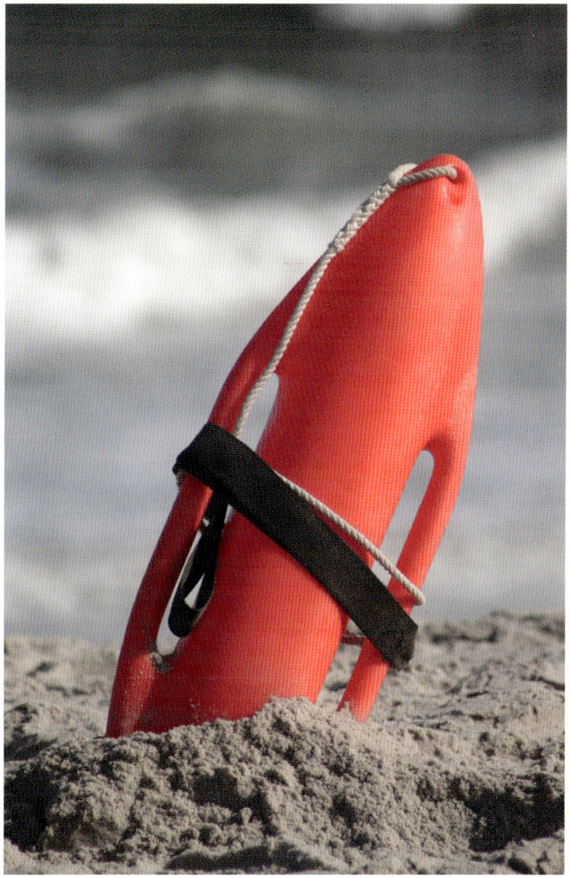

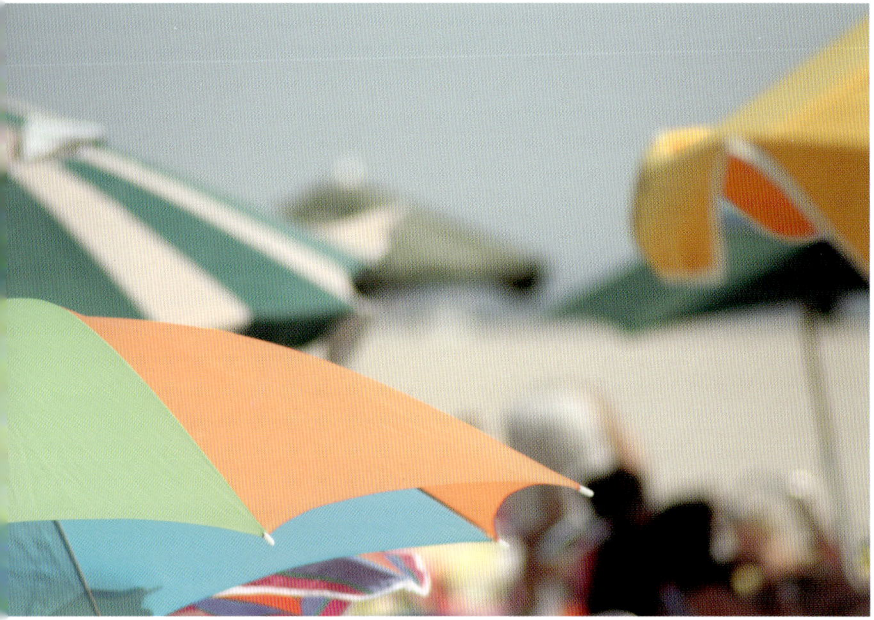

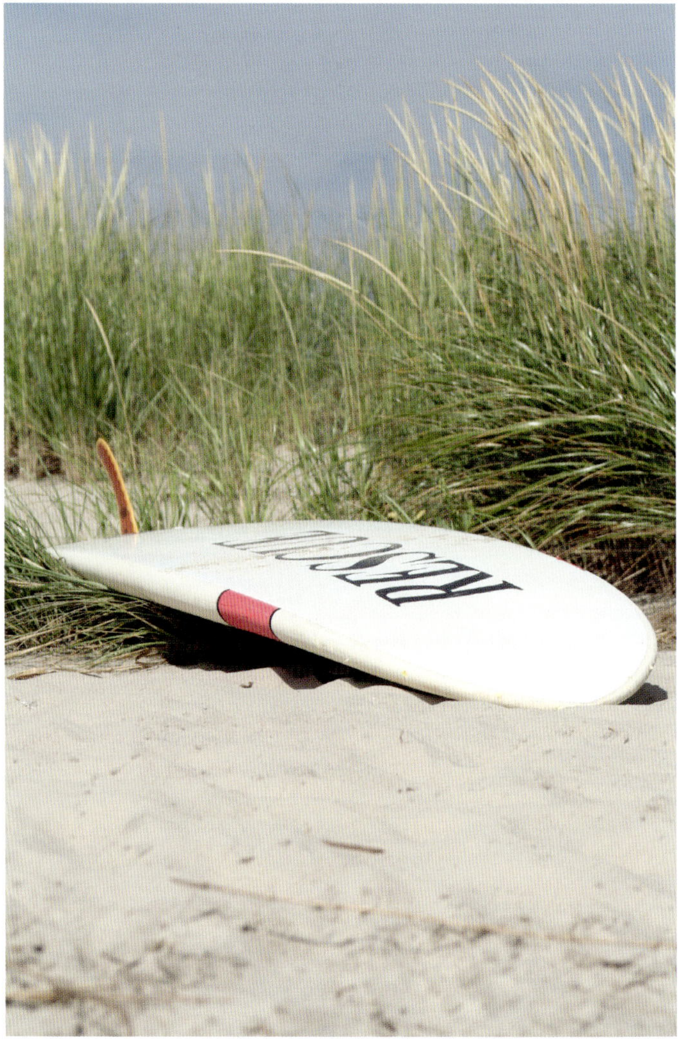
RESCUE

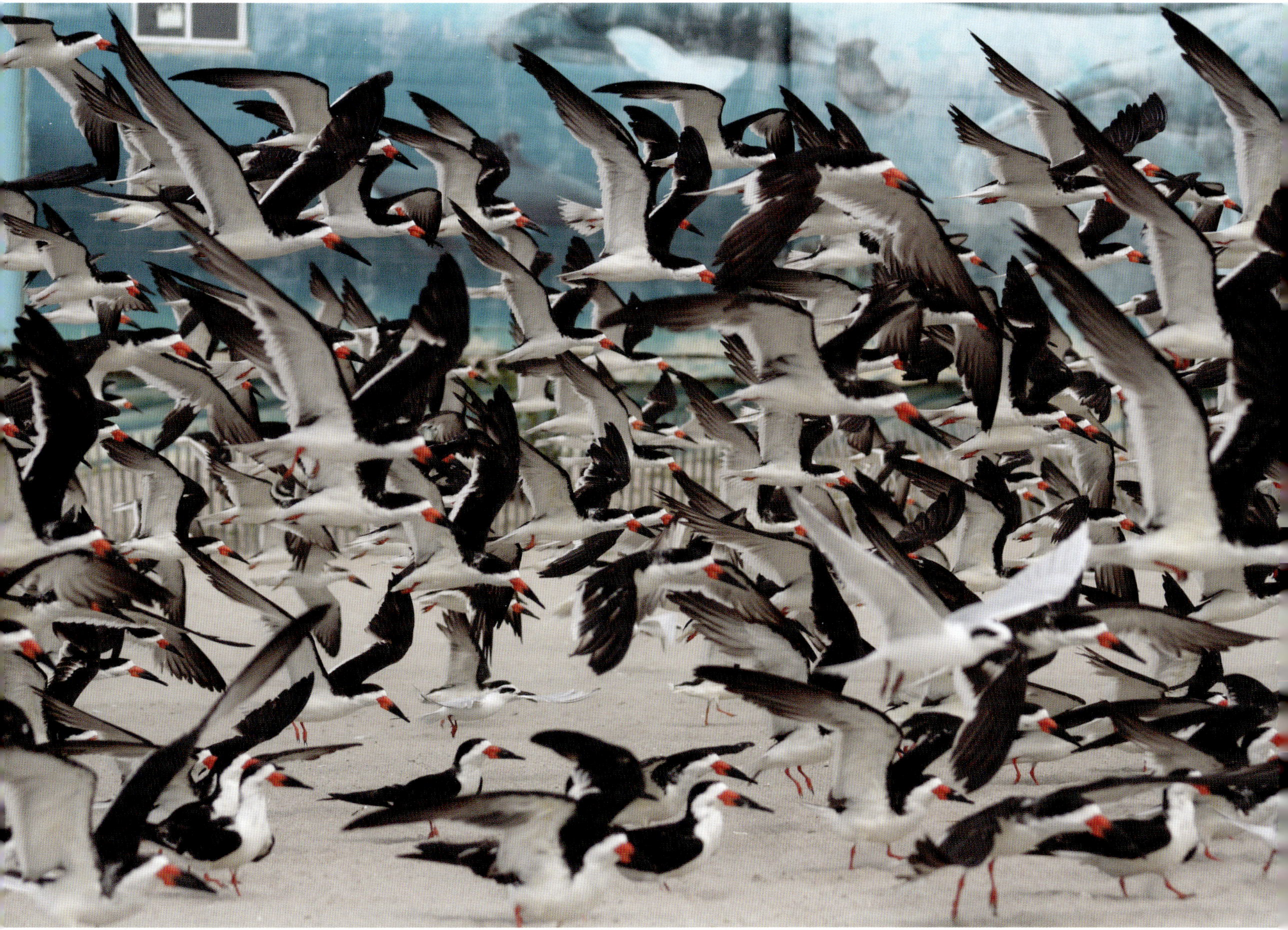

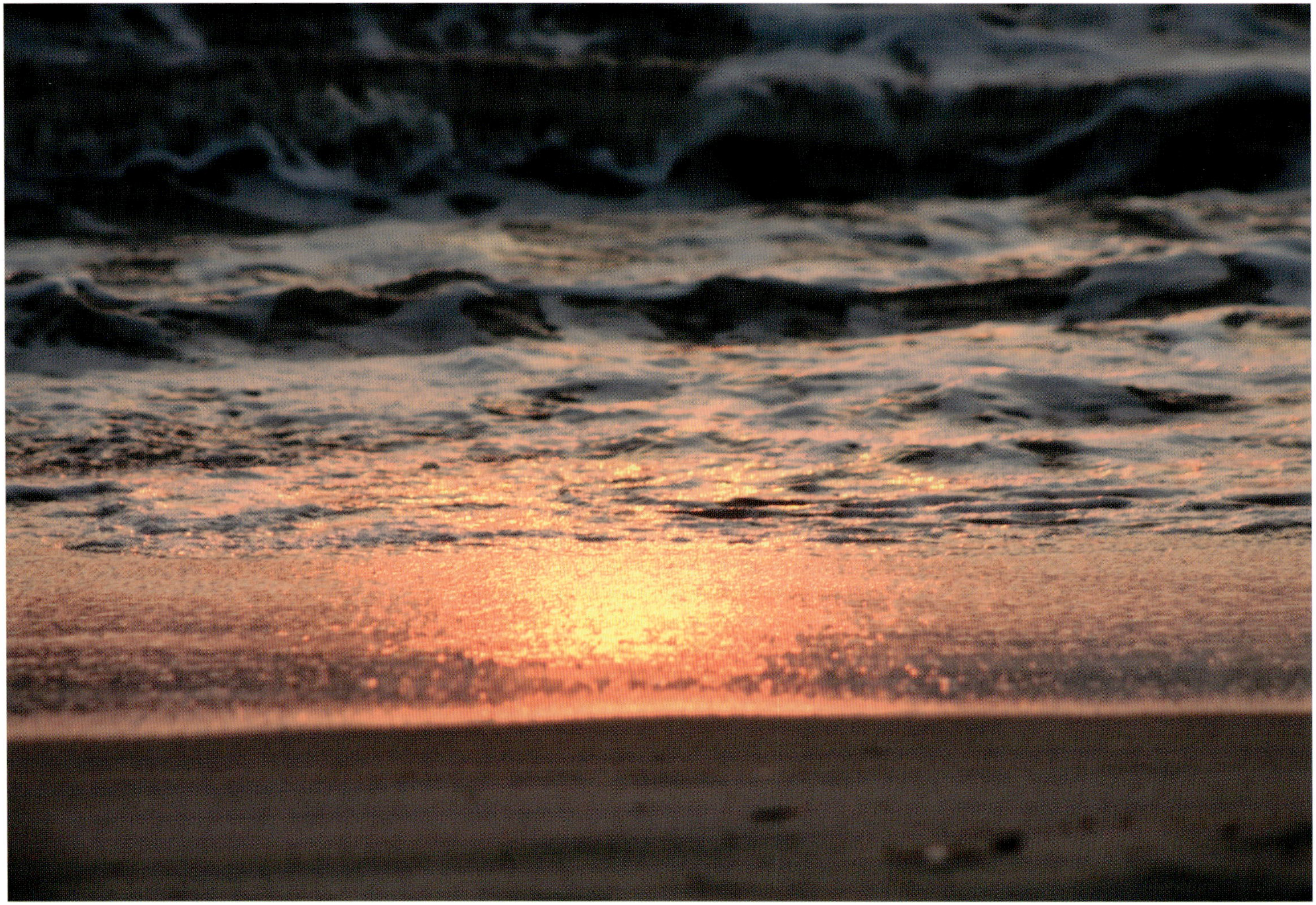

*"When anxious, uneasy, and bad thoughts come, I go to the sea, and the sea drowns them out with its great wide sounds, cleanses me with its noise, and imposes a rhythm upon everything in me that is bewildered and confused."*

~ Rainer Maria Rilke

# The Cove

When you have, quite literally, reached the end of the road, you will find The Cove. Somewhere out there in this almost bay-like break in the shoreline once stood the site of the small town South Cape May. A victim of the relentless eroding power of the sea, the town is now but just a memory. If you have a bit of imagination, you can look out into the surf and imagine where the trolley tracks once ran along the beach from the city of Cape May to Cape May Point. The ocean has since reclaimed this stretch of beach, returning it to an undeveloped state. The handful of South Cape May homes that managed to survive the surf and were not smashed by the sea were moved to safer ground; many of these can now be found along Sunset Boulevard and in the area of Second Avenue to Broadway. Even today this highly dynamic beach is the victim of erosion and the forces of nature. Other forces are at work here too. The United States Army Corps of Engineers has returned time and again to undertake beach replenishment projects. And so man, or occasionally a storm, deposits great amounts of sand, building the beach back up, while the next storm erodes it further; back and forth the battle rages. One can often watch this part of the shoreline change dramatically in a single year. The area behind the dunes, also once part of the town of South Cape May, is now a nature preserve known as the South Cape May Meadows.

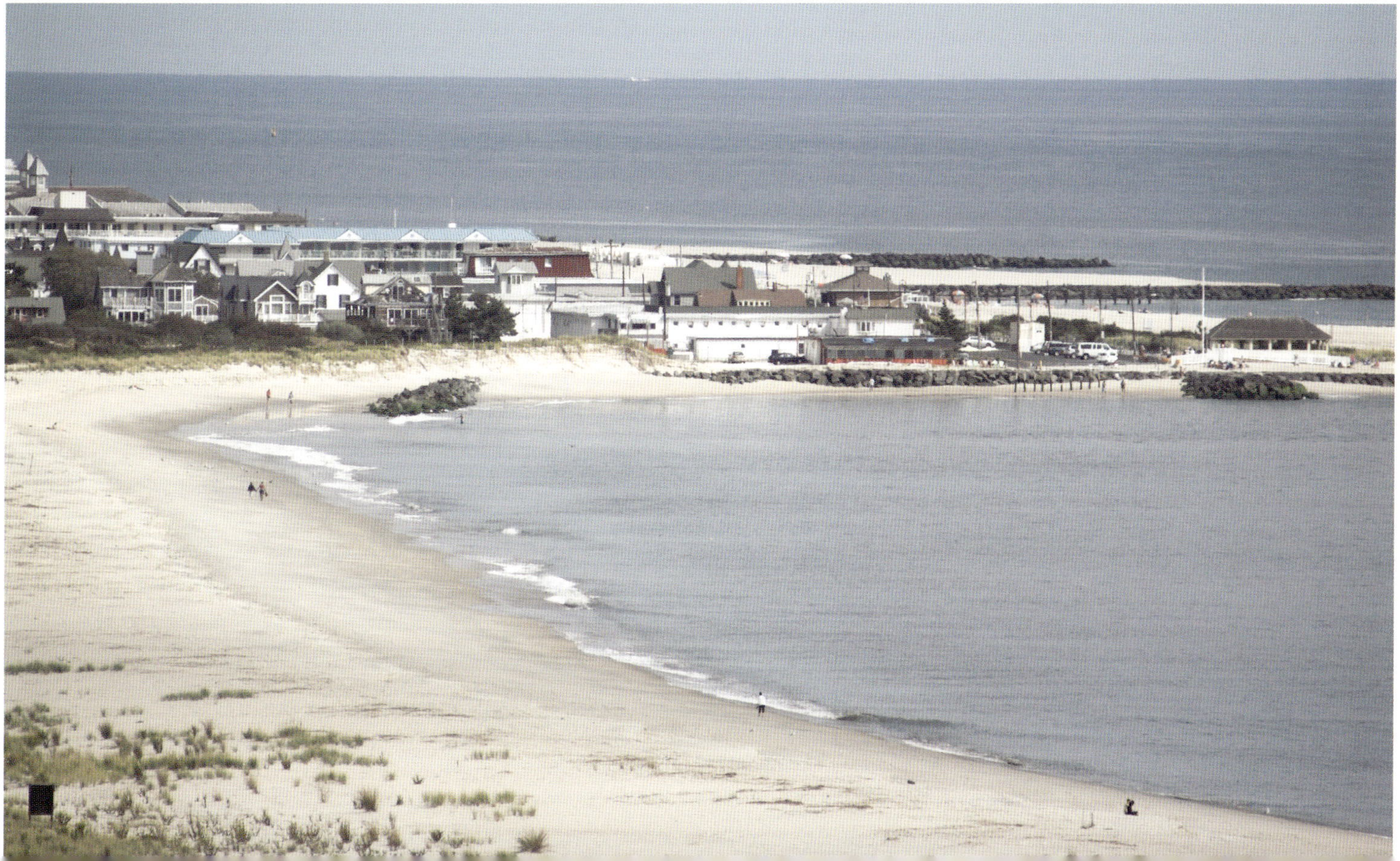

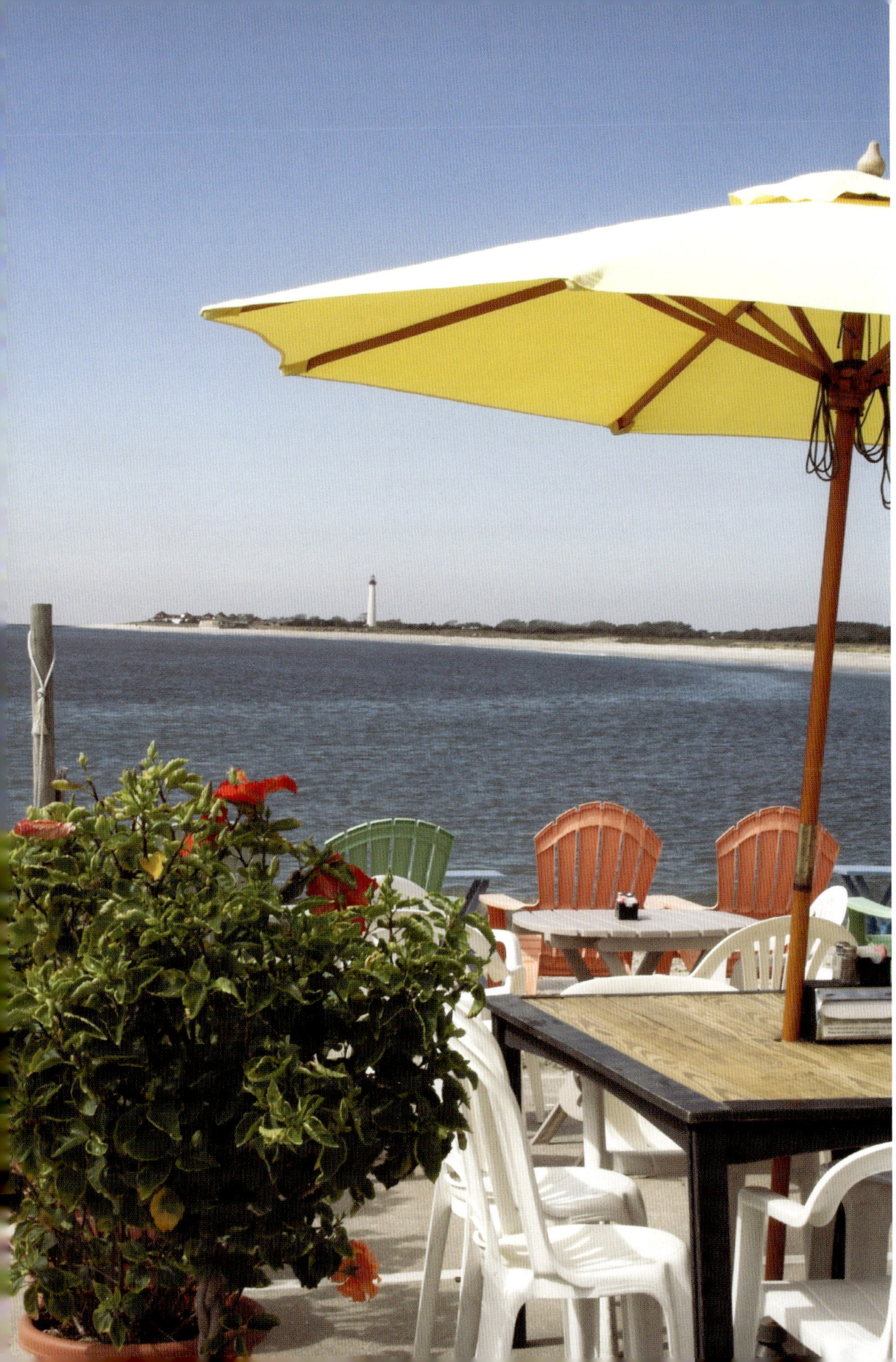

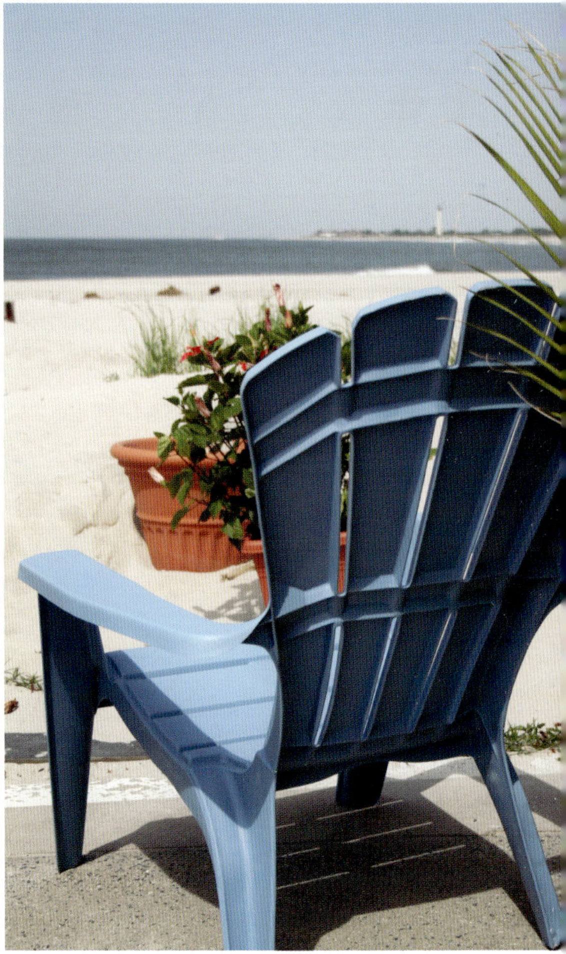

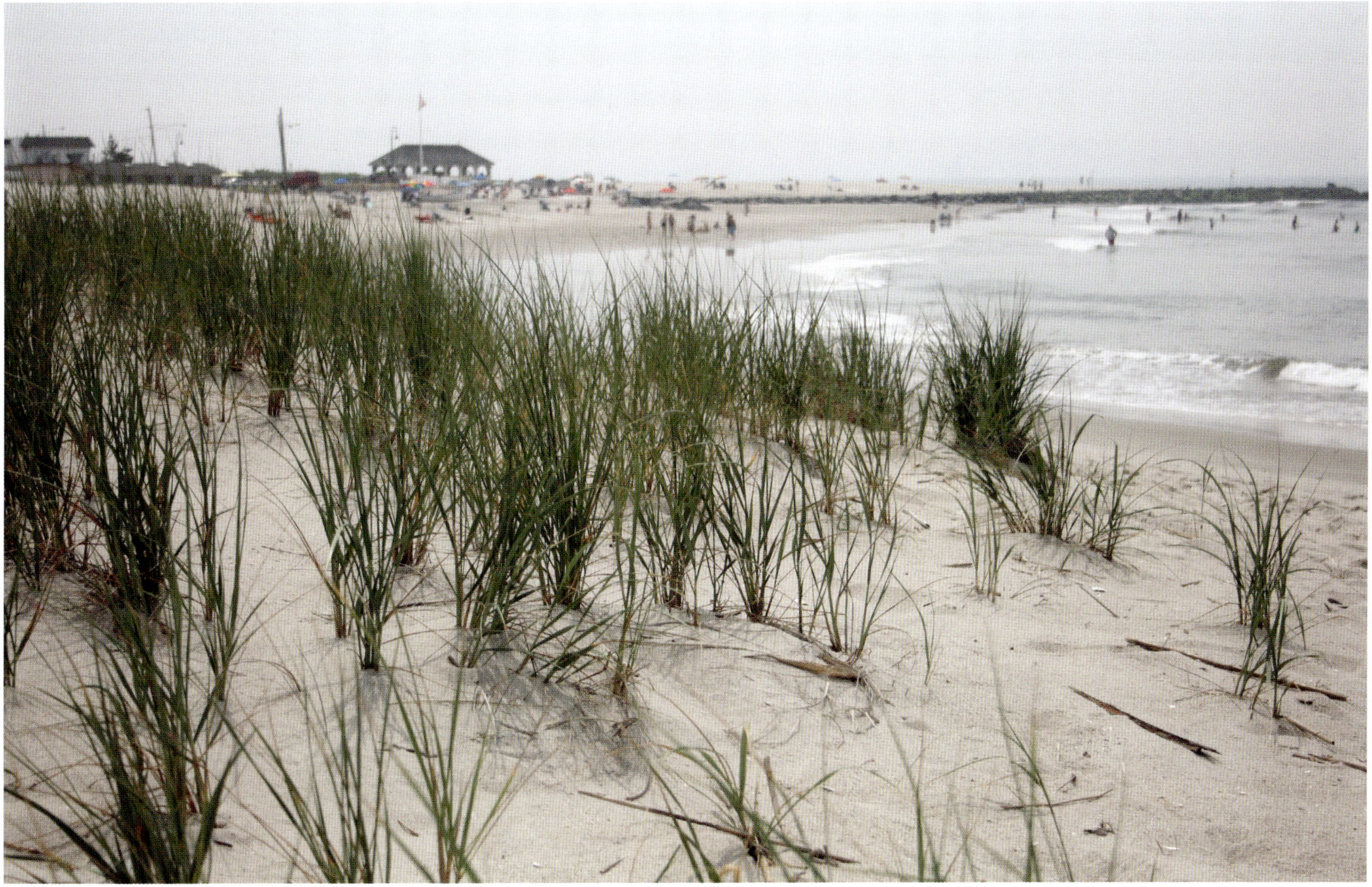

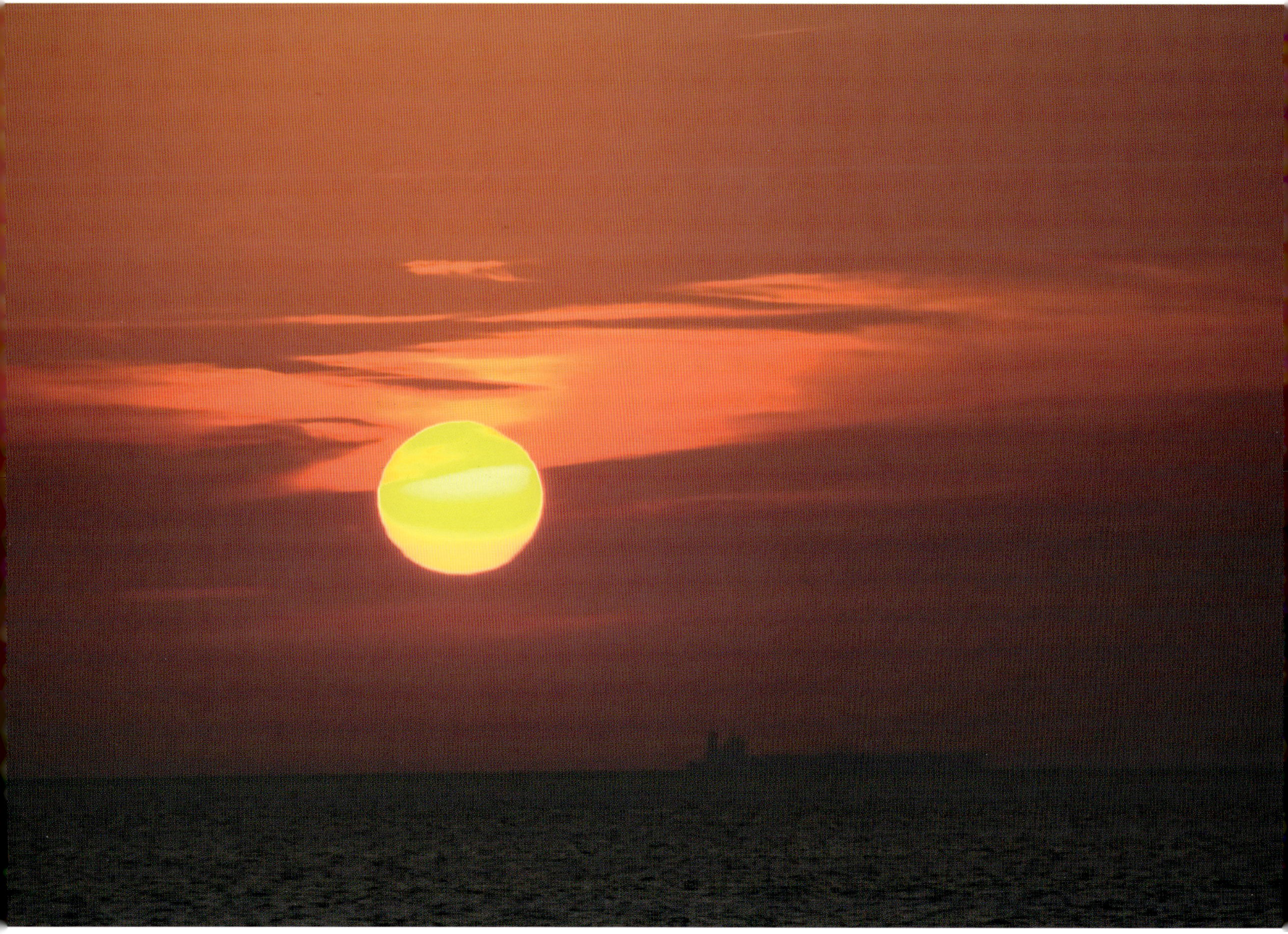

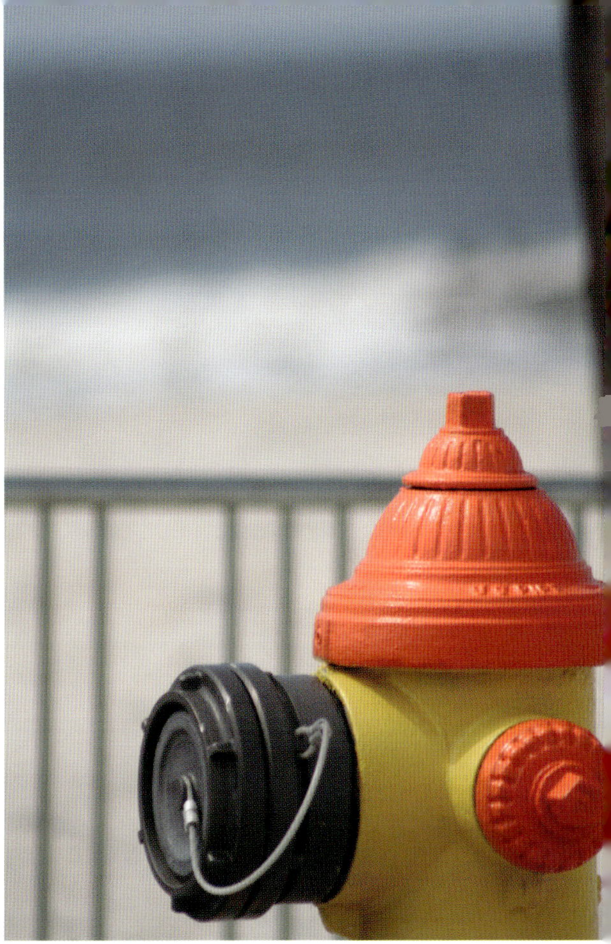

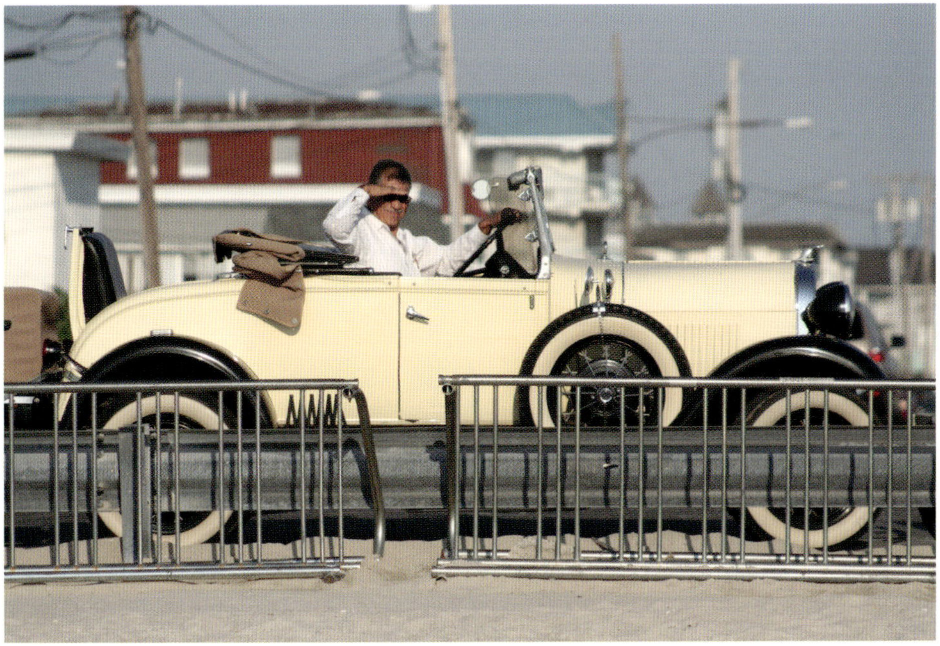

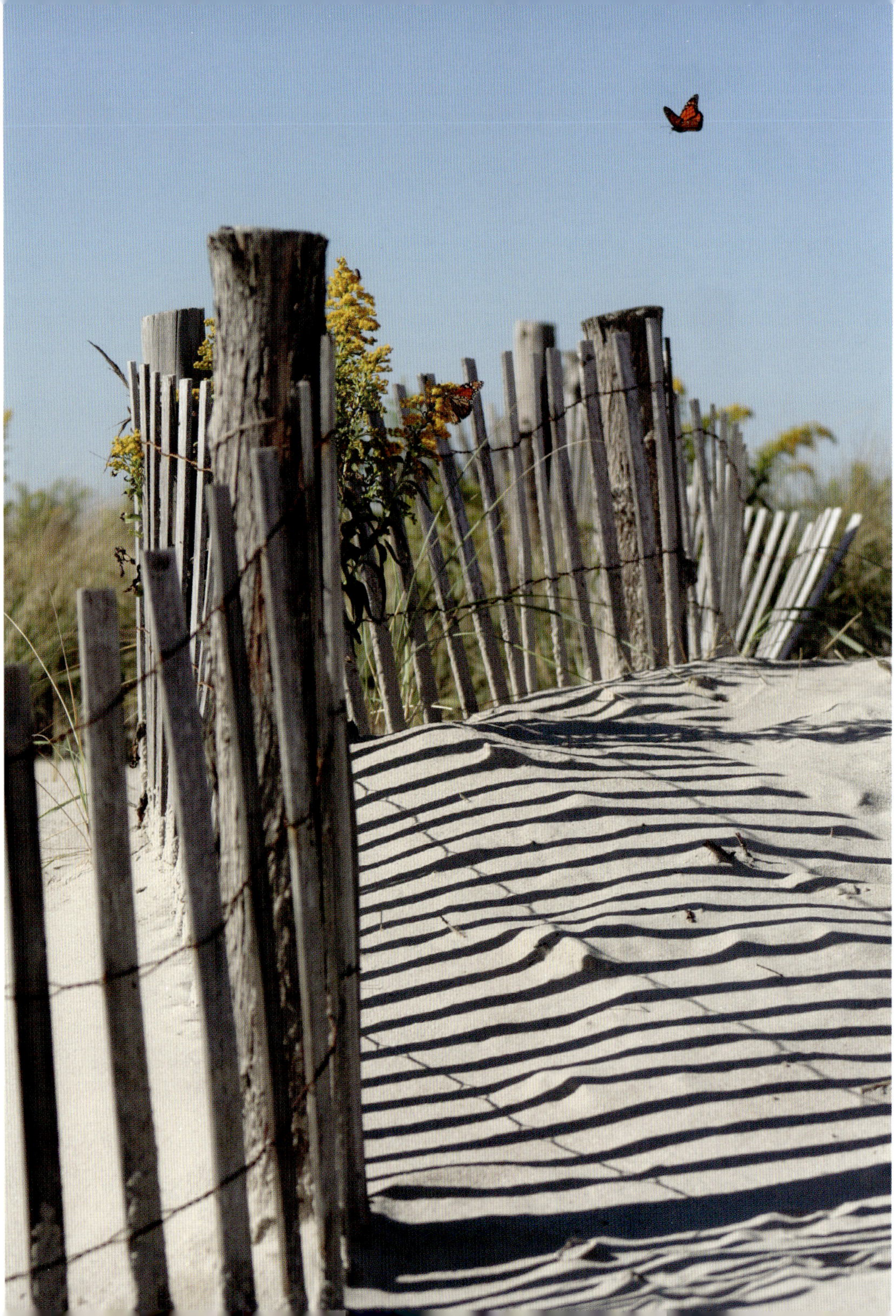

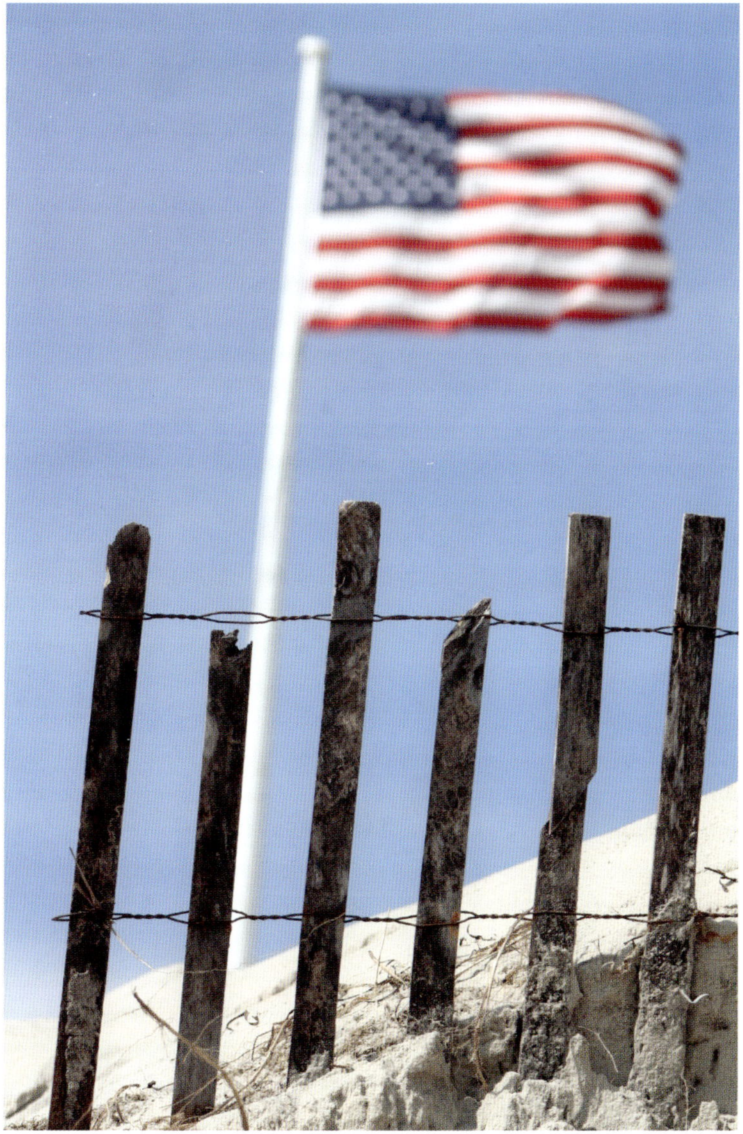

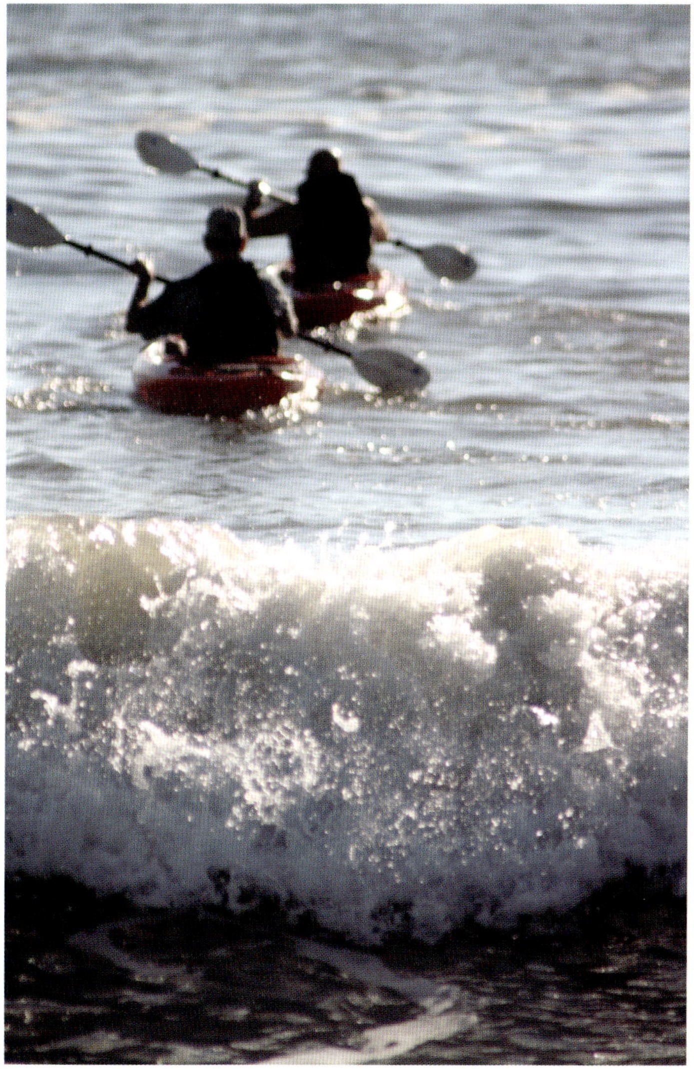

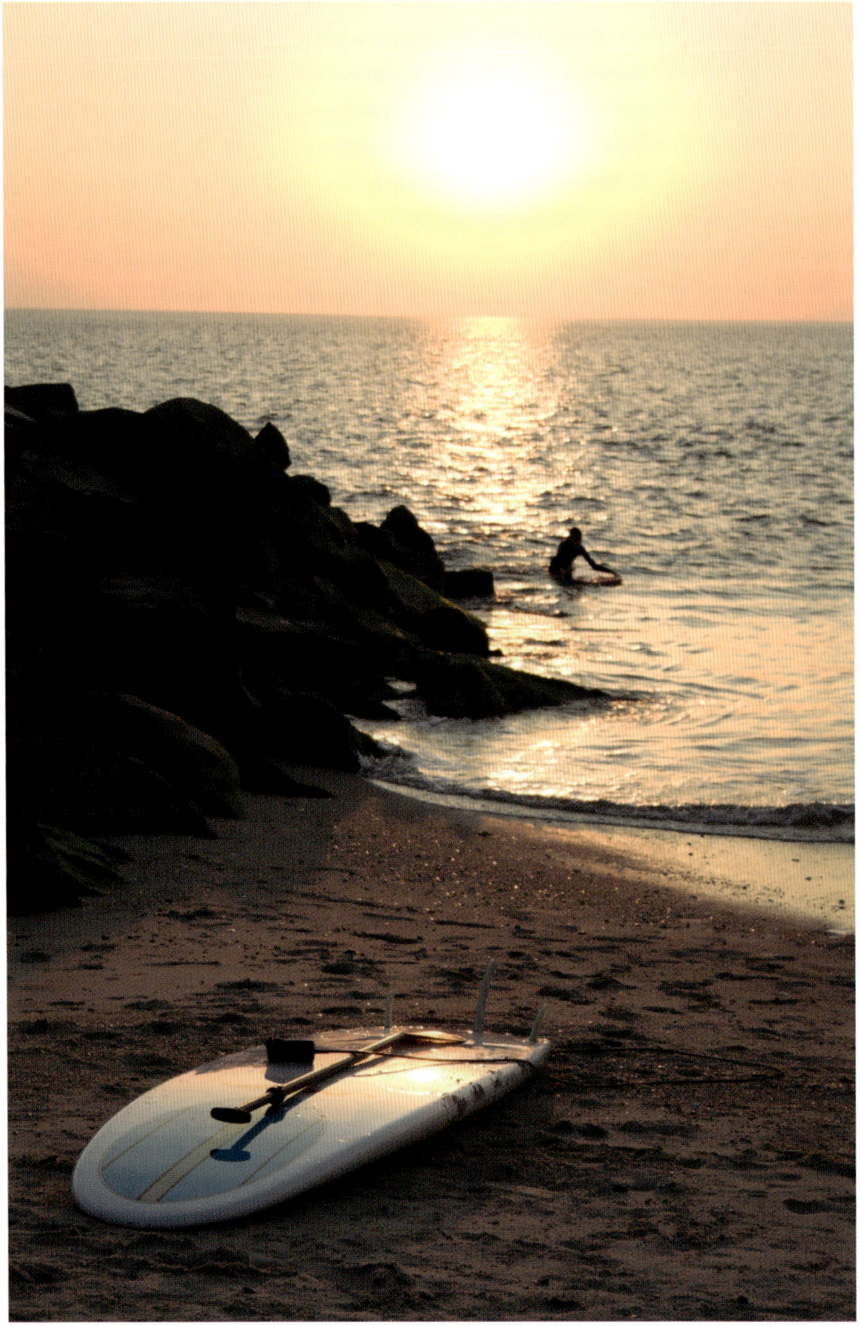

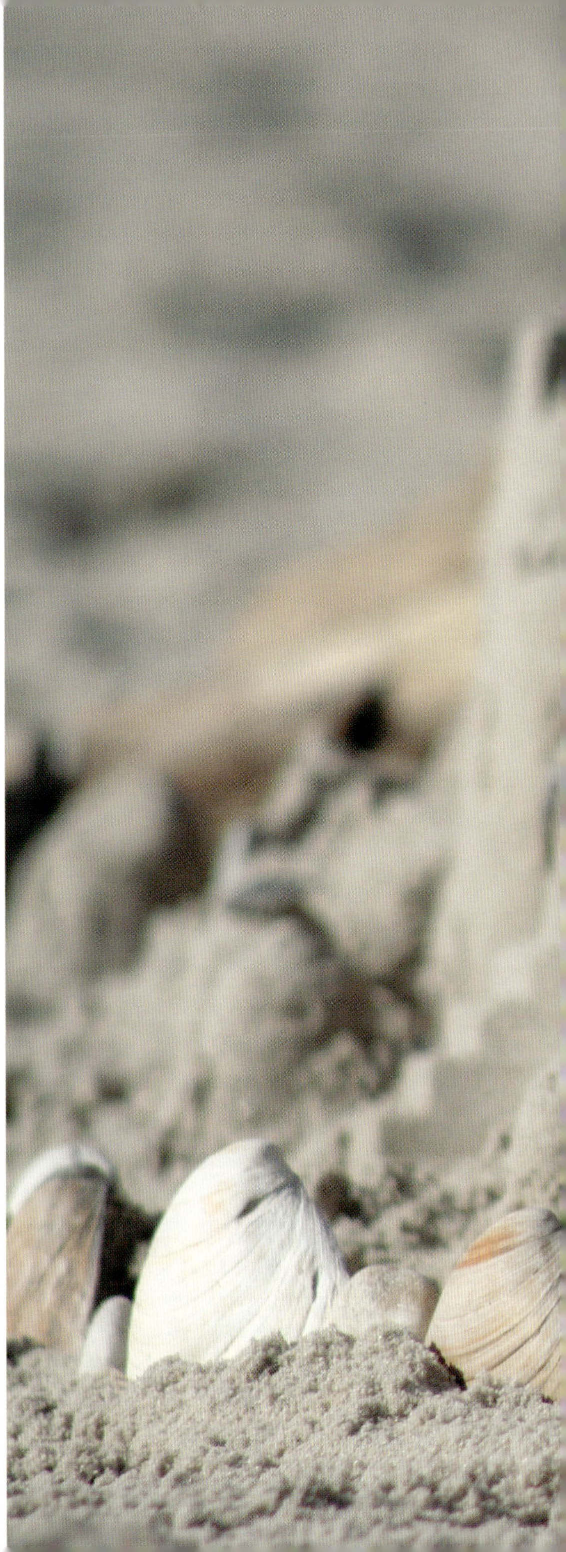

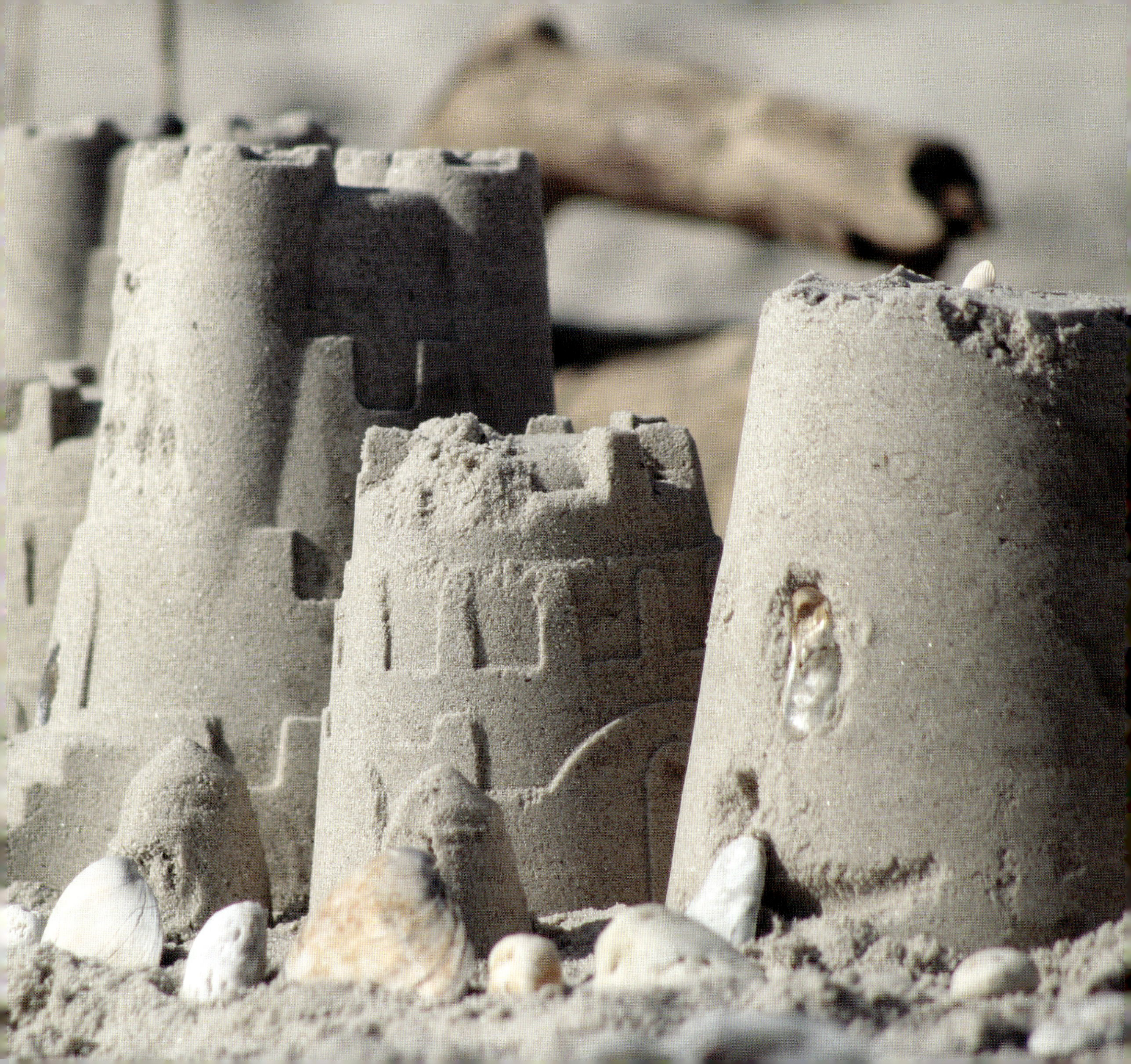

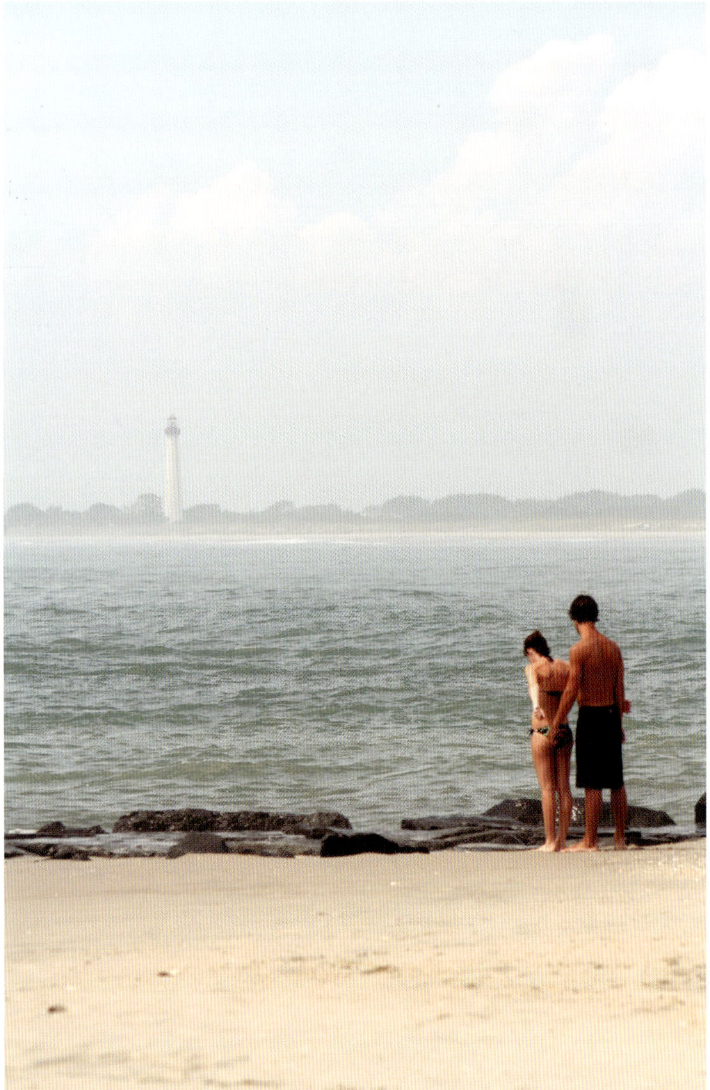

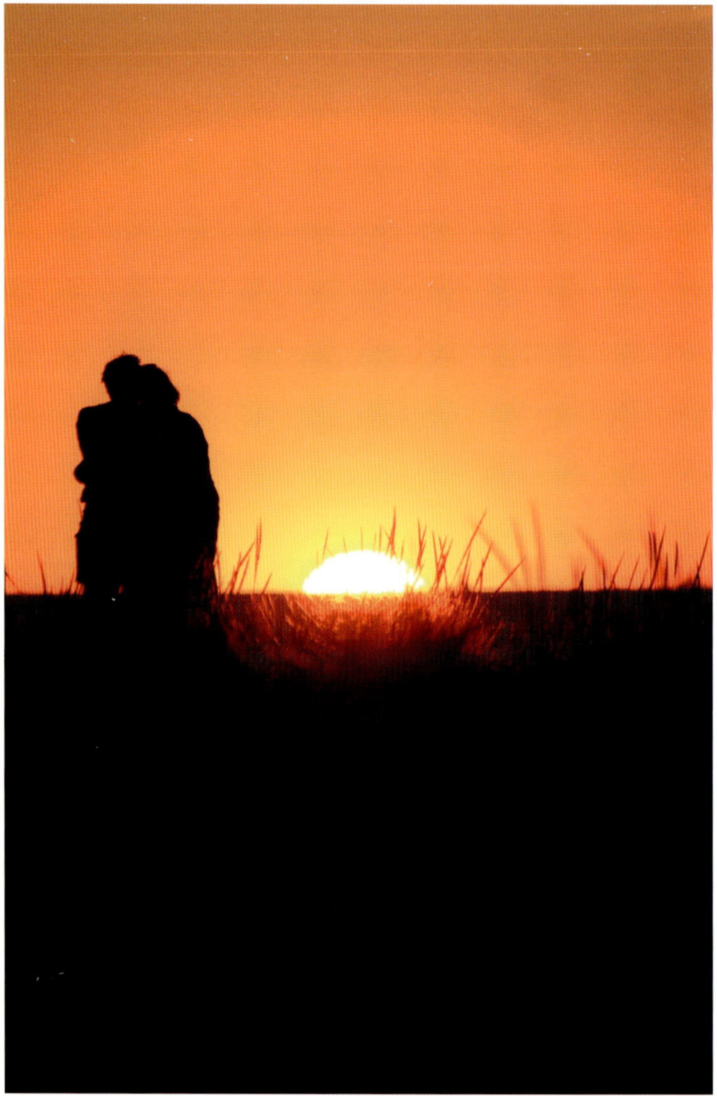

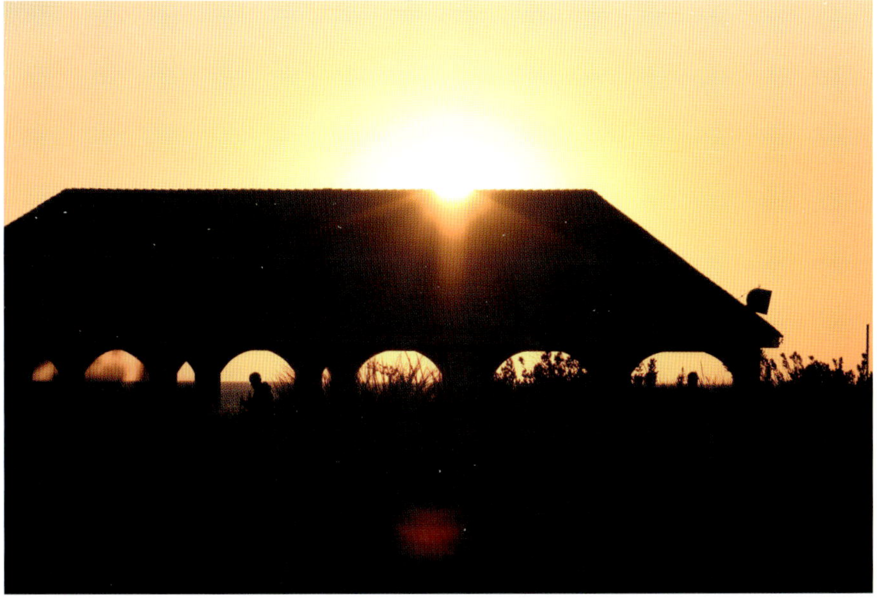

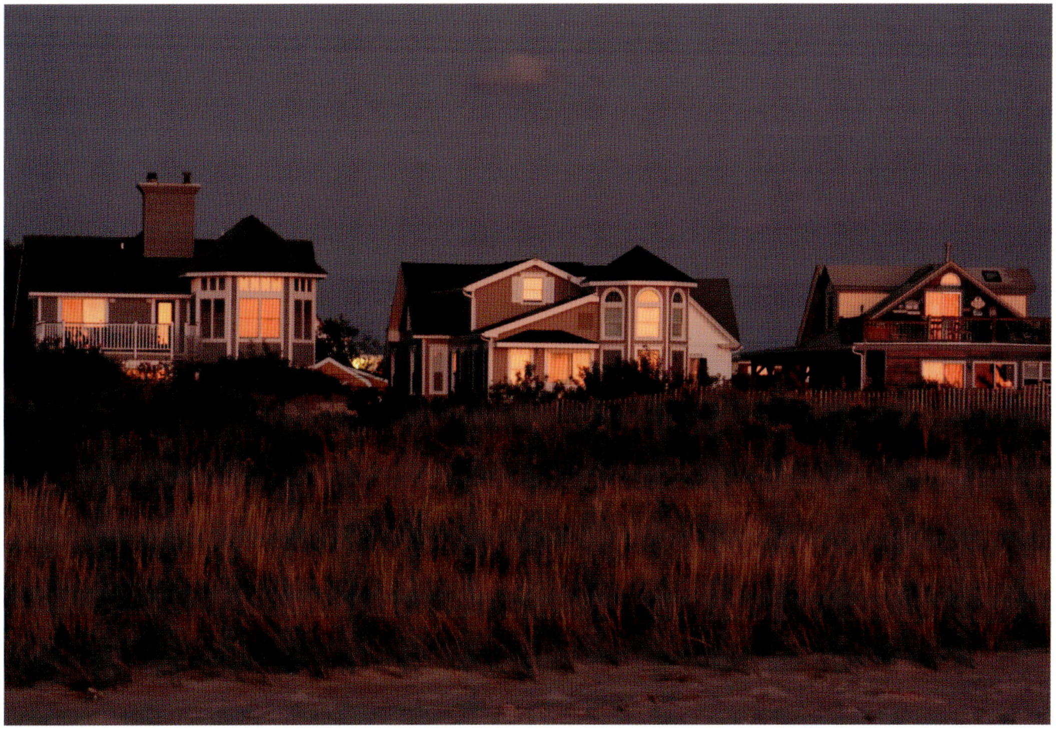

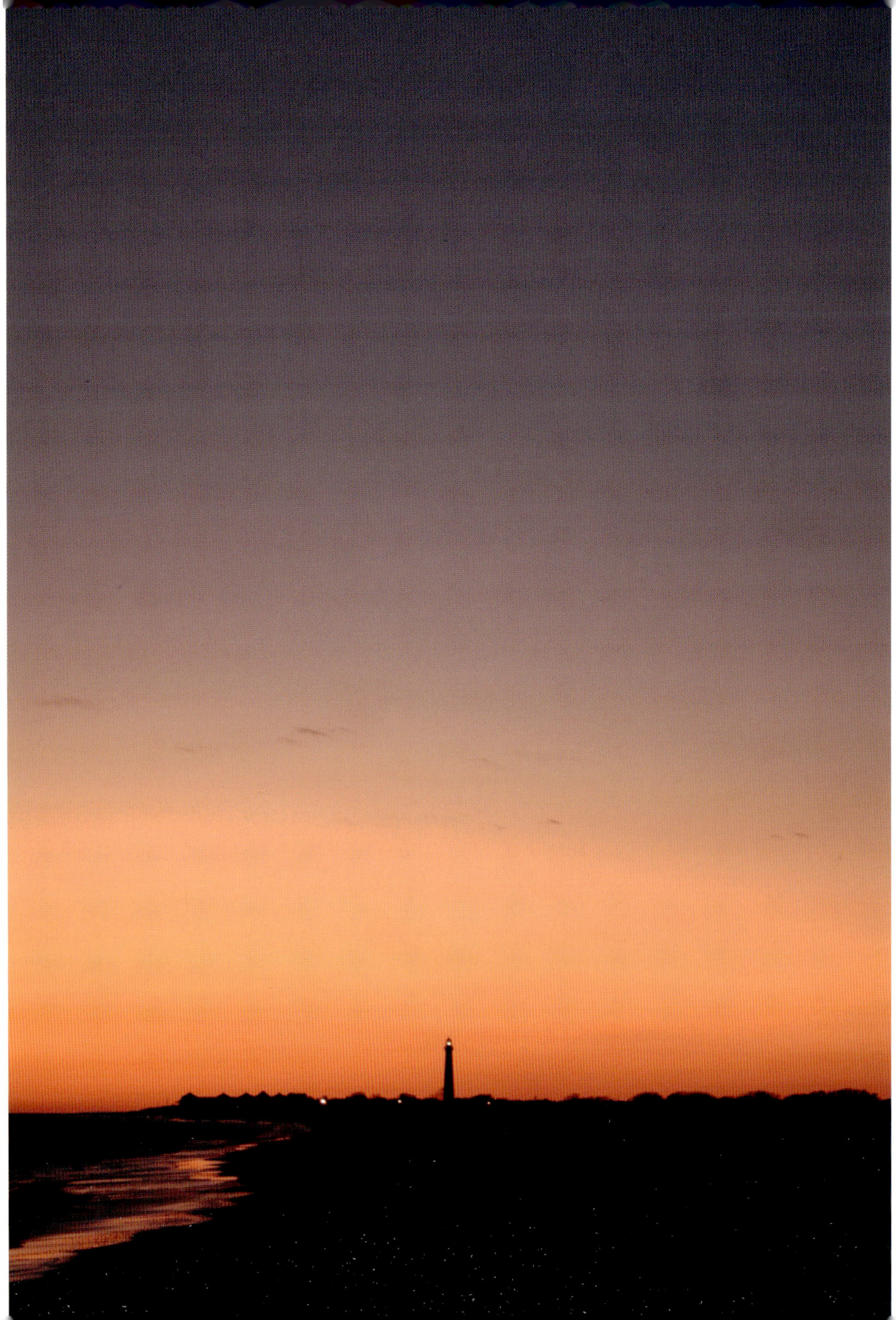

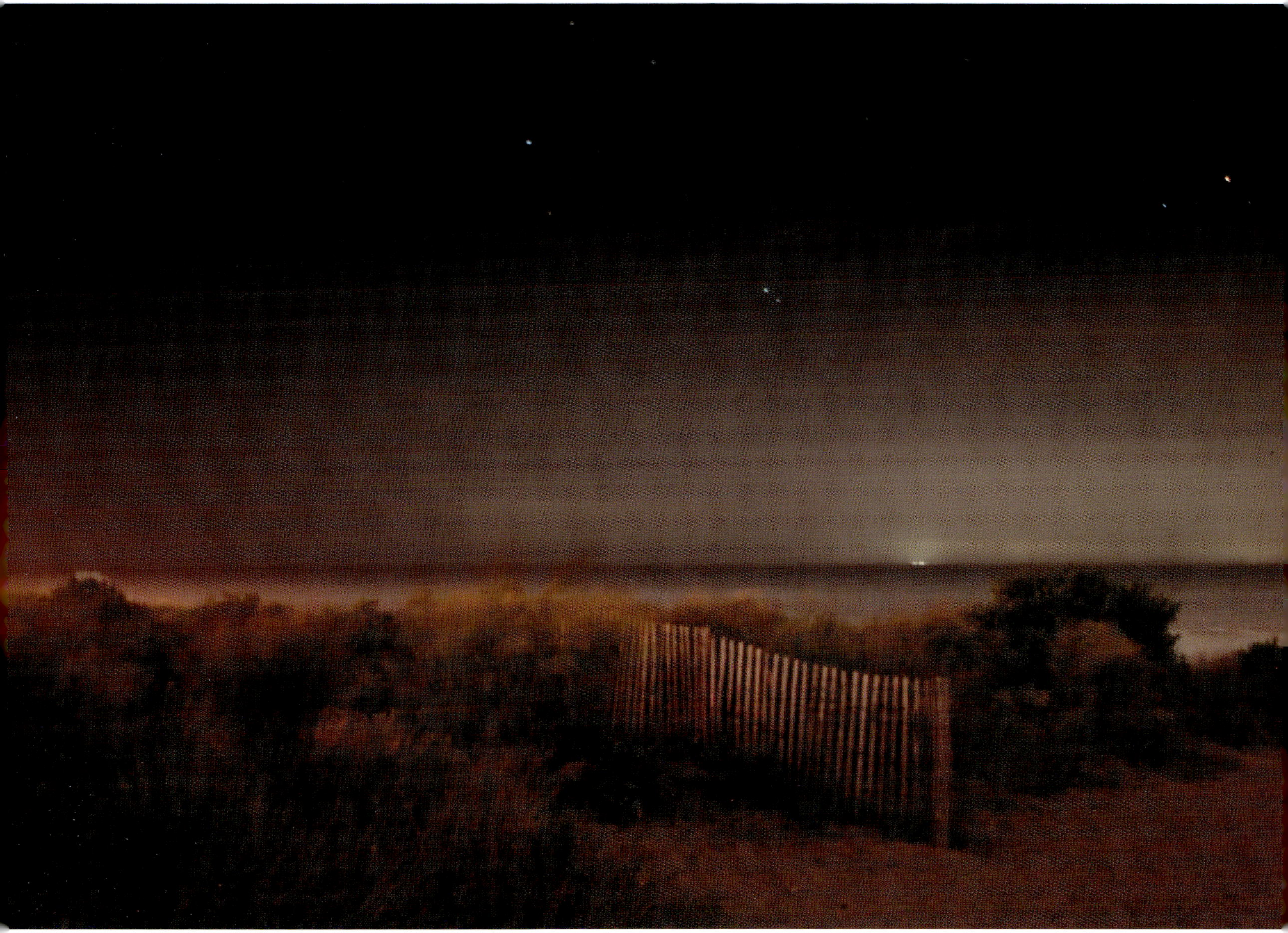

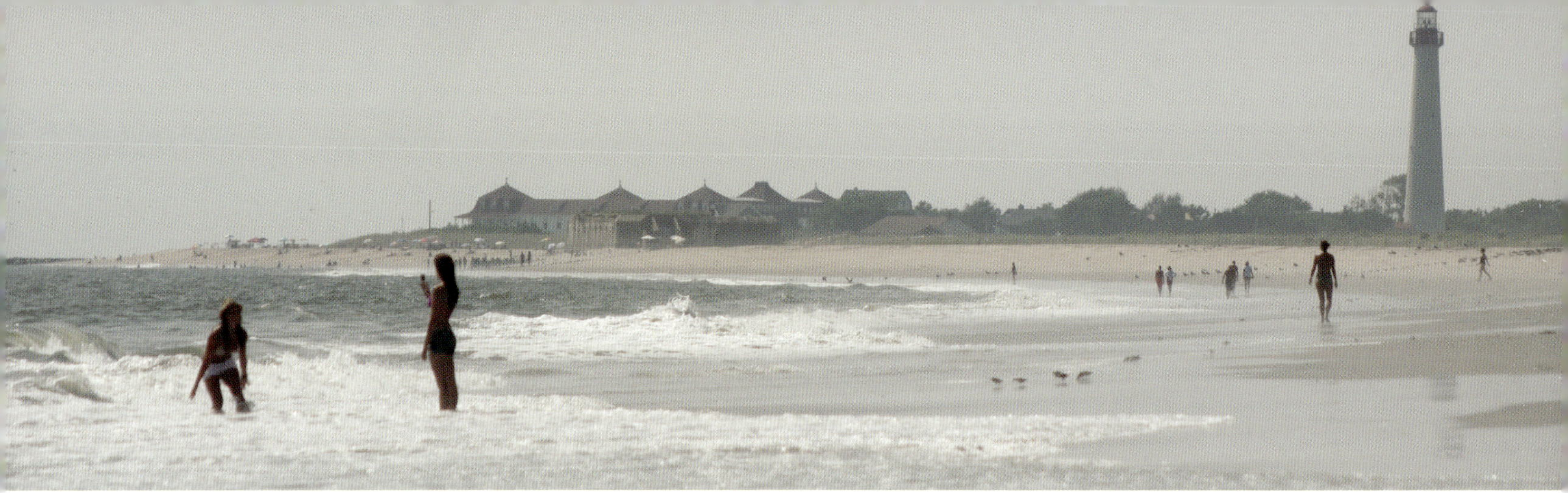

# Cape May Point

Cape May Point, or simply "The Point" as it is known, is a unique community that sits at the confluence of the Delaware Bay and the Atlantic Ocean. In addition to its beaches, The Point is home to a New Jersey state park featuring marsh and woodland walking trails, a nature museum, look-out decks for birding, a World War II concrete bunker, and, of course, the famous Cape May Lighthouse. It is exceedingly challenging to take a photograph at The Point that doesn't in some way include the lighthouse.

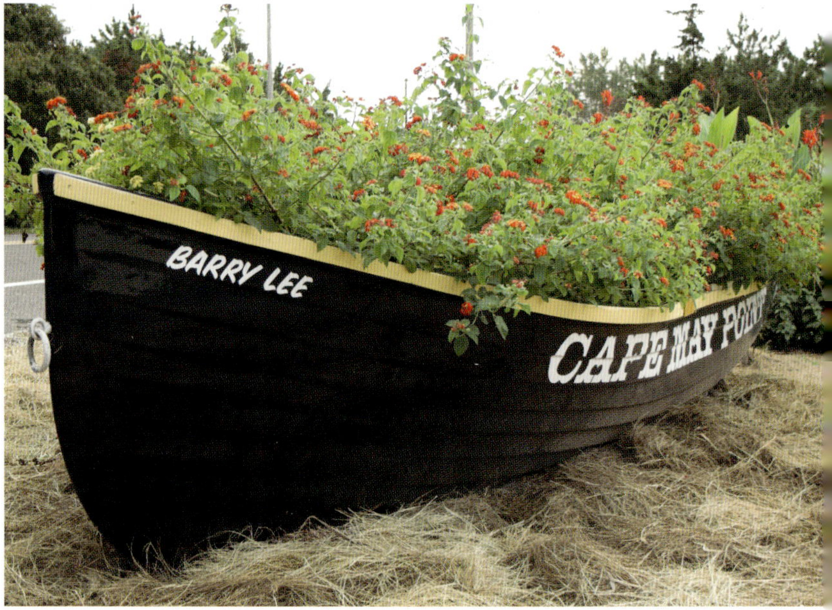

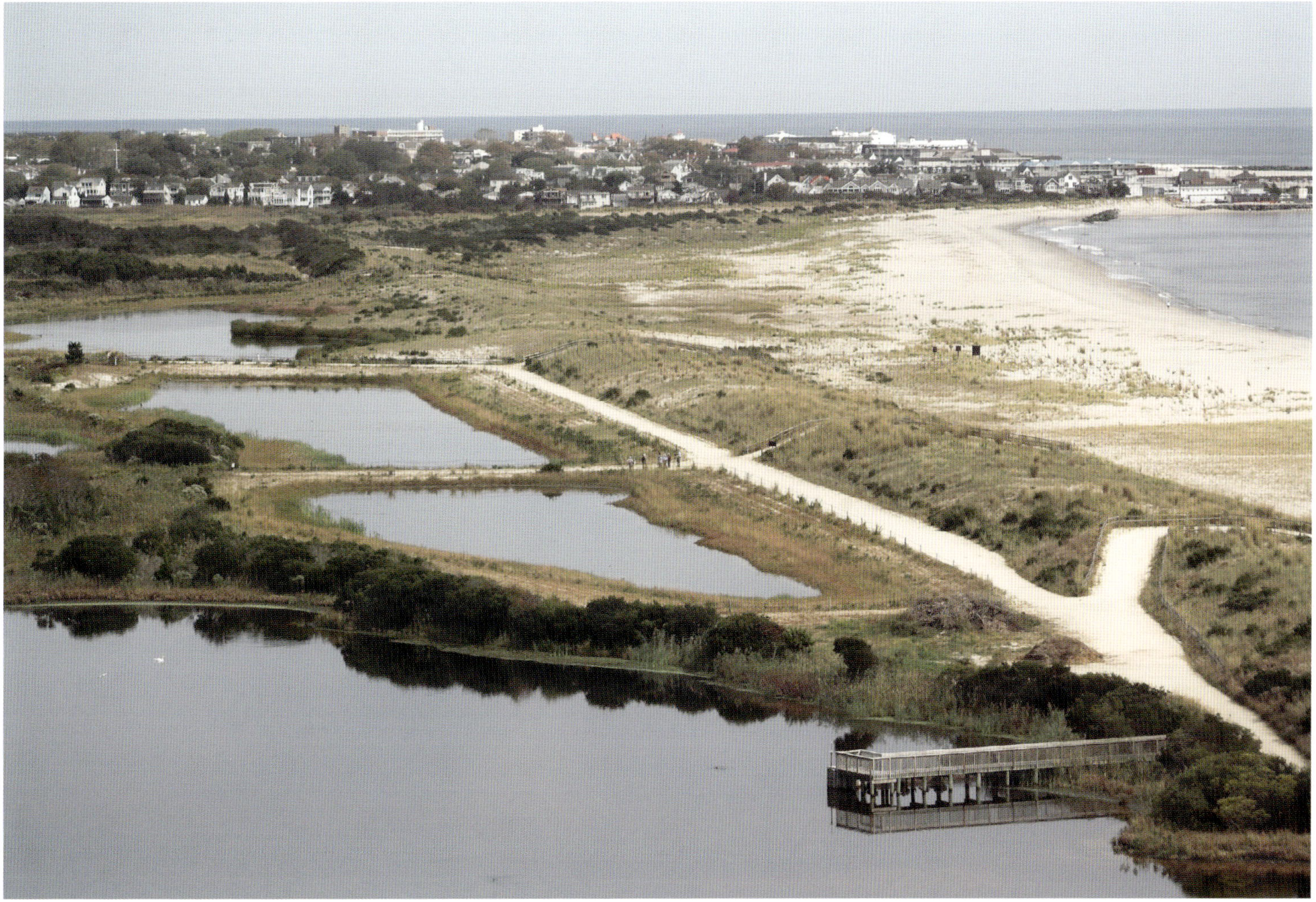

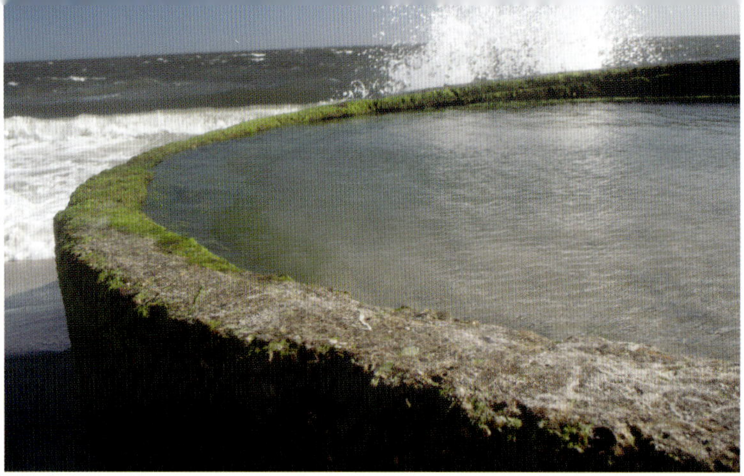

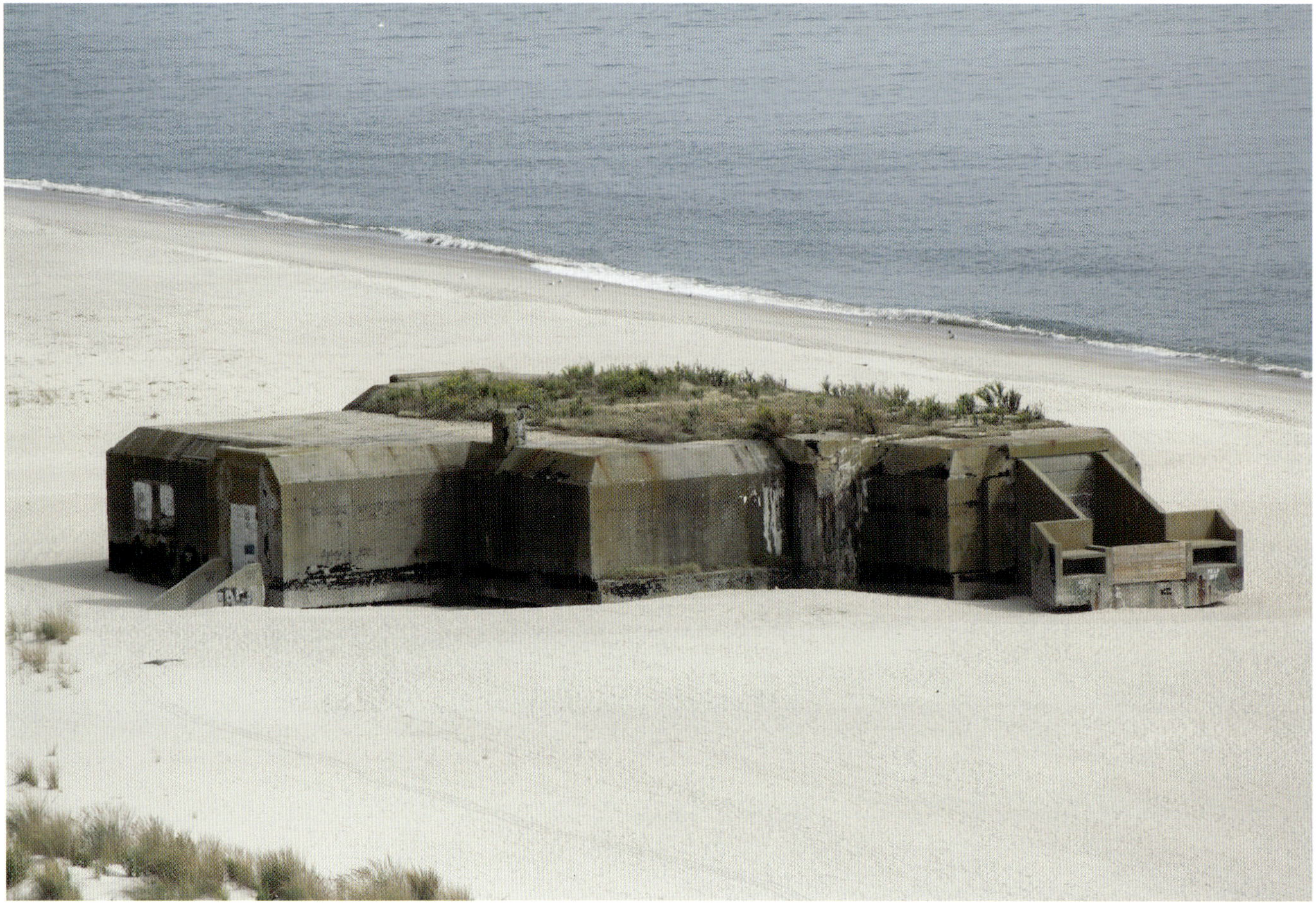

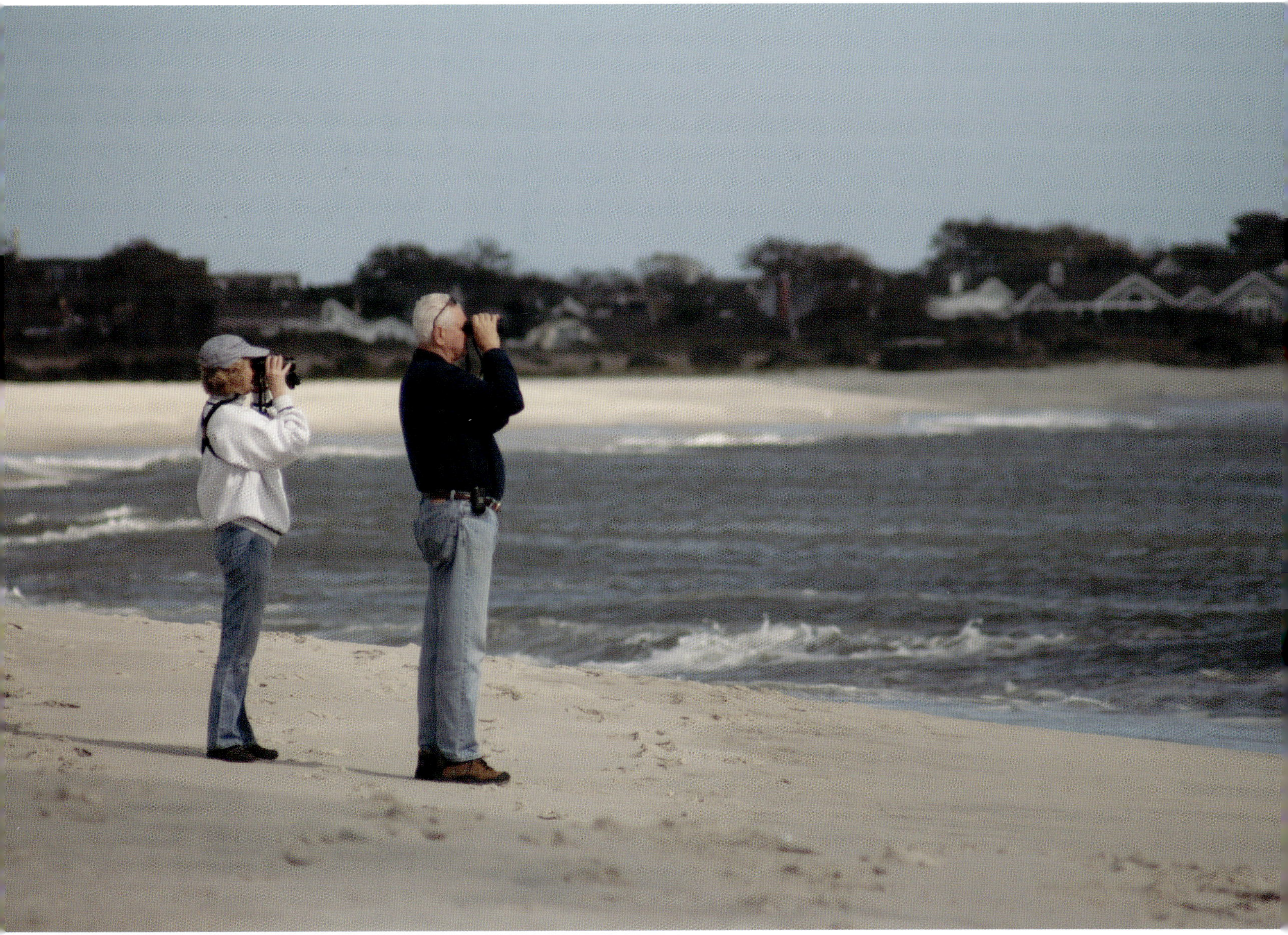

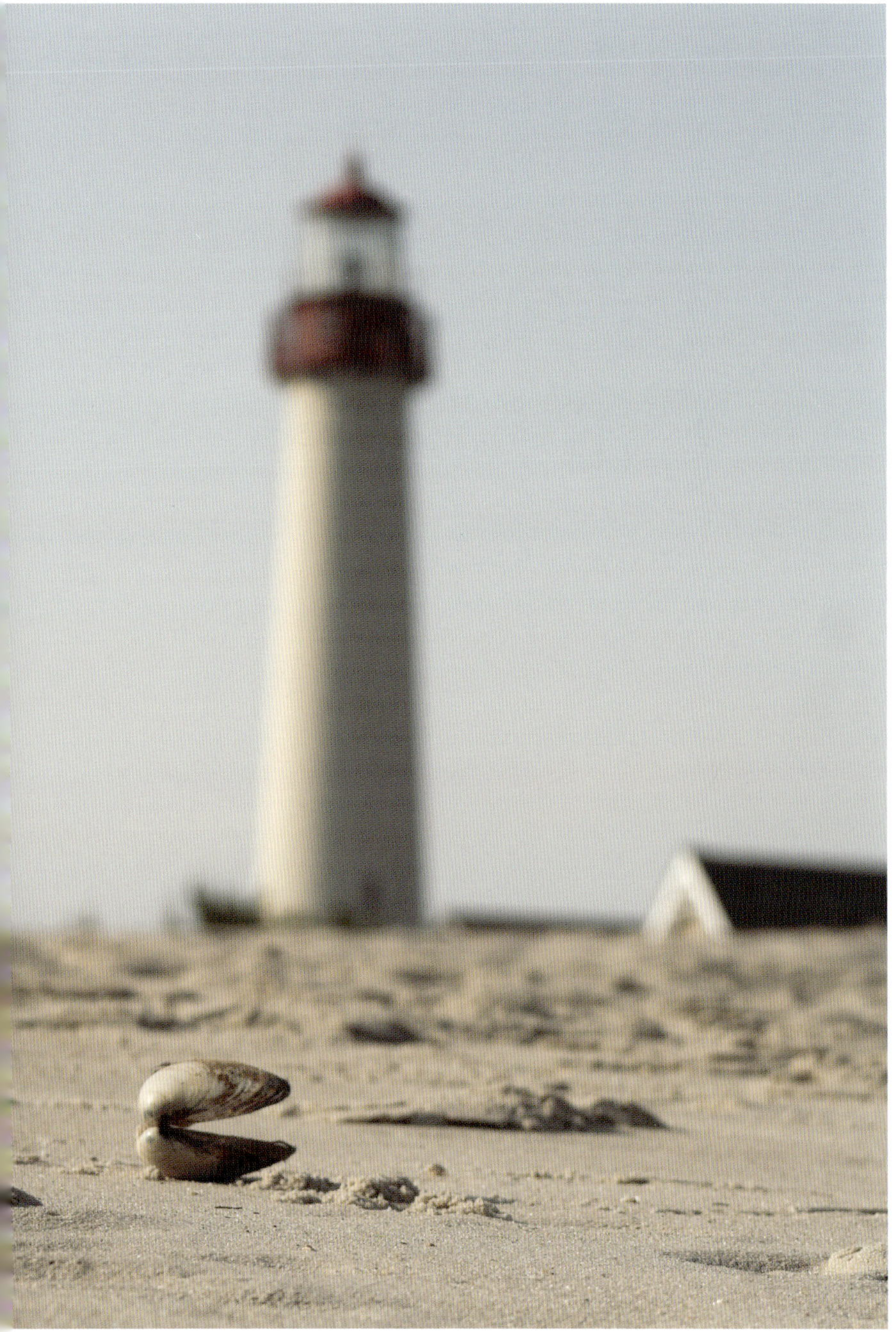

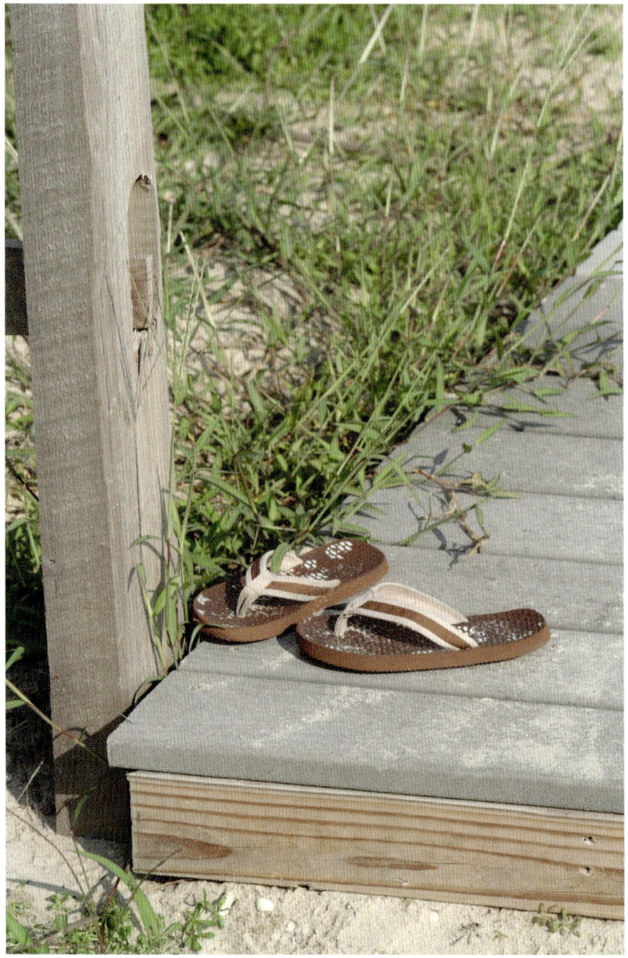

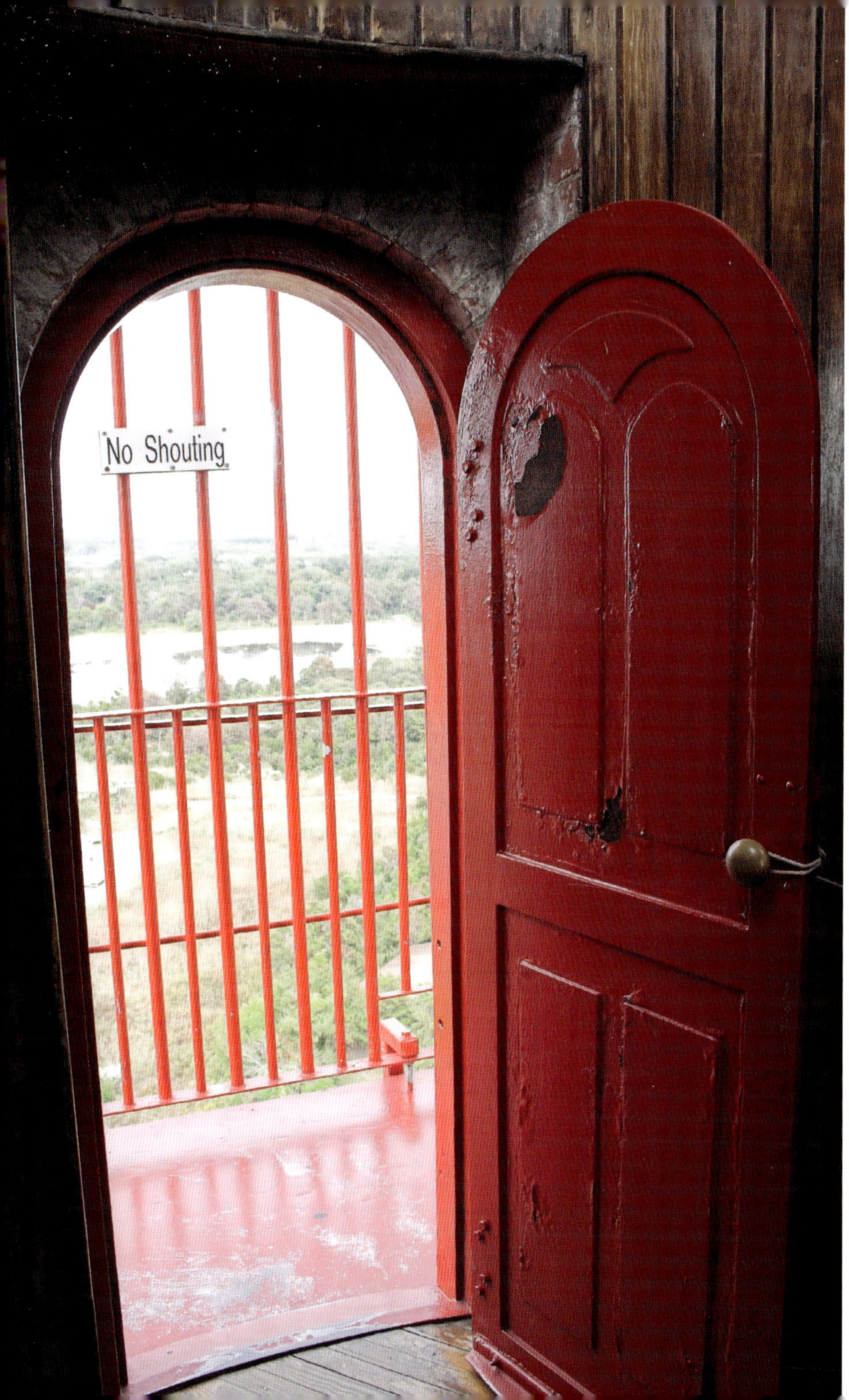
No Shouting

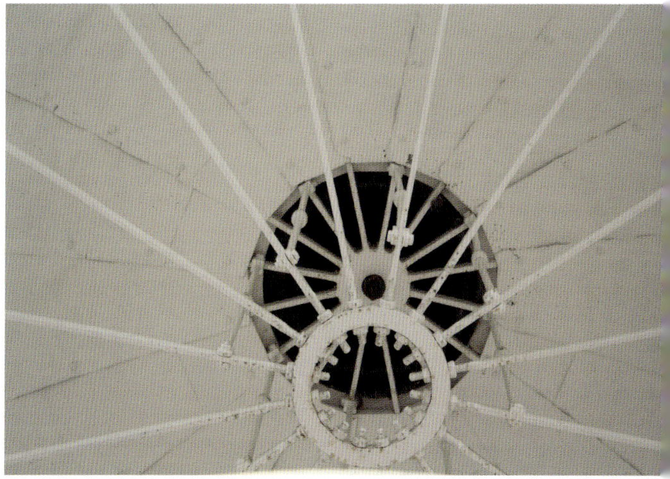

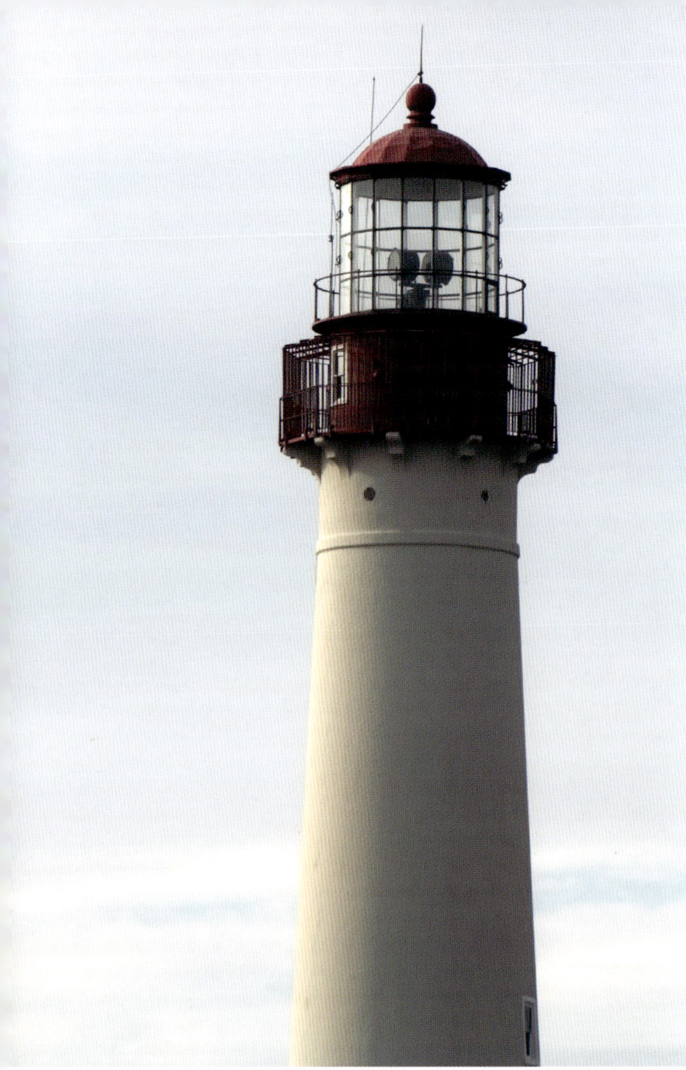

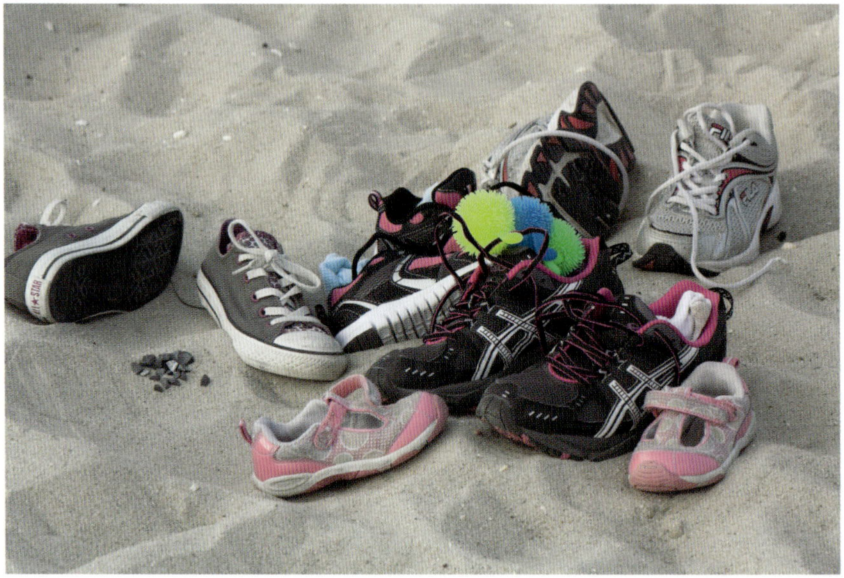

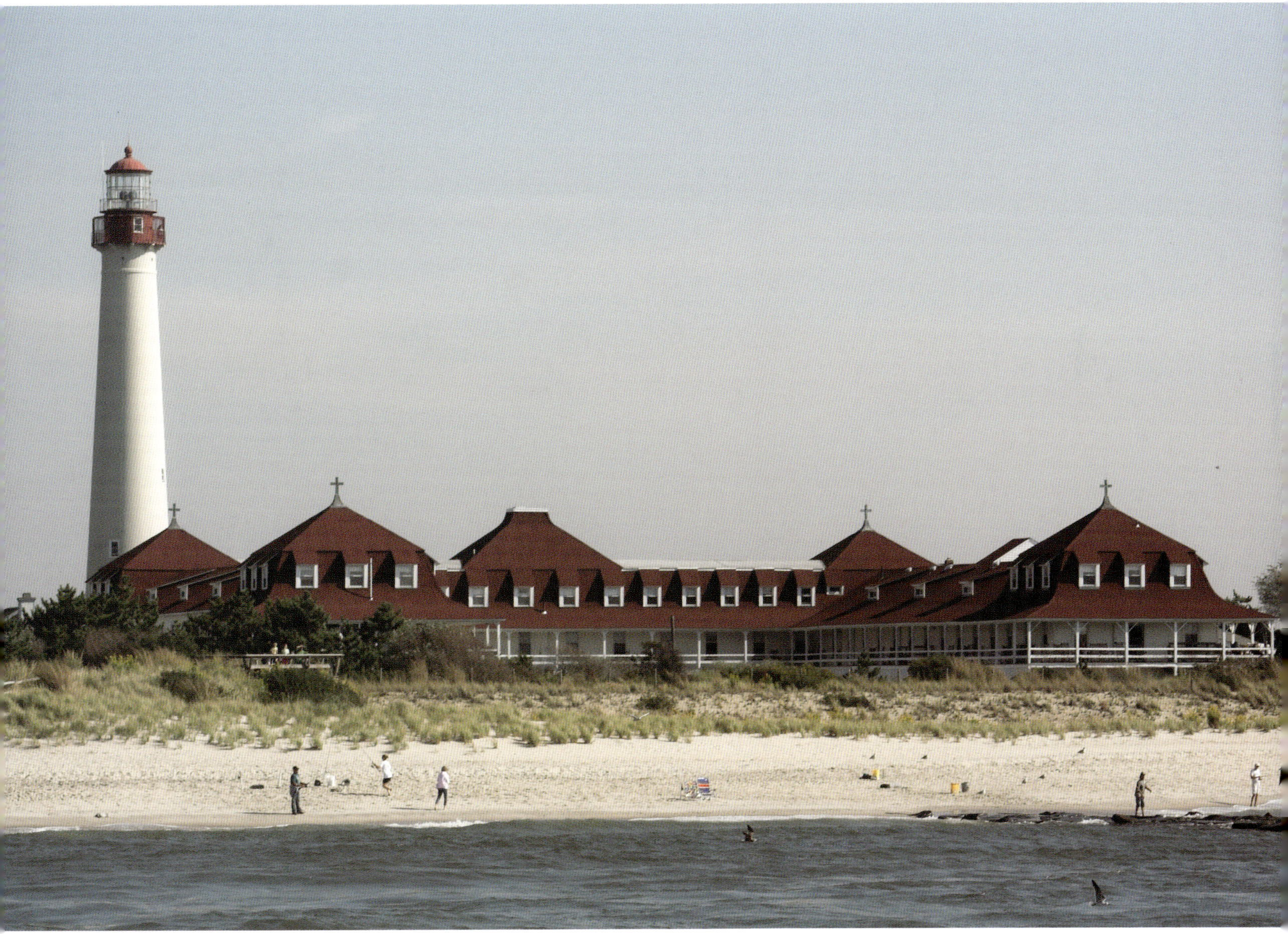

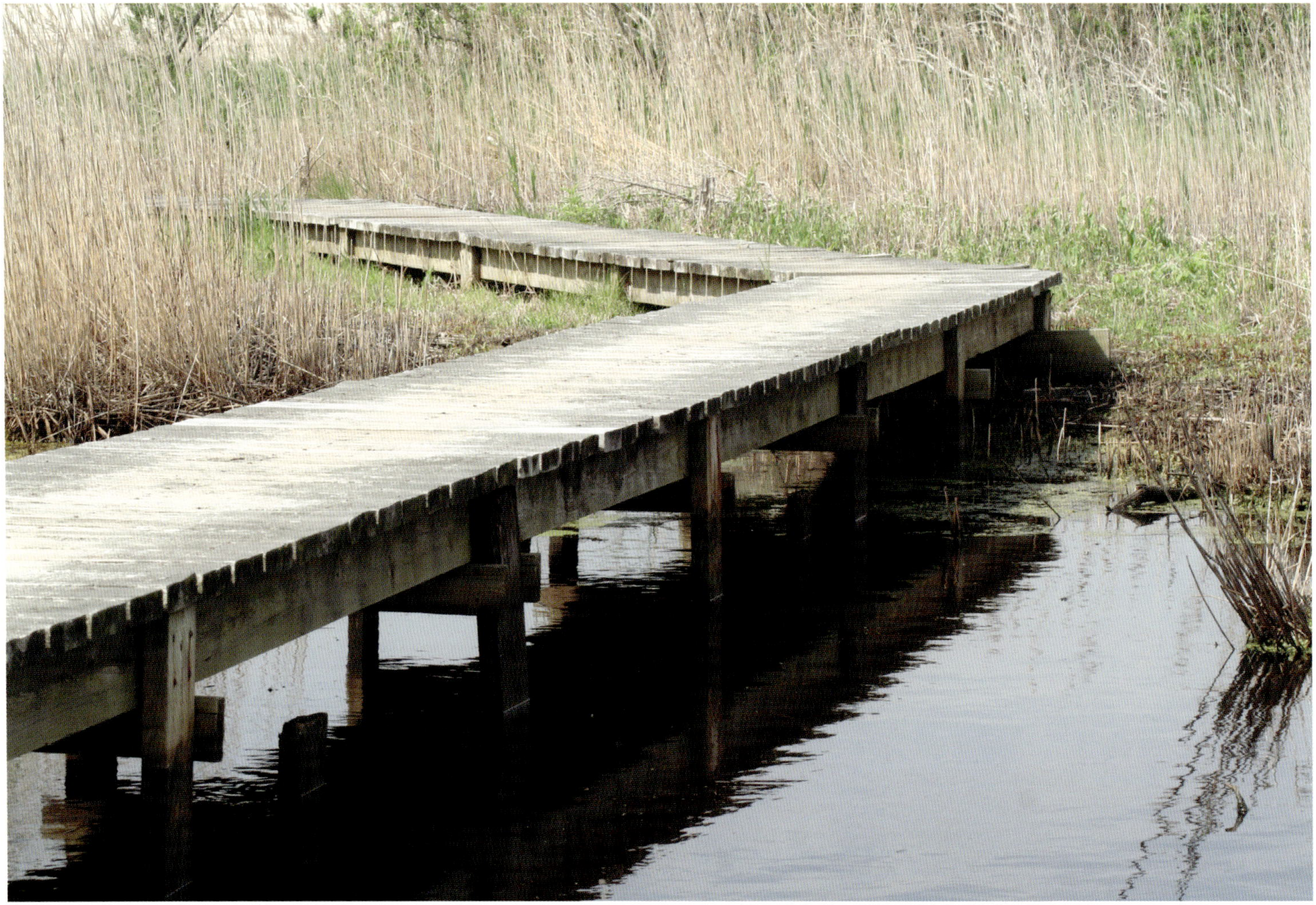

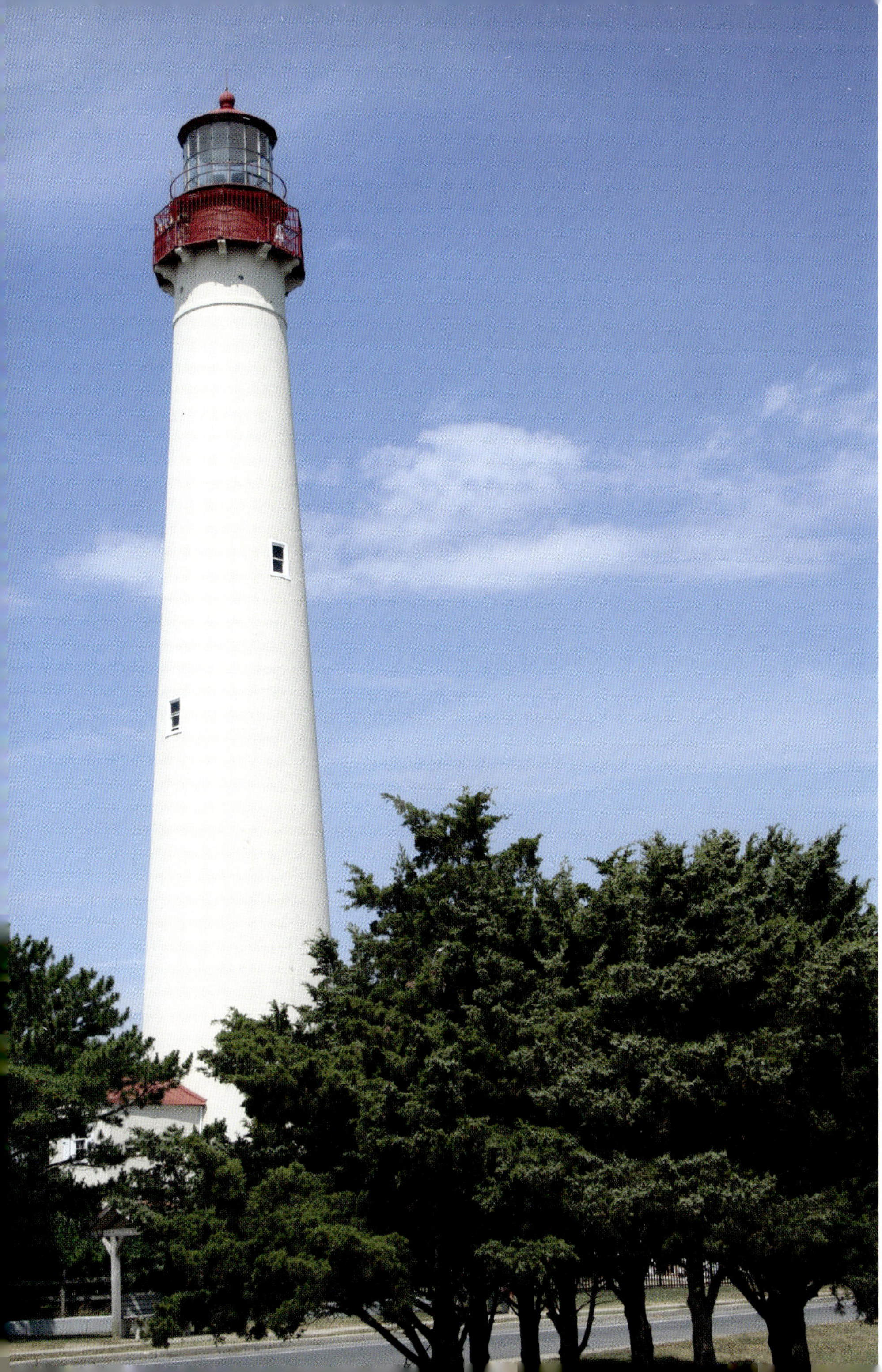

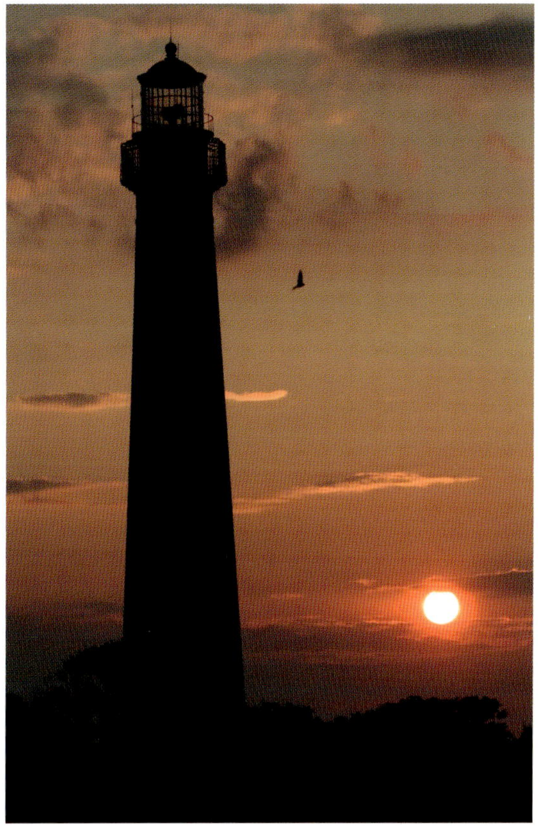

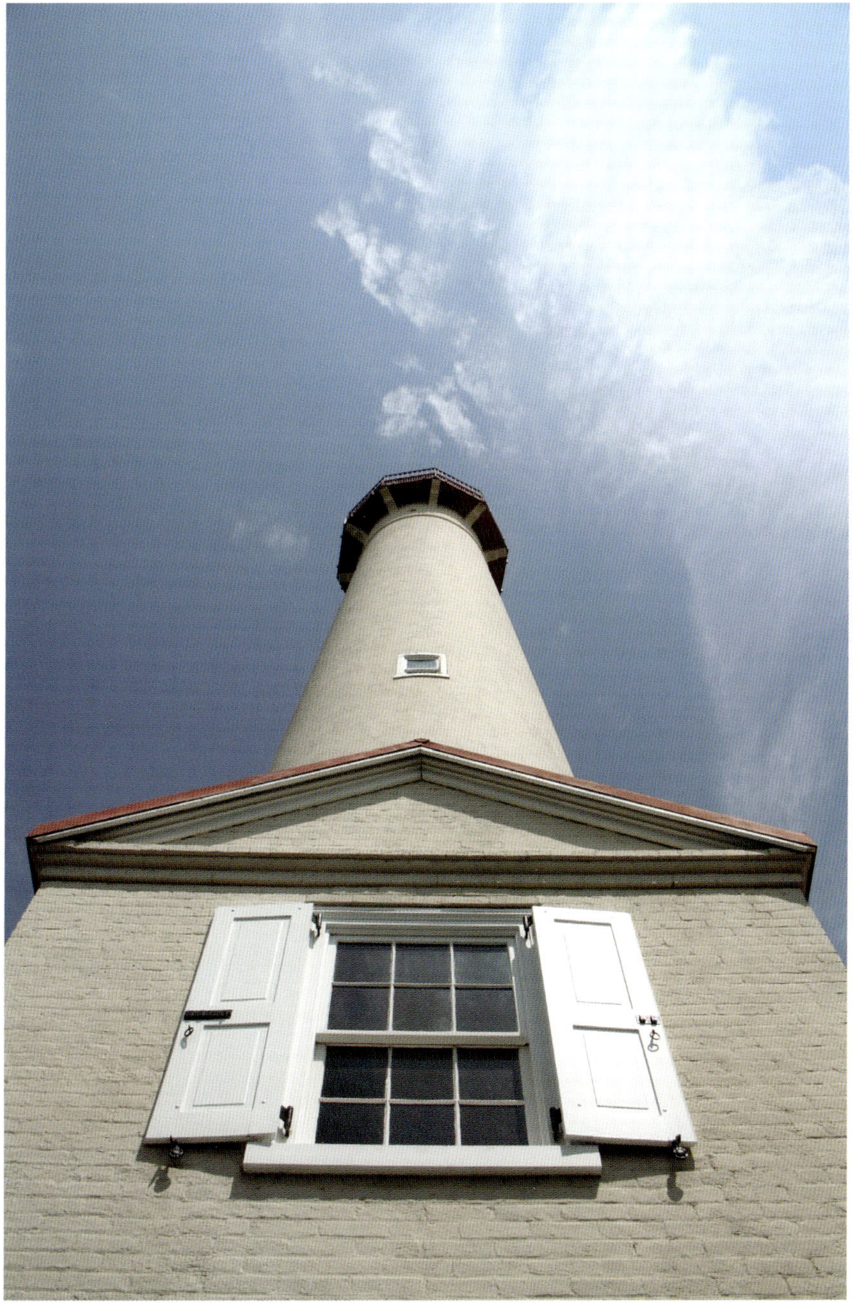

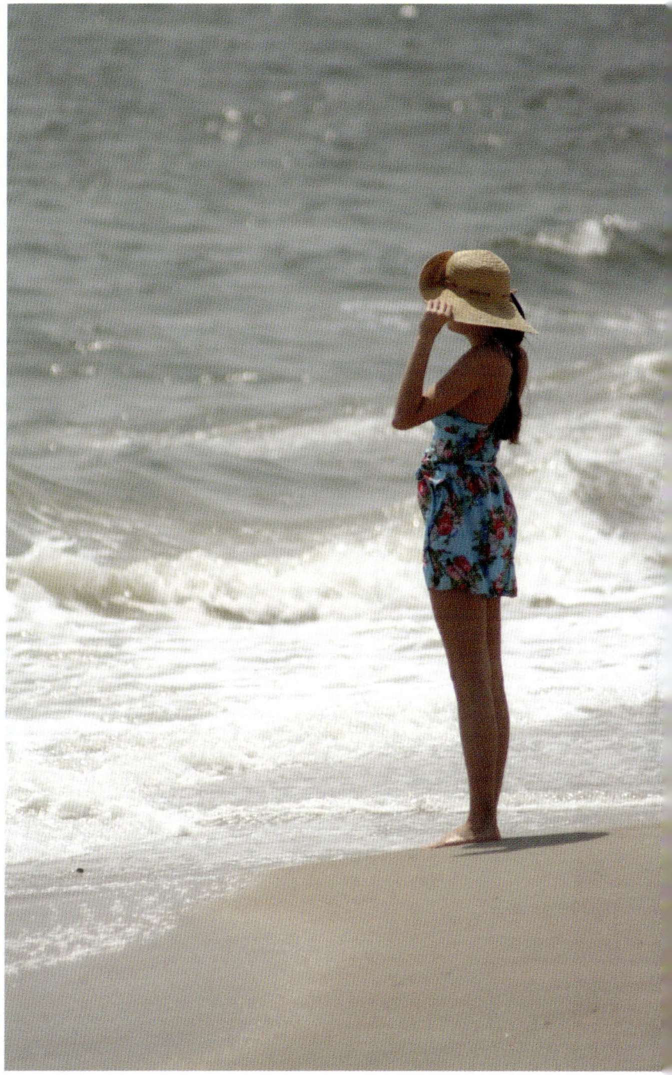

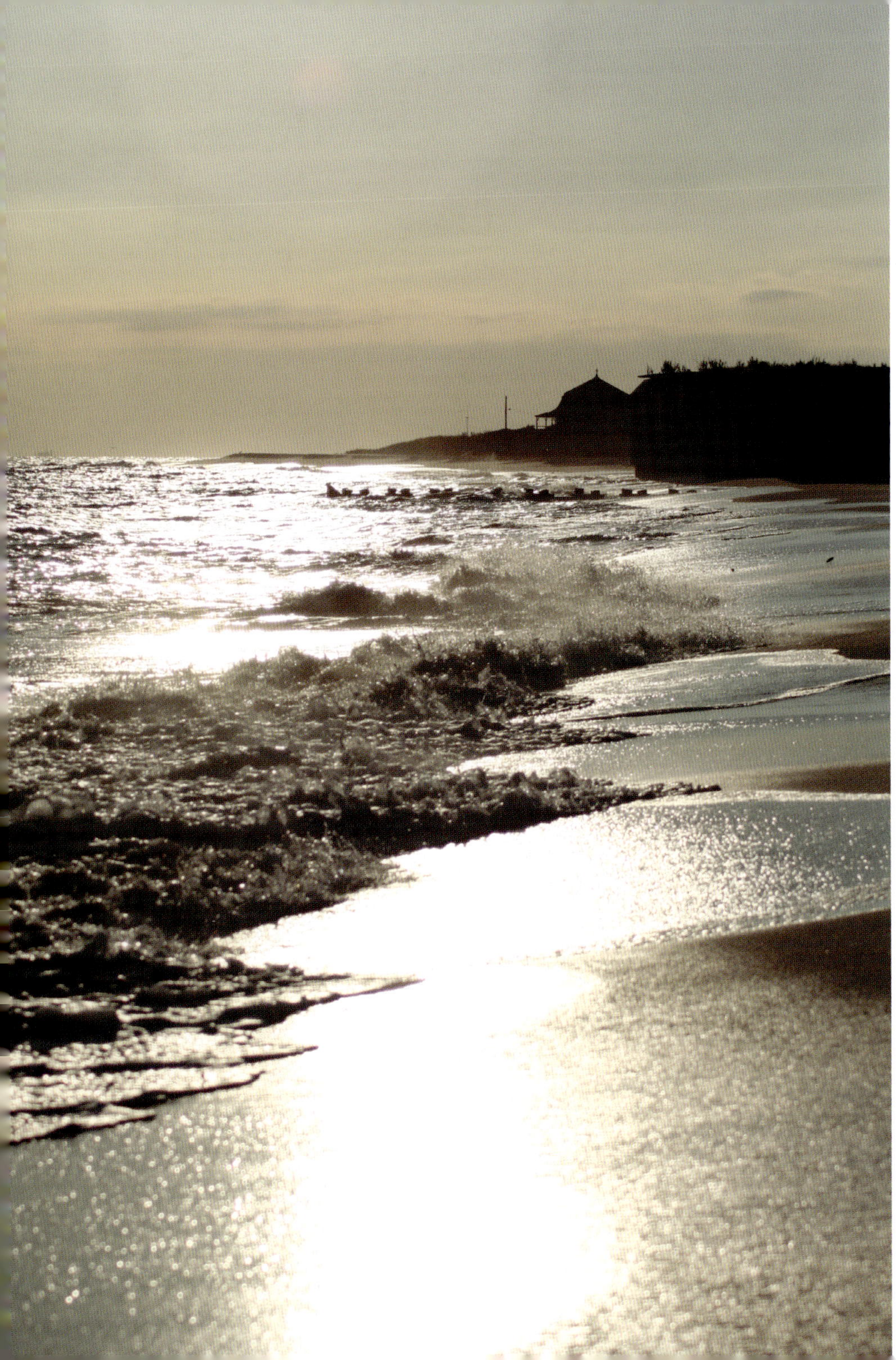

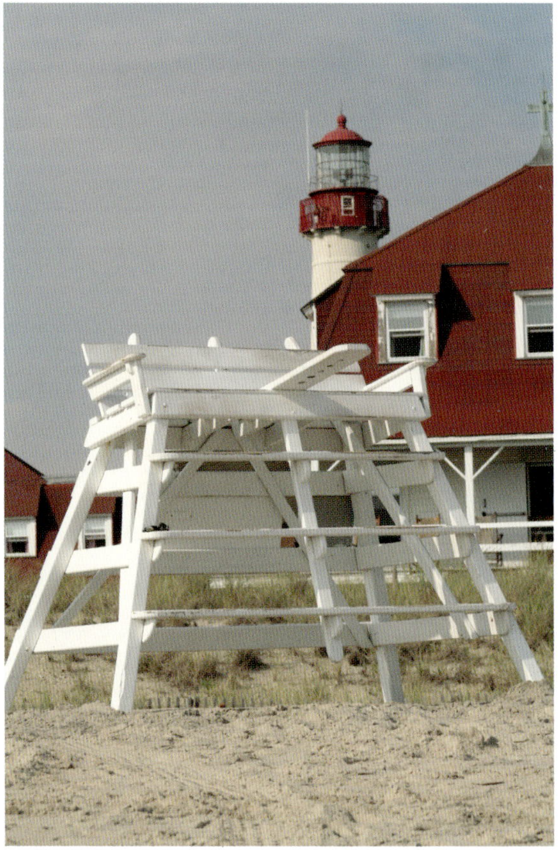

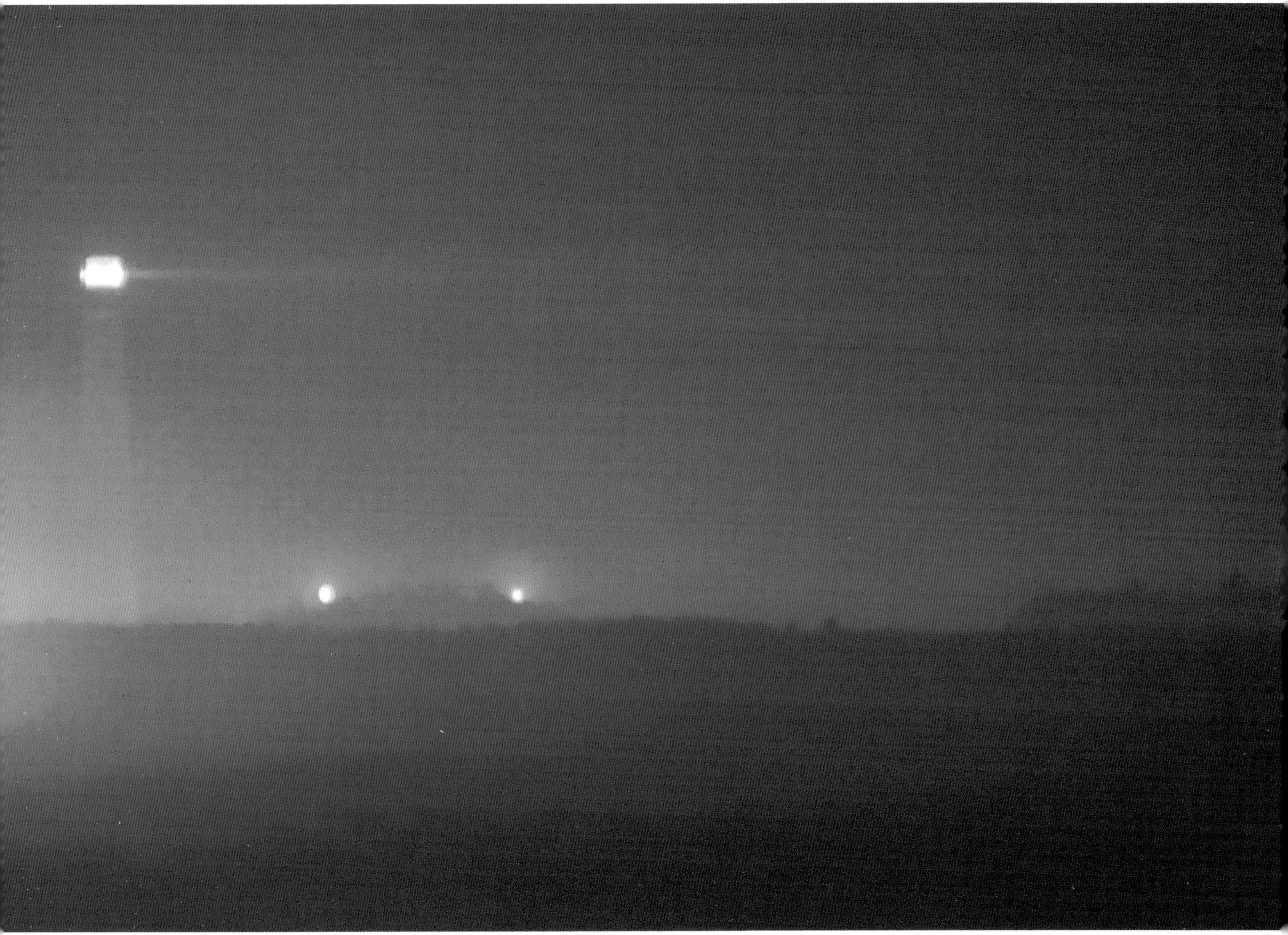

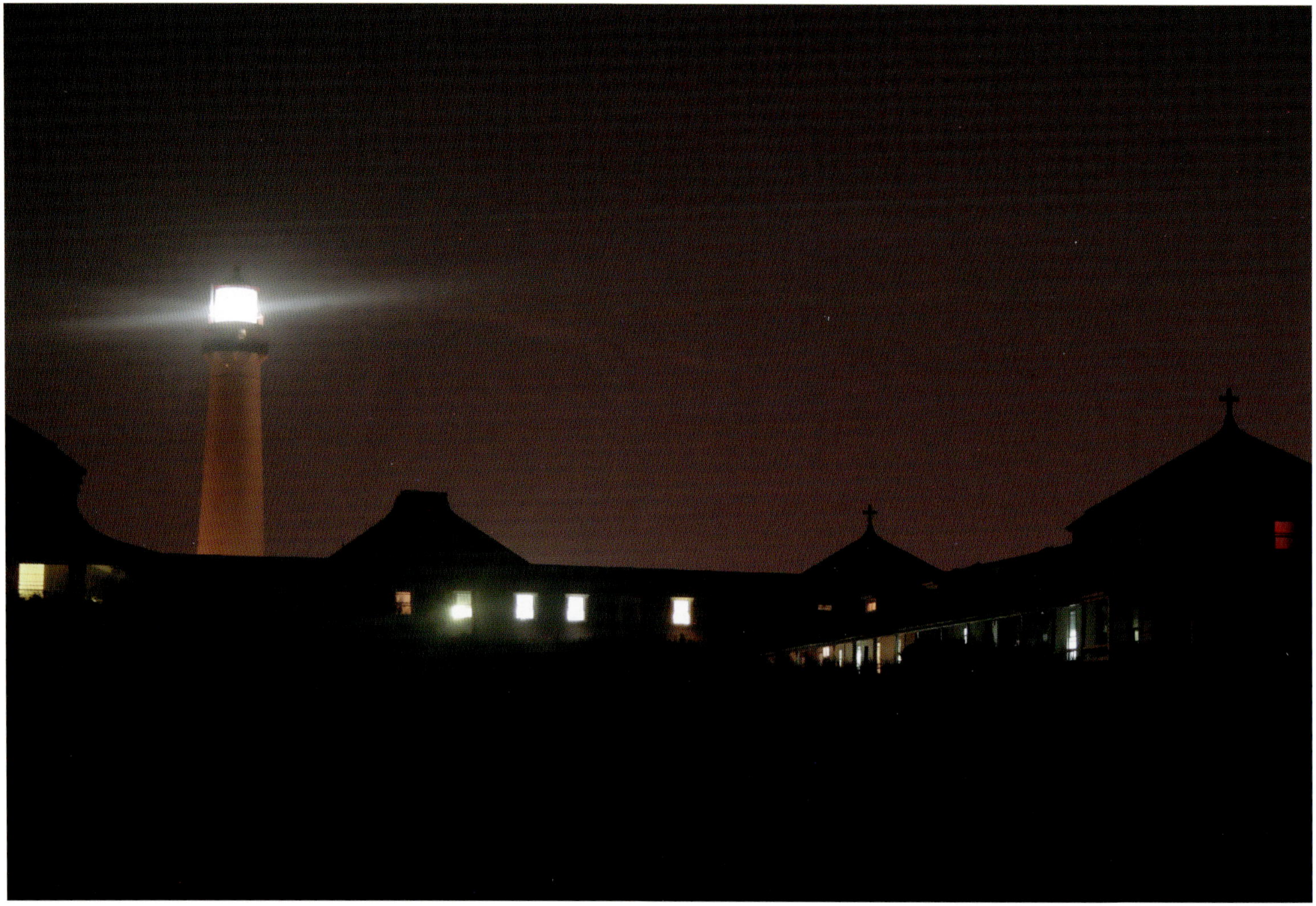

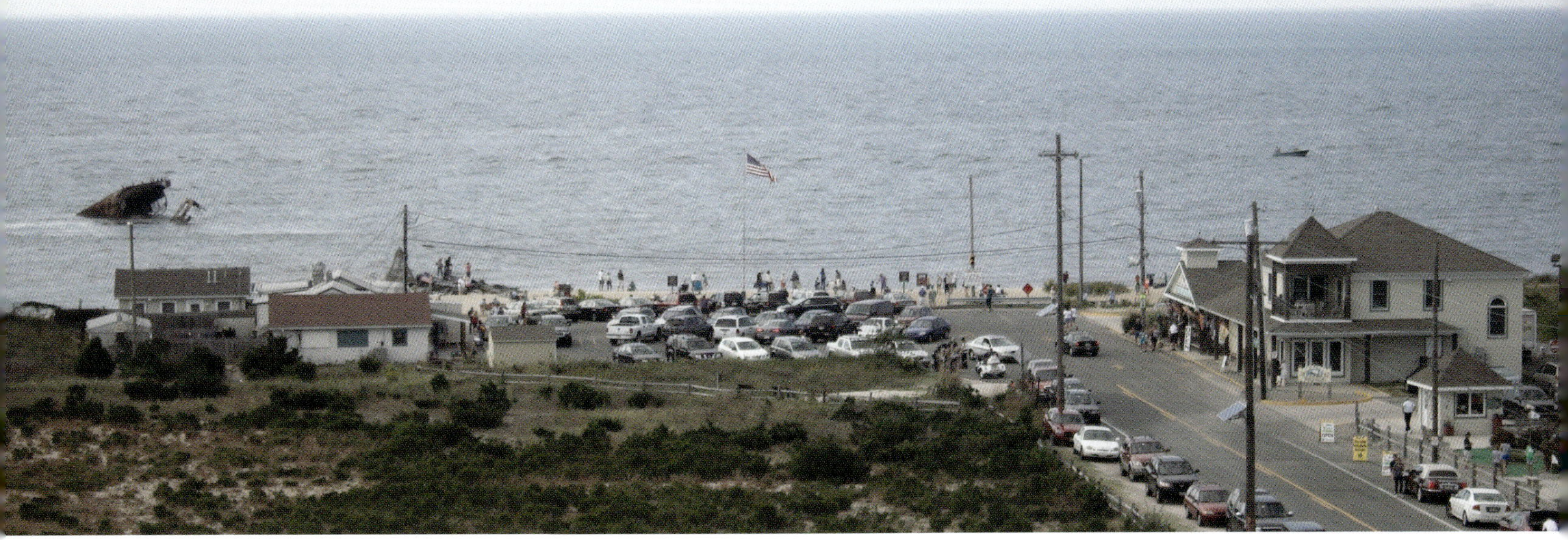

## Sunset Beach

Sunset Beach is home to gift shops, a World War II-era fire control tower that was once part of the network that protected the shipping lanes up the Delaware Bay, the shipwrecked remains of the concrete ship S.S. *Atlantus* (yes, you read correctly, a *concrete* ship), nightly flag-lowering ceremonies, and, of course, spectacular sunsets. Visitors enjoy scouring the pebble beach in search of the legendary Cape May diamonds, clear quartz crystals that when polished, cut, and set make for respectable imposters for real diamonds.

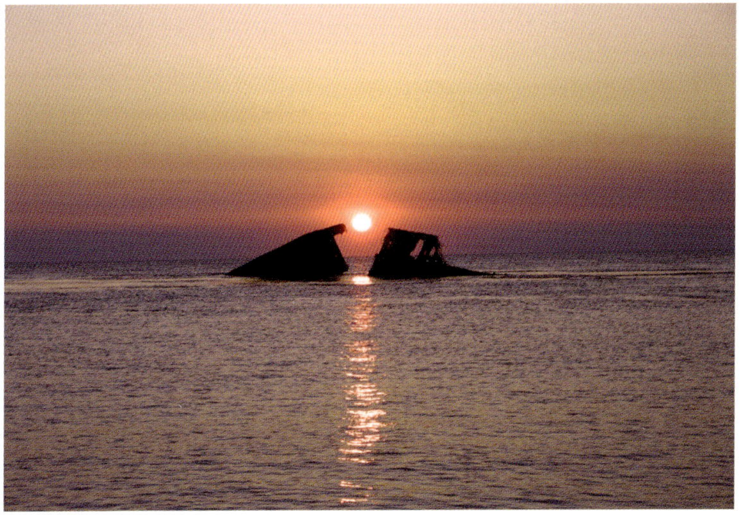

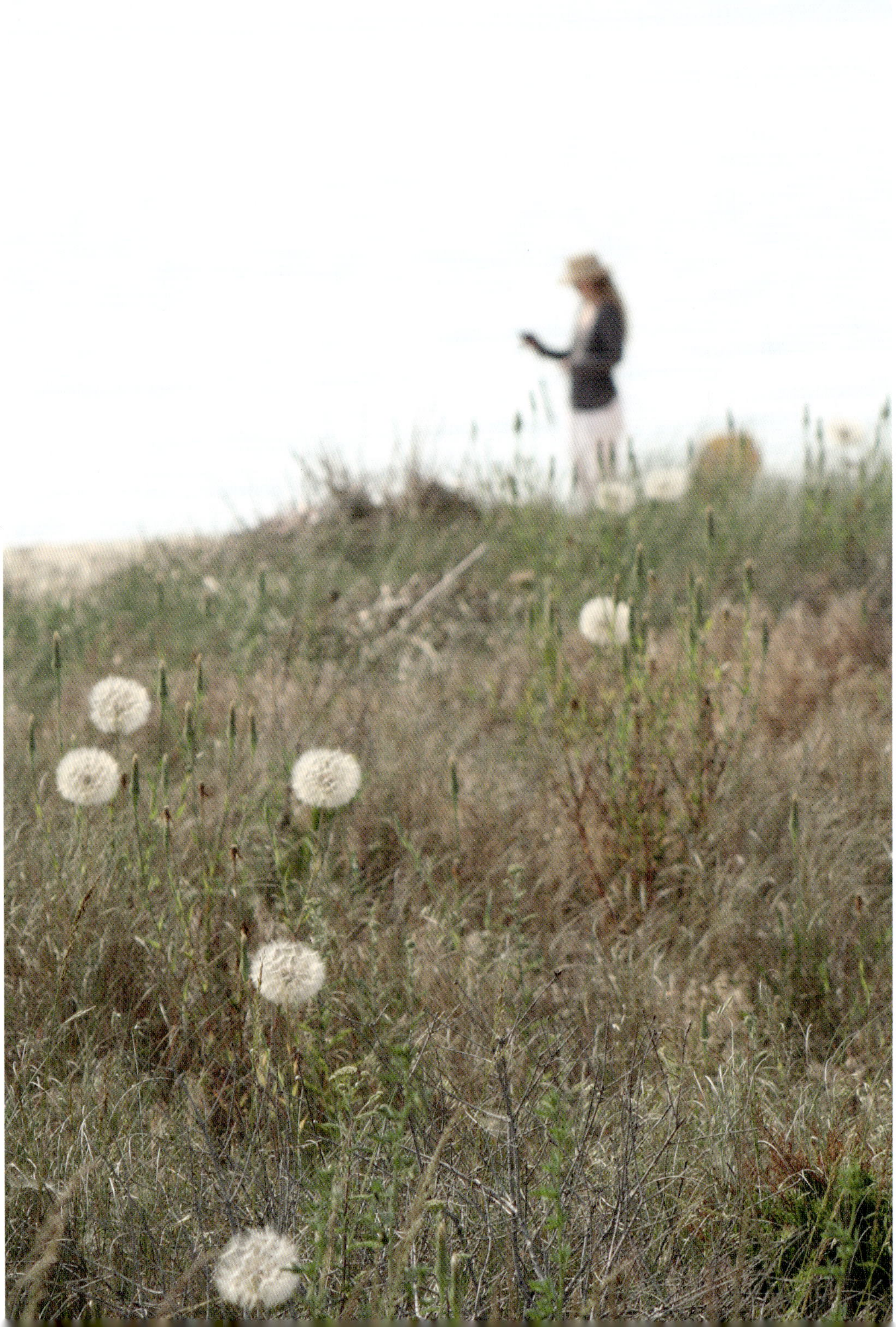

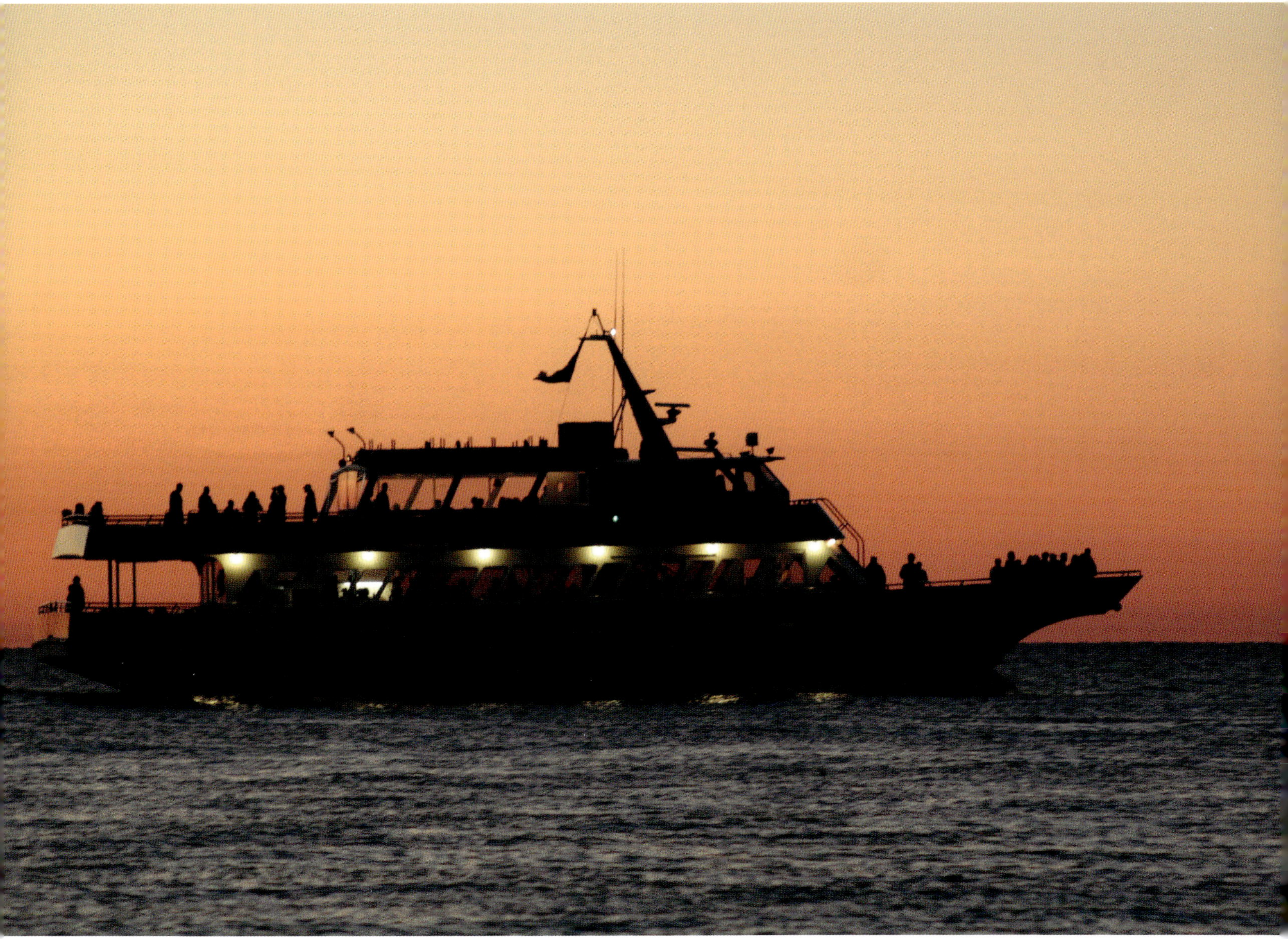

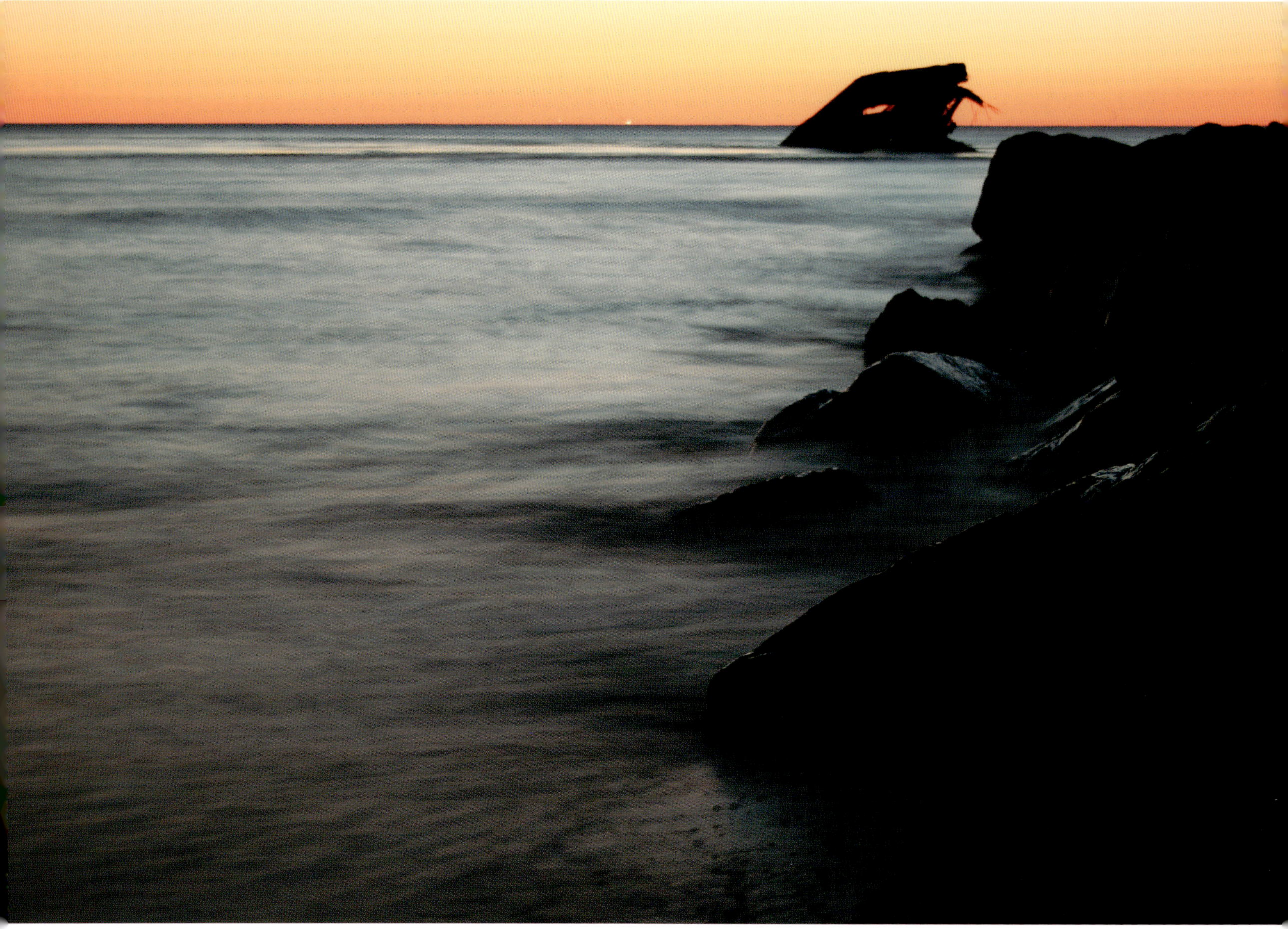

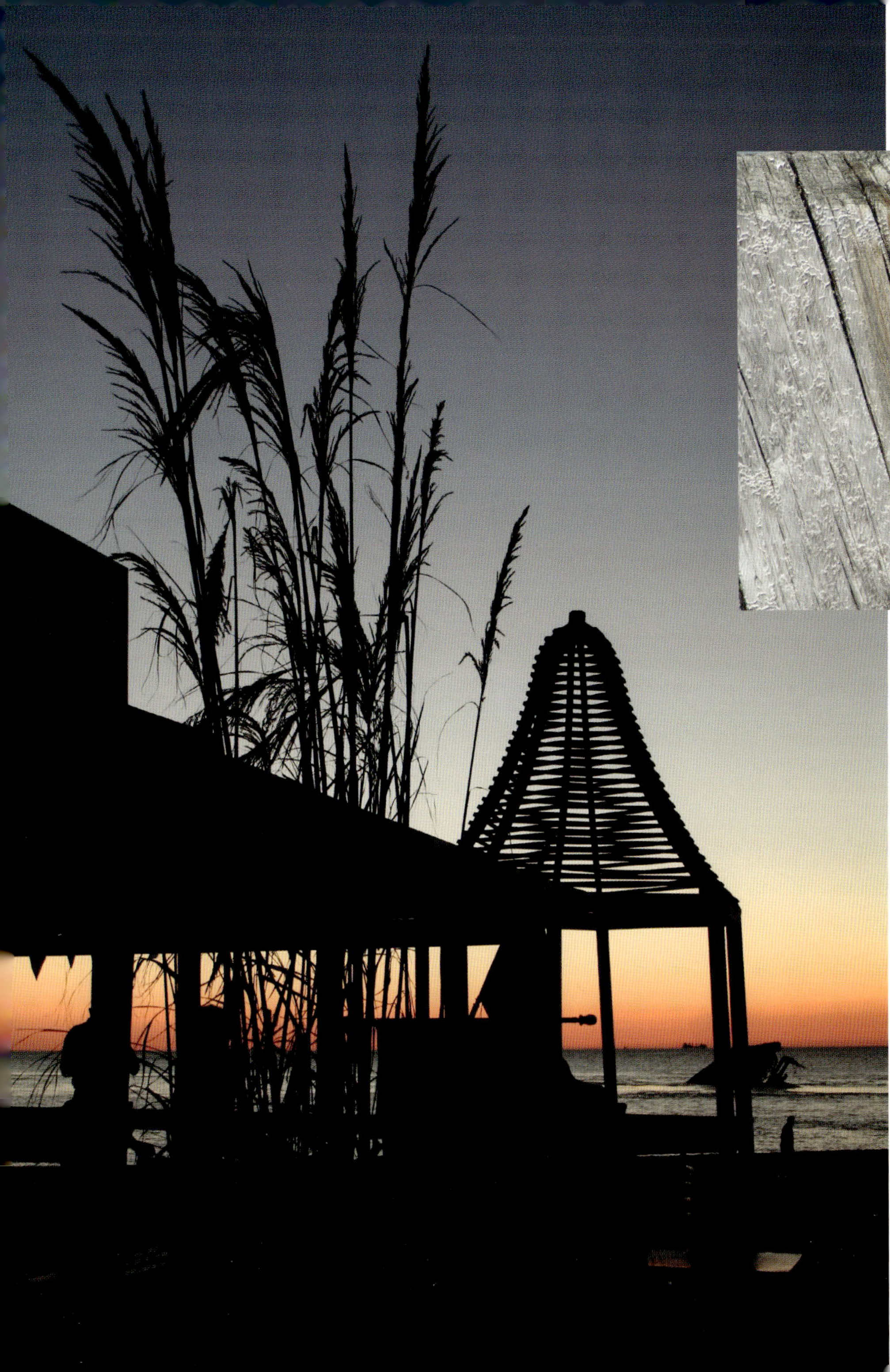
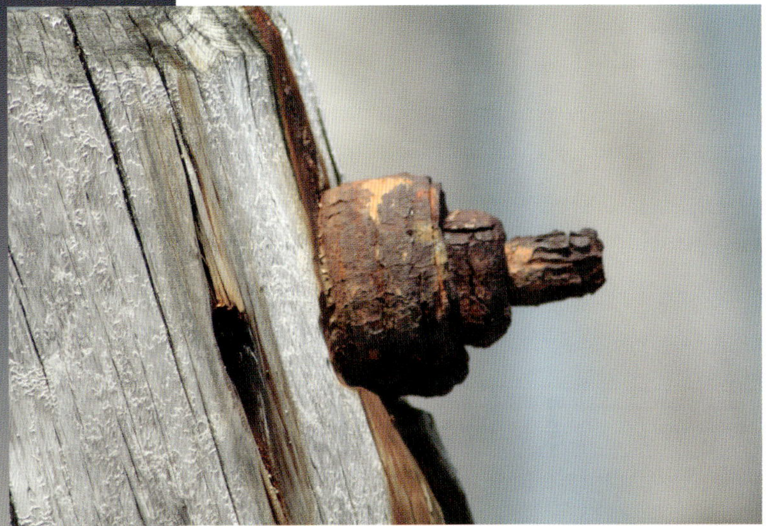

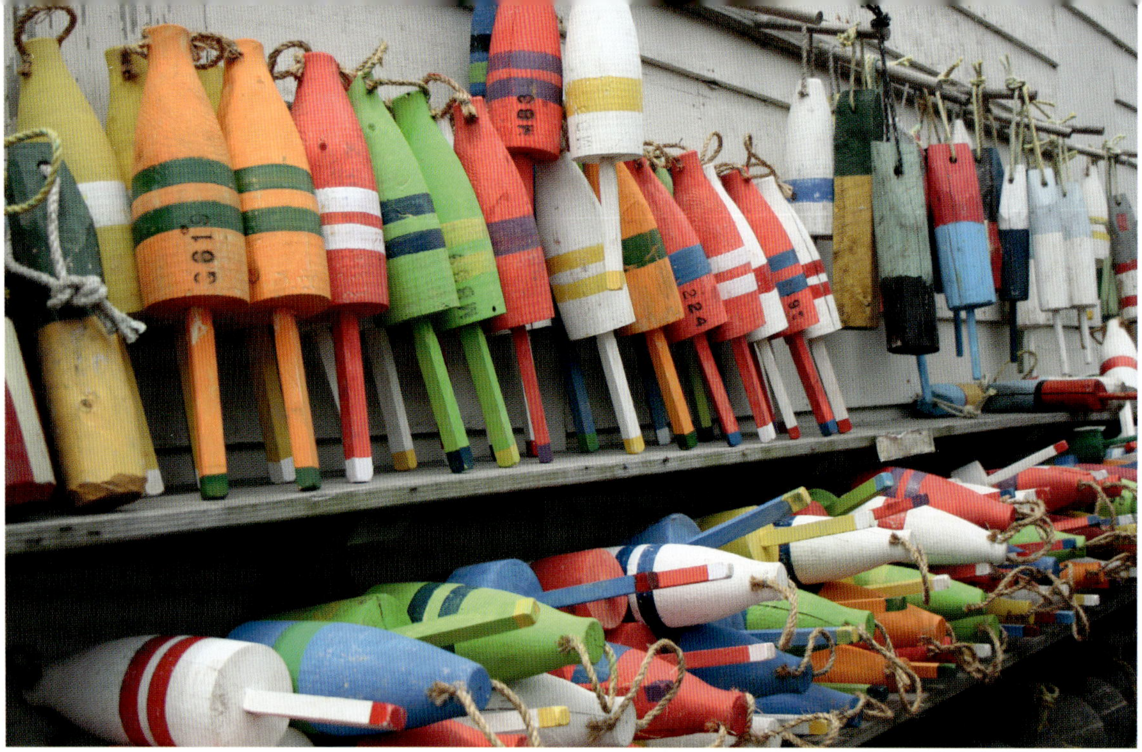

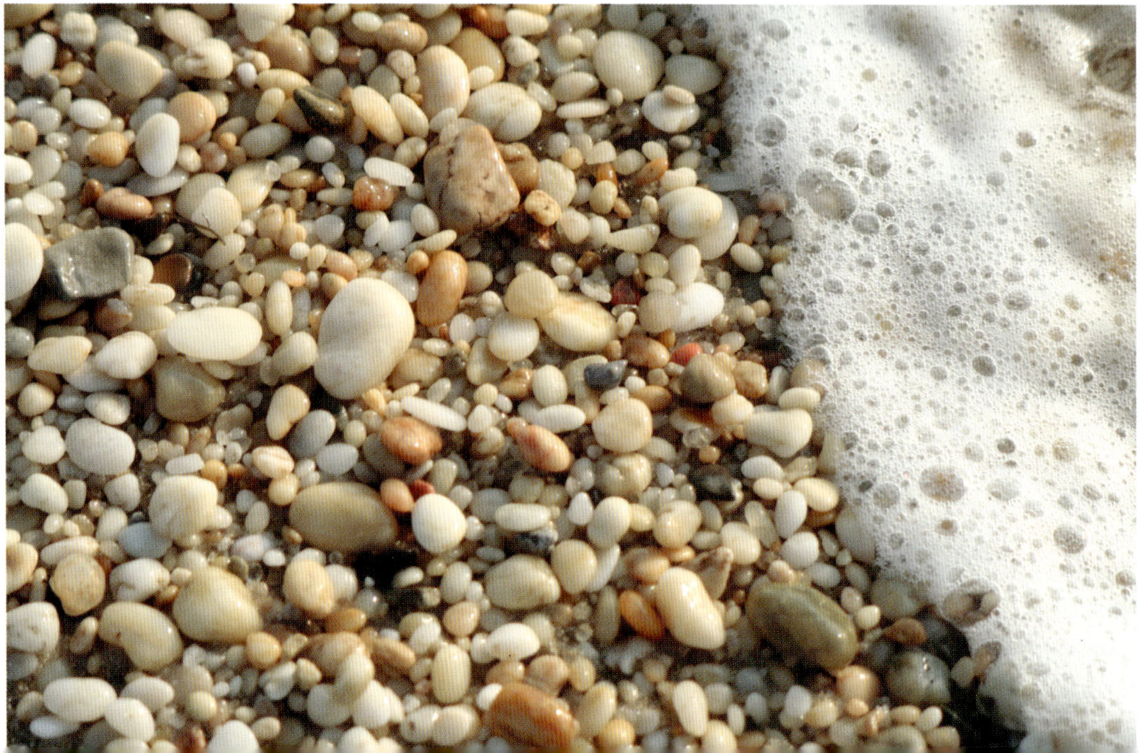

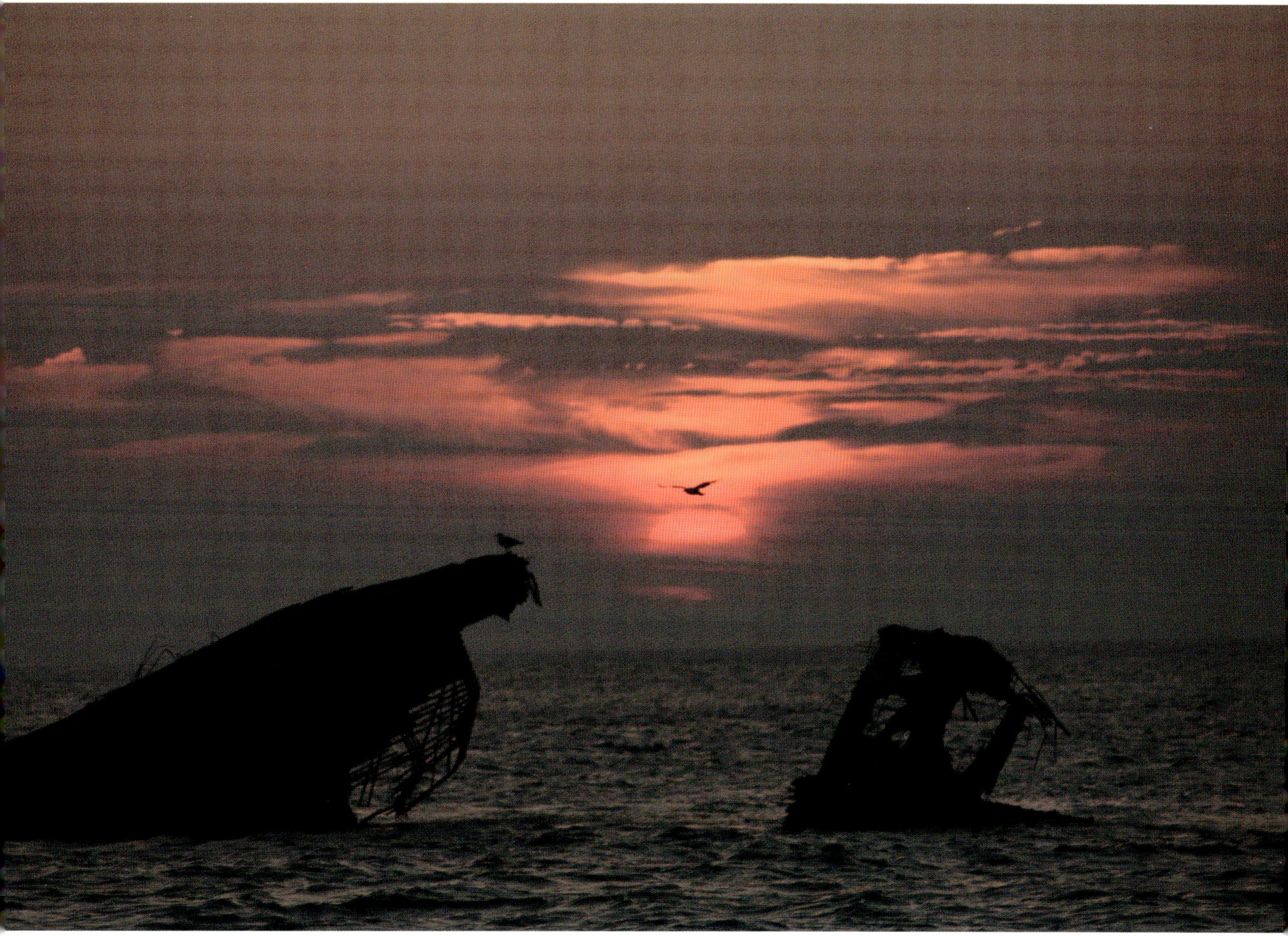

# Higbee Beach

I am going to share with you one of the rarest gems of the Jersey Shore, but you must be sworn to secrecy and promise that you won't let the great masses in on our secret. If you have ever wondered what Cape May looked like when Captain Mey first explored its shores, Higbee Beach is probably the closest we will ever come to seeing the view that greeted the good captain. As part of a state Wildlife Management Area, Higbee is one of the last truly wild expanses of shoreline in this area. High dunes and sun-bleached, twisted driftwood dominates the landscape. If you are fortunate enough to visit the beach on a quiet day and find that you have the beach to yourself, you could easily begin to imagine that you are happily lost on a deserted island.

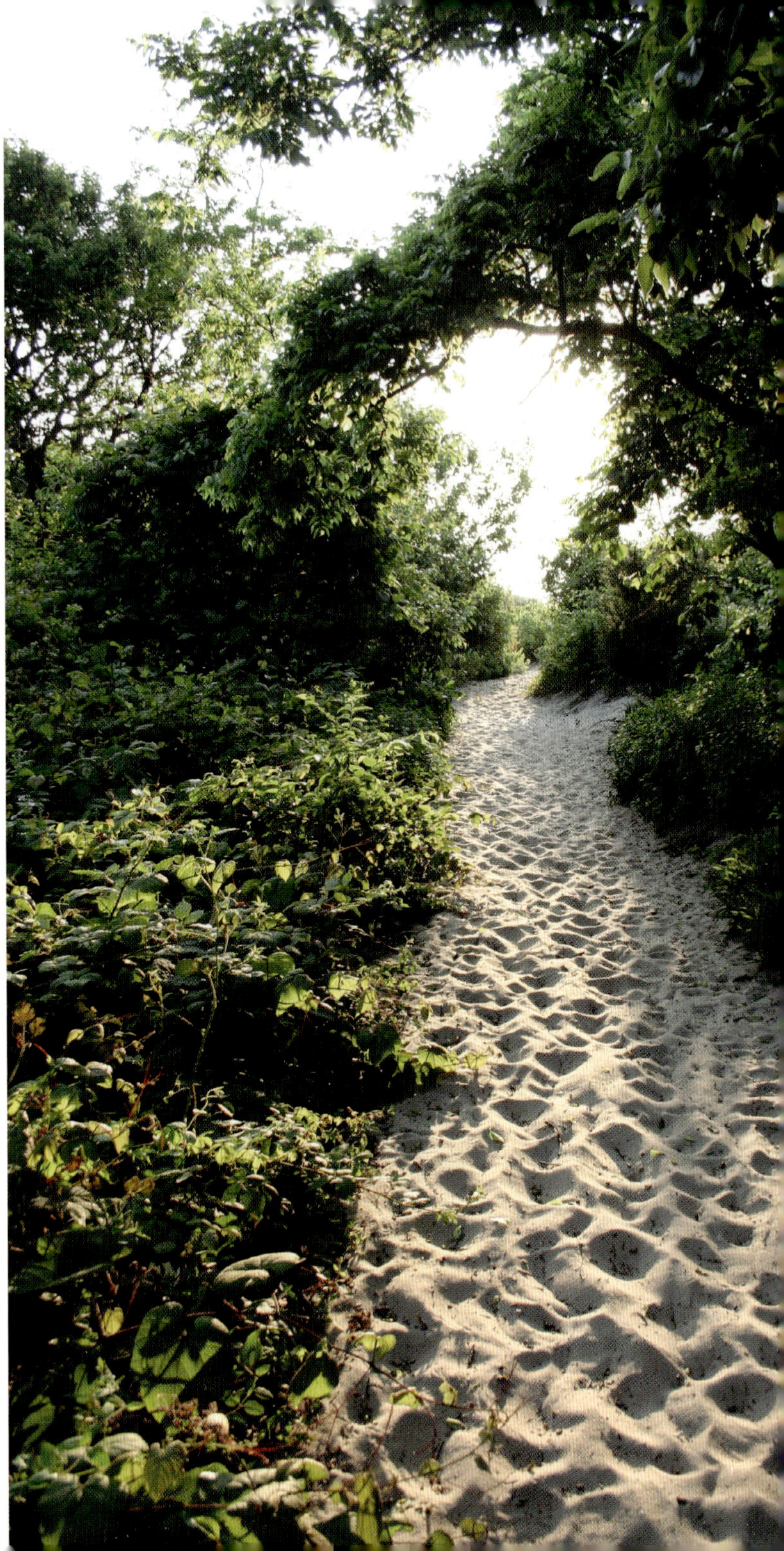

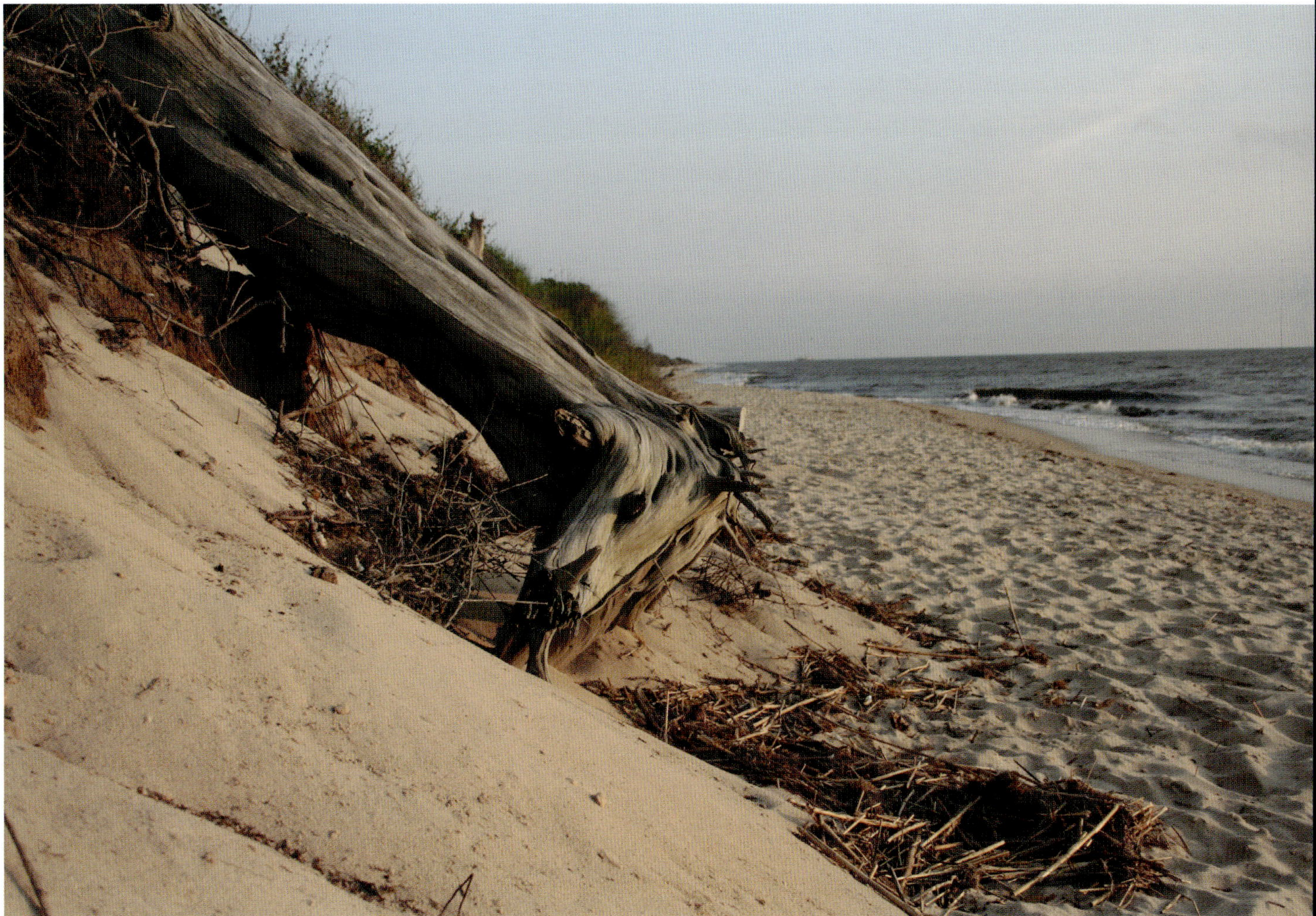

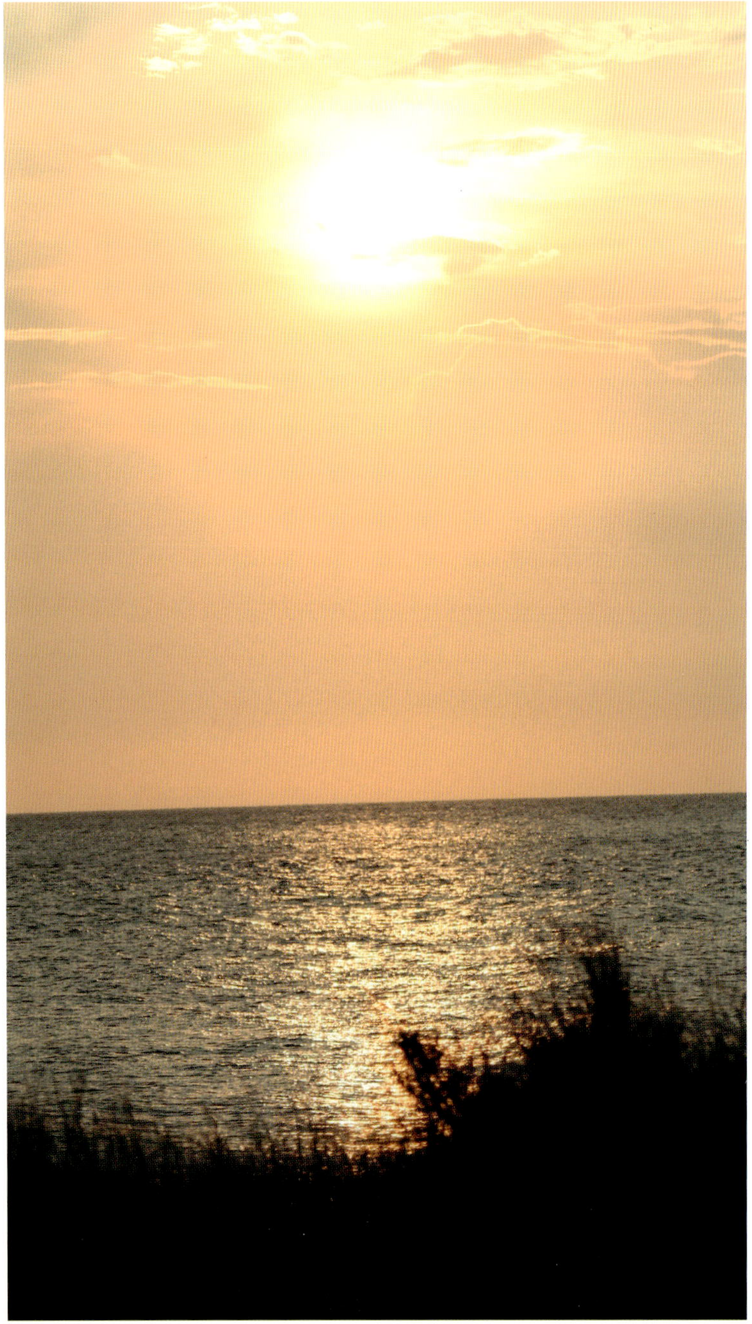

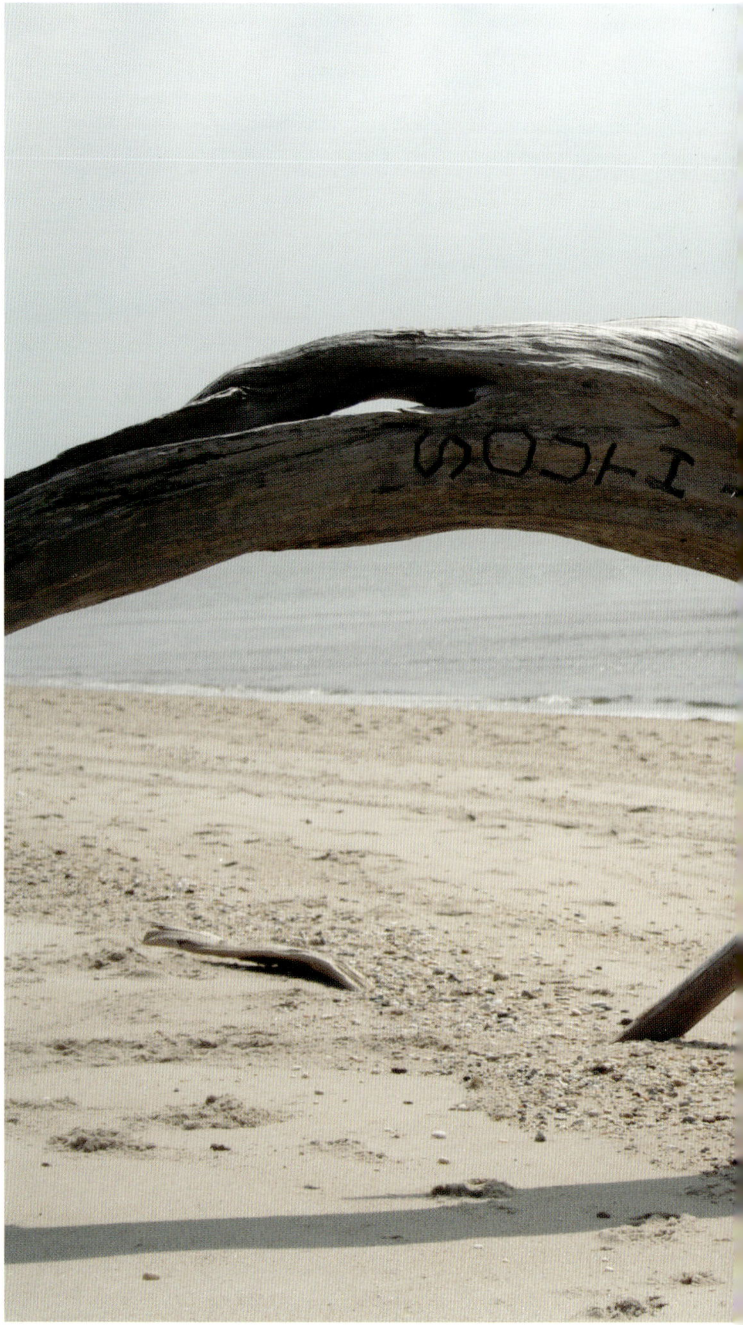

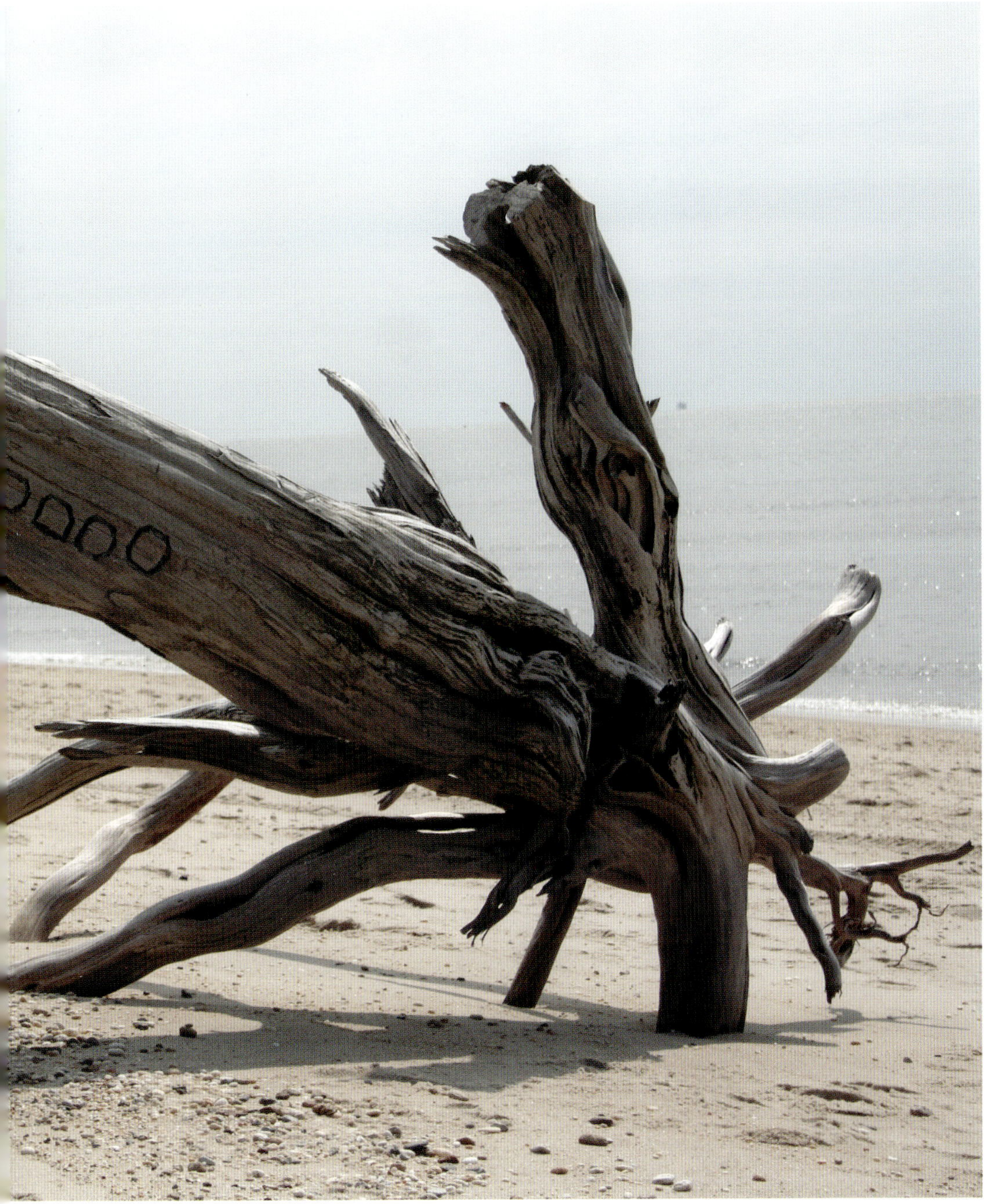

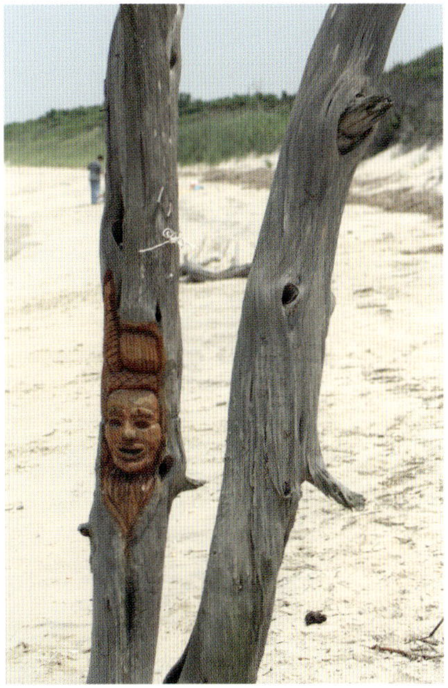

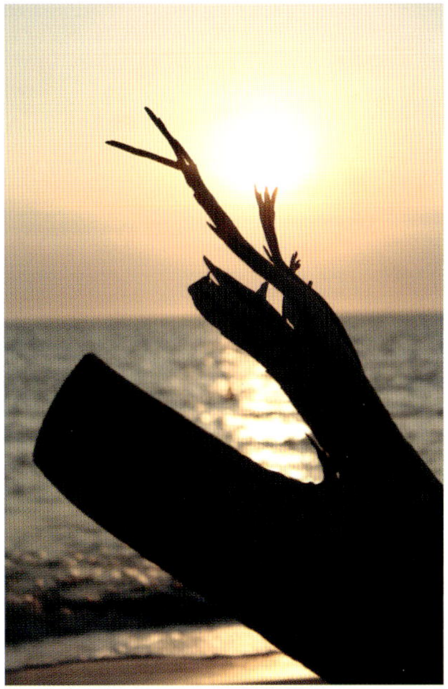

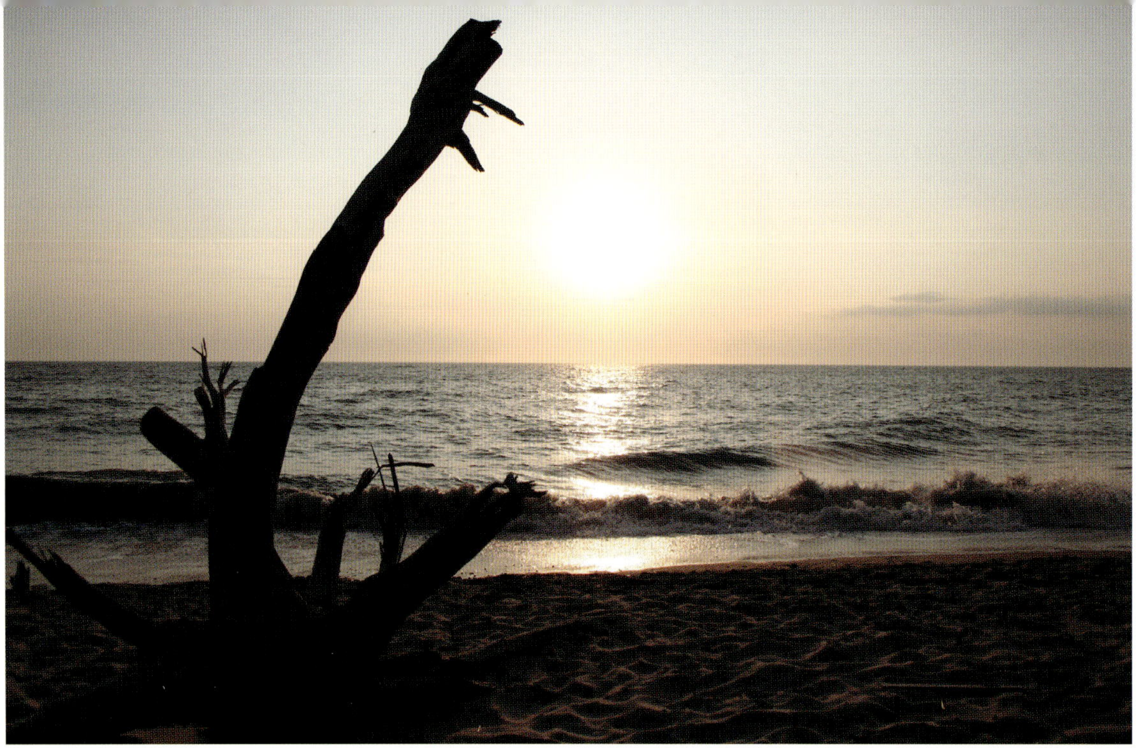

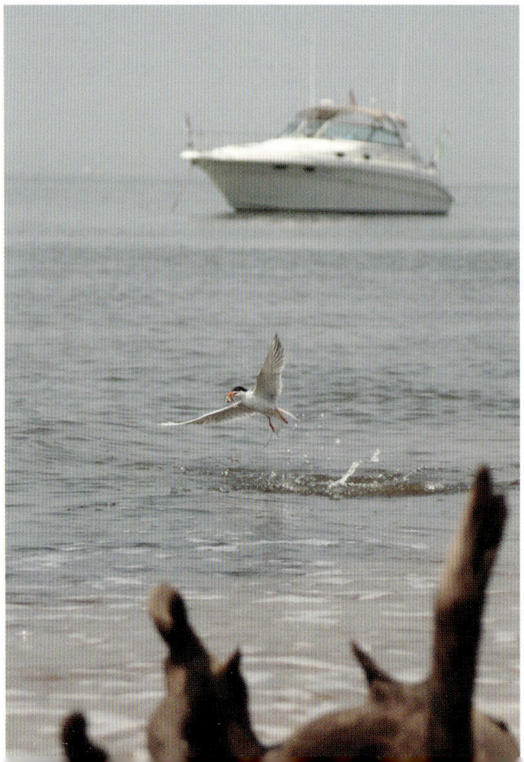

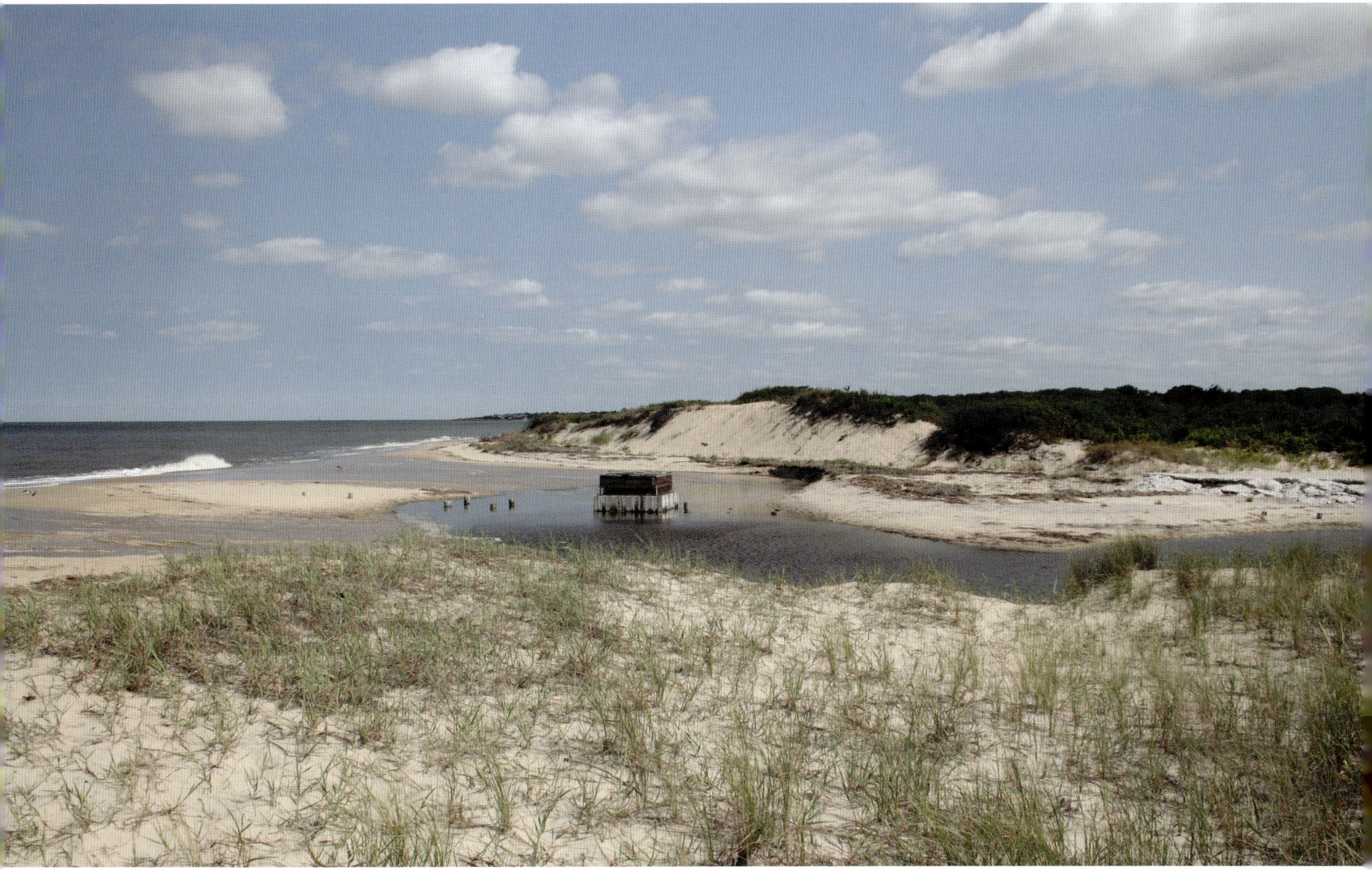

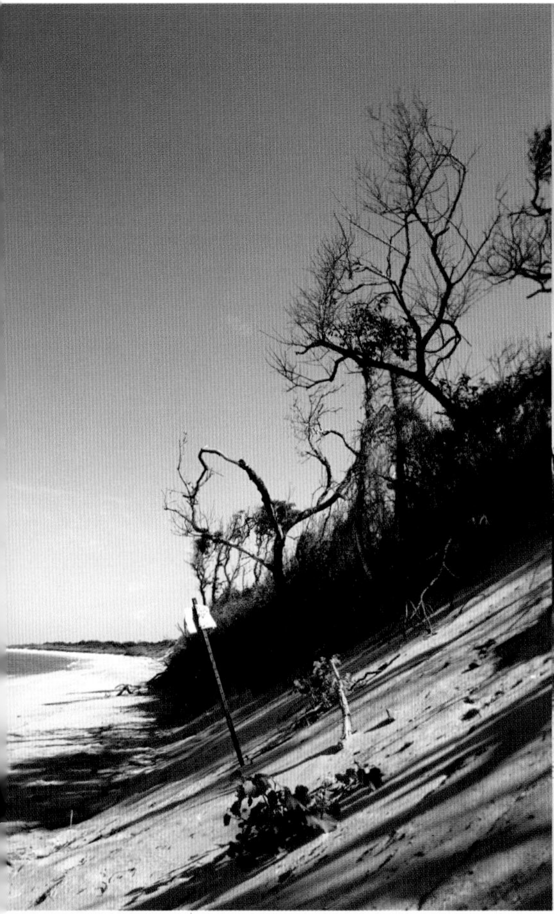

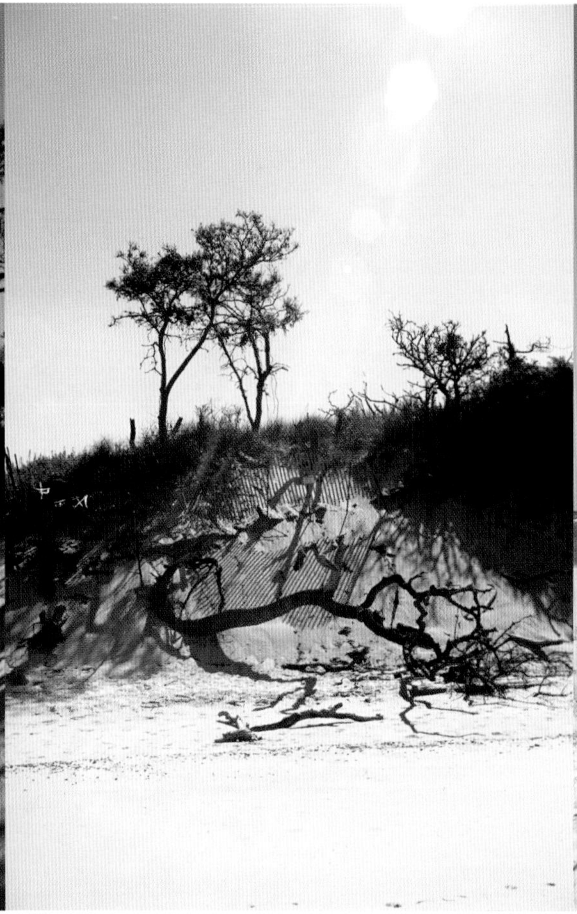

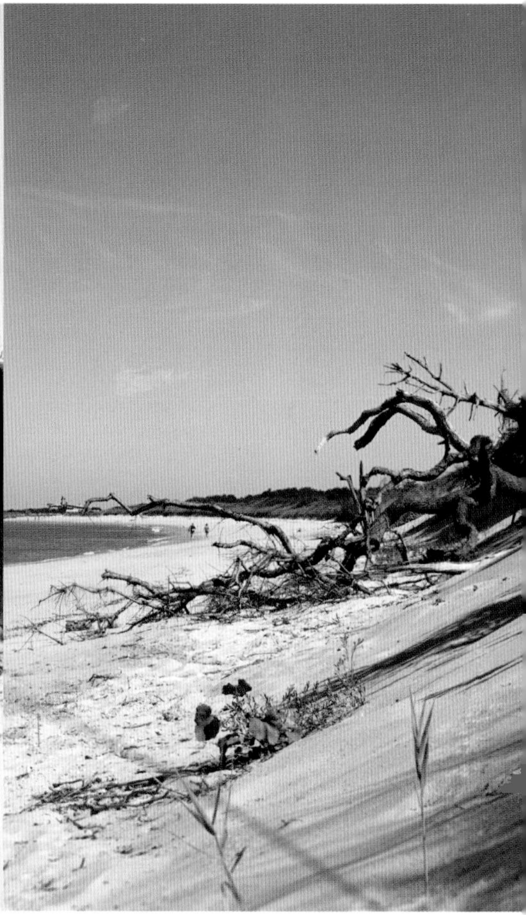

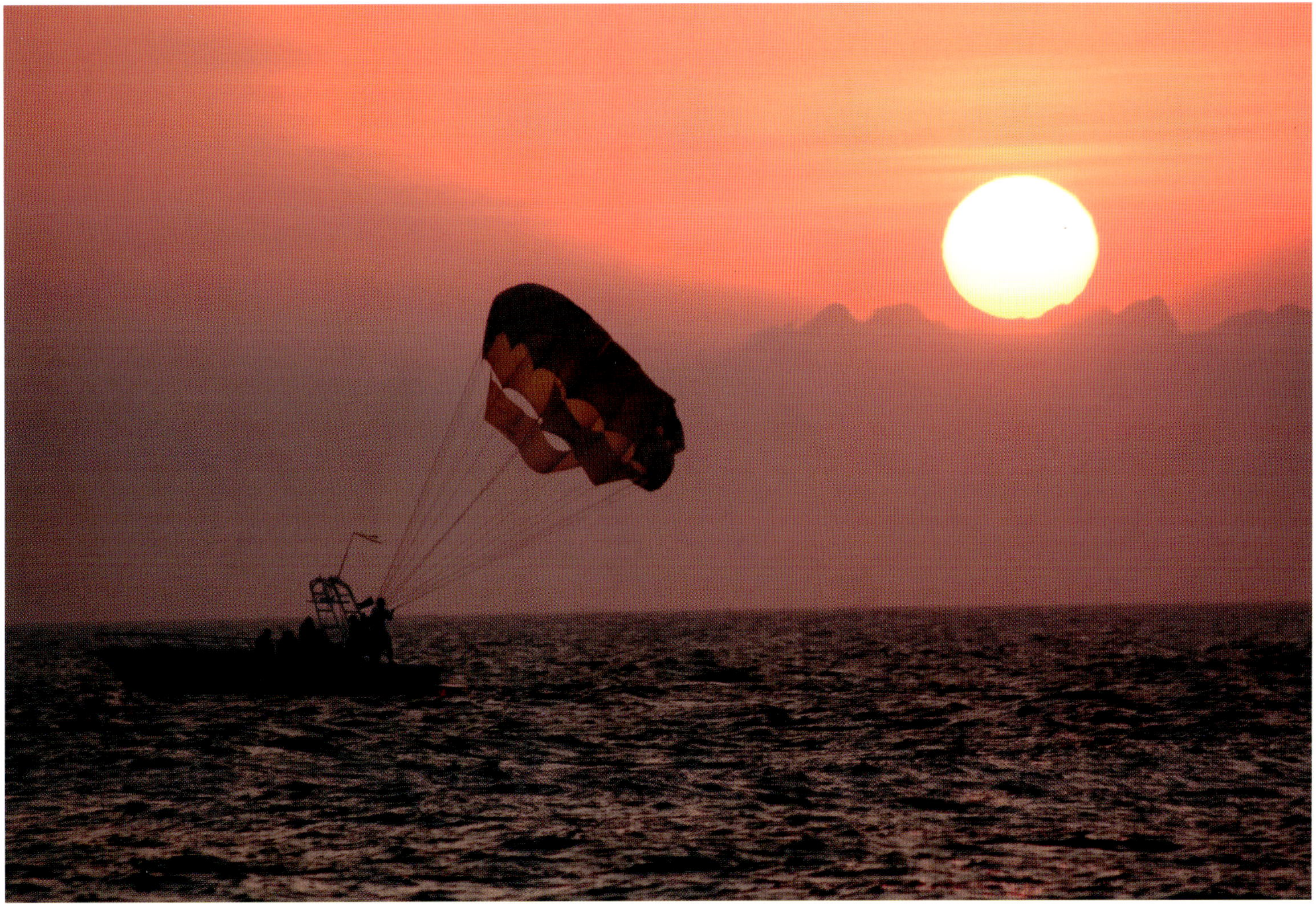

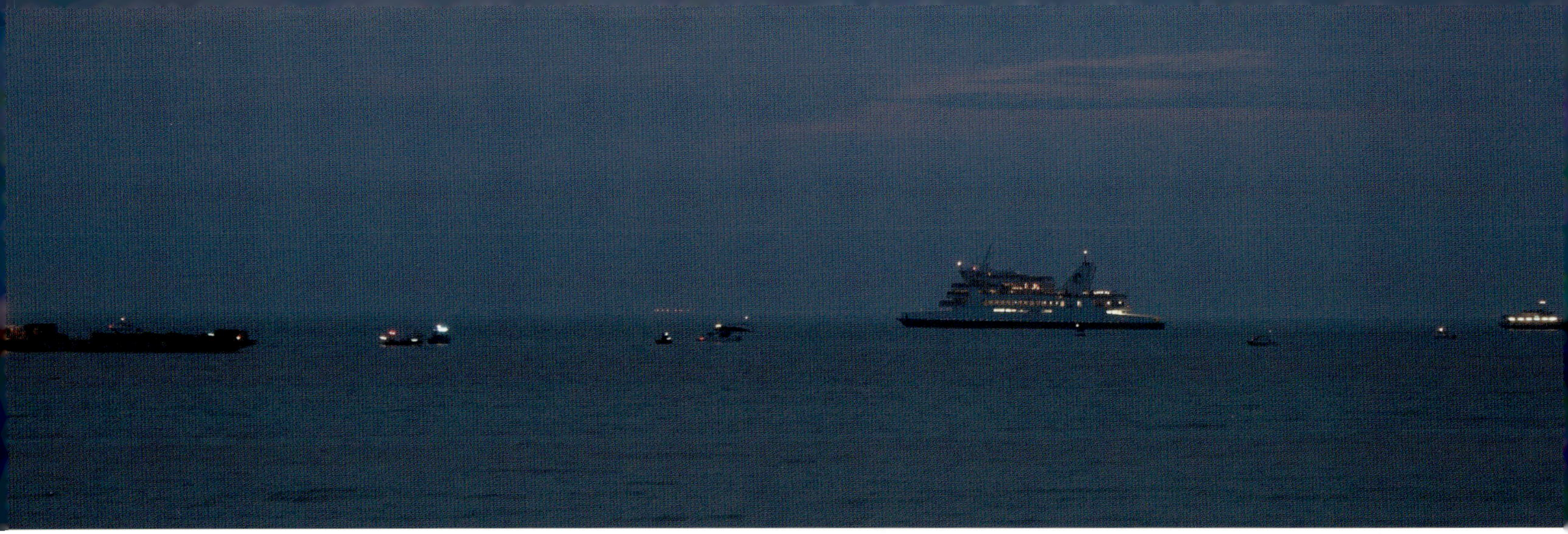

# The Bayside and Beyond

From the Cape May-Lewes Ferry landing near North Cape May, northward to old fishing villages turned into an eclectic mix of full-time residences and vacation cottages, the "quieter" side of the Cape May County peninsula is an important part of the Cape May experience for those who enjoy wandering a bit off the beaten path.

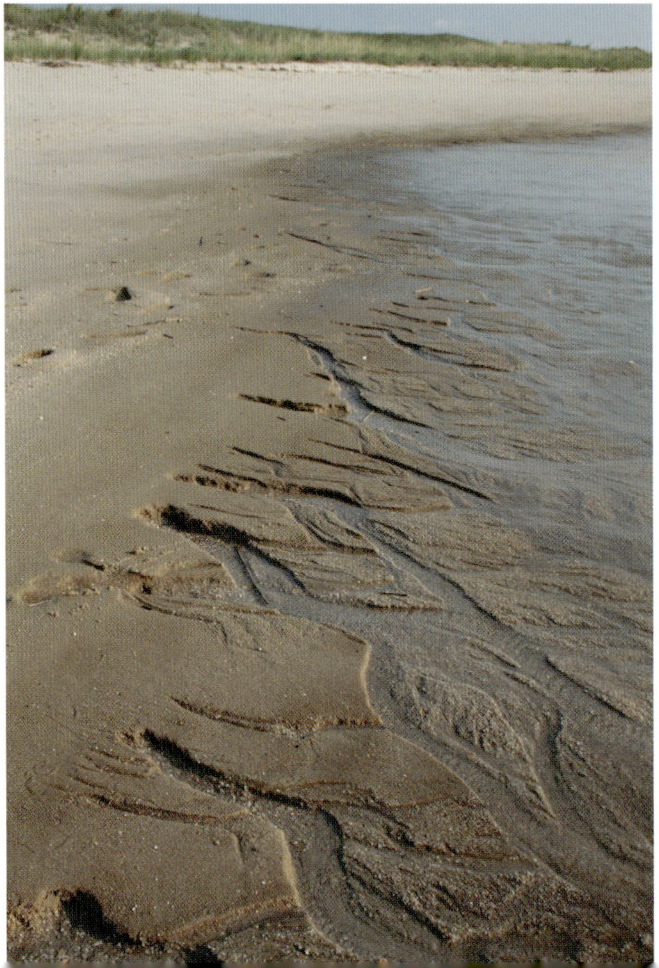

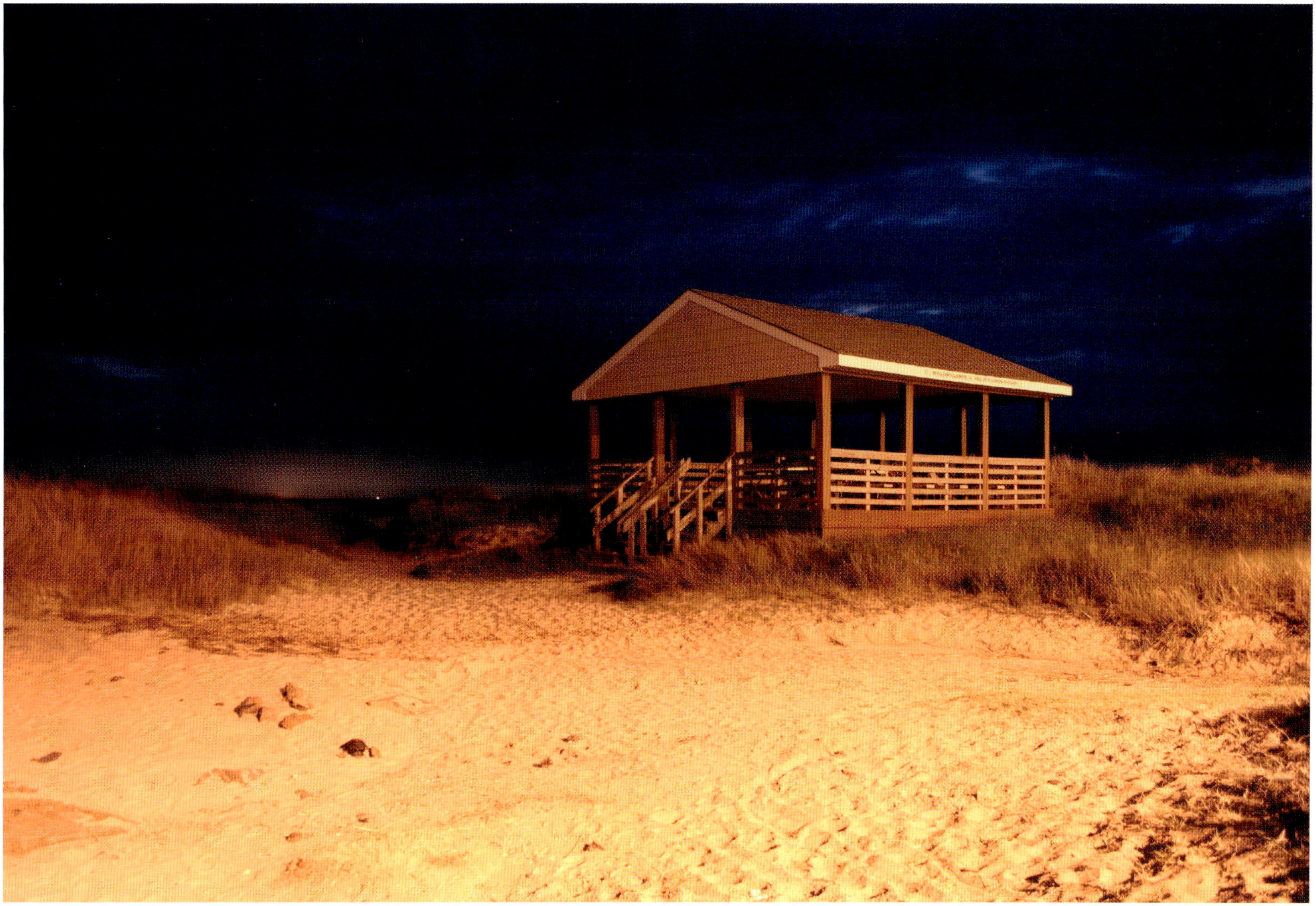

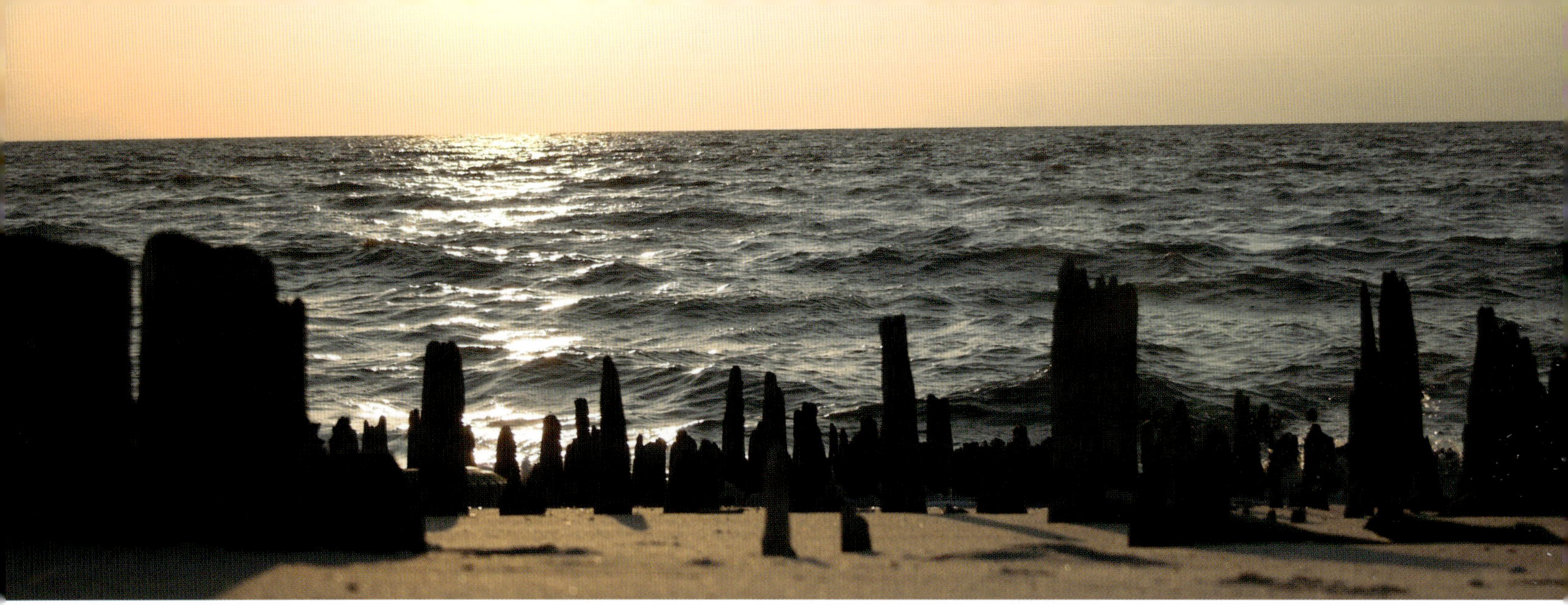

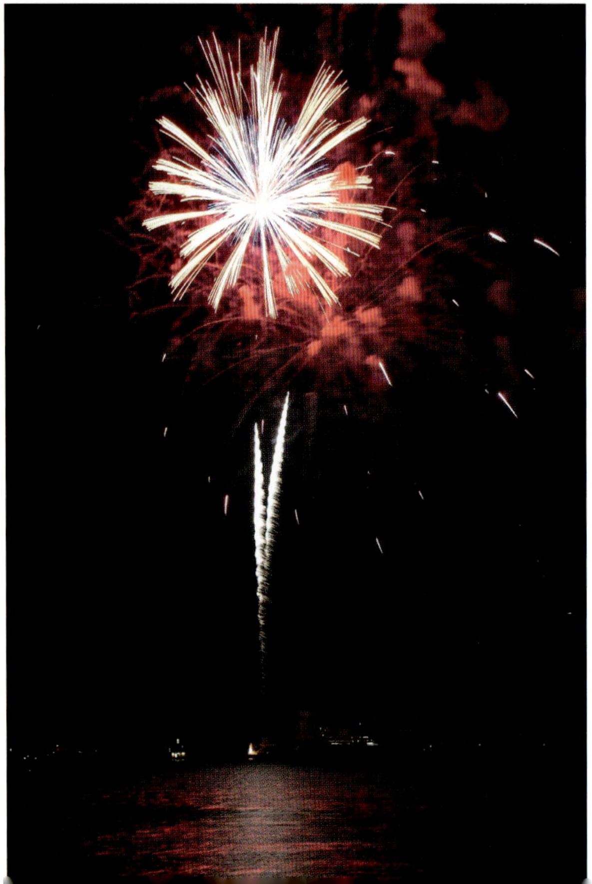

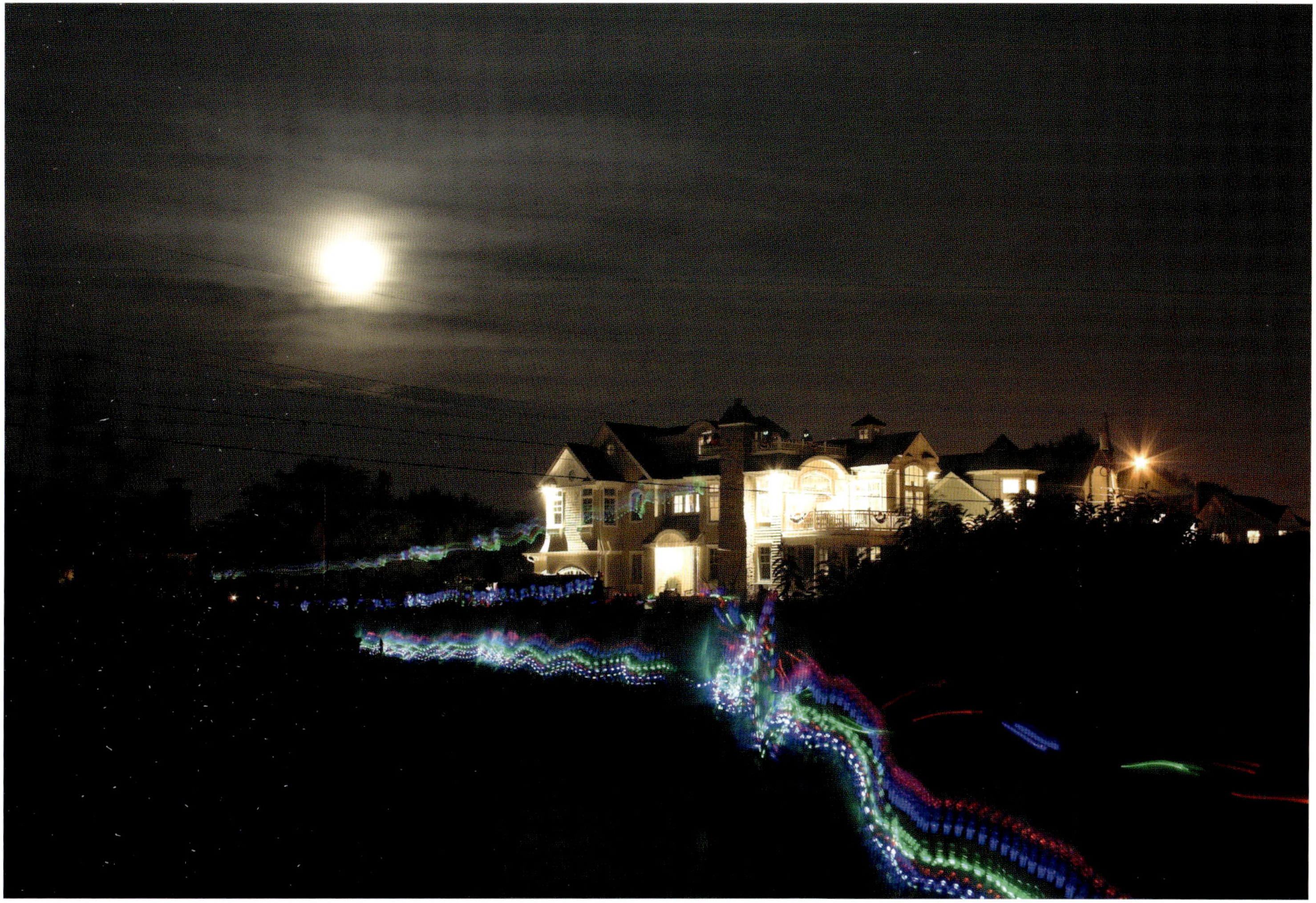

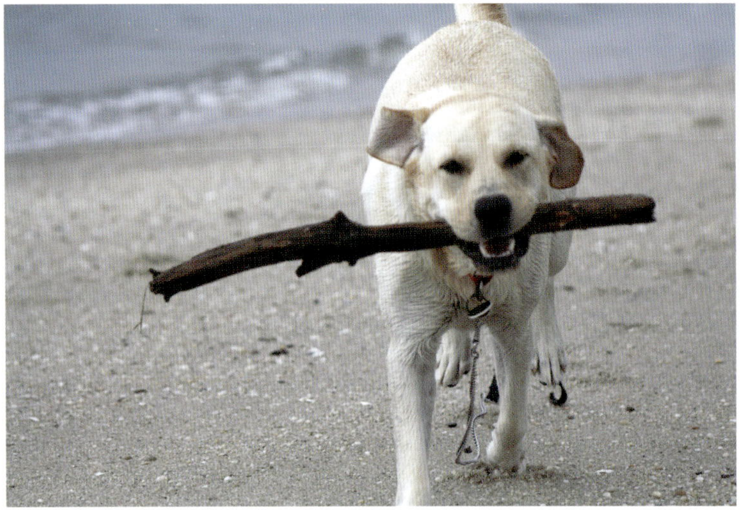

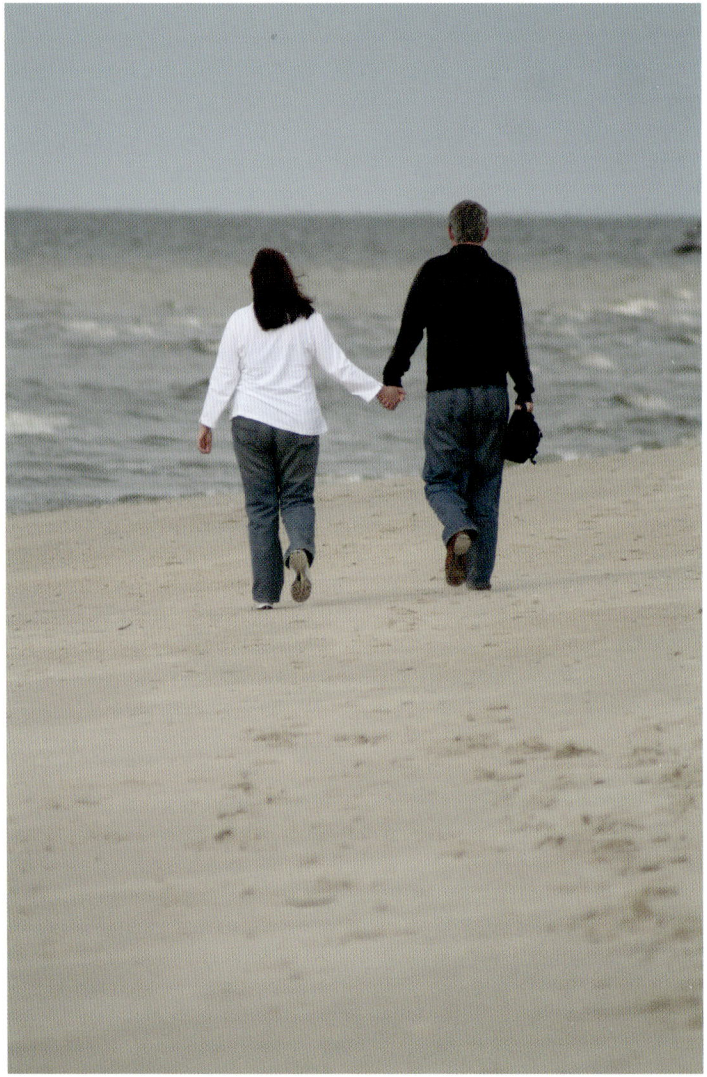

*"For whatever we lose (like a you or a me),*
*It's always our self we find in the sea."*

~ E.E. Cummings

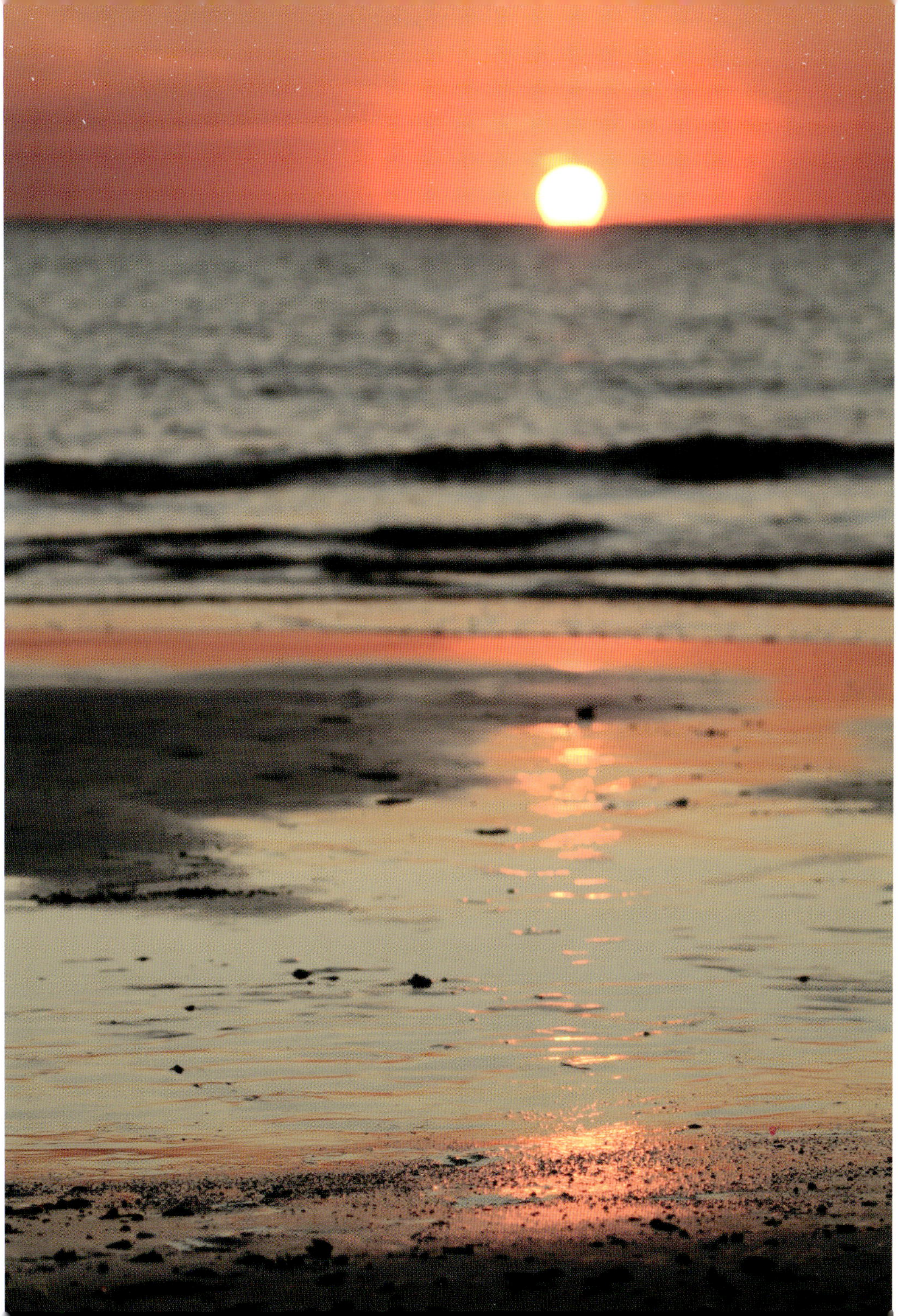

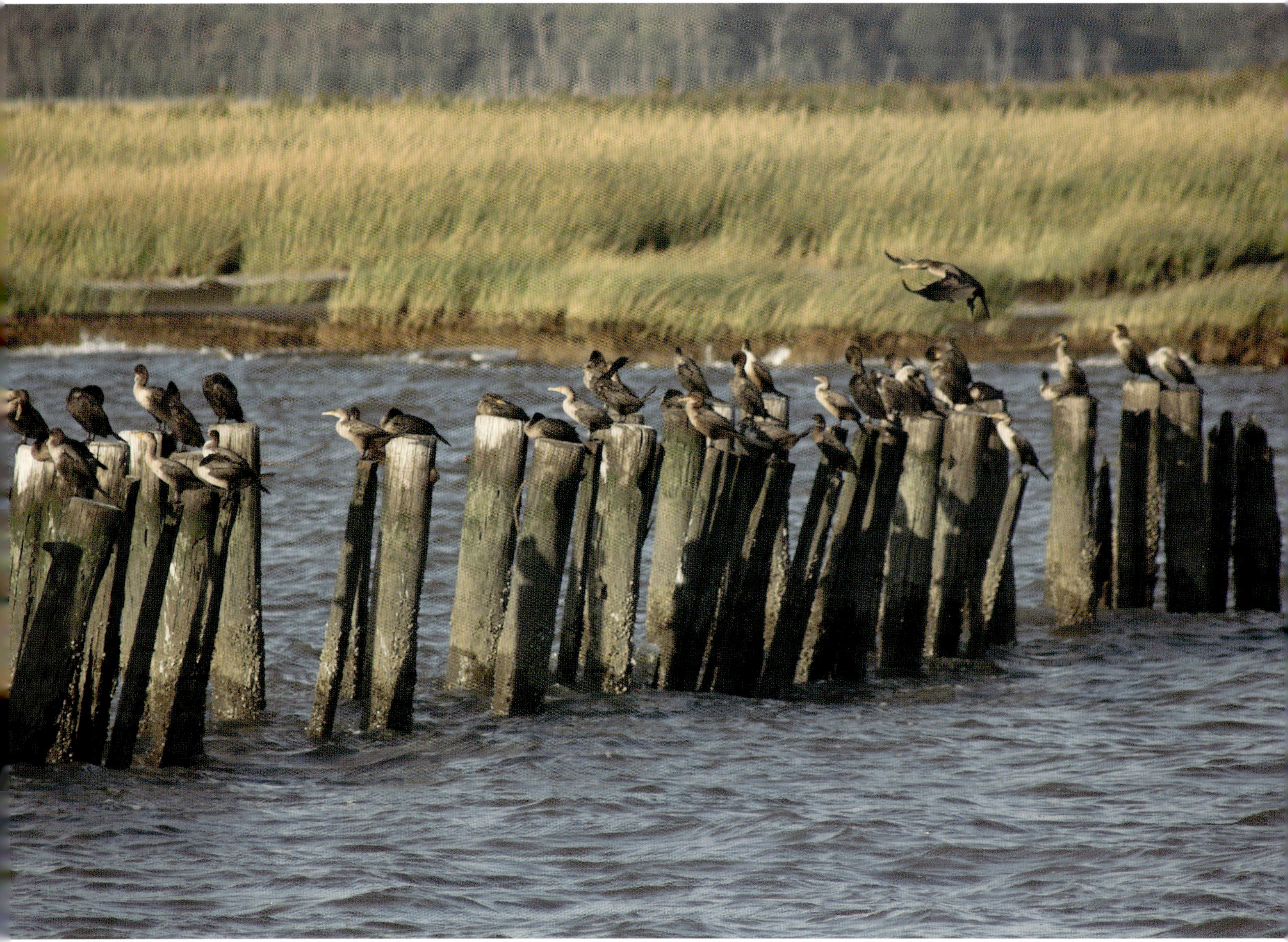

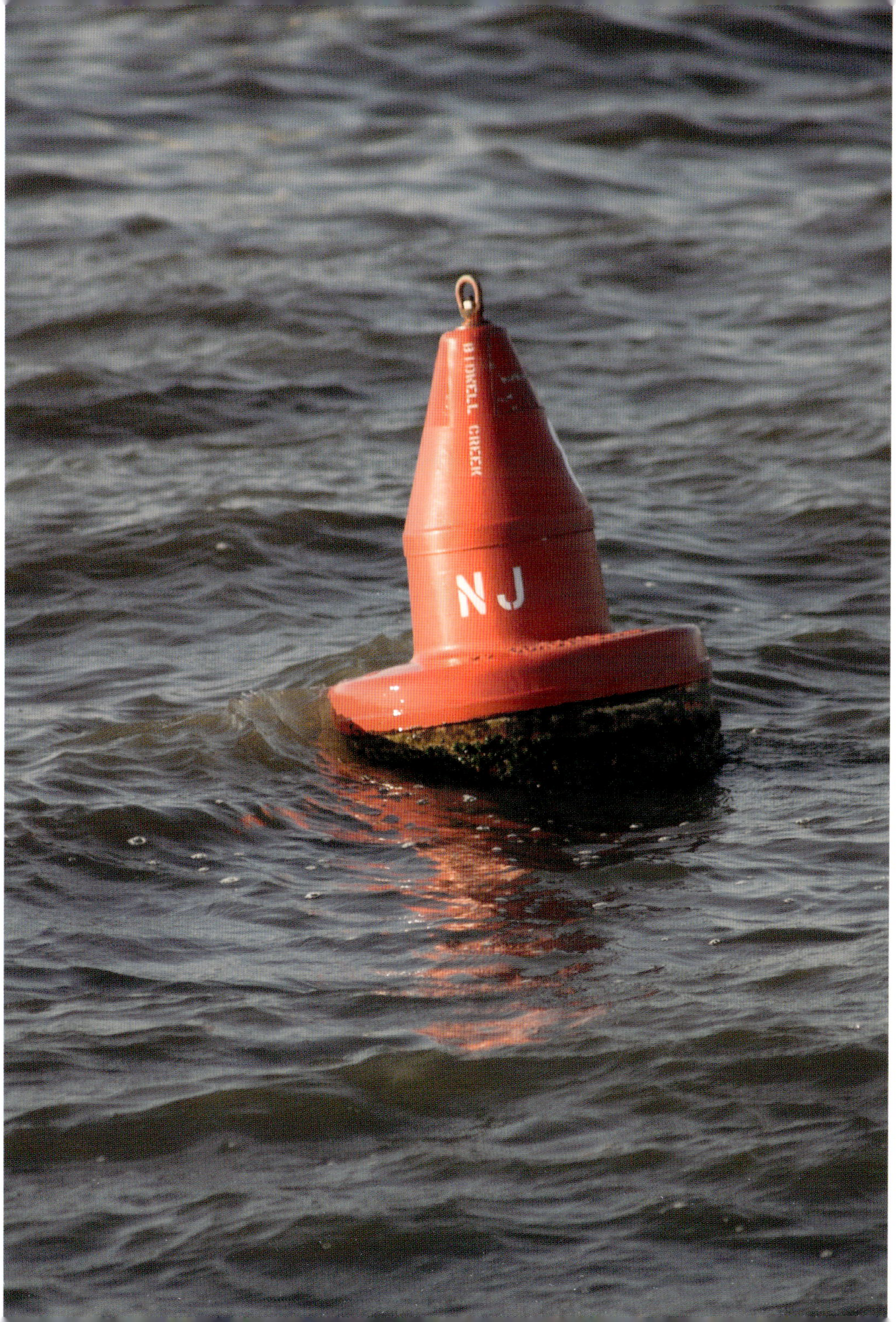
BIDWELL CREEK
NJ

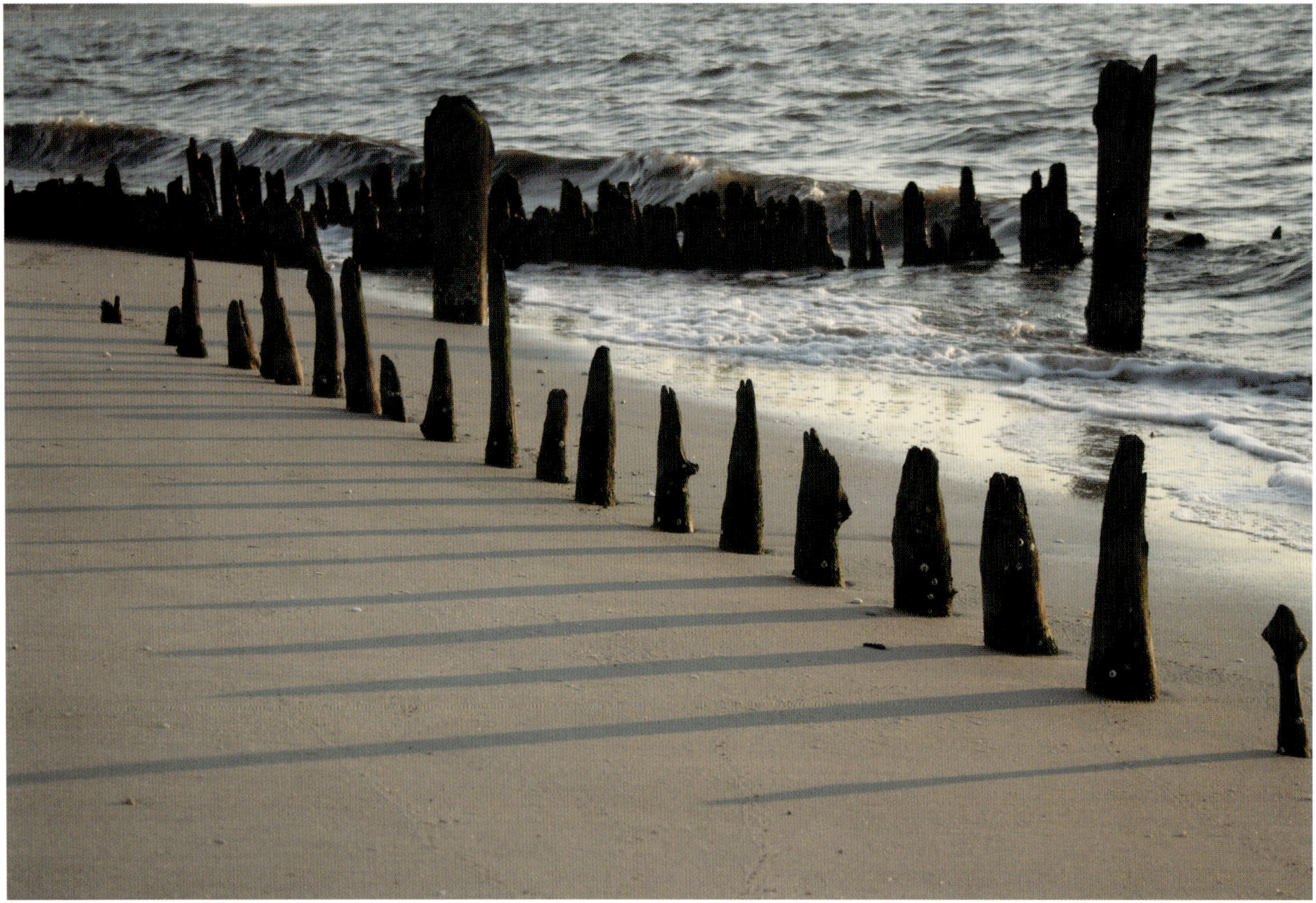

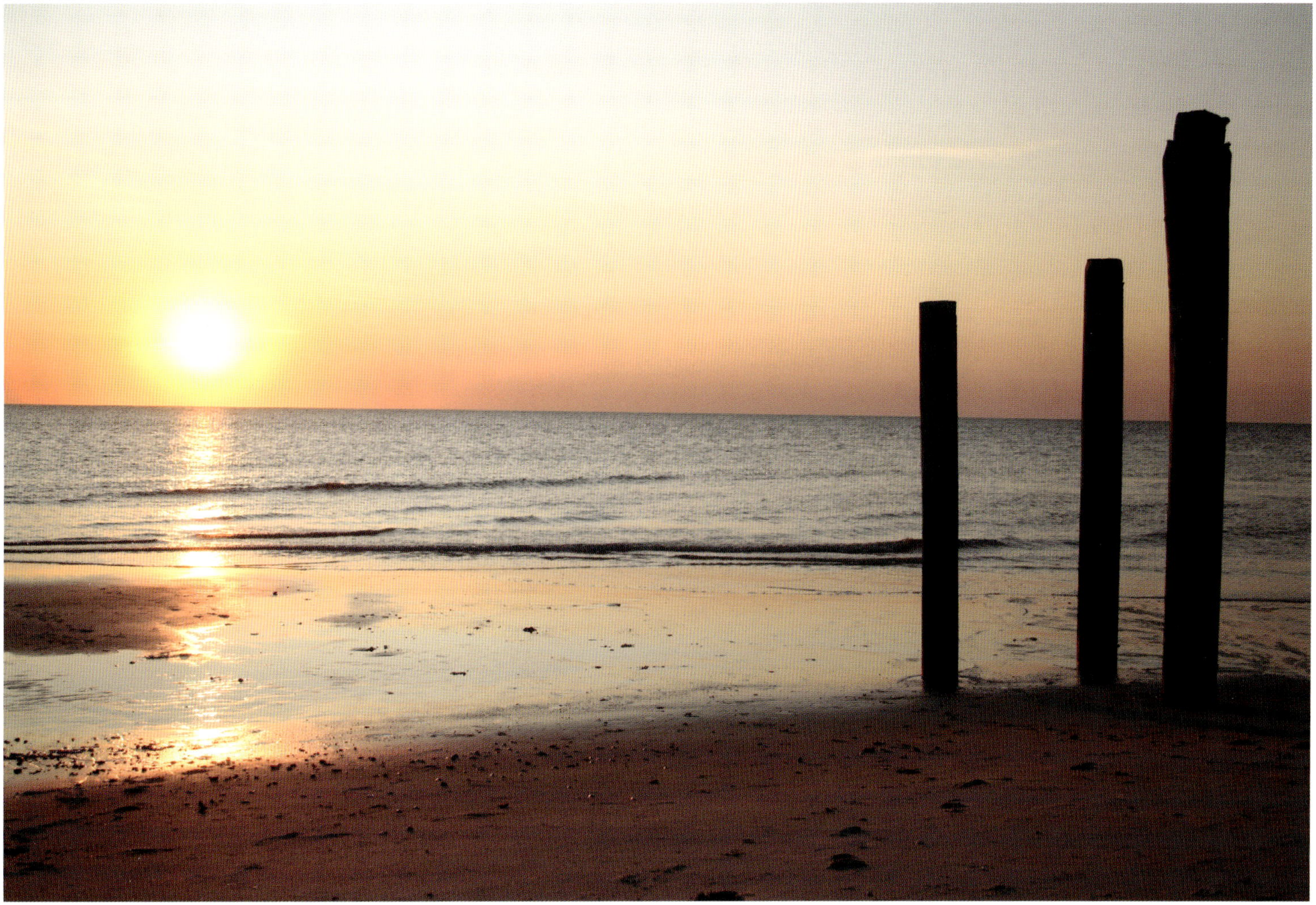

## Chapter Four

# Wildlife and Natural Beauty

Cape May is blessed with an abundance of wildlife and natural beauty. In addition to the inherent beauty that is found almost anywhere water meets land, the Cape May region has an abounding collection of flora and fauna native to the area. As if there wasn't already enough to take in, Cape May's geographical placement puts it in the path of countless species of migratory birds, butterflies, and other creatures every spring and autumn. Each migration cycle, birders and nature enthusiasts descend upon the Cape in numbers almost as great as the migratory species they come to observe. You don't need be a naturalist or a birder who knows the difference between an *Ardea alba* and an *Egretta thula* to appreciate the beauty found on the Cape. *Anybody* can be held spellbound by the natural beauty of Cape May. To find that beauty, one needs only to stop long enough to look around.

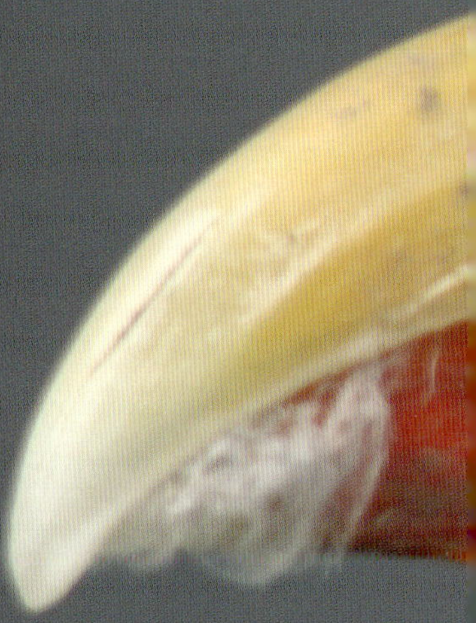

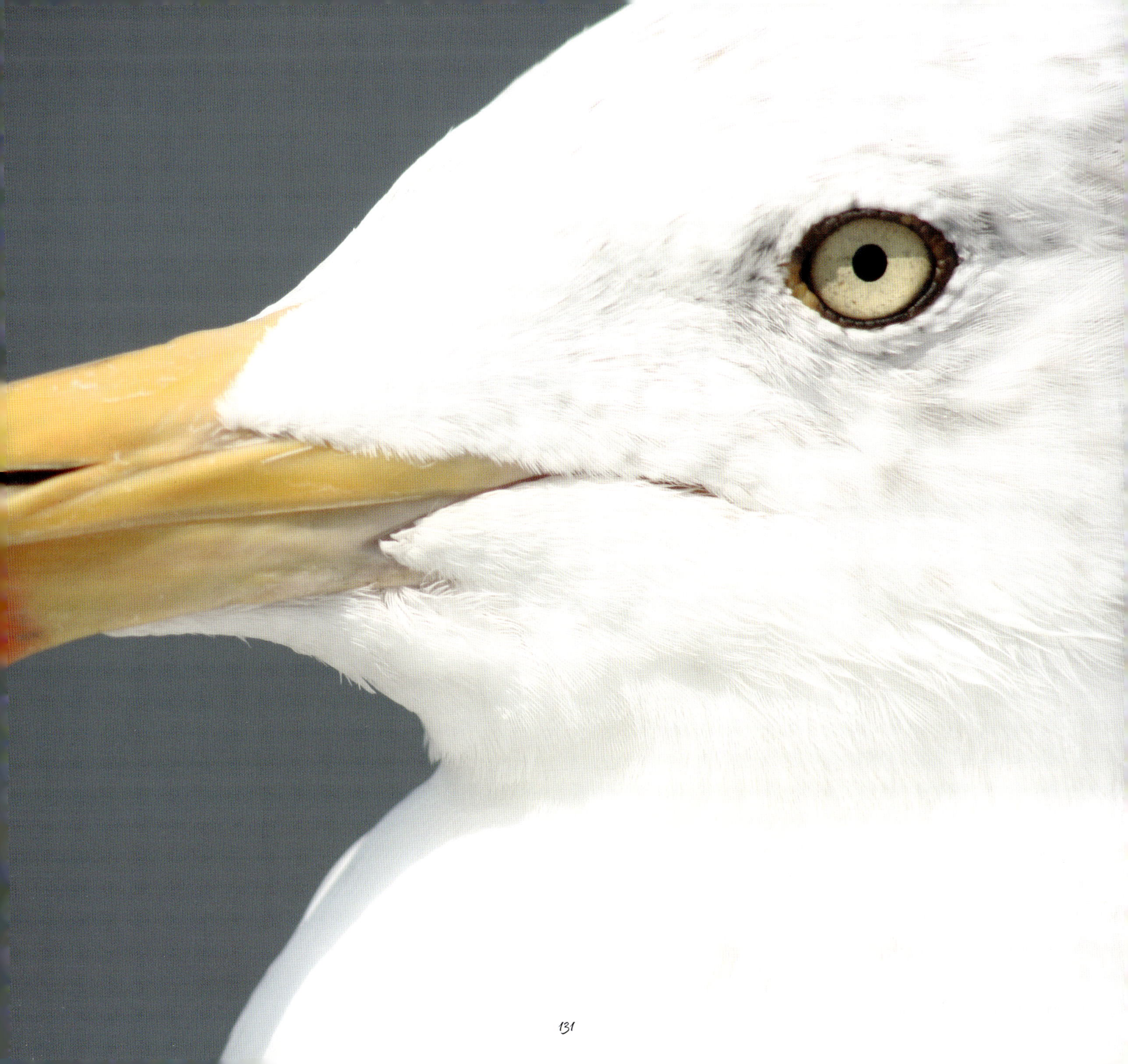

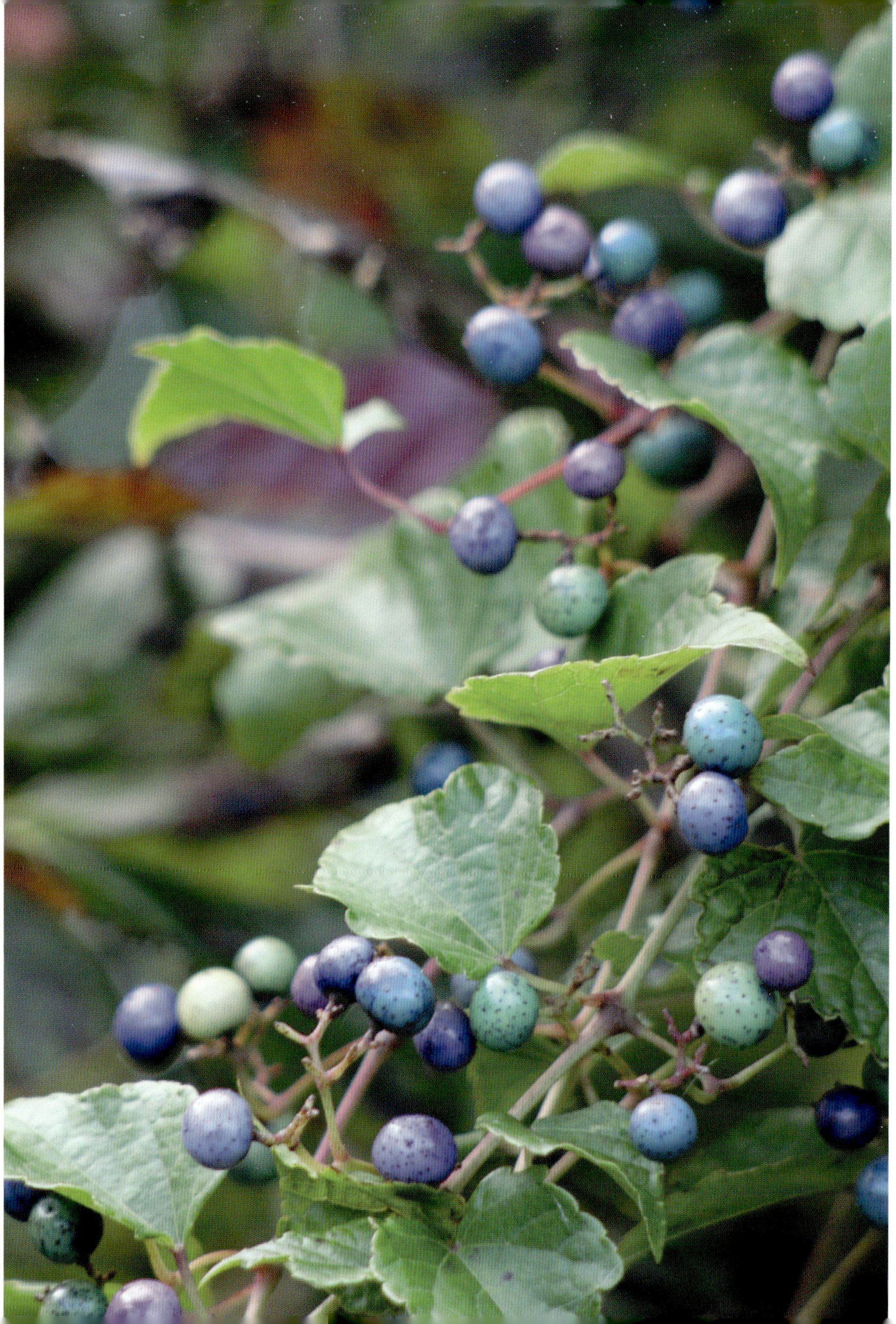

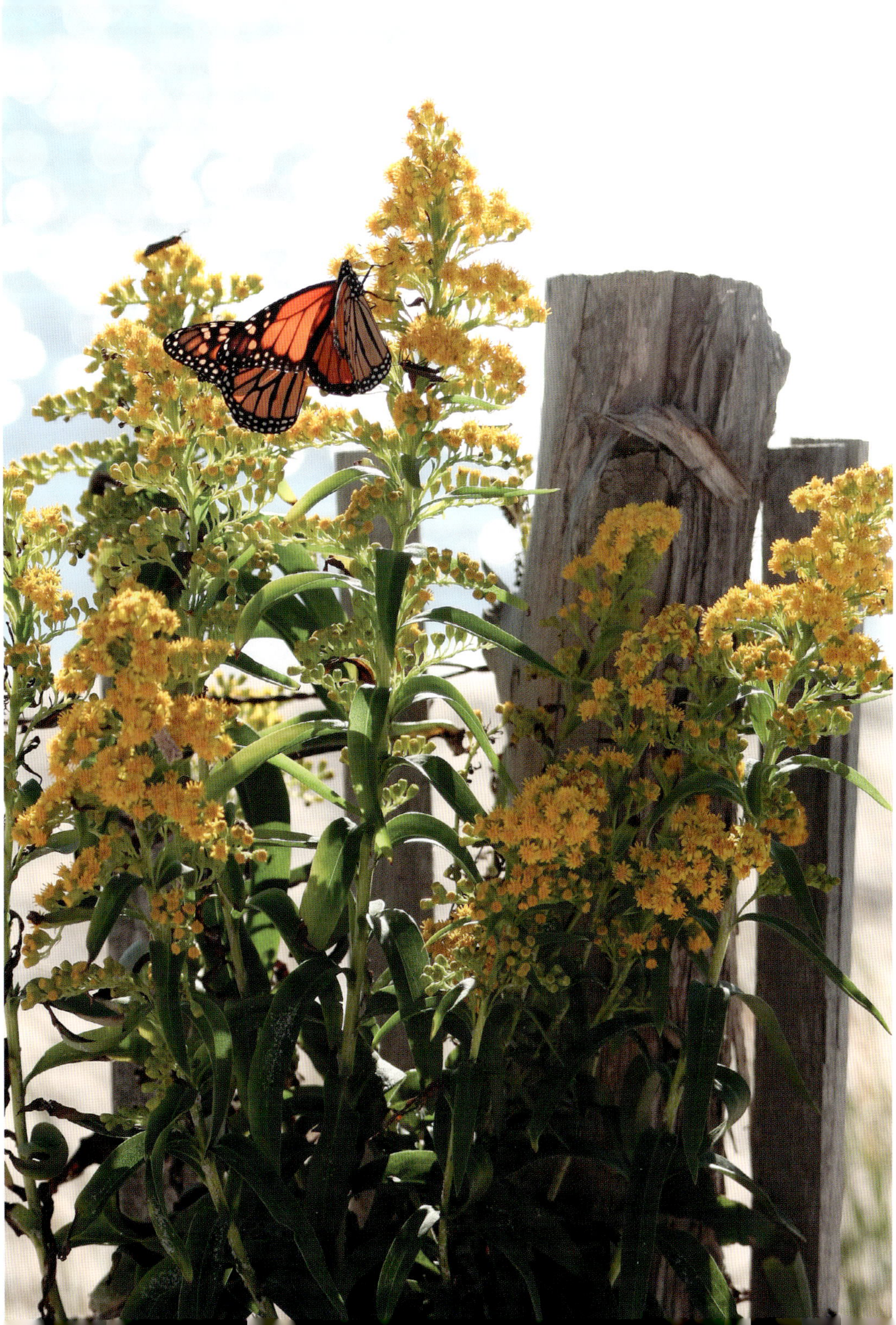

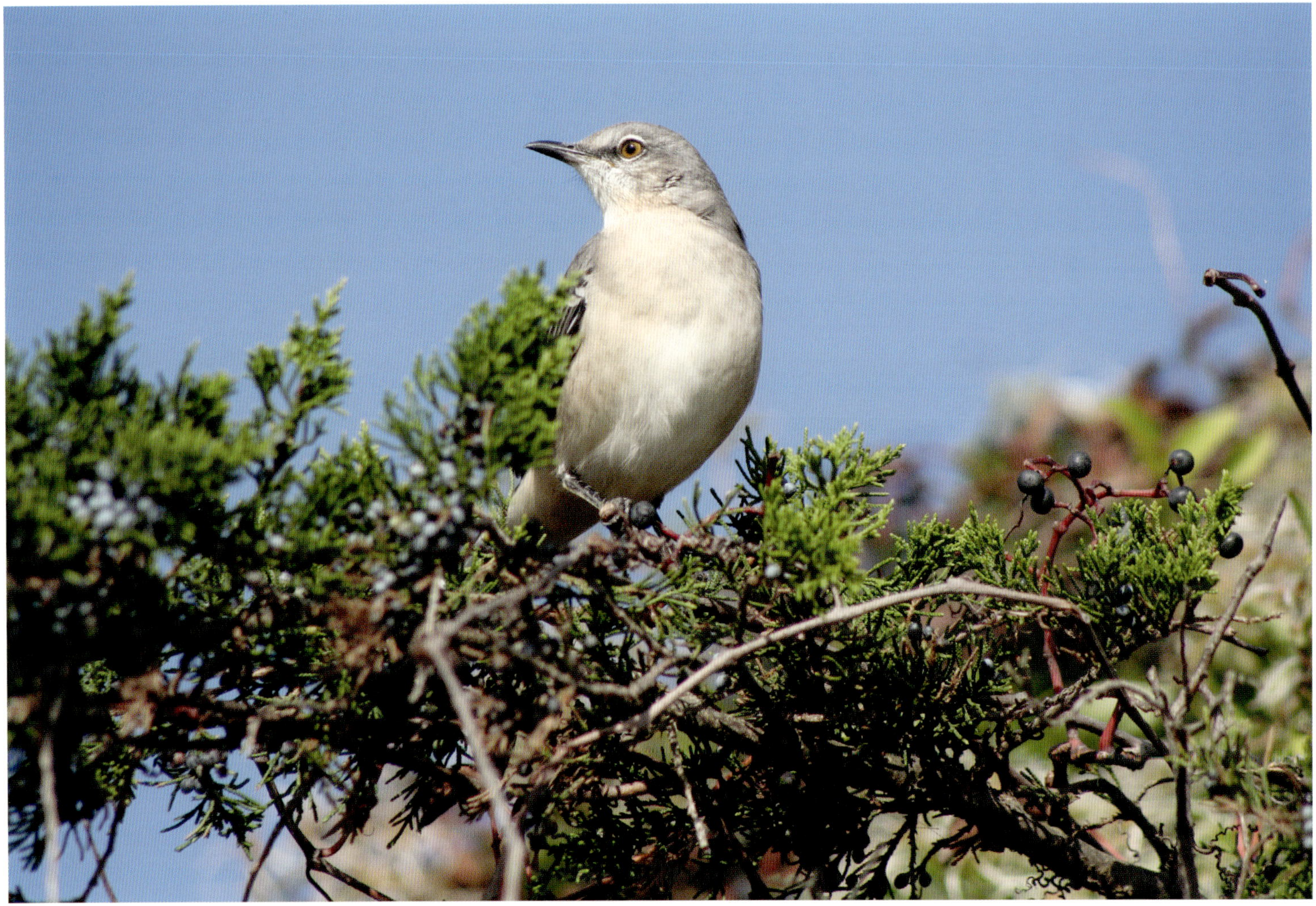

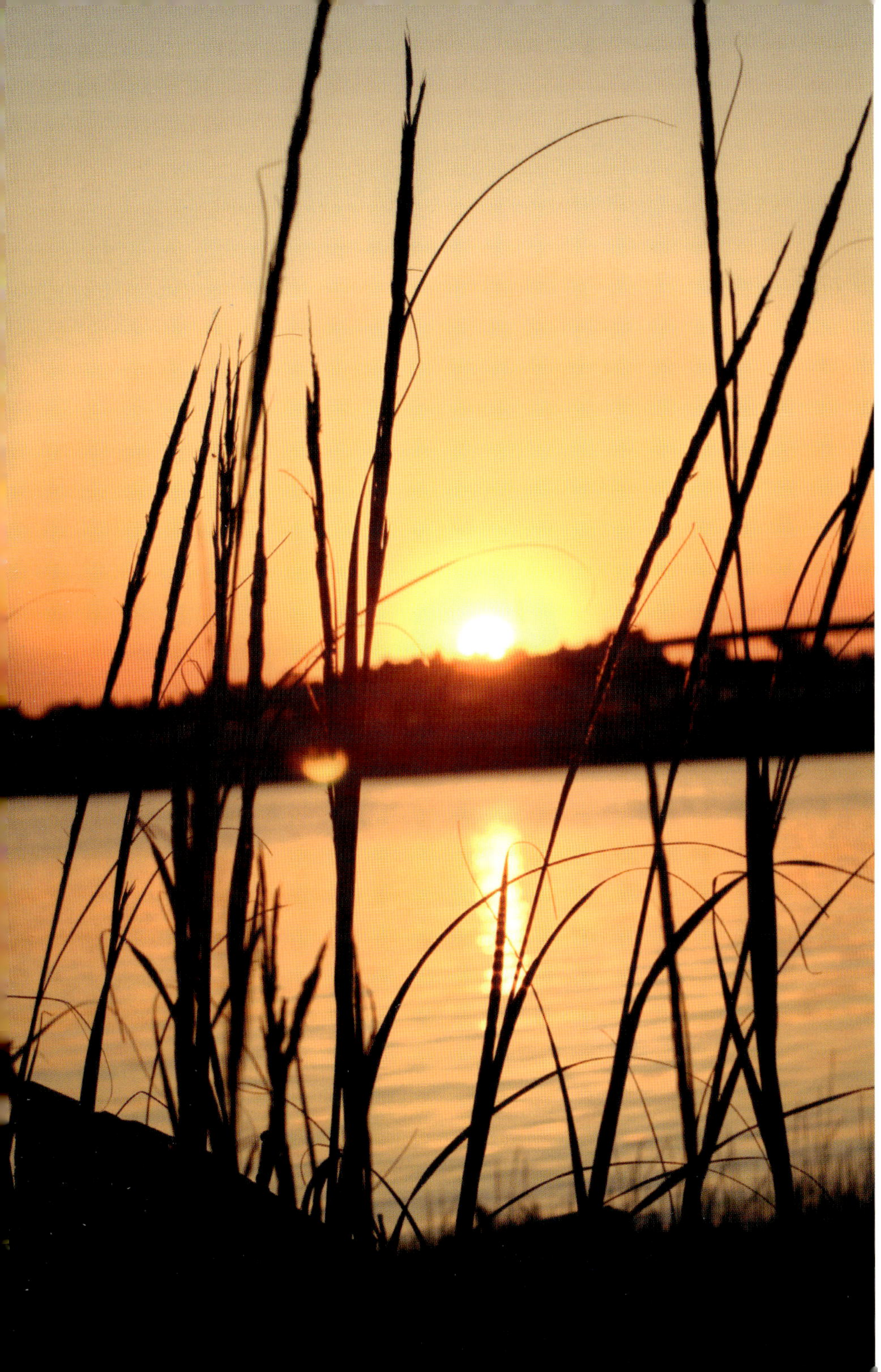

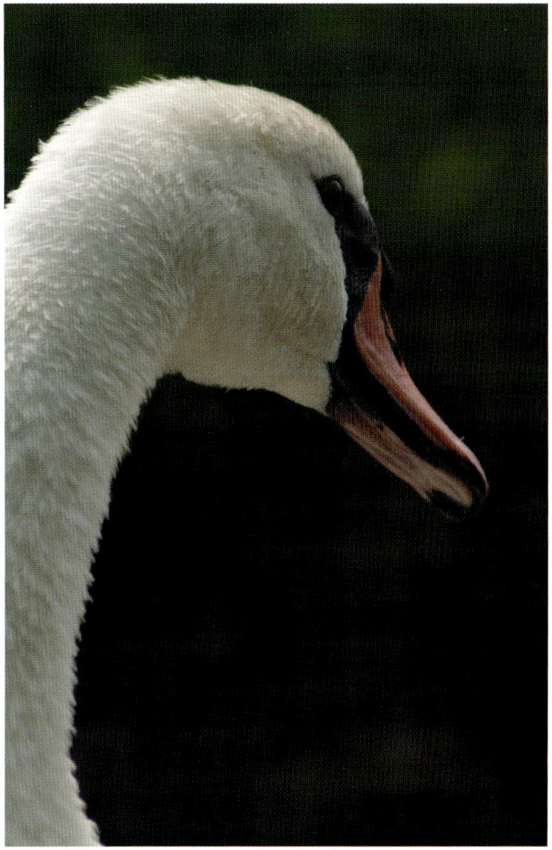

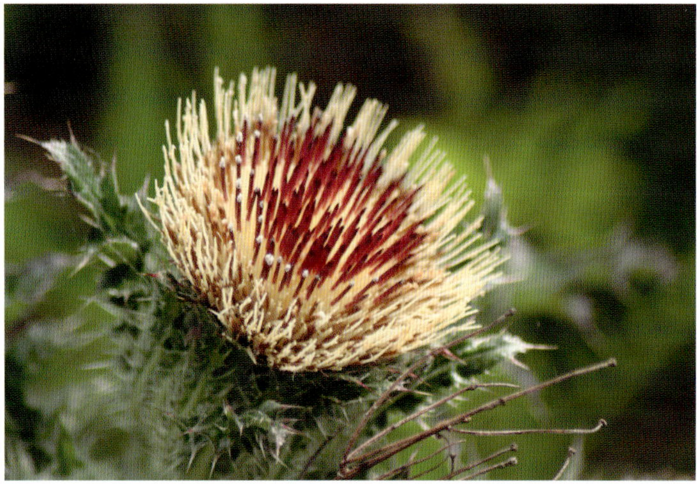
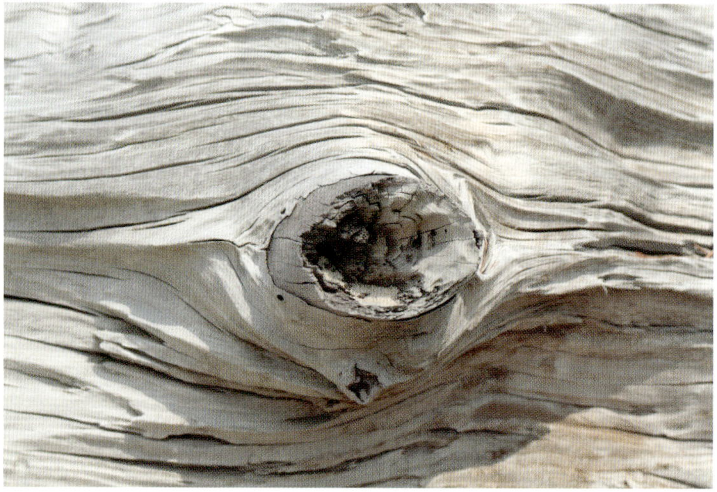
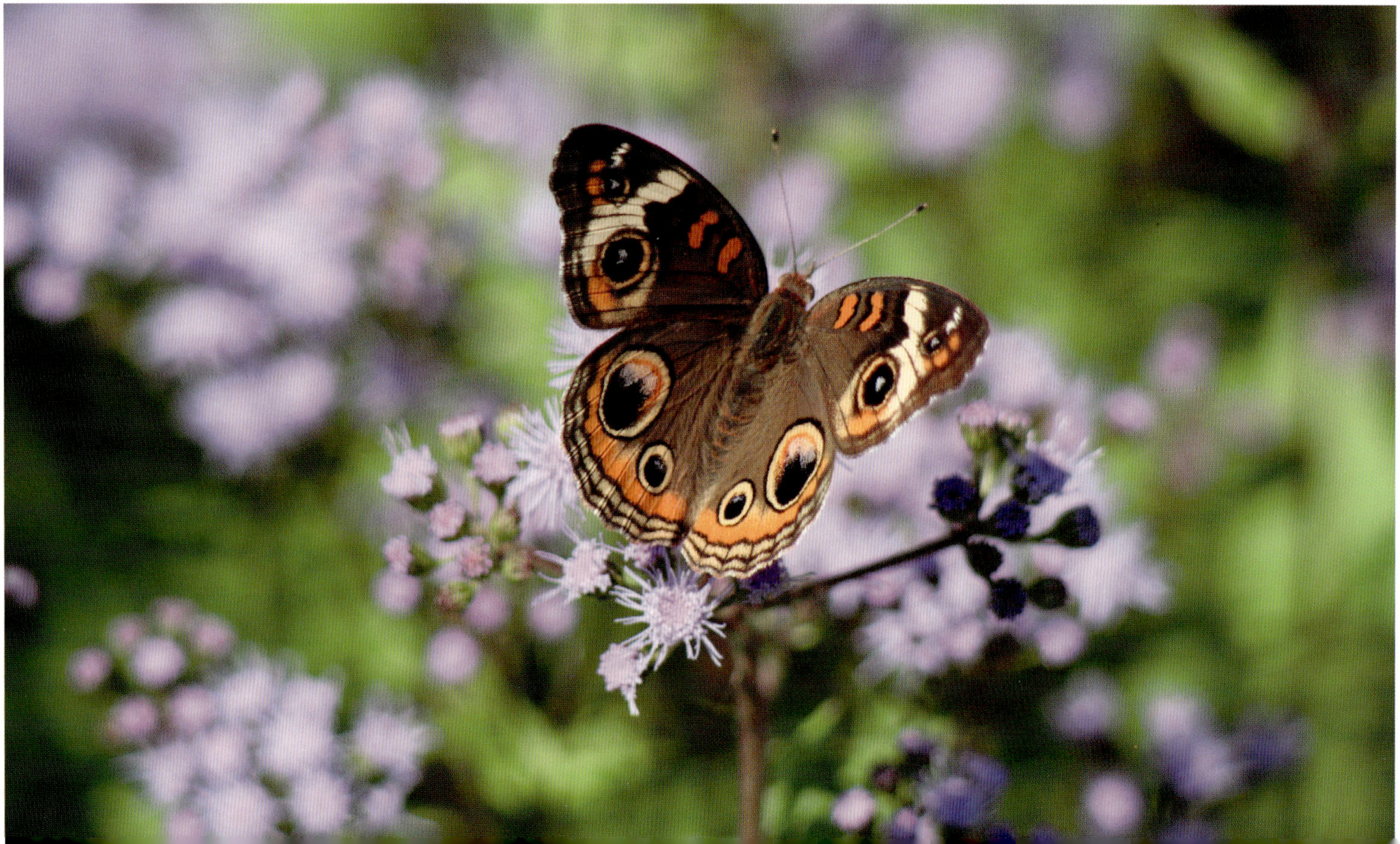

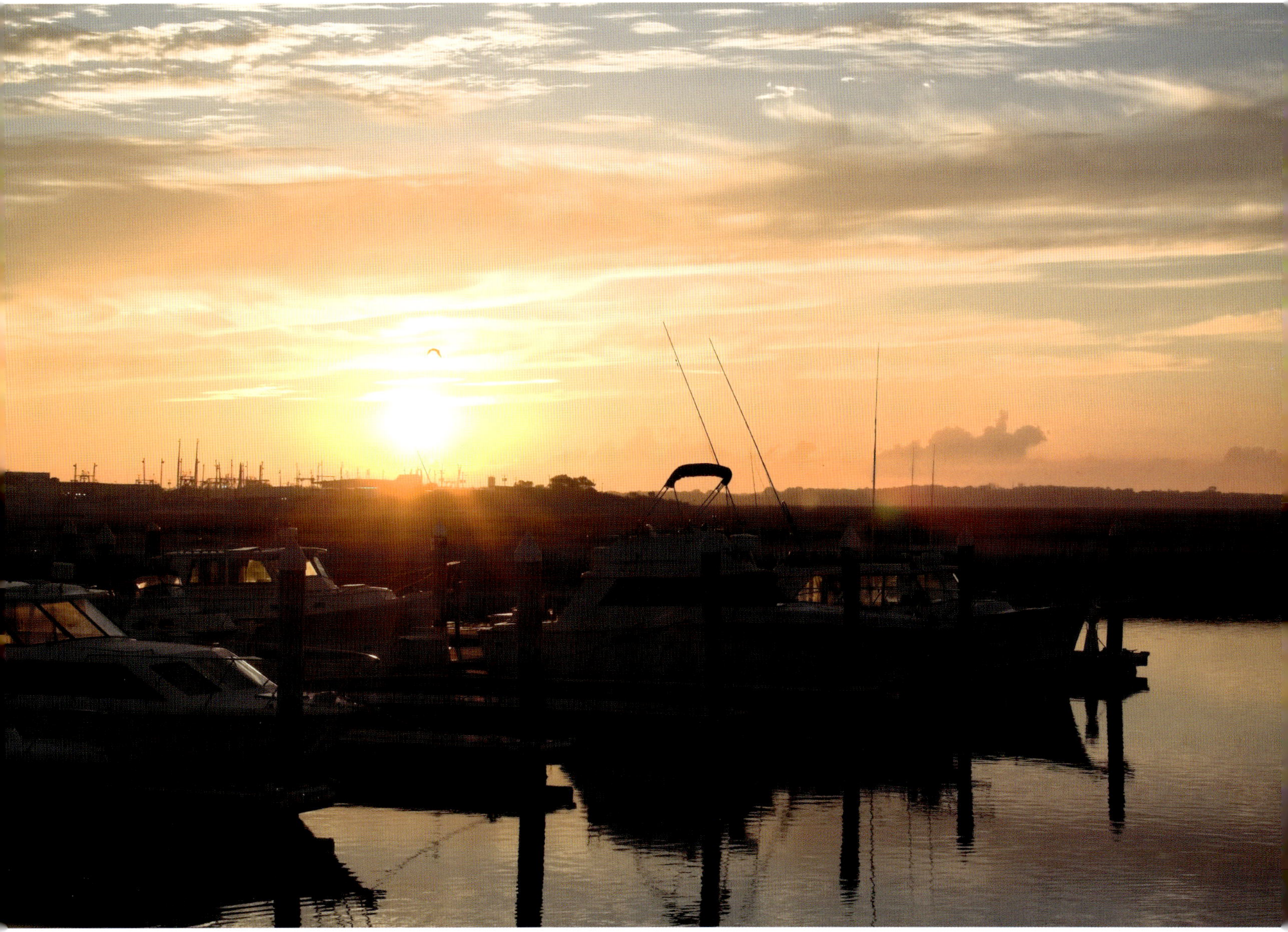

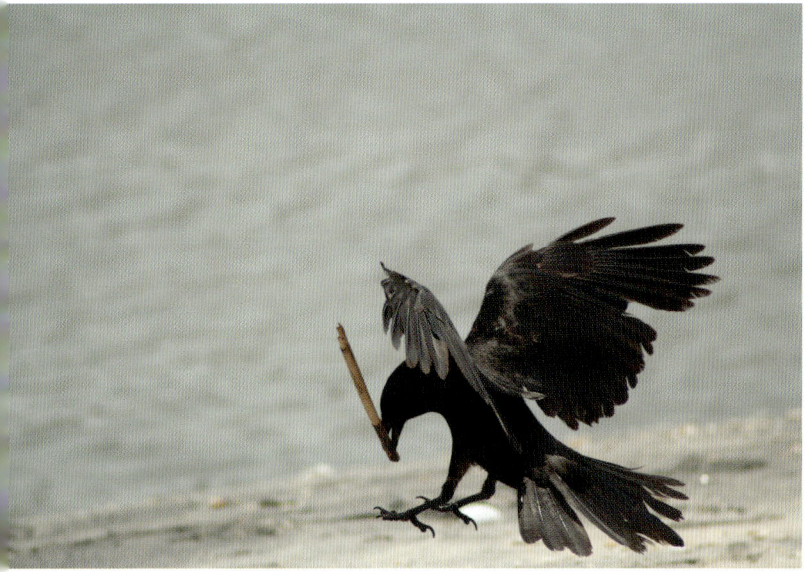

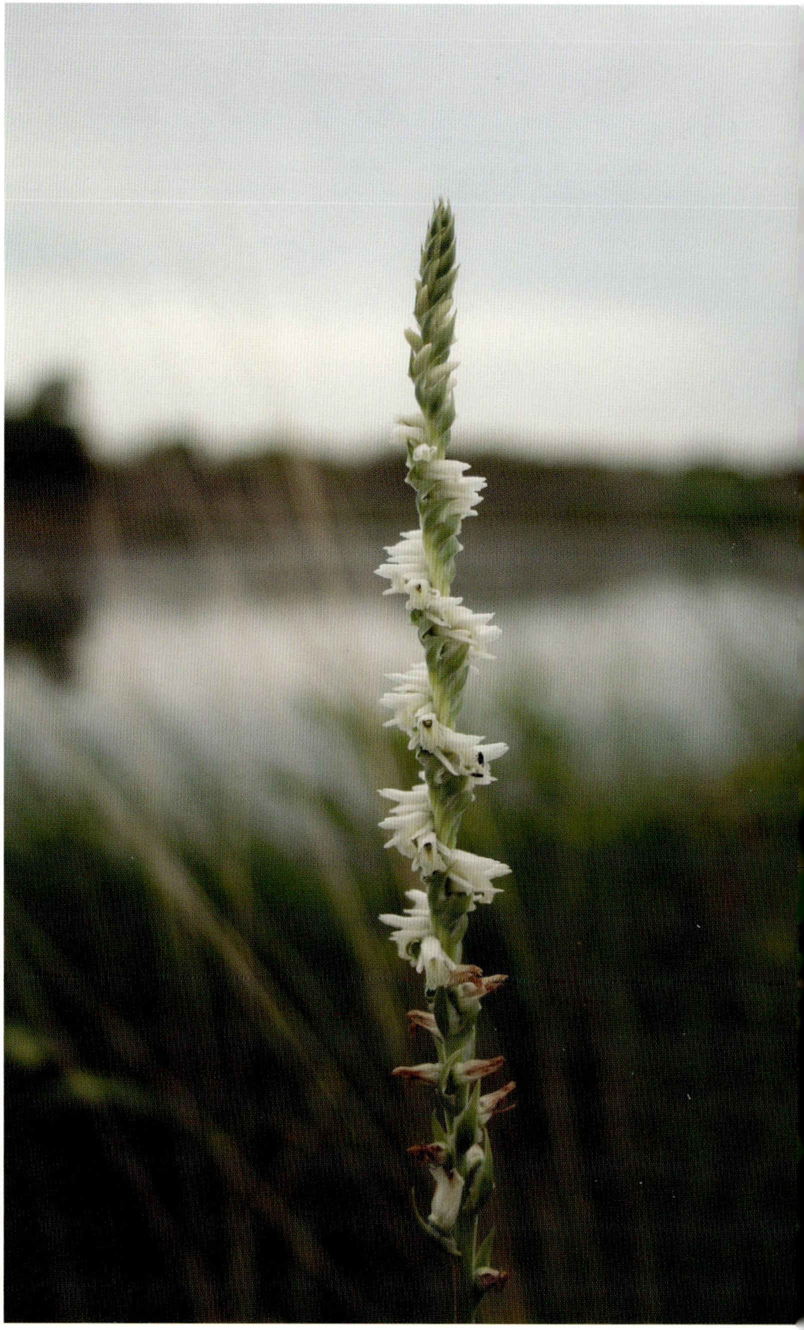

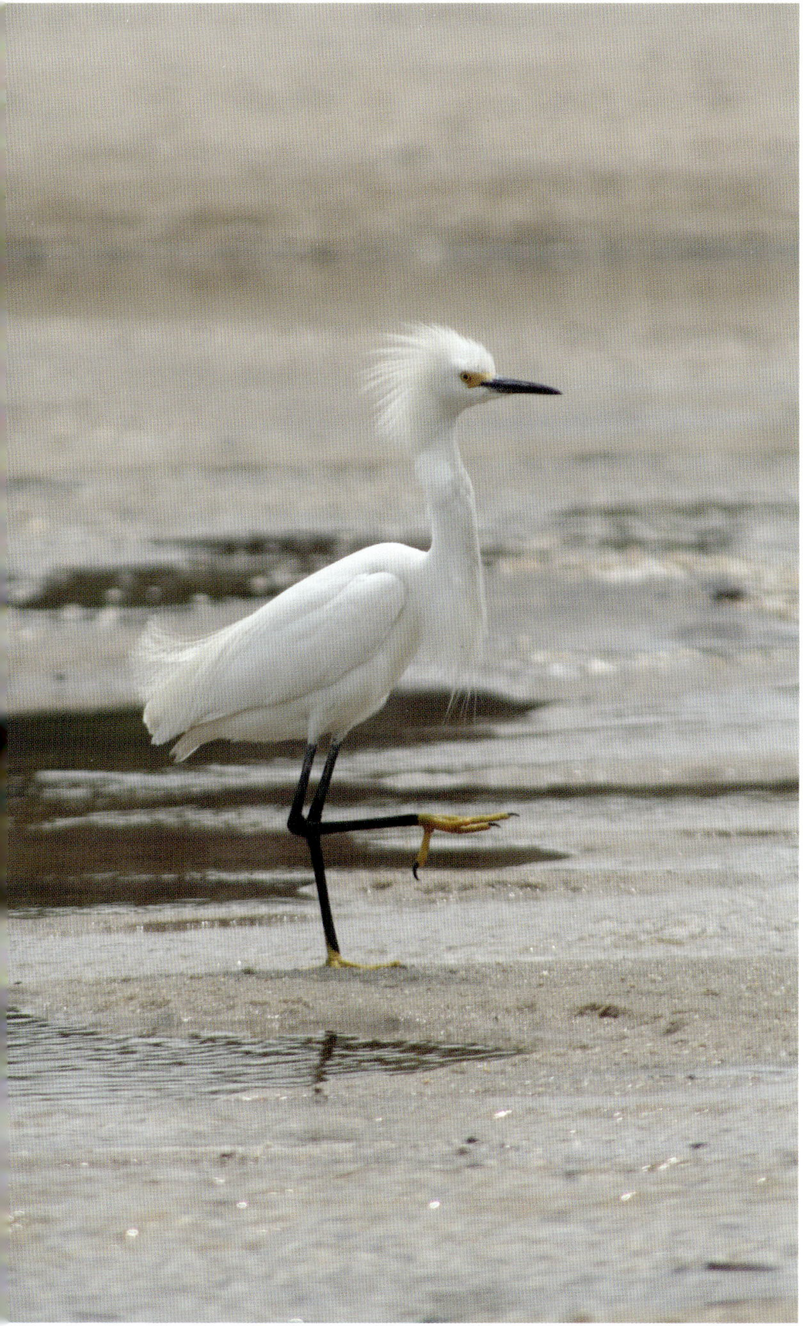

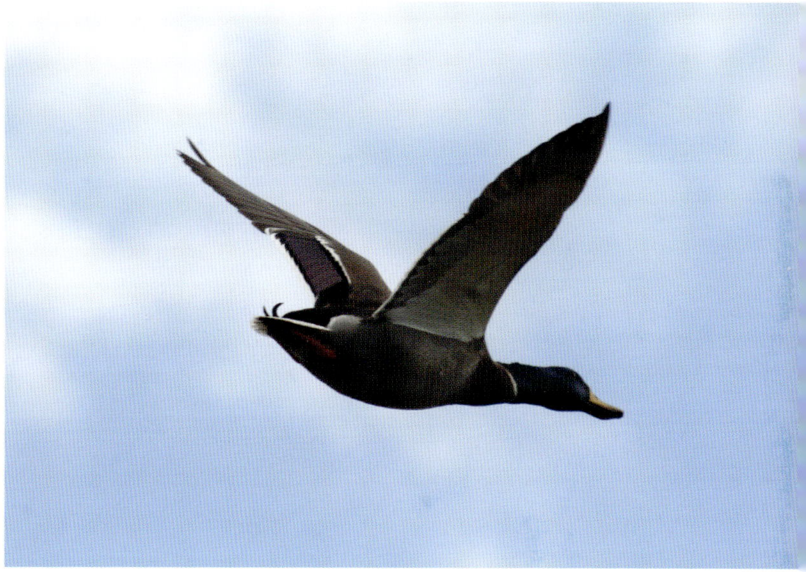

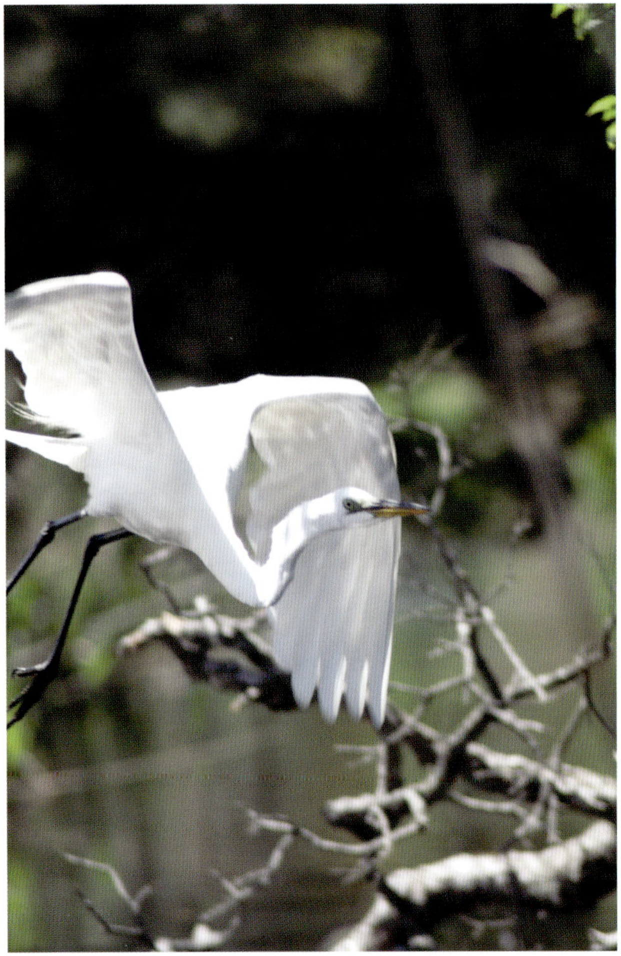

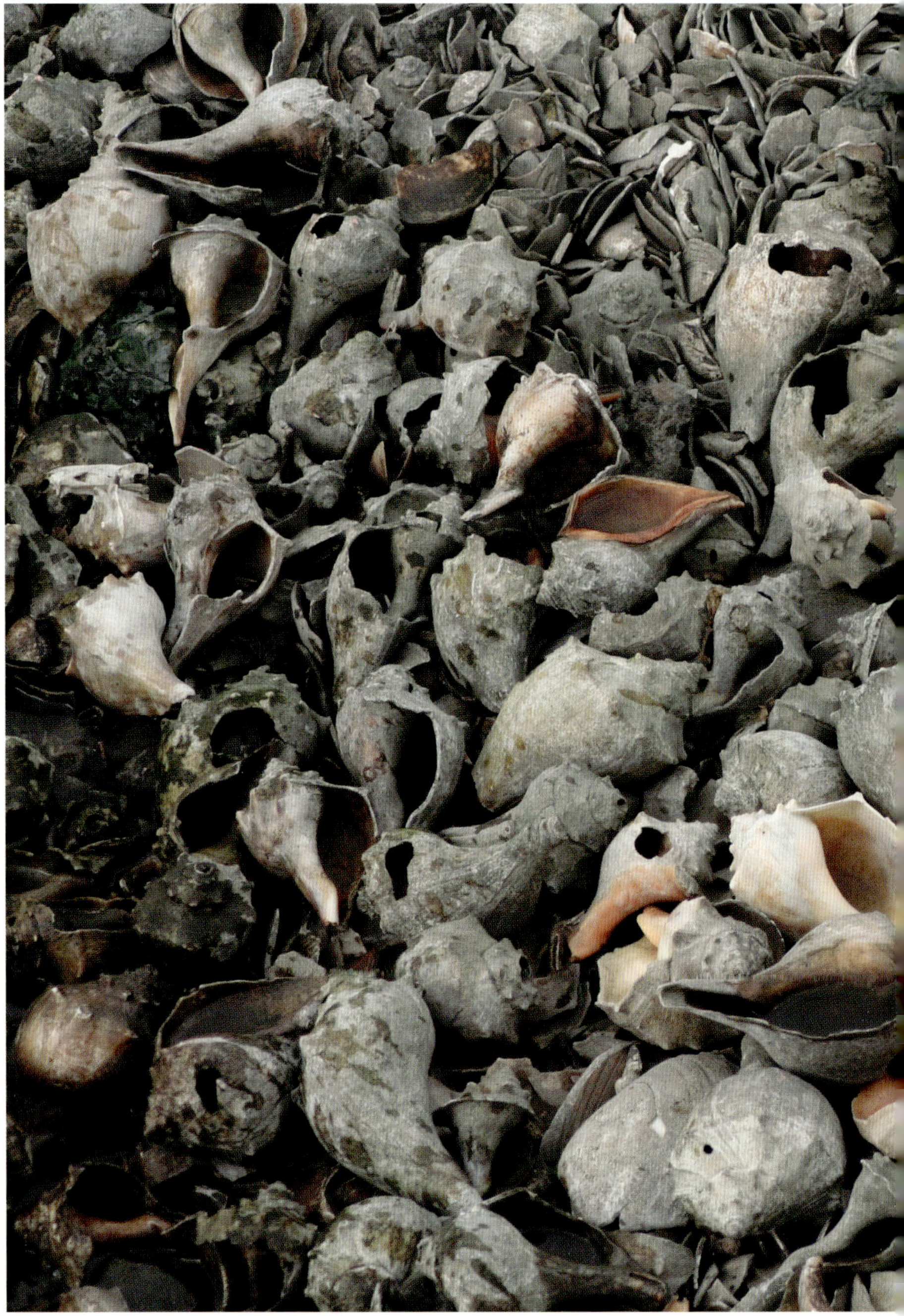

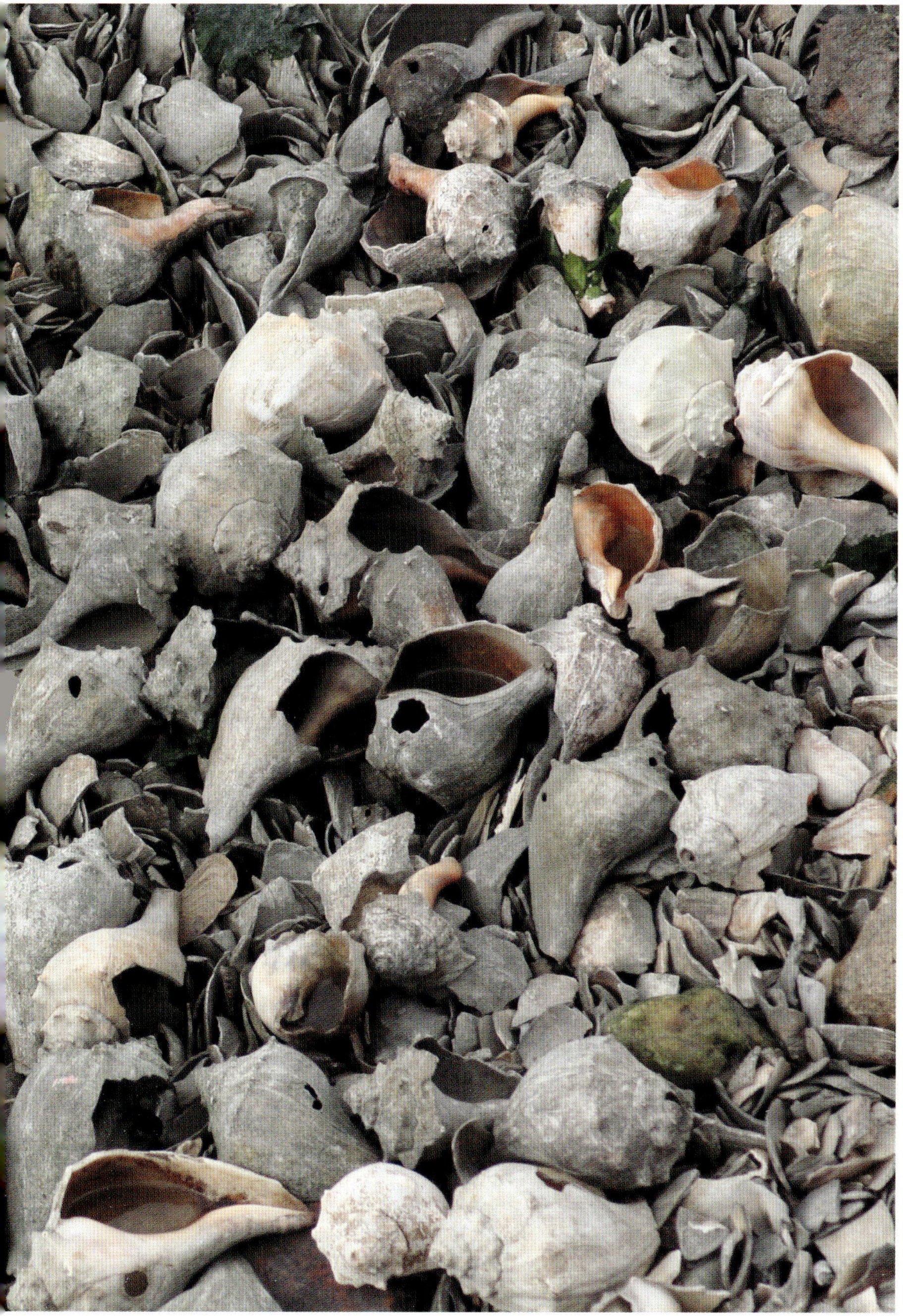

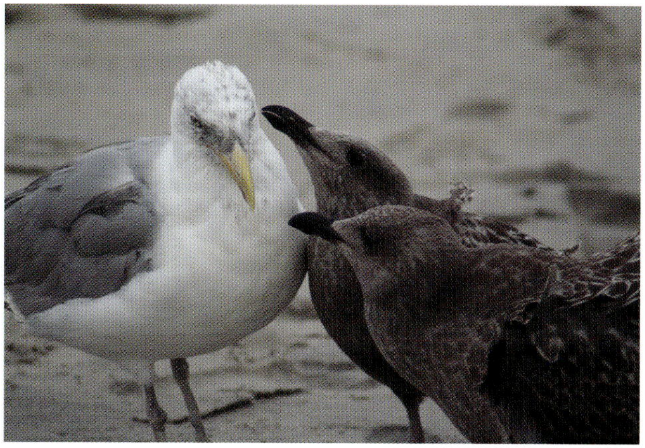

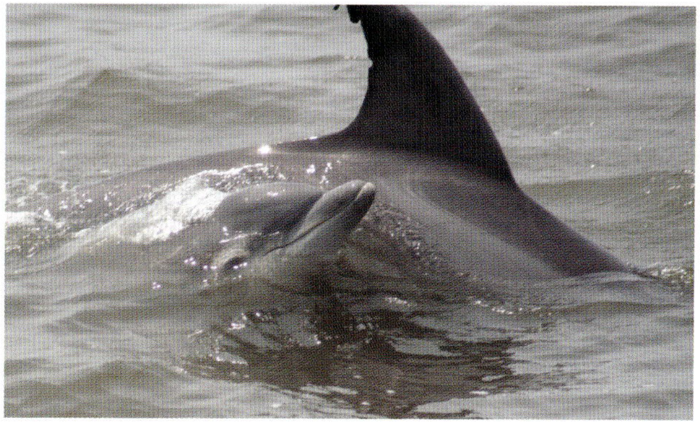

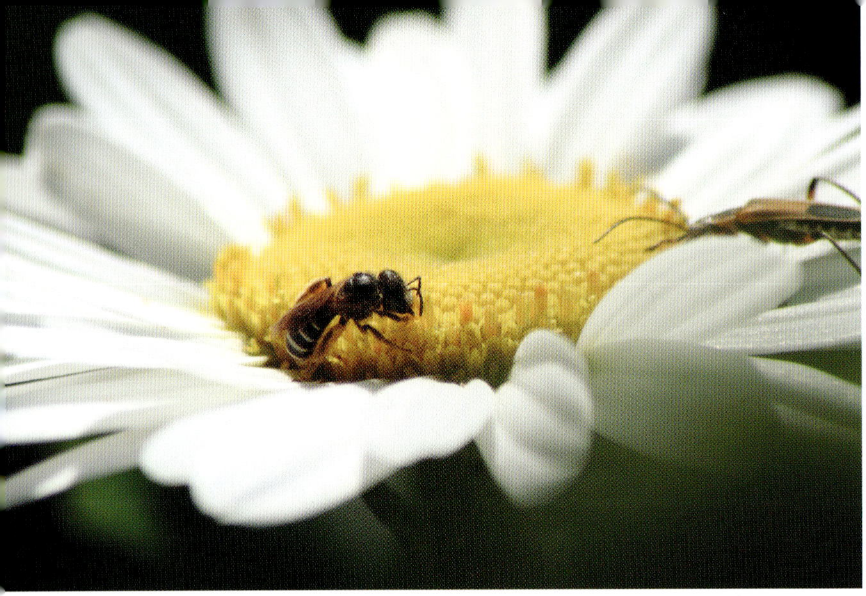

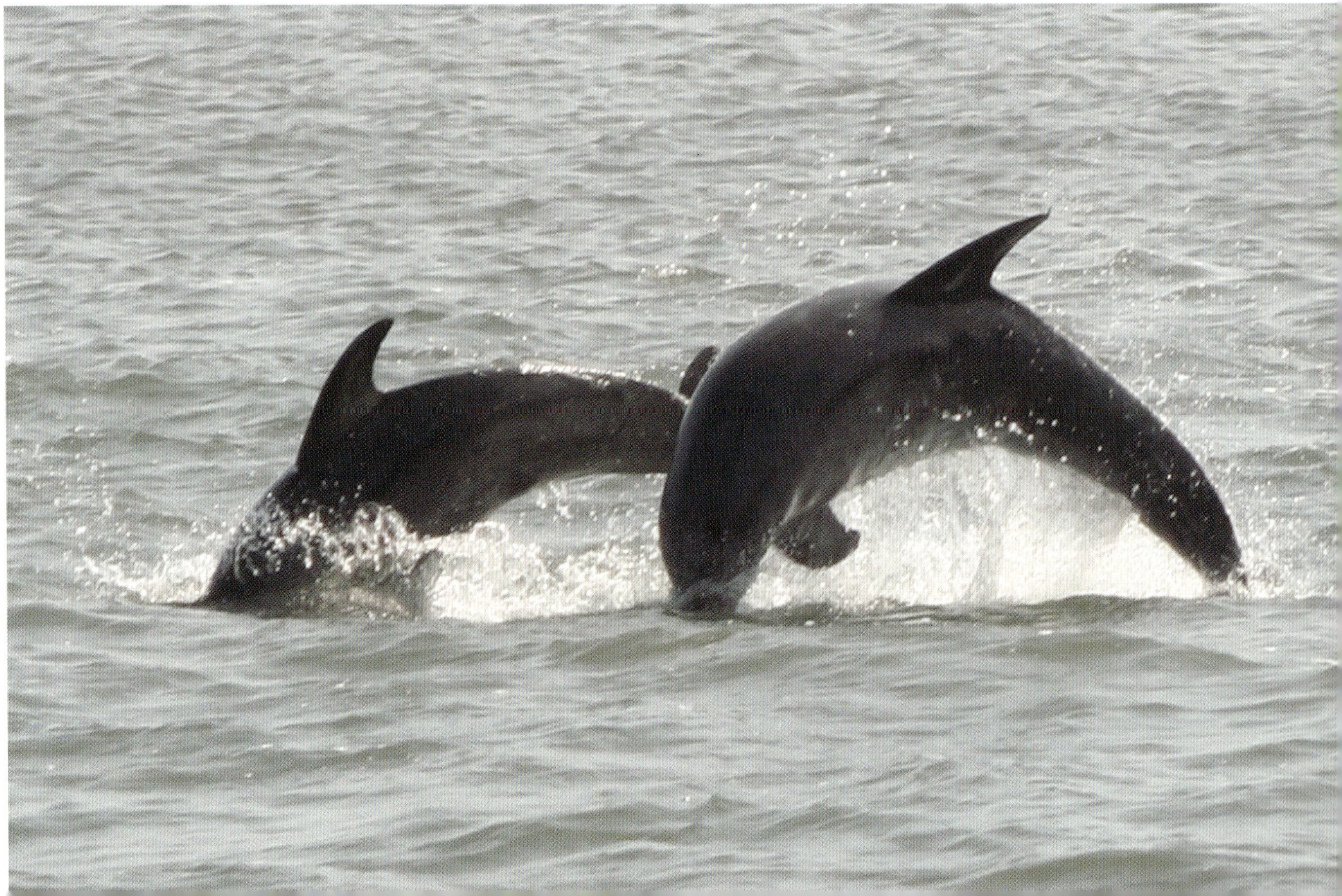

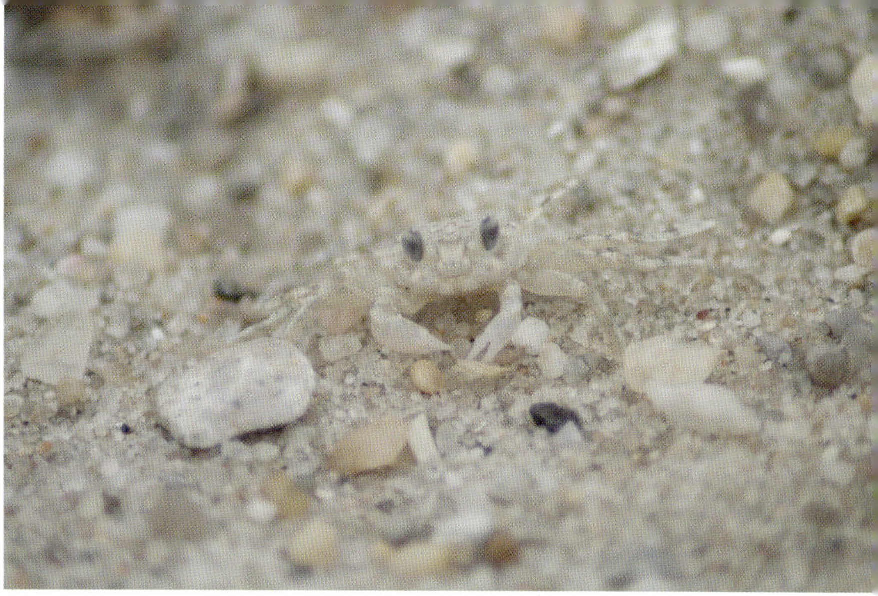

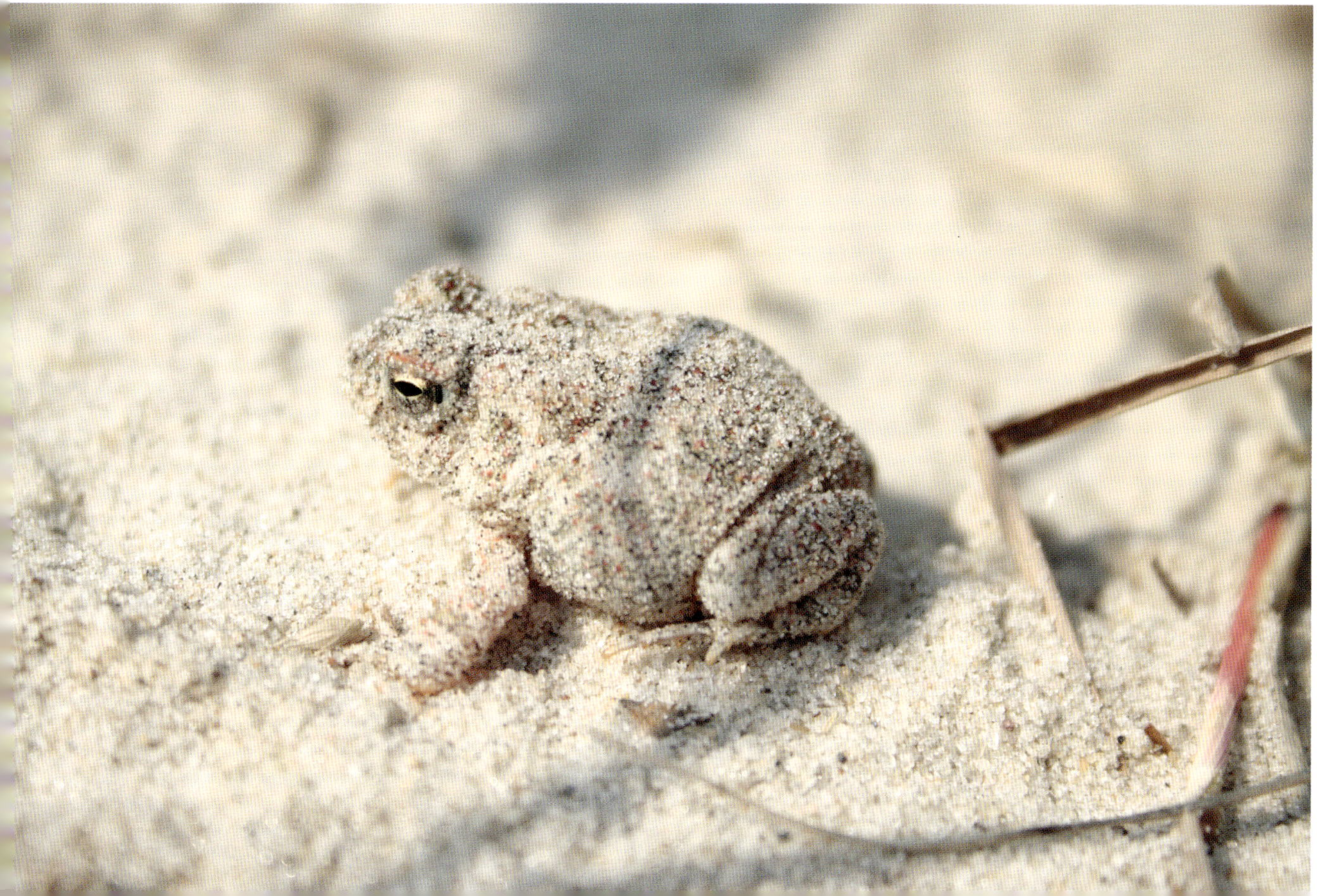

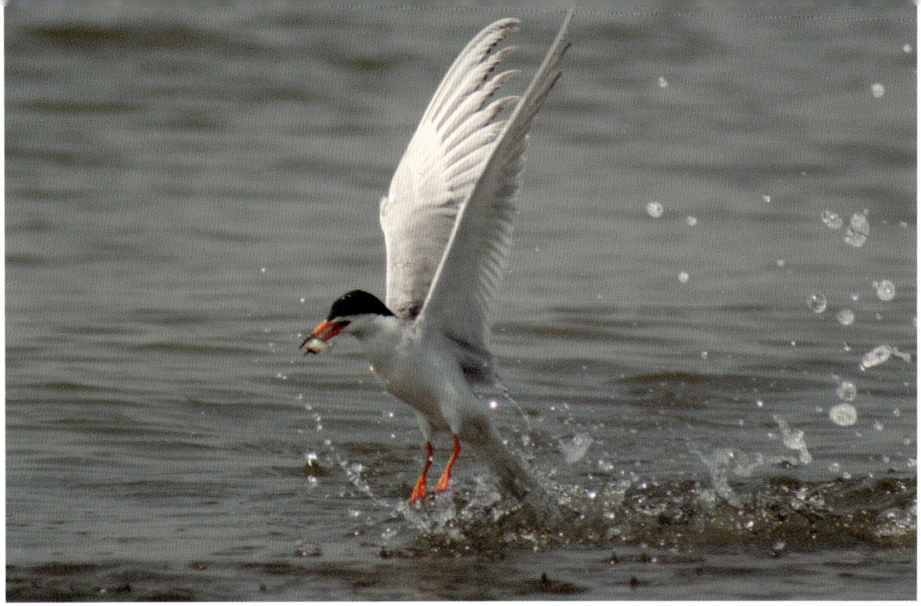

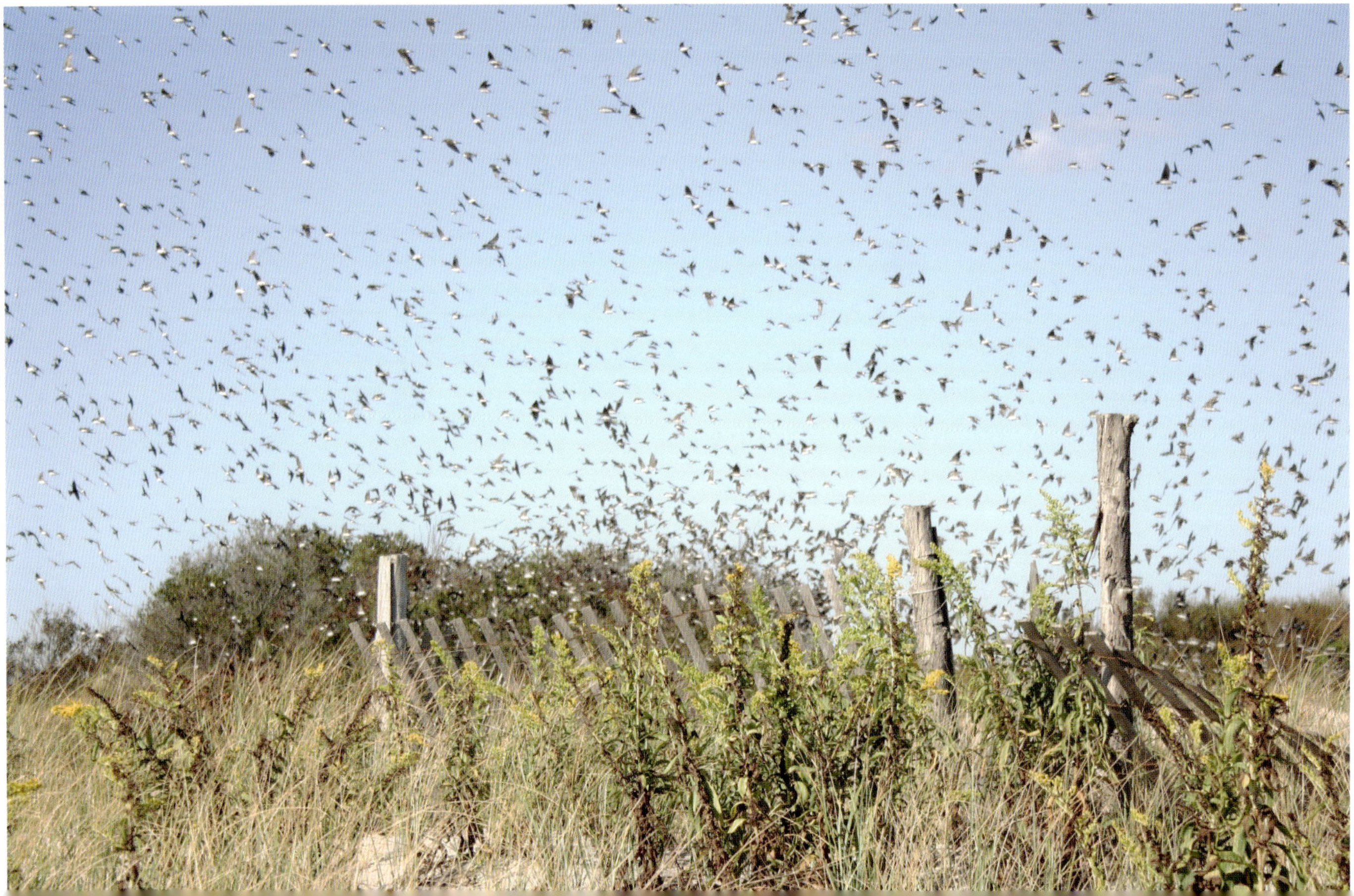

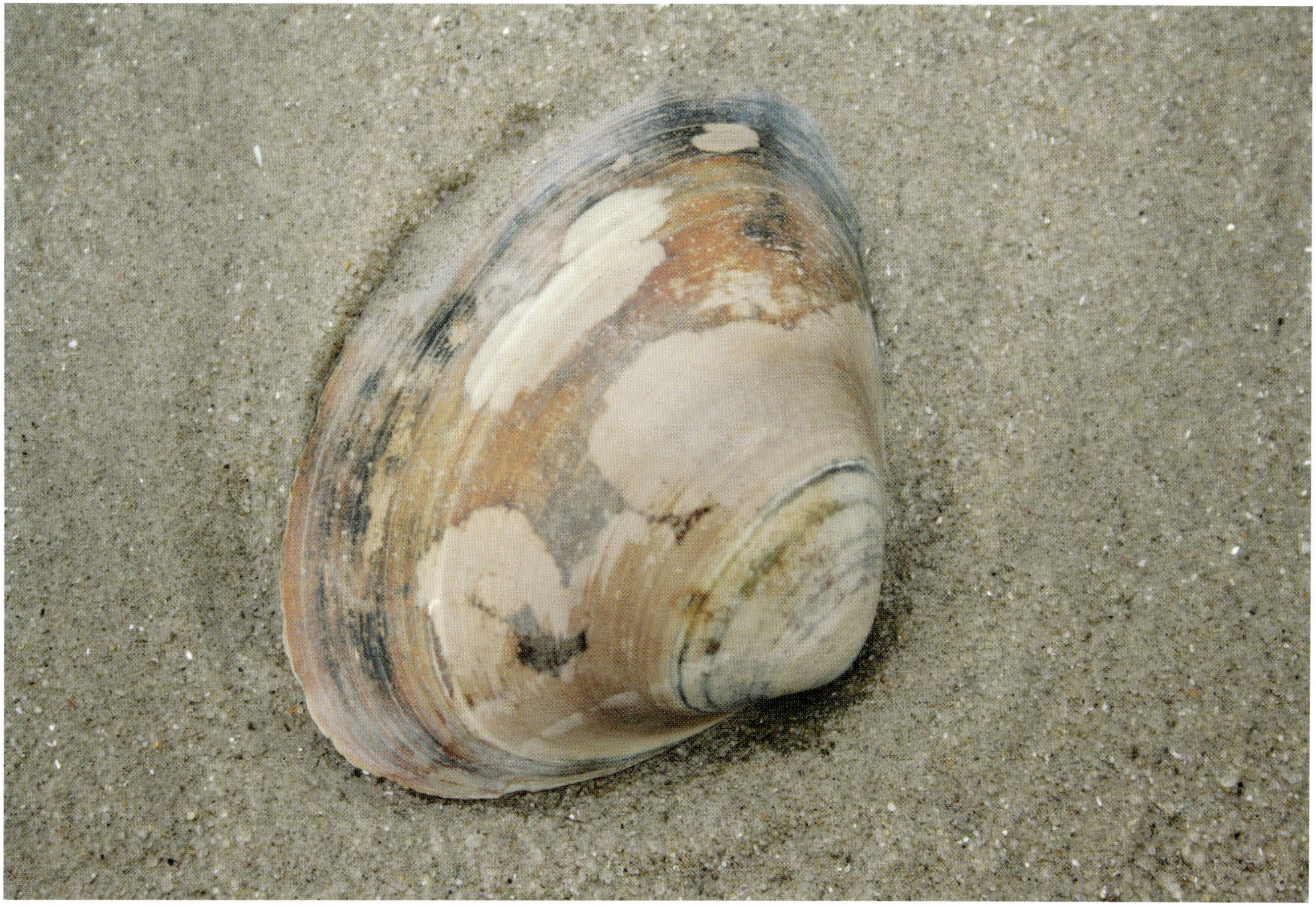

*"One cannot collect all the beautiful shells on the beach; one can collect only a few, and they are more beautiful if they are few."*

~ Anne Morrow Lindbergh

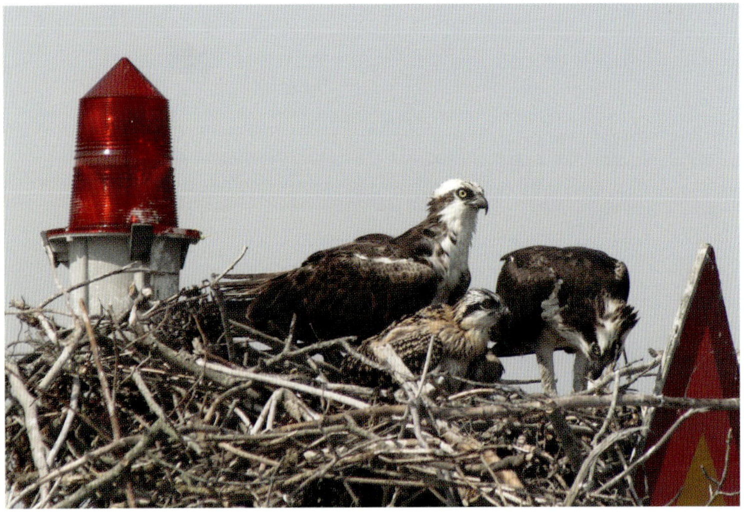

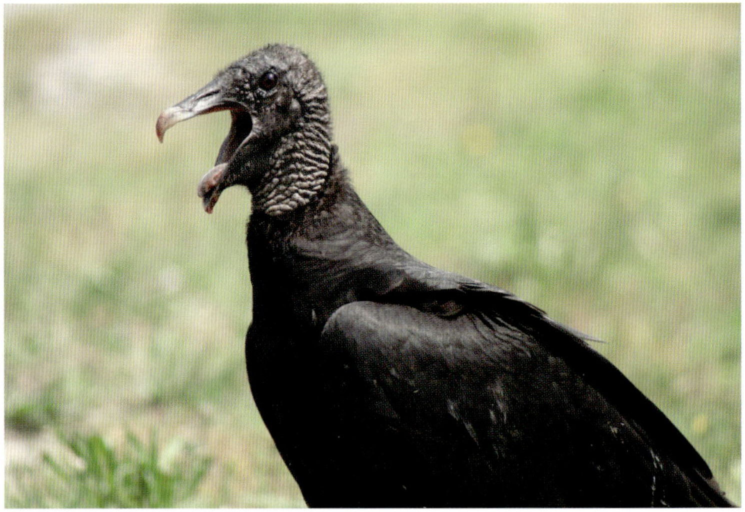

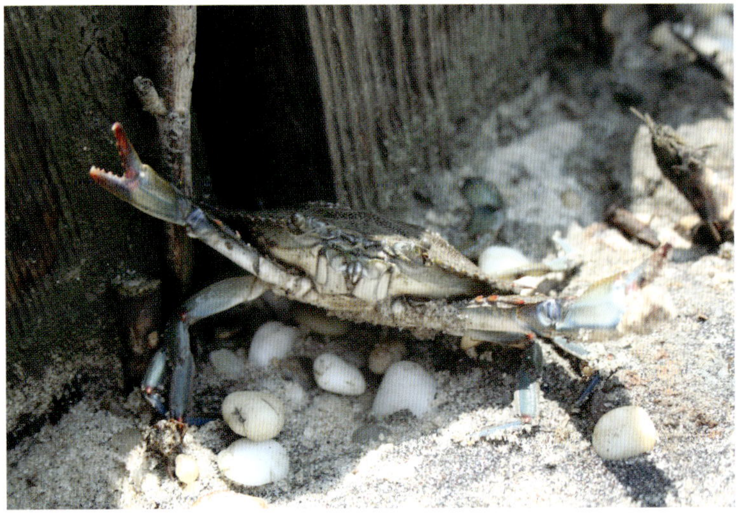

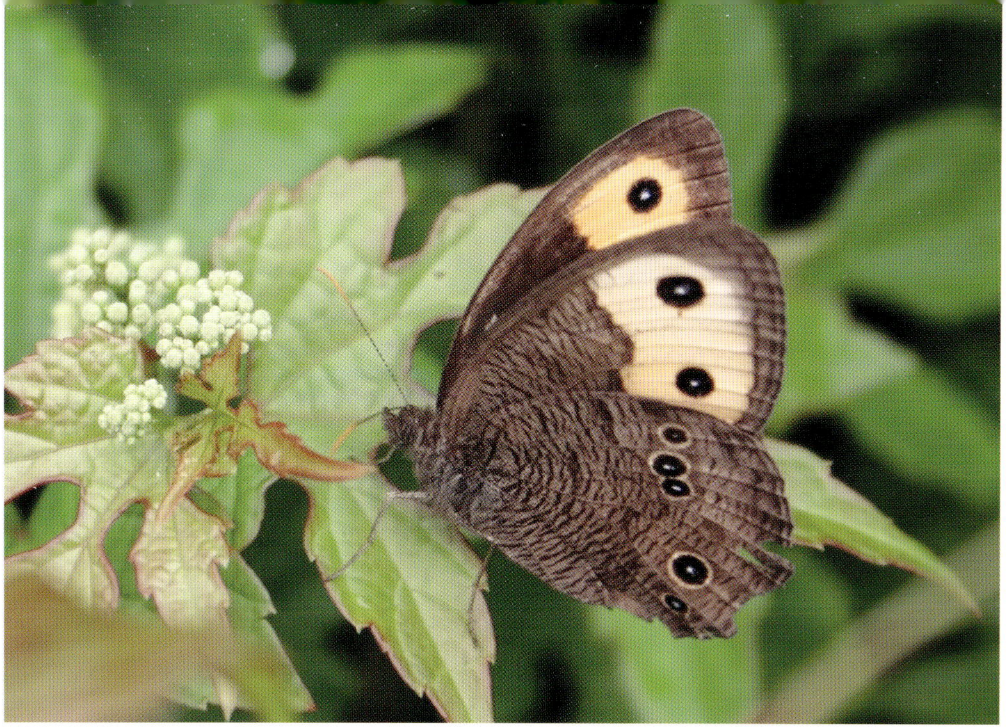

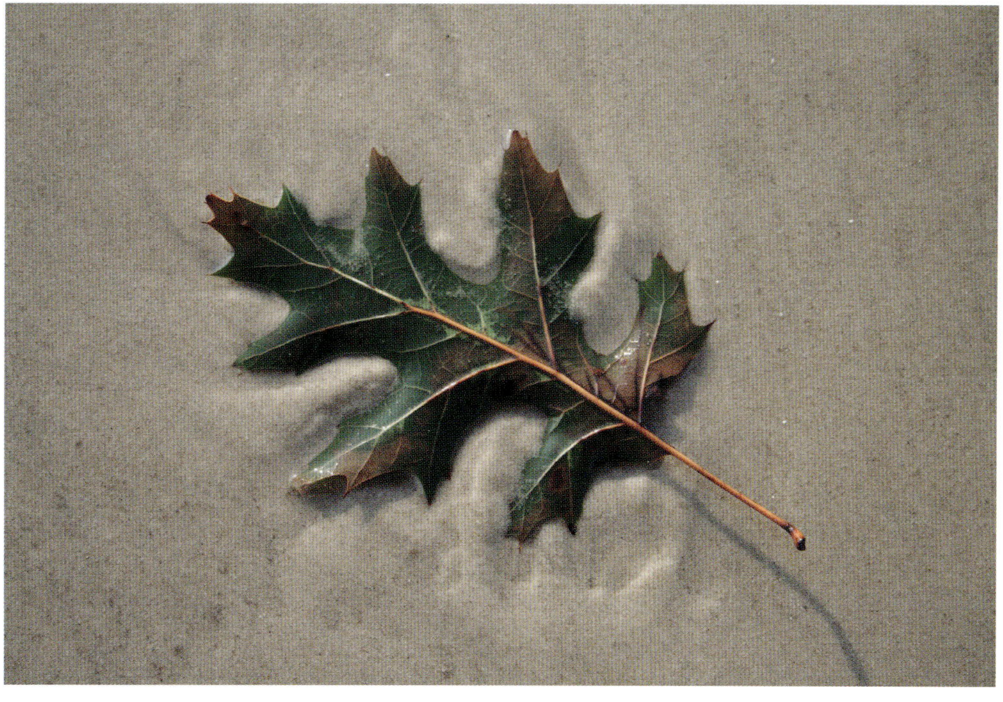

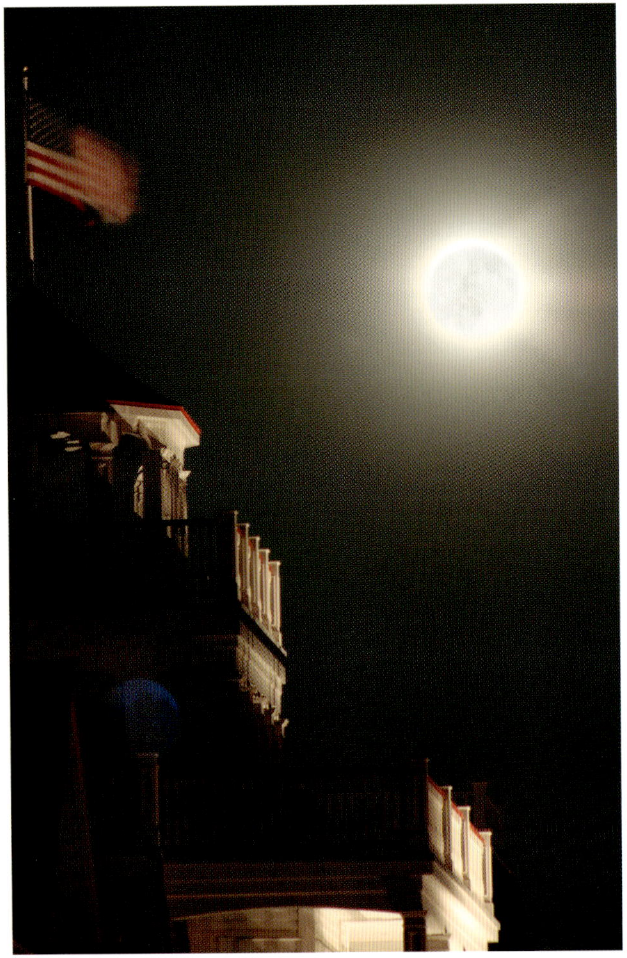

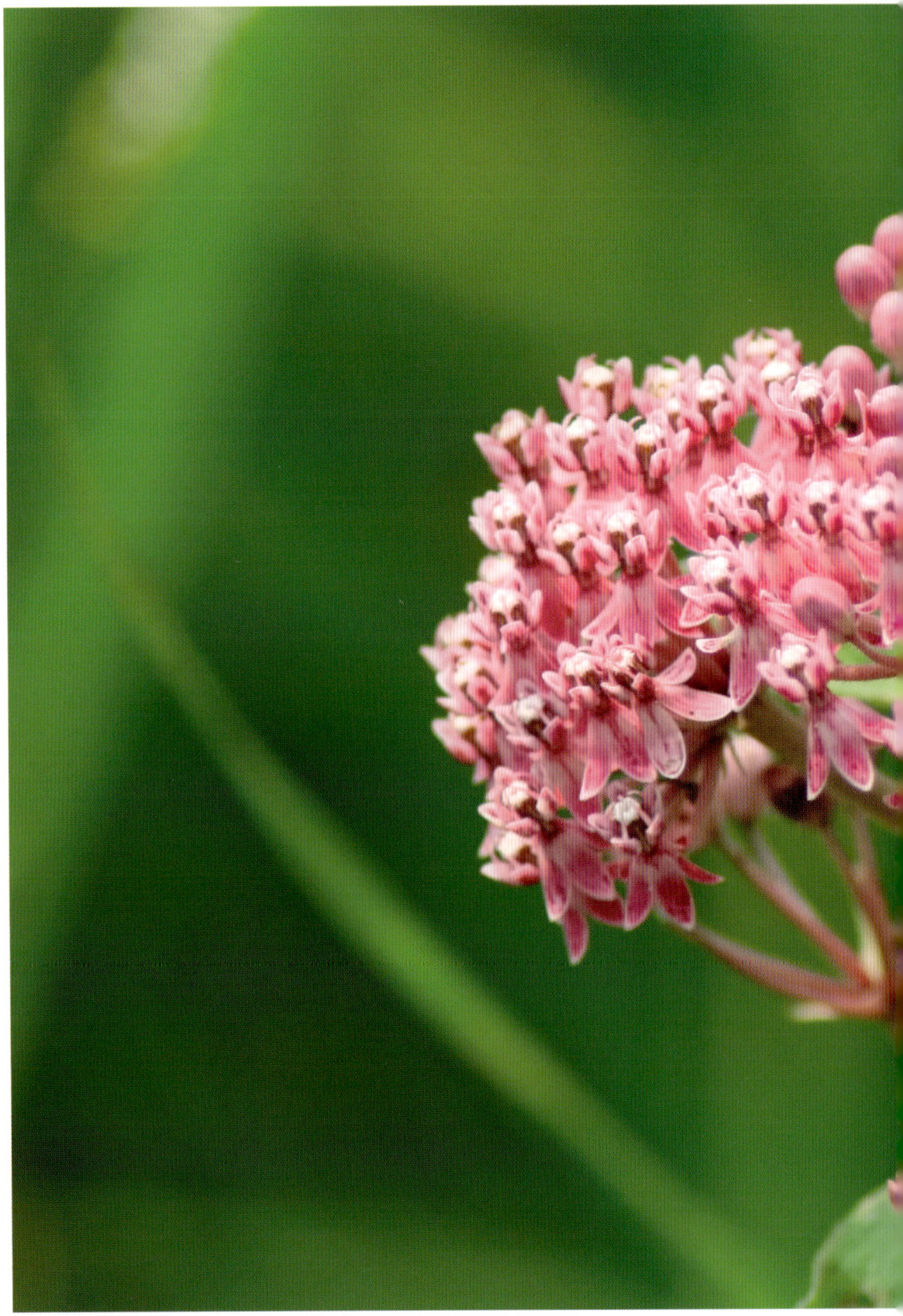

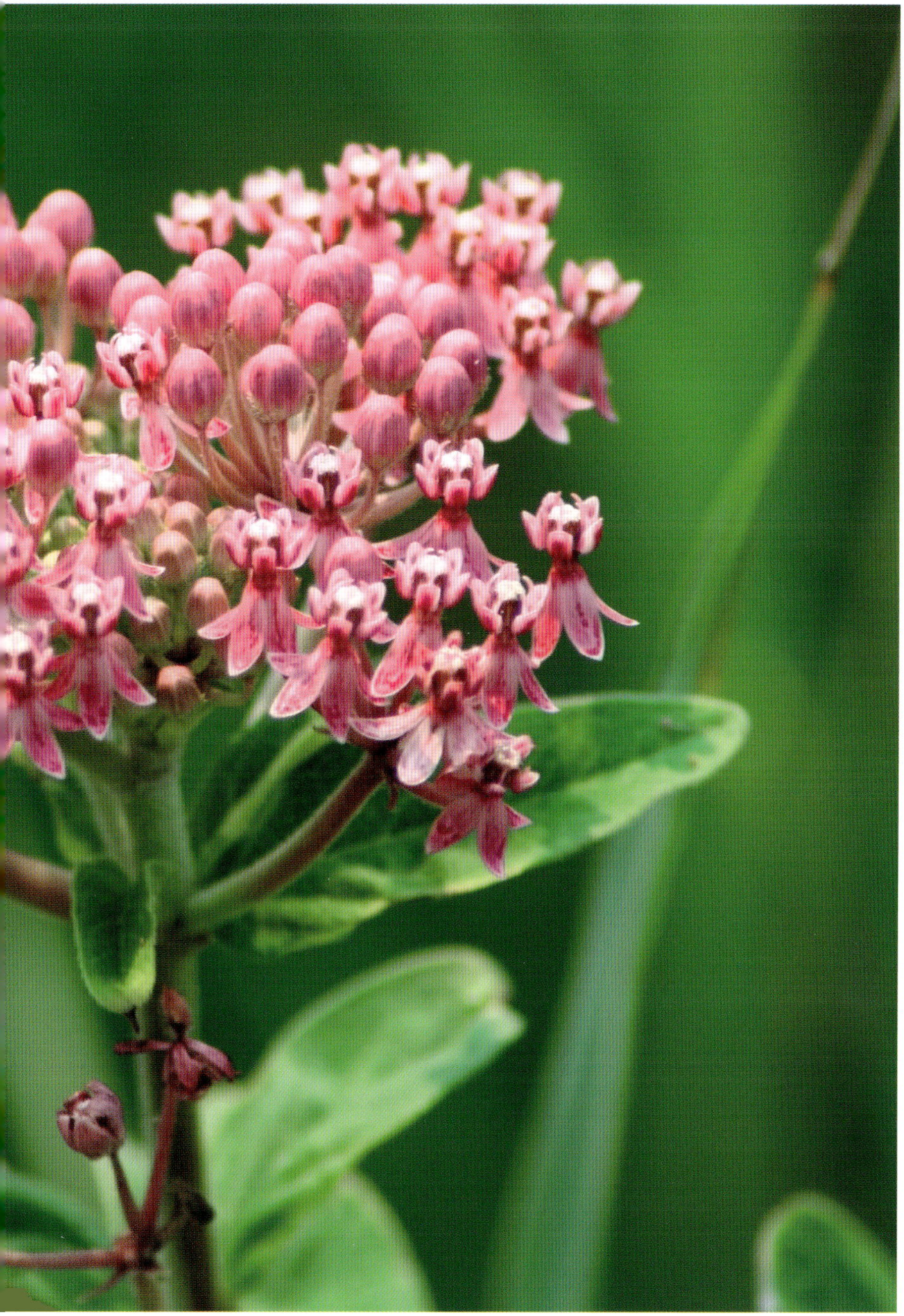

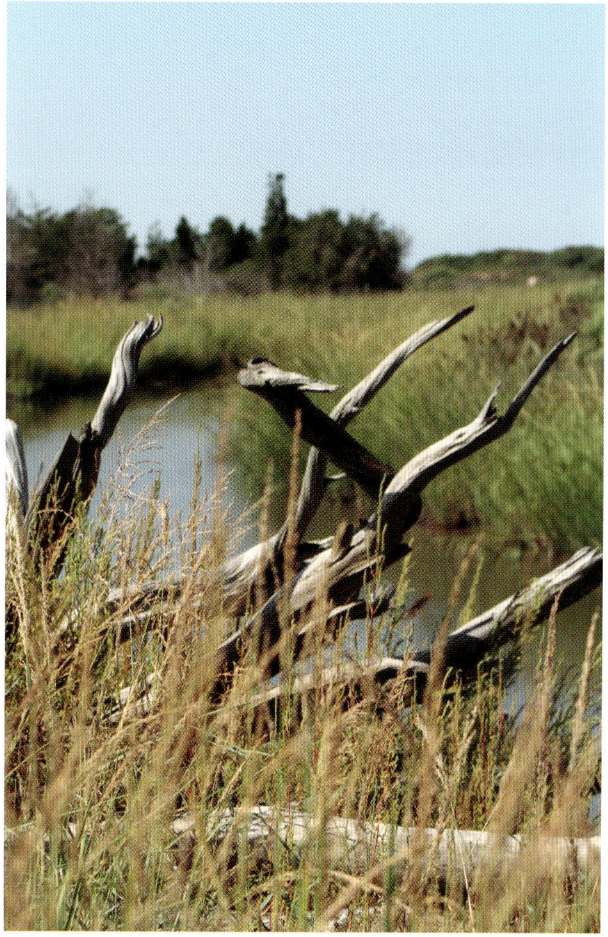

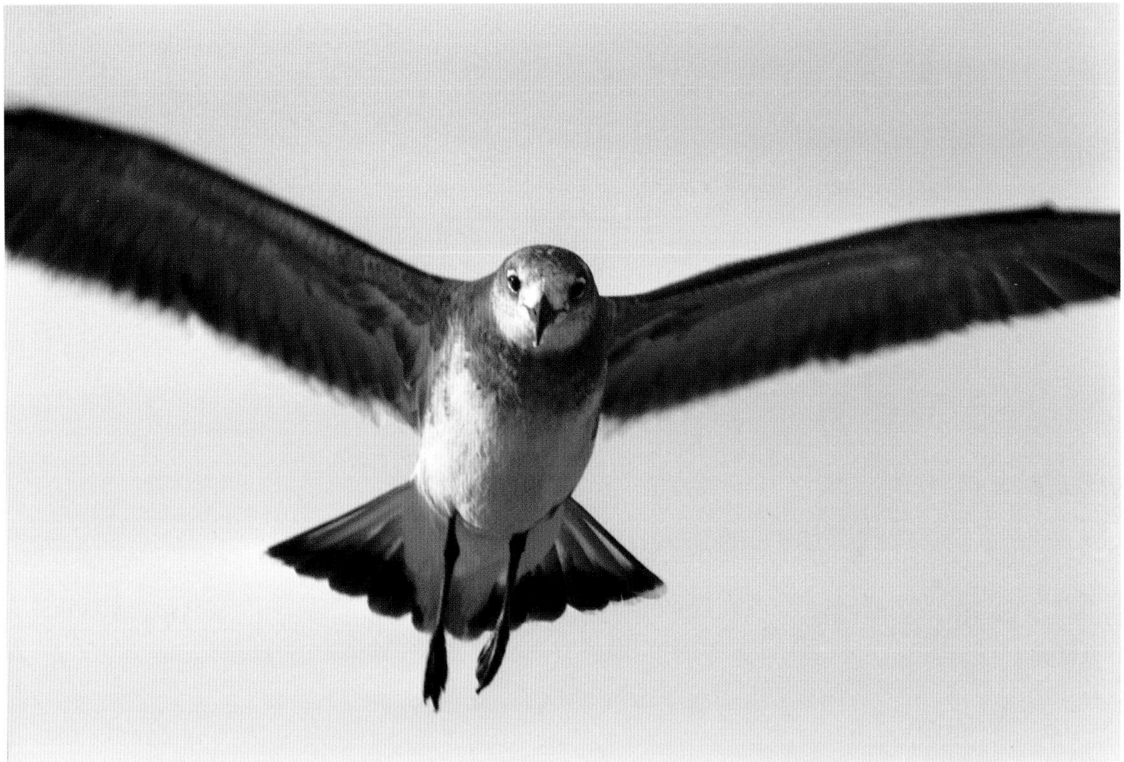

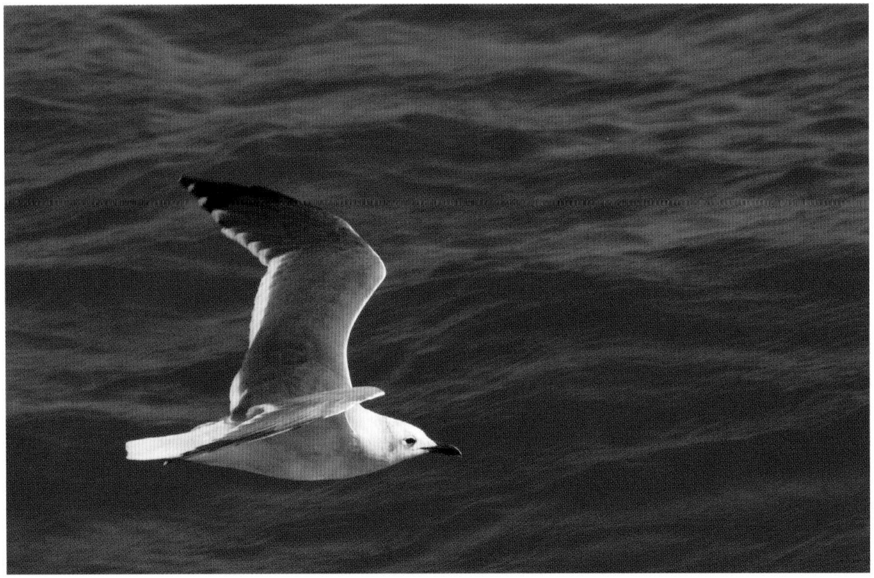

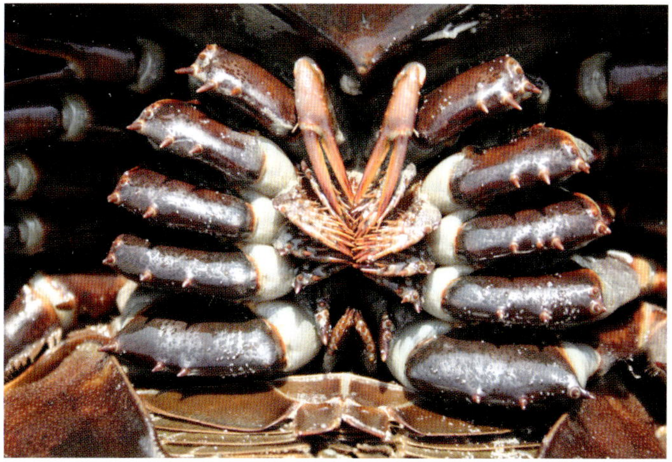

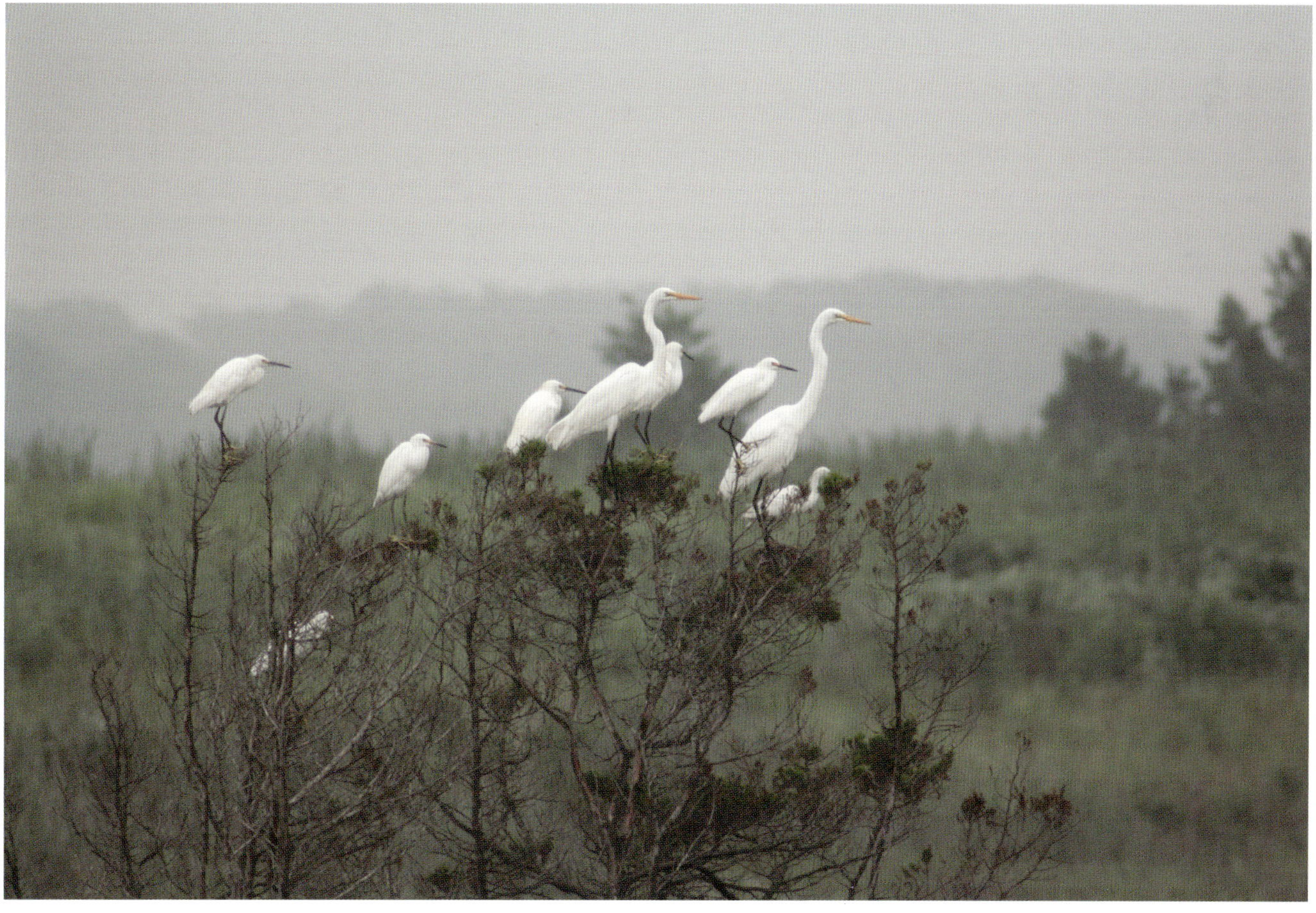

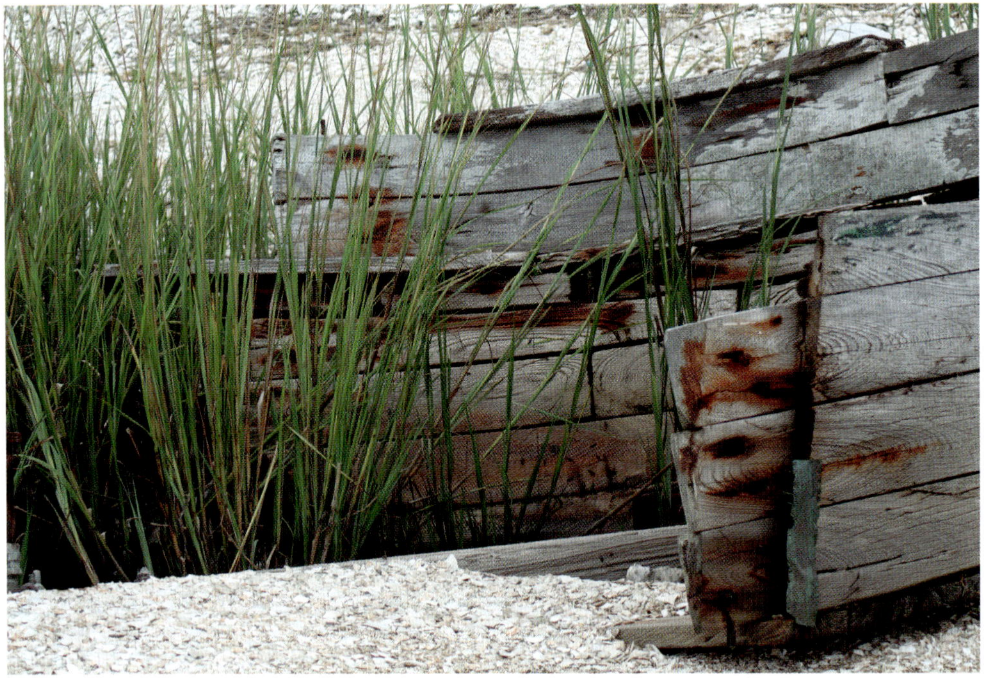

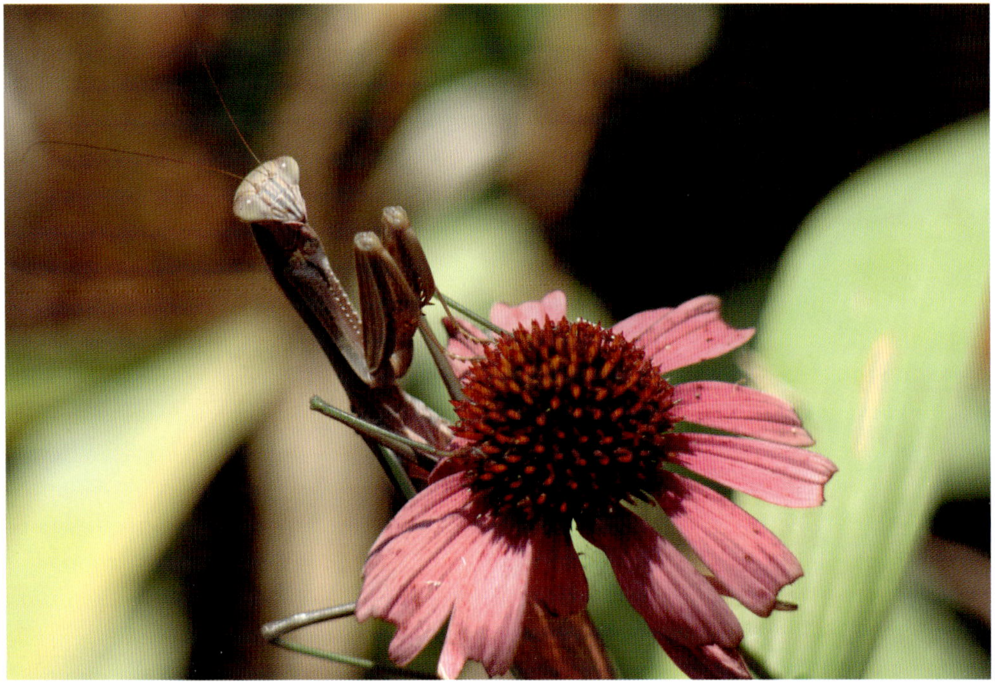

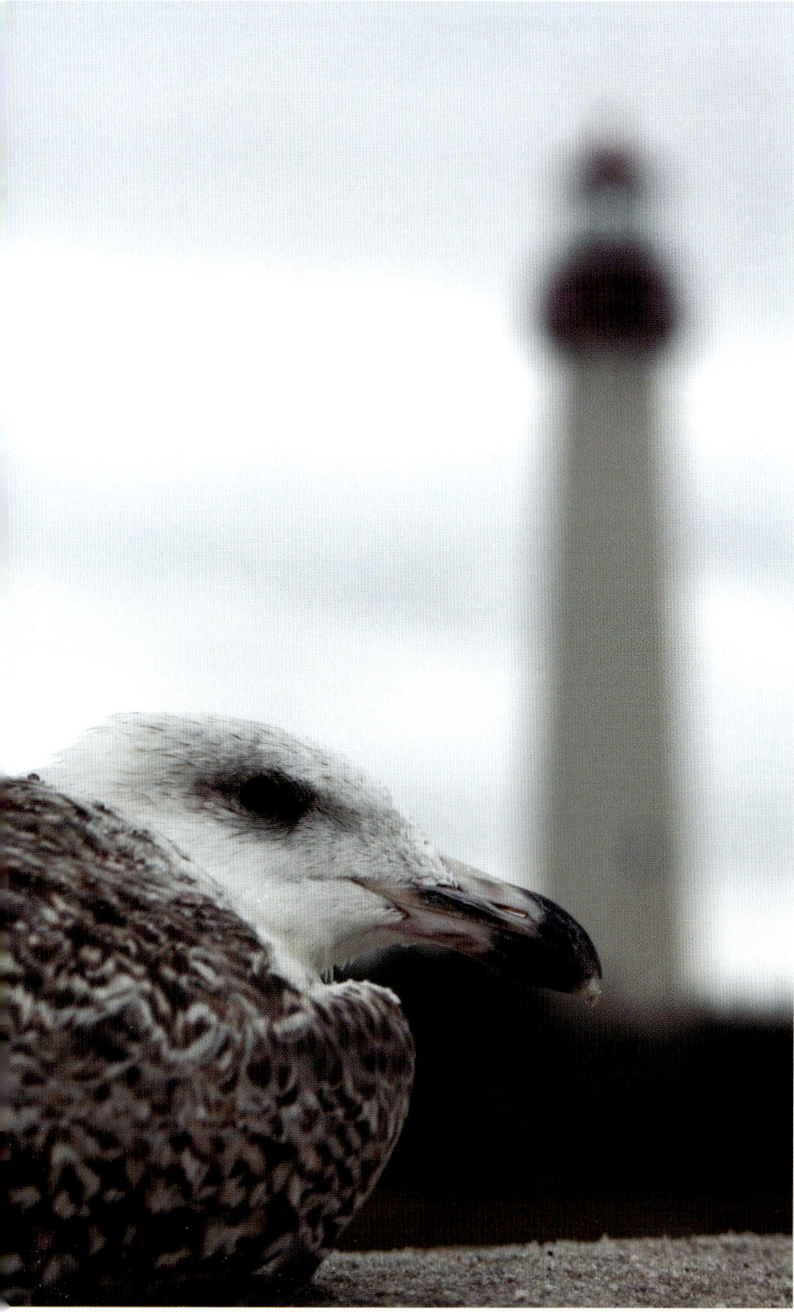

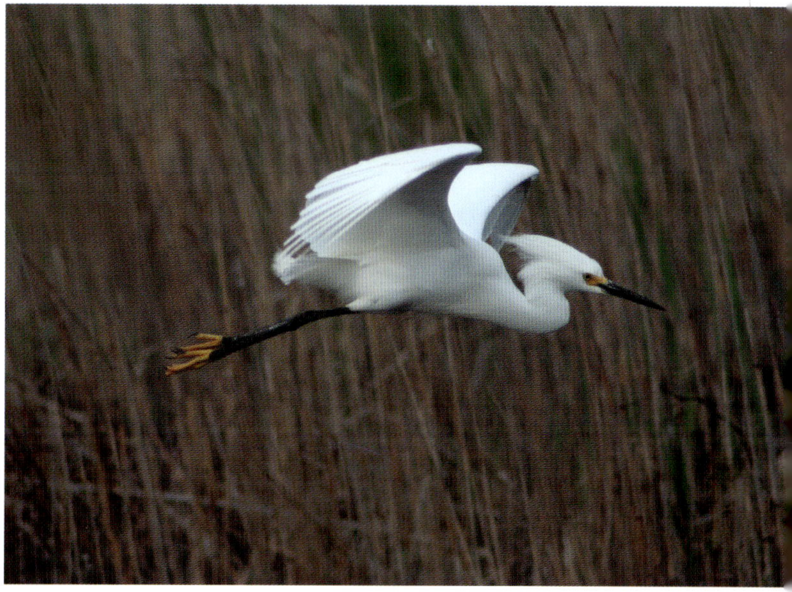

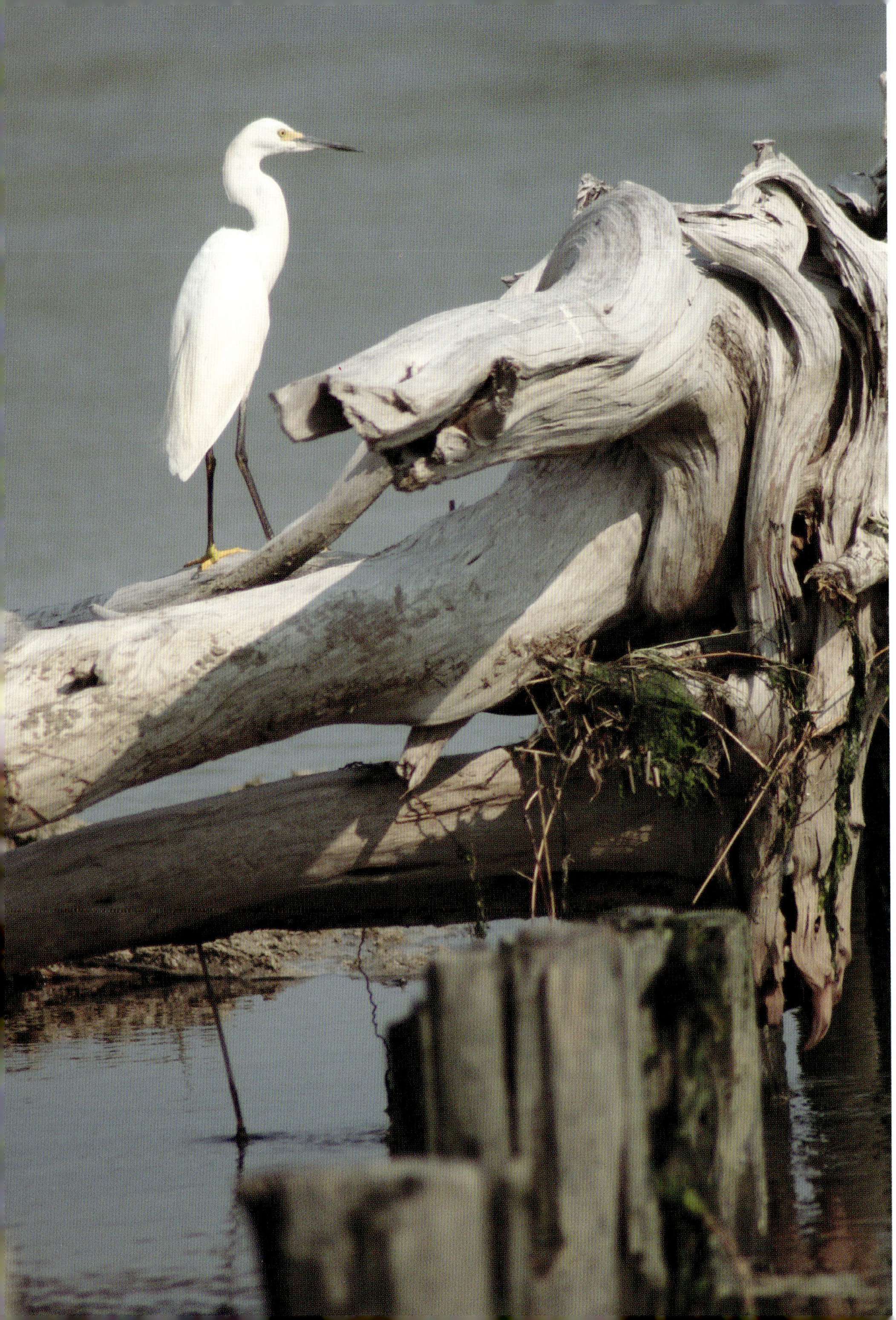

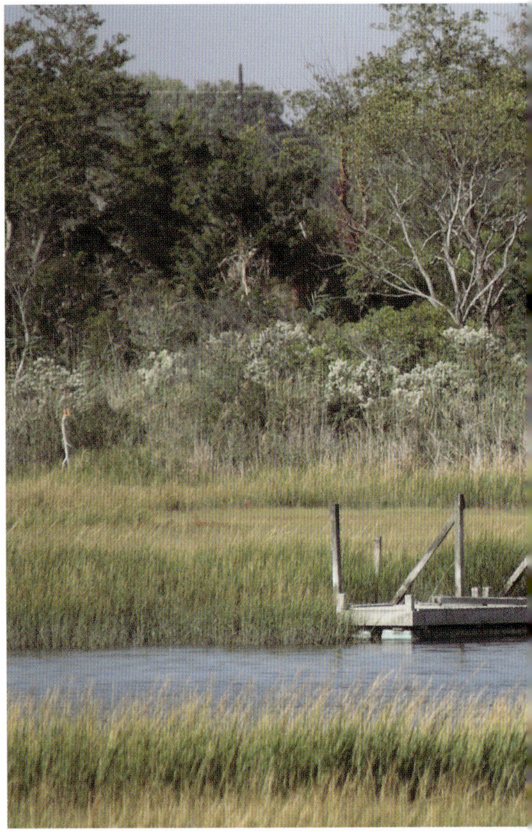

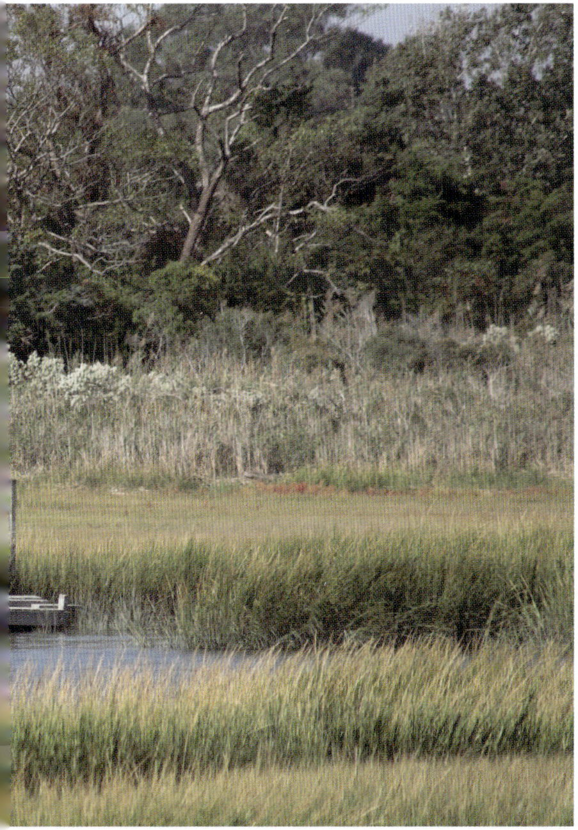

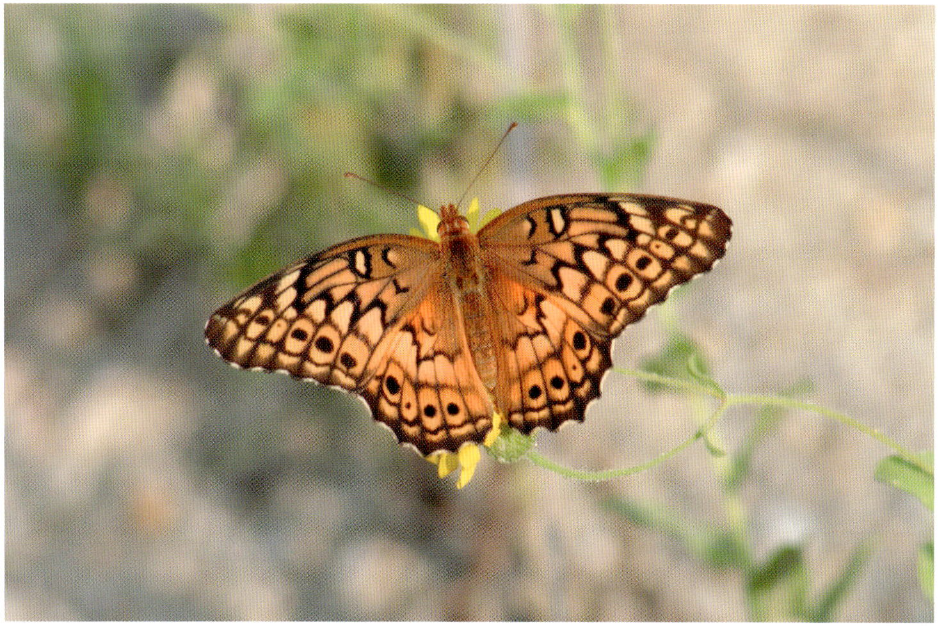

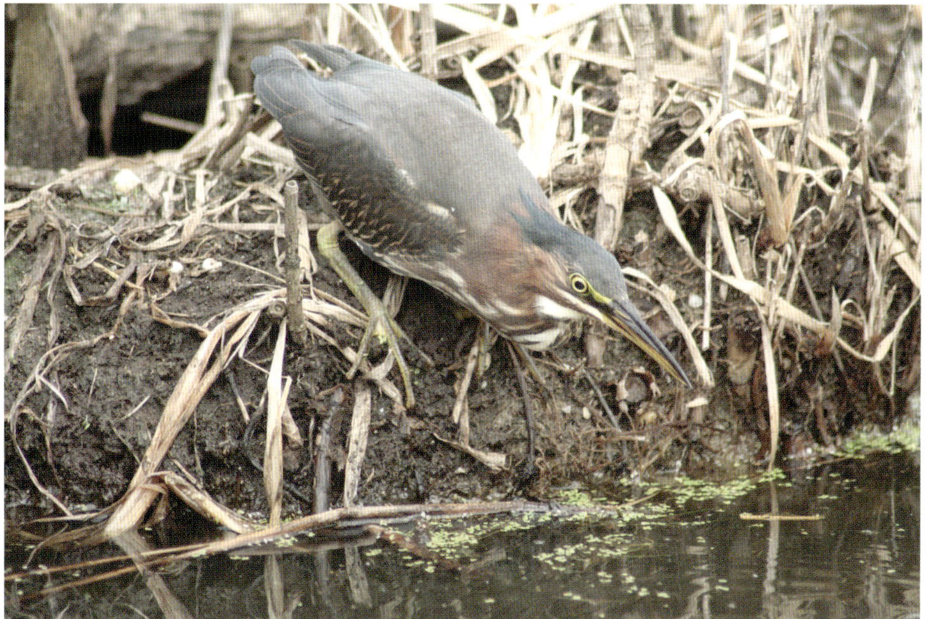

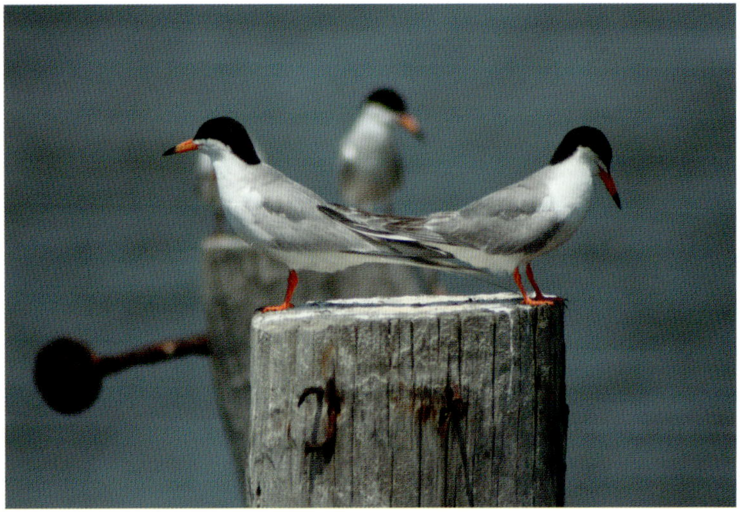

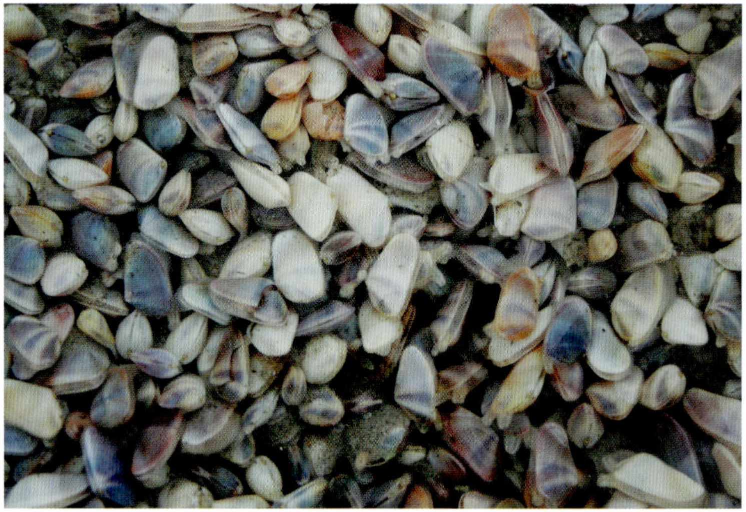

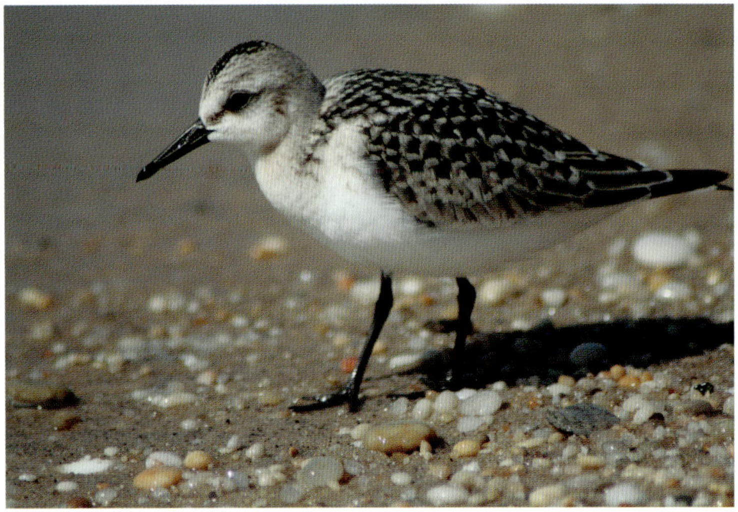

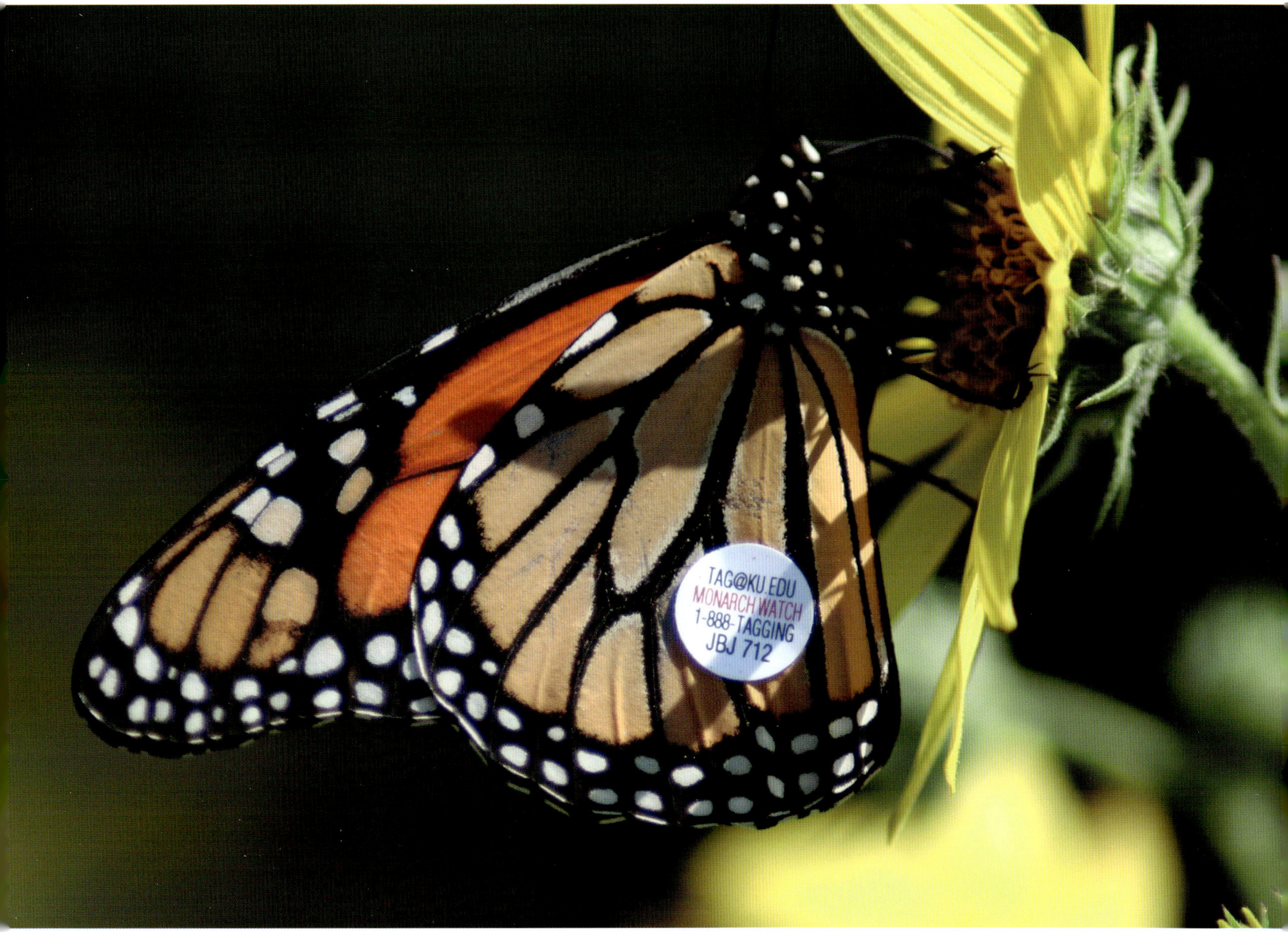
TAG@KU.EDU
MONARCH WATCH
1-888-TAGGING
JBJ 712

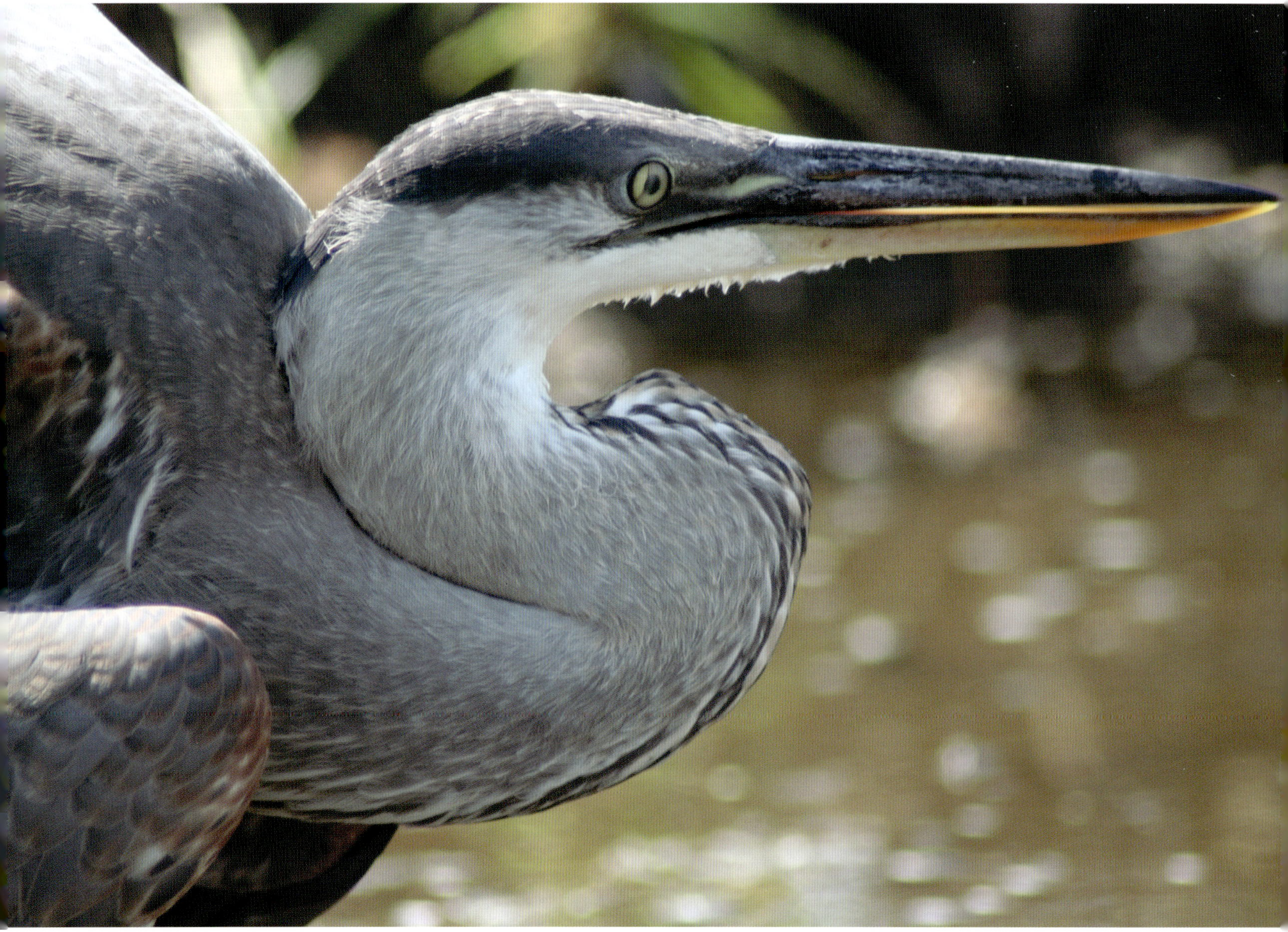

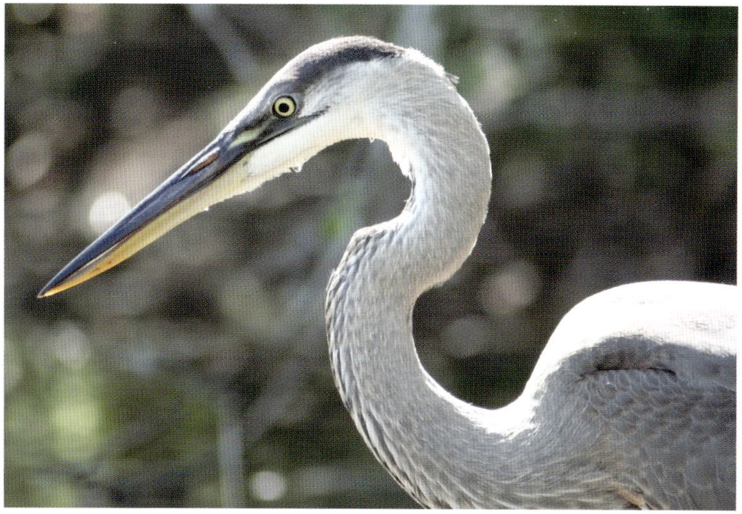

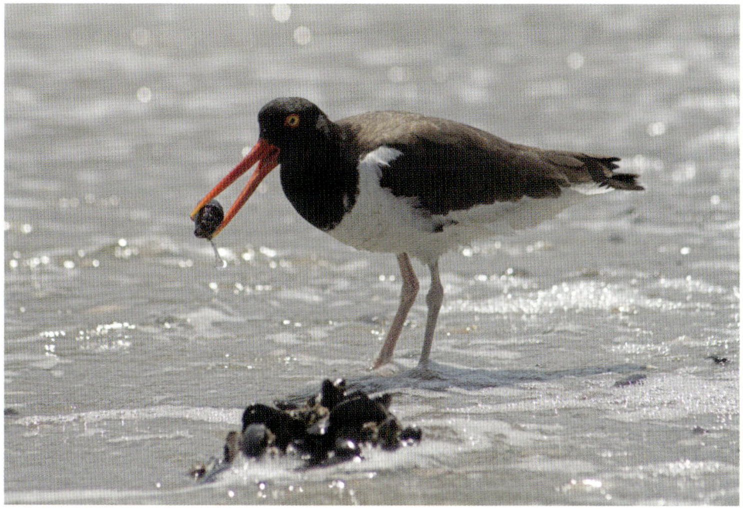

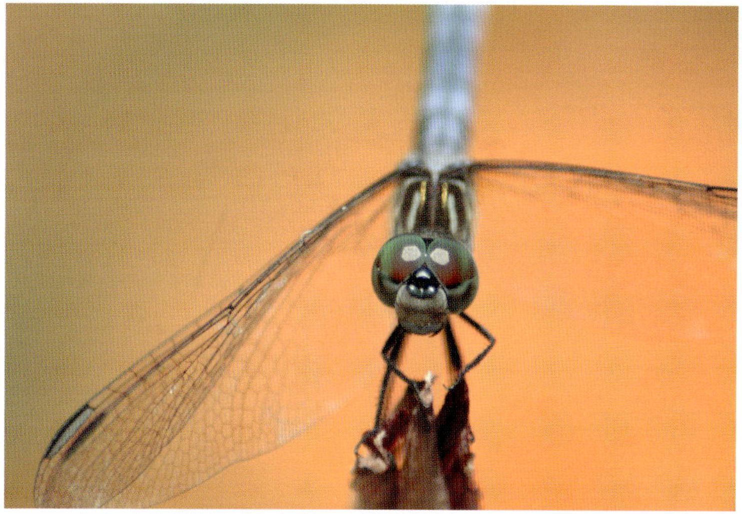

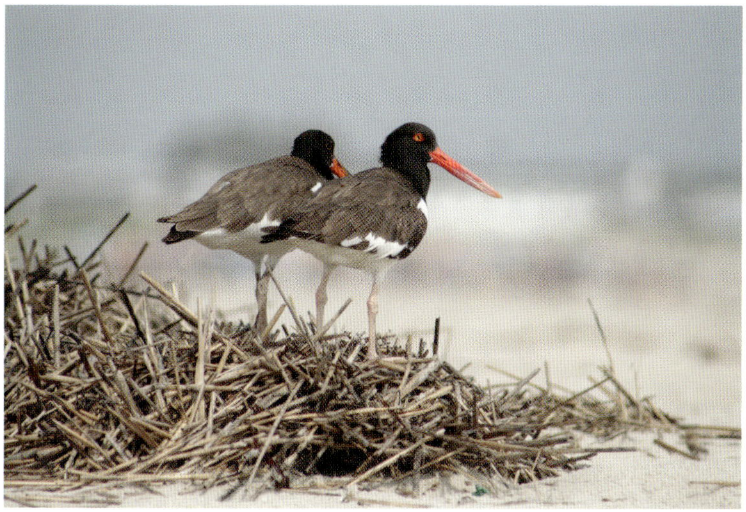

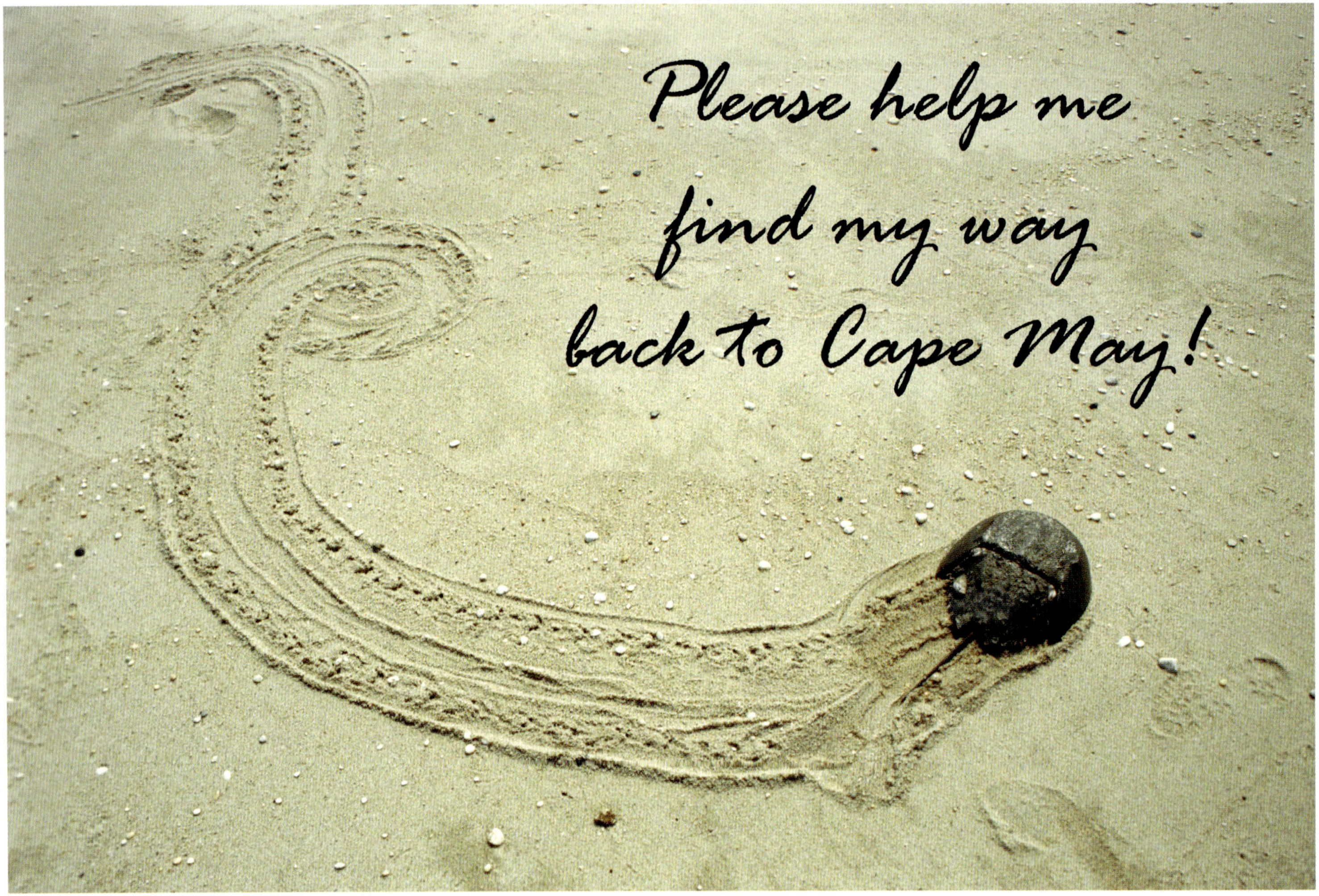
Please help me
find my way
back to Cape May!